THE WILD GENTLE ONES; A TURTLE ISLAND ODYSSEY

(TALES OF A LONE MYSTIC CELT)

BY

Jerome «Twin Rainbow» Irwin

VOLUME TWO

(The Ancient Spirit & Wildness of Native North America)

Wild Gentle Press

BRITISH COLUMBIA, CANADA

2006

To contact author or purchase additional copies of: Vol I & Vol II of *The Wild Gentle Ones* ; the CD *The Singing Drumsticks; Spirit Songs & Stories For The Earth & All Earth Peoples* ; or the blank journal *Pioneer Remembrances Of The Odyssey* ; go to: **www.turtle-island-odyssey.com**

Direct all correspondence to: **tri@turtle-island-odyssey.com**

First Edition

Cover Art Design: Carl May, True Colours Ltd, North Vancouver, B.C., Canada
Cover Photography: Stuart McCall, North Light Images Ltd., Vancouver, B.C. Canada
Graphic Consultant: Aroon Masand, Desktop Design, Berkeley, California
Turtle sculpture/sketch on cover & in text: Charles Van Sandwyk, The Fairy Press,
North Vancouver, B.C. Canada

Library and Archives Canada Cataloguing in Publication Data

Irwin, Jerome, 1940-
      The wild gentle ones: a Turtle Island odyssey: tales of a lone mystic celt /
Jerome "Twin Rainbow" Irwin

Contents: v.1. Immigrant legacies & heritage of Native North America – v.2. The ancient spirit & wildness of Native North America – v.3. Ireland & South Tyrol: a return to the ancestors.

ISBN 0-9739179-3-8 (set) – ISBN 0-9739179-0-3 (v.1).   SAN: 119-0296
ISBN 0-9739179-1-1 (v.2) – ISBN 0-9739179-2-X (v3)

    1. Irwin, Jerome, 1940- –Travel. 2. Deep ecology. 3. New Age movement.
4. Indians of North America. 5. Indigenous peoples. I. Title. II. Title: Turtle Island Odyssey. III. Title: Tales of a lone mystic Celt.

BF648.179A3 2005   299'.93   C2005-905943-5

THIS IS WRITTEN FOR
THOSE OF YOU
WHO WOULD GO

UPON AN ODYSSEY:

*THAT IS LESS AN HISTORICAL RECKONING
THAN A SPIRITUAL LONGING;*

*OF ADVENTUROUS TRAVELS
MARKED BY MANY CHANGES OF FORTUNE;*

*UP AND DOWN THE LAND
AS A JOURNEY WO/MAN WAYFARER;*

*UPON A WANDERING QUEST
OF MIND AND SPIRIT;*

*NEGOTIATING STRANGE PASSAGES
THRU TIME AND SPACE;*

*AMIDST RANDOM AND VORACIOUS
LIFE EXPERIENCES;*

*THROUGH INSIGHTFUL EXPLORATIONS
OF THE SOUL'S ROOTS*

*EVER IN SEARCH: OF LIFE'S MYSTERIES;
OF TRUTH, BEAUTY & WISDOM
WITHIN BOTH THE SHADOWS AND LIGHT.*

– Acknowledgements –

This work never would have been possible were it not for the ever-abiding love and forbearance of my Australian soul-mate, Beverley Ann Phillips, who not only encouraged me To Go but To Stay, always keeping the door open between us.

As with any artistic project, this never would have been possible without a host of guides in this world and beyond who played a part in the dream-vision becoming a reality.

I send into the world of spirit much love to the host of nameless, faceless ancestors and spirit guides who have faithfully stayed by my side every step of the way and whose ghostly spectres lounge and play between every line herein.

Especially warm thanks go to Alex Gyongyosi and the Kinko Family of Vancouver, British Columbia and to Aroon Masand of Desktop Design and the Copy Central Family of Berkeley, California who became the northern and southern 'electronic oases' of the odyssey. Without their generous technical support and high-caliber of professionalism this would not have become anything near the work of art that it is.

Special accolades go: to Cap Lavin, a native San Franciscan, high school English teacher whose zany spirit early on transmitted a love of words and desire to write; to Charles 'Baby Brother Bear' Van Sandwyk, artist and friend extraordinaire, of Fiji and British Columbia, for his inspirational input on the work's cover art design, and for his sculpture and drawing of Turtle that became the writing's guiding spirit; to Hoopa spiritual man Jack Norton for the gift of a Spotted Eagle feather that many times over has helped translate the odyssey's confusion and pain into much joy, laughter and healing; to Dave Larson, a graduate music student of the University of British Columbia, for those balmy nights spent drumming with him and his young son Craig on their back porch, and for his sensitive ear that lent itself to the transcription of the work's musical notation; to Annie Sajdera-Barron of San Francisco's Conservatory of Music for her assistance in musical notation in-between a busy schedule of recitals and jazz workshops and to Ernie Mansfield of Mansfield Music in Berkeley for his expert typesetting of the works's musical epigrams; to Pat Smith of Yellowbellydesign in Berkeley who created a beautiful website to showcase the work; to Carl May and True Colours Ltd in North Vancouver, B.C. for their artistic rendering of the book cover; to painter Suzanne deVeuve, for her permission to use her Bear-Man artwork; to Randy Milliken for granting the use of his brilliant Master's thesis on the Native peoples of the San Francisco Bay Area; to Kazuhira Tsuruta, who accompanied me on the Rock to photograph The Occupation; to Sasha Shamszad of Ziba Color Lab in Berkeley for for his masterful touchup of old photos and creative brainstorming on Volume Two's cover art design; to Thom Henley and the Rediscovery International Foundation Family for putting me closer on the path to find my real indigenous roots; to Jerry Kamstra, 'The Frisco Kid', for those rainy 'Beat' days on 'Pot Hill' in San Francisco, sharing our love of words, reading one another's works-in-progress while giving mutual succor to the lonely life of the struggling writer. Last, but by no means least, to: Alvin Warwas - part owner of Blooms Saloon and Finnegans Wake in San Francisco; Patti Dunsmuir - school teacher and artist extraordinaire in Vancouver, British Columbia; Dave MacDonald – Chilcotin frontier pioneer-husband-father par excellence in British Columbia, for their acerbic editorial comments as they plowed through the writing in its different evolutionary stages of development.

As you turn the cover of this book, think of it as a window you've just thrown open wide. A window within the home that is your own body. mind and spirit.

Imagine the time to be the midnight hour of Winter Solstice – The Eve of Christmastide.

Unable to sleep because of all your excitement thinking about the wondrous gifts lying beneath the holy tree of life – newly brought into your home from the wild forest outside – you throw open this window of your dream-time place to catch some sense of the night's magic.

Outside, in the crisp, cold, cobalt-black sky, thousands of stars twinkle in gay profusion amidst pale green, red, blue and yellow flashes of the aurora borealis. Dazzled by their brilliance and mystery, your thoughts begin to wander as far out into space as they all are.

Suddenly it's as if you all at once are visited by the spirits of the past, present and future – *Your* past, present and future – each offering up flashes of your life: as a youth; as an adult; an elder; and finally as one standing before the open grave that somewhere awaits.

Each fleeting image represents some ultimate truth of life. Some truth's bright, happy, expectant ones. Others dark, sad and foreboding. All nevertheless seeking to aid you in either the reclamation or redemption of some aspect of yourself.

Each, in turn, now patiently awaits you to gaze – to venture – ever deeper inside and outside the window's view here.

VOLUME ONE

Immigrant Legacies
&
Heritage of Native North America

– Part One –

EXPLORING OUR YOUTH

– Part Two –

SEARCHING FOR RITES OF PASSAGE INTO ADULTHOOD

VOLUME TWO

Understanding
The Ancient Spirit & Wildness
of Native North America

ACKNOWLEDGING THE MOST SIGNIFICANT EVENTS IN OUR LIVES

– Part Four –

INTEGRATING OUR LIFE'S LESSONS IN SEARCH OF BALANCE & HARMONY

VOLUME TWO

Understanding
The Ancient Spirit
&
Wildness of Native North America

"AHO!", ROARS BEAR MAN,
"AND SO CONTINUES
THIS EVOLUTIONARY
TALE...

artwork: www.deveuve-kelly.com

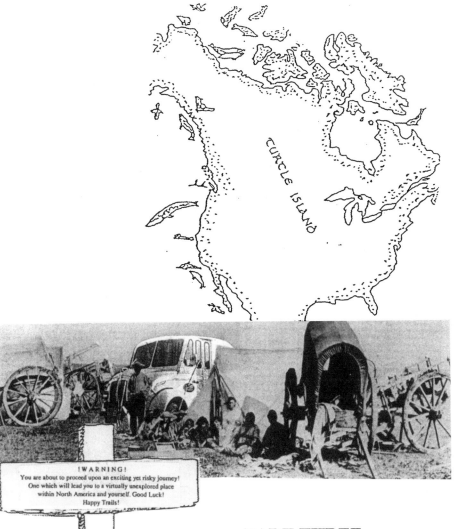

!WARNING!
You are about to proceed upon an exciting yet risky journey!
One which will lead you to a virtually unexplored place
within North America and yourself. Good Luck!
Happy Trails!

PART THREE

ACKNOWLEDGING THE MOST SIGNIFICANT EVENTS IN YOUR LIFE

The nations I draw upon
for my ancient roots and heritage
are

The place where I was raised
that I would call my
sacred homeland is

_____

_____

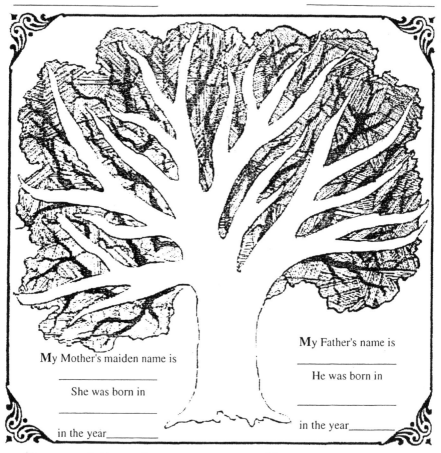

My Mother's maiden name is

_____

She was born in

_____

in the year_____

My Father's name is

_____

He was born in

_____

in the year_____

The one spot in Nature where,
as a youth, I received the
greatest emotional & spiritual nurturance

is_____

My favorite animal/s, bird/s, reptile/s,
insect/s, plant/s of that spot were the

_____

Of all these life forms, those I feel most related to, as if they
were part of my own family tree are the _____

_____

TURTLE ISLAND

PRELUDE

WHERE DID YOUR

LIFE'S ODYSSEY BEGIN?

In light of 1992, we are here to celebrate the
beginning of the next 500 years for the Western
Hemisphere. I'm part of the first generation
willing to leave behind European, African
or Asian identities, and enter fully into being as
inhabitants of Turtle Island.

(Gary Snyder, **Poems From Turtle Island &
Other Collections**)

- Song Of The Turtle –

Words & lyrics
by
Jerome Twin Rainbow Irwin

– THE MYSTIC SHADOW SIDE TO LIFE –

"PILGRIM", heralds The Great Voice Of The Turtle, *"As a pioneer of the next 500 year cycle of North American society, what part of your Old World identity are you willing to forget as you set out upon this odyssey to get to know who I am? What part of it are you willing to remember? For Remembering or Forgetting is everything. The one you daily choose will determine the degree of pleasure and pain - the heaven or hell, as you humans call it - that you will discover during your life's journey upon me. Listen to my many voices that sing of a mystic tale that first began in the long, long ago time... Long before those invaders among your kind first came to my shores and began to artificially rename my native lands and people to suit their whim and fancy. In the East, humans once gathered upon my back, like to turtles, and the spirit of the place called itself - Turtle Island. In the distant West, they gathered upon me at a place calling itself Haida Gwaii, or 'Land of The People'. In the far North and South they gathered at still other wild places, each with its own natural name that spoke of the homelands of 'The People'. Today, there still exists as many different spirit names within me as there are nations of indigenous humans and non-humans upon my body. But thousands of alien names like 'North America', 'Canada', 'United States', 'British Columbia', 'District of Columbia' enshroud me and all my native life in darkness. For you to reach beyond their shadows toward the light my names represent, is to undertake a healing within yourself, your nation, me and all my minions. This is the ultimate odyssey you now must create for yourself."*

———————➤●⊂———————

"**W**HERE ON EARTH DID THIS CRAZY ODYSSEY REALLY BEGIN?", I shouted aloud to The Great Turtle. For hours I silently sat with my back up against my medicine tree's rough trunk spine – my body cushioned by a lush green carpet of thick sphagnum moss – imploring any spirit who heard my thoughts for some counseling to this quest. The shouting: a final act of frustration when no solace was forthcoming.

Yet just as fast as the words passed from my lips, were they swallowed up by the ponderous silence of the dense, sunless forest.

A sudden, Biblical-like shaft of sunlight, appearing as if out of no-where as it brightly shone through the thick canopy overhead, mystically highlighted a twenty-foot wide fairy ring of stark white pine mushrooms that thrust their heads above the mossy forest floor.

Inspired, I once more shouted aloud, "So, pray tell me, Sacred Forest! Sacred Tree! Oh Holy Ring *of* Mushrooms! You Unseen Ones! Where in the name *of* Heaven or Hell did all this begin?
My mind began to wander thru time and space:

Was it some twenty years ago when first I learned *of* you, Turtle, through those traveling Mohawk's on their White Roots *Of* Peace tour? Maybe it first began over a half-century ago in San Francisco when a half-feral youth set out to explore the tiny, wondrous wild hills, vacant lots and hidden backyard gardens *of* his Cow Hollow-Union Street universe? Was it when that wild child heard a spirit voice whisper in his left ear, "Lad! I would have you become another Johnny Appleseed!" Or perhaps it was when, as a Catholic altar boy, he stood in the great oak-lined sacristy *of* Daly City's Our Lady *Of* Perpetual Help church and heard the mystifying sound the sides *of* his starched white vestment made as they tore apart, shattering the awesome silence *of* that man-made holy place?

Then again it could have begun the day that lad abandoned his altar boy duties and headed into San Francisco's San Bruno Mountains in search *of* a more natural spiritual retreat. Or possibly it all started when, as a young adult, he underwent a Lacotah vision-quest with the guidance *of* Joe Thunder Hawk and saw – after standing naked and shelterless for three days and nights without food or water – an apparition upon a holy hill that spoke *of* his faerie spirit's intimate name for him. Sure now, it still might have been during that next flash *of* consciousness atop the hill when he recognized himself to be a relative *of* Bear, Eagle, Hawk, Wolf and Elk.

Still again, this odyssey could just as well have first begun in that blinding moment of revelation when years later, as a grown man in quest of the truth, while wandering along the Capilano River of British Columbia, Canada, he spied a driftwood sign that read *The Elves Inn*, hanging above the gate of a magical cottage straight out of *The Hobbit*. The cottage's resident elf someone who spoke of leprechauns and UFO's and beckoned to him to enter the Inn and stay for the next twenty years in the hope of meeting up with them both.

Or did this odyssey really begin on that more distant day of the man's youth when he first sensed that he himself, somehow strangely, was part leprechaun as well as part intergalactic voyager who was only briefly passing through this Earth realm one last time, never again to return? Or did all this rather start on the day that grown man's Turtle Island meditation ended and he opened his eyes to see a Red-Tailed Hawk feather drop out of the sky from some mystic place, landing beside his hand as he started to scribble down the dedication page of his odyssey's strange account?

Yet what if the origins *of* this mysterious odyssey indeed go back to an even more ancient time when his Celtic ancestors, filled with the same wanderlust, set across yet another continent in search *of* the emerald-shelled isle *of* their own dreams?

But if all these things be true, is this not then a pilgrimage that knows no boundaries between sky-middle-underworld's, time or space?

Years later, these same '*quest*-tions' all surged back into conscious thought the day a mysterious-looking, leather-bound wicker trunk was happened upon in a Northern Californian auction house.

The 18th century steamer – its aged brown wicker lid trimmed with thick strips of steel-hard, bone-dry parfleche and securely latched by two hand-forged black metal hasps – had once belonged to a New World pilgrim-immigrant-refugee from parts unknown, who came to North America with whatever imaginable fears and dreams for the future.

Barely discernible in chipped black paint that skipped and hopped over the uneven ridges and valleys of the wicker, were the words: "W.A.S. – Red River Country, Rupert's Land – Osborn Gally – Captain's Cabin – Settler's Effects."

Whoever 'W.A.S.' had been in life, who the trunk's new settler was and why they left it unclaimed for nearly a year, or how a once Red River-bound trunk upon the deck of the Osborn Gally ended up in a warehouse in an industrial park on the edge of the San Bruno Mountains, were all equally unsolved mysteries.

At the time, I didn't know why I decided to buy the beat-up wreck of a trunk except that I felt drawn to it, as if something or someone were compelling me to take possession of it or it of me.

Once I got it home and opened it up, I found inside nothing more than a heap of threadbare, antique peasant clothing too far gone to even recycle. But in amongst the rags, wrapped carefully in a faded red nightshirt, tied with two strands of red-dyed buckskin, was a thick, weatherbeaten leather journal. A journal chock-full of visionary-dream notes, musical fragments, ancient myths, sayings and drawings of all kind.

On its parchment skin cover was the faded, water-colored image of a classic volcanic-shaped, snow-capped mountain set in the background, below which lay a thick, verdant green forest. At the edge of the dense forest were several strange androgynous-shaped rocks and trees on either side of a rough, pot-holed road that disappeared straight into the forest towards the mountain. Above the faint, hand-tinted scene were the scroll-like words: 𝔄 𝔖𝔱𝔯𝔫𝔤𝔢 𝔑𝔢𝔴 𝔗𝔢𝔯𝔯𝔦𝔱𝔬𝔯𝔭𝔢; 𝔗𝔥𝔢 𝔉𝔯𝔲𝔫𝔱𝔦𝔯 𝔍𝔲𝔯𝔫𝔭 𝔬𝔣..................

But the name was gone! The journal's author unknown forever, for the ravages of time had obliterated any trace from the cover.

"Hey, c'mon! Hold it!", moans a Doubting Thomas somewhere at this early twist in the tale, "Is all this true or just a leg-pulling fable?"

"SKEPTIC!", snaps back Turtle's Voice without a moment's pause, "Read not one word more without oft recalling the wise saying of that cartoonist-columnist Robert Ripley whose daily by-line once declared, 'BELIEVE IT OR NOT! BUT TRUTH IS OFTEN STRANGER THAN FICTION!'"

Given the fabled bed fellows that truth and fiction often make in life, the chance discovery of the trunk and its strange contents at times seems as if nothing more than a figment of an over-active imagination of one wondering how his immigrant ancestors, a century or two before, would have written of their own Turtle Island odyssey. Or how some young seeker, a century hence, might react to stumbling across these scribblings in the same wicker trunk with only the initials 'J.F.I.' or 'T.R.' to go by as clues to the identity of its original owner-pilgrim.

As I turned the journal's brittle, water-stained cover to a place marked by a moth-eaten, hawk feather bookmark, a passage declared:

View thee here but the shadow of me servant hand, what with pen to paper on this new yeare eve night of Samhain, in the one thousndth seven hundrd an seventith yeare of Our Lord, humbly dedicates this shrine of me thoughts to the abrigine of this land an me ancestors. Ay, an to me DALg CAIS clann what first came to these shores, as our seanachies tell it, six hundrd or more yeare before the birth of Our Lord an now degn me return to explor new fruntirs of these lands.

Ay, be it known to what eyes read these words of wit and drama that I speak as one Gael what longs to feel in his heart the holy grail of these lands. Ay, an longs, too, for the cool refreshment in a tear of joy recevd as a gift from all the spirits what would attend the jurny behin the writin of these few foine words. To all this - gratefulness is sent to the four corners of the earth.

Following upon the heels of the passage was an epic-size poem, whose opening stanza's proclaimed:

(1)
I speak to thee
From beyond the veil of time
As a lone,
Wanderin,
Countae Claireman.
Foine taproot
Of a new Gaelic tree of life
In this faire land.

(2)
I, too,
As Amairgen
What first set foot
On Dear Olde Eire -
Am a wave of the sea,
A hawk on the cliff,
A teardrop in the sun,
The fairest of faire flowrs,
A stag of seven tines,
A salmon in a pool,
What sets wing, hoof an fin
Upon a new isle of our people.

(3)
Aoibheall -
Bright faerie
Clann protectress -
Follow me
To this new land.
Abide with me
In me evry thought.

(4)
Cinneide -
Oh, great clann chieftain!
Help me
To be thy voice
Of those livin an dead.
What are The Law,
What protect The Law.
What teach The Law.

(5)
Aoibheall! Cinneide!
Guide me destiny
Upon these lands
With this hope
An covnant's desire
Of our clann
Goin back to a time
Beyond mind.

(6)
Aoibeheall -
Guide me
Over this bridge of life.
Grant me the courage
To pass thro its lands
Of spirit an matter,
Between two worlds
Of eternal life an death.

(7)
𝕬 man
𝕹o abrigine inbian
𝕺r european pet knows -
𝕳as begun a jurny
𝕭etween two races,
𝕺n a path of blinb trust,
𝕮ross an untrobben chasm.

(8)
𝕳oly worbs
𝕹ow sent.
𝕬ncestors listenin.
𝕴 seek me power
𝕿hrough sacreb
𝕭obhran brum songs
𝕬nb great breams.

So it was that the partial identity of the original settler-owner of the mysterious trunk came to light. This seeker dubbed here – *Dreamer-Of-The-Great-Migration*.

Closing the journal's fragile skin cover, I retied its long strands of red buckskin, slipped it back into its faded red nightshirt wrap and returned it to its resting place within the wicker time-capsule.

Reading the *Dreamer-Of-The-Great Migration's* hopeful expectations led me to ponder my own grandparents rite of passage from Ireland and the Southern Tyrolean Alps to the New World. I at once retreated to a meditative place in Nature to seek the counsel of its resident wise ones.

All of a sudden, as I nestled my back into the spine of another medicine tree helper, I heard the Great Turtle's Voice again implore:

PILGRIM! The time has come to close your new-found journal and spend some time with this new listening post in my body. Once you've settled yourself, imagine travelling with this wicker steamer and journal to all those spiritual places in your life that you deem significant. See, too, all those wild, gentle humans of each place who have had the most impact on your evolutionary tale. Take whatever images reveal themselves as the opening passages of your odyssey atop me.

As your mind is drawn back, take note of the benchmark events that occurred around these people and places. Allow the years to fade in and out of focus as if they were scenes from some old familiar movie watched many times. Allow the one scene that keeps drawing you back to itself to be where your odyssey's tale begins.

See the pages of your new-found journal already chock-full of visionary-dream notes, fragments of music, ancient myths, sayings and drawings of all kinds. Note especially some love's gentle touch or fond memory of an unforgettable relationship. Imagine what they all are.

The first entry to visualize is the one on its fly-leaf. Use this as a medium to receive some communiqué from a long deceased grandparent or ancestor from your peoples' place of origin. Even if you are clueless as to who they were or what they looked like just allow your imagination to create whatever figure comes forth.

Passively observe your aboriginal image of them writing upon the fly-leaf something about why they left their beloved native homeland and came to the New World. As if peering over their shoulder, notice the one dream above all others that they hoped to realize as they set out upon their odyssey across this new continent.

It was hours later before I suddenly realized I'd drifted into a reverie that led me off to so many different places. Countless faces at each spot filled my thoughts.

It was then that I again heard The Great Turtle's Voice continue:

PILGRIM! if you are the first generation of your people to have emigrated to the New World then the initial entry in your journal will be a different one. You will have to imagine yourself as the ancestor, writing of your own dreams or fears for having come to this new land. Your mind's eye instead will have to create the image of a descendent peering over your own shoulder as you scribble upon the journal's fly-leaf.

Next is the journal's opening passage. Imagine your grandparent-ancestor or yourself jotting down as a legacy to some unknown future descendant how their dreams or fears were realized. See each word as if spoken aloud as it's written. Listen for the music of your peoples' native inflections and mannerisms expressed through each word.

Turn your thoughts towards the journal's end. See yourself or some descendant discovering the postscript notations that sum up the essence of what was learned in the act of trying to realize these dreams or dispel all the fear. What was the one most important pearl of wisdom – after all of life's trials and tribulations, joys and jubilation – that was learned about this new country, land, love and life. Apply that pearl of wisdom to what you and your family or clan have since experienced in the place where you now live and then project those experiences into the thoughts of an imaginary grandparent-ancestor as he or she concludes their entry. Place these thoughts on the fly-leaf, opening passage and postscript of your journal. Think of these entries as pioneer remembrances of the odyssey.

Once again I drifted off, wondering about all those ancestors before me who I now represented. I wondered what all it was that they wanted me to share with those who were passing through this same living time. Turtle's Voice soon declared in my thoughts:

Lad! Begin to sketch your *Family Tree*. Let the ground upon which this tree draws its life be where you found your wicker steamer. Make the trunk and roots the places you draw upon for your heritage. Include on its branches all those towards whom you feel most akin amongst the non-humans who walk the earth, swim in the water or fly through the air.

Next create a *Medicine Wheel* to live by. Place upon the spokes of the wheel how you intend, each morning as you rise from your place of dreaming and each night before returning back to the dreamtime, you will honor the: *Yet Unborn* so they may find a beautiful world to enter into; *Young Children* so they can live a good, healthy, peace-ul life; *Old People* that they are respected and cared for; *Native*

Peoples that their time-honored ways of life are protected and preserved; *Animal People* that their inalienable rights to life, liberty and the pursuit of happiness are acknowledged; *Mother Earth* that she be duly honored and obeyed as the mother-of-all-mother's that she is; *Water Of Life* in your body and that of the planet's remains pure; *Air Of Life* in your lungs and beyond stays fresh and clean; *Fire Of Life* and its spark within you burns forever bright and intense. List, too, the ways you will daily humble yourself as you honor each remembrance. Explore how to turn each one into a meditative song, chant, ritual or silent affirmation.

Even if your journal never finds its way into published form, see these first entries as a tiny book, unique unto itself, with a beginning, middle and end. Immediately publish it in a simple way.

Transcribe these opening entries onto a piece of acid-free parchment. Slip the parchment into a stout glass, tightly-corked bottle and then take it to some great body of water and set it adrift in the universe, like a time-capsule, for whatever distant, future eyes to read. Look upon this act as symbolically sowing the seed of the odyssey's tale.

Try to imagine what the accumulative effect would be on the human psyche if millions of these time-capsule bottles suddenly began drifting all about our planet's watery body, washing upon the shores of every continent.

Like the wandering, migrant, cosmic spirit that every human life is, they would speak to that secret, knowing, inner place of human thought that acts upon the truth when it hears it.

For a split second I once more found myself sitting with my back up against that medicine tree's rough trunk spine atop a lush green carpet of thick sphagnum moss. My thoughts swallowed up by the ponderous silence of the dense, sunless forest that surrounded me. Another Biblical-like shaft of sunlight, once more appearing as if out of nowhere as it brightly shone through the thick canopy overhead and mystically highlighted a twenty-foot wide fairy ring of stark white pine mushrooms that thrust their heads above the mossy forest floor.

"BUT ENOUGH TALK!", bellowed The Great Turtle's Voice at that moment. **"WHENEVER YOU SEE ME APPEAR, STOP WHAT YOU ARE DOING AND BE OFF WITH YOU! GO, I SAY, IN THE MOST LOVING WAY POSSIBLE! RETURN NOW TO THAT PLACE AND TIME WHERE THIS HEAVEN OR HELL, AS YOU HUMANS PUT IT, FIRST TOOK ONE OF ITS MOST PIVOTAL TURNS!"**

CURTLE ISLAND

ROAD SIGN # 10

WHAT NATURAL
OR HUMAN-MADE
THING SYMBOLIZES
YOUR WILD GENTLE VOICE'S
IMAGE OF ITSELF?

Our stories are as if the limbs and branches of a tree. All emerge from the main tap root and The Old Wise Ones, when shown a limb or branch, can recount what came before, what after and what yet will be.

(Anonymous 19th century Irish Seanchai)

– The Circle Is Unbroken –

Now over the skyline –
I see you're traveling.
Brothers from all time –
Gathering here.

Come let us build –
The ship of the future.
In an ancient pattern –
That journey's far.

Come let us set sail –
For the always island.
Through seas of leaving –
To the summer stars.

(**The Big Huge**, Robin Williamson)

ALTA-DENA;
A NEW FRONTIER COVERED WAGON

"PILGRIM", probes The Great Voice Of The Turtle, *"What forms and shapes, what sounds and images has your spirit used to make itself known to you? Does it speak to you through one of my stones, feathers or plants? Or maybe it speaks to you through some human-made object in your world? How have you used these things in your daily life to honor its presence inside you and carry out what it would have you do with your life's limited time, energy and resources? How have these symbols of who you are helped you to better know me, all my native human and non-human children and the ancient patterns of life they represent?"*

Every generation has its own special way of defining who they are, of setting the beginnings and endings of each significant era in their emotional and spiritual evolution.

For my generation, the late 60's and 70's were legendary benchmark years in so many different, often conflicting, ways as we rushed about in search of purpose and meaning. The Great Mystery of Life causing each of our odyssey's – our own peculiar notion of what we felt needed to be done to bring about a healing of ourselves, our nation and Mother Earth herself – to take all manner of strange direction.

As the odyssey took me ever deeper on a spiritual journey to slay yet one more newly-uncovered dragonish inner shadow, there were those others who instead rushed off elsewhere. While young defiant idealists, on one side of the world, were busy throwing up barricades in Paris and Prague, idealists of a darker sort, on the other side, were storming Phnom Penh and Phong Duc, to slay or be slain in steamy jungles and muddy rice paddies. As each seeker responded differently to the shadowy demands of their own dragonish-demons, Turtle's Voice asked of me, "Lad, which side are you on?"

While young and old of all colors and creeds chose to 'circle the wagons' in Asia, in last-ditch stands to fend off "the enemy's" takeover of their hard-won territories, still others, in hippie covered wagons, instead began circling 'round a Medicine Man's Sun Dance at Wounded Knee. Rather than destroy someone else's sacred circle of life, they were helping to reform and heal the Seven Circles of The Great Sioux Family and so reclaim their own heretofore lost spiritual territories.

As the first dying gasps of the beginning of the end of a violent Old World 'Dry-Rot' Order could be heard making its machine-gun death rattles from along far, distant Asian shores, Life's Great Mystery was causing some of us on our own shores to instead shake our dance rattles in honor of all life. A mysterious force was directing us to explore still unknown frontiers of the human mind and heart.

In the fall of '69, this force drew us from all directions to the Pacific shores of California, to join together with *Indians of All Tribes, Inc* in the peaceful occupation of Alcatraz Island in the middle of San Francisco Bay. Alcatraz a symbolic Turtle Island in microcosm.

We felt ourselves, at that unique juncture in time and space, being called upon to take to heart the sacred charge we each had been given by The Great Spirit to begin in earnest a spiritual renaissance movement. A world-wide movement among those of us of the first 'Four Worlds' whose collective vision looked to a futuristic One World Order that ultimately could bring peace and harmony to our tiny, troubled, warring planet.

The first stirrings of this historic new epoch began to sweep up in its wake many New Frontier peoples whose appearance upon the scene had long been prophesized as "The Return of the Seventh Generation".

– THE SACRED POWER OF SEVEN UPON TURTLE ISLAND –

When first I heard Oglala wise man Joe Thunder Hawk speak of the return of the Seventh Generation, I was reminded of a similar prophecy among traditional European peoples about how auspicious it is to be "The Seventh Son of the Seventh Son" among one's lineage.

During my time with the Hunkpatina at Crow Creek and the Oglala at Pine Ridge, I heard much talk about a native philosophy that some referred to as *The Seven Drums* religion, which others spoke of as Turtle Island's *Seven Commandments*. Or, as Thunder Hawk simply put it:

(1) To Live with *HEALTH* (Physical, Mental & Spiritual)
(2) To Live with *QUIET* (Keep still and holy each breath)
(3) To Live with *HAPPINESS* (Seek it not for oneself but for others)
(4) To Live with *SACRED POWER* (Allow Creator to use our body, mind & spirit as channels for healing)
(5) To Live with *KINDNESS & RESPECT* (Practice total non-violence towards all life forms)
(6) To Live Life as a *GIVEAWAY* (Sacrifice personal needs and wants for those of one's own people)
(7) To Live Life with *HONOR* (Follow the ancient wisdoms of the land as taught by the elders.)

Sitting 'round native council fires in South Dakota, I often heard much talk about the magical power of seven in all things. I was reminded of how our life cycles, if 'on schedule', take seven full years. Or how, at other times, if 'ahead of schedule' – depending upon the positive or negative physical-mental-spiritual energies we attract to ourselves or project into the world – they can take only a few short months or years to complete. Yet if 'behind schedule' they may take still many, many years or even lifetimes.

Just as *The Indian Drum* record, that arrived on my 7th birthday, proved to be the first of many benchmark cycles of the longings and aspirations stirred up inside me by the Great Voice of The Turtle, so, too, did the appearance of dear old Blue in all its Comet Caliente, hardtop convertible, sky-blue splendor.

The saga of how that '62 Comet and I came together in the summer of '68, in San Francisco, speaks to an earlier time and place of the odyssey's many unexpected turns. Blue magically made her appearance as one cycle reached its natural end and a fresh one was about to start up.

But like the opening and closing of still another one of life's earlier stages – when the time came to trade in my racy, red Schwinn racer for a stout walking stick, and begin an exploration of the San Bruno Mountains of my youth – it was Blue's turn to give way. The time had come to put my trusty 'New Age Steed', as I called her, out to pasture. Unbeknown to me though, Blue was about to be replaced by yet another mystical conveyance whose intimate name this time was *Alta-Dena*.

In those days, hippies treated their cars, vans, combos and trucks as if they were sentient beings, with unique personalities and identities full of magical import. As the saying went back then, "To behold a hippie with his truck is a beautiful thing!"

Blue, who acted as an outer image of an inner spiritual force that incessantly drove me forward, willingly gave way, without a whimper, to Alta-Dena on the day she made her sudden grand appearance.

Like Blue, Alta-Dena was about to become my new 'Indian scout' pony, hippie-version of an old Metis Red River Cart. This strange New Frontier covered wagon entity, whose name in Spanish meant 'a high place', soon would wildly carry me off to many high, distant places within myself and the Great Turtle's body.

Alta-Dena's unexpected arrival became another *of* The Voice's declarations that within some loftier plane, the star-bound sacred circle upon which I journeyed with so many others, no matter how often it might be broken and reformed, would forever remain strong.

It was Alta-Dena's turn, on the next leg *of* the odyssey, to spirit me away to many holy places to put into practice what I'd learned during my vision-seeking ceremony with Thunder Hawk. It was she who would soon take me to the Four Directions to join up with the large columns *of* other New Frontier hippie covered wagons that were beginning to wend their way through Indian Country. We modern-day *coureur de esprit bois* ('explorers *of* the spiritual woods') driving our wagons ever onward, eager to learn what we could *of* Turtle Island's basic, simple yet lofty wisdoms.

The dramatic way the two *of* us came together to explore this ancient world *of* reality that parallels the White Man's world, is typical *of* the always wondrous, natural way The Great Mysterious Force *of* Life seeks to raise our consciousness *of* such things as it subtly moves through us.

– ANOTHER MYSTIC TALISMAN OF THE OPEN ROAD –

I couldn't even begin to fathom the import *of* the two-decades long journey in Alta-Dena that was about to unfold on the day she whizzed by Blue and I on one *of* San Francisco's legendary, steep hills.

At a glance, that ordinary, '40's-style, DIVCO milk truck: made from a hodge-podge *of* GM parts; its comical old-fashioned snub nose, friendly squat body; 16 inch, split-rimed tires, gracefully-curved aluminium fenders, huge panoramic windows, bulbous headlamps and heavy, mouth-like bumber; looked more like a smiling White Buddha-Earth Goddess than just another run-o*f*-the-mill delivery truck.

Blue and I had earlier settled in San Francisco's Castro District where I secured a job as a teacher in a nearby public school; eager to teach The City's youth – through my self-styled 'Organic Classroom', and its Shannachie-Bardedashe-Socratic process – what all I'd learned about Turtle Island's Seven Commandments.

I'd found a place to live in a quasi-communal house with two couples and another single man who were all teachers. One couple was Dave and Sago Benson, who already had a DIVCO milk truck, ala hippie covered wagon, named *Blewett*, who, though larger, was a spitting-image *of* Alta-Dena. Several months before, Blewett had brought Dave and Sago out to the West Coast from Dave's family farm in Minnesota.

Eager to find a truck like my two new-found soul-mates, I at once committed to do a battery of guided-imagery and positive visualization exercises, each morning and evening, in the hopes of materializing my own 'Blewett'.

After several months of religiously applying these daily meditative exercises, Blue and I were driving home from school one day when – It Happened!

As we drove through the Castro, up Divisadero Street, a white, snub-nosed DIVCO suddenly crested the hill above us. Thinking it was Dave and Sago in Blewett, Blue and I honked at them in friendly salutation.

But as the DIVCO flew past, the sign on its side didn't read, "Blewett Dairy! You Can Whip Our Cream But You Can't Beat Our Milk!" Instead, it boldly declared, "Alta-Dena Dairy! Direct From The Farm To You!"

With that, The Voice gleefully shouted aloud, "AH, HAH, LAD! There's your dream-vision chariot I promised you! Direct From The Spirit Farm To You!"

Before realizing what I was doing, I whipped Blue 'round mid-block and set off in hot pursuit of that strange white dream-vehicle come true.

Yet how could I even remotely know that this innocent-looking milk truck Blue and I were madly chasing through the streets of San Francisco wasn't a truck at all but a mystical mixture of a talisman and a life goal.

This huge, two-ton mass of steel, glass and rubber indeed about to become one of life's awesome medicine charm-amulets that would lead to the discovery of a multitude of other magical charms that yet awaited up ahead on the open road.

Talisman-charms like the carved wooden plaque, depicting *Ophelia* from Shakespeare's *Hamlet*, still to be discovered some fourteen years later, that patiently awaited my consciousness at the entranceway of yet another seven-year cycle. That futuristic spiritual benckmark plaque itself visualizing into reality *The Elf Inn*, a Tolkien-like, fairy tale of a dream house in British Columbia, Canada.

That green and gold-painted Elf Inn talisman serenely waiting as an advanced lesson of the kind of First Nation committments that naturally come from rooting long enough in one place. Whereas Alta-Dena still had so much to teach me about another First Nation understanding that everywhere one travels to in life is a *living-in-a-sacred-place* experience with its own innate responsibilities.

Alta-Dena's conjuring powers, like those of The Elf Inn's distantly waiting, were about to demonstrate just how much, as Shakespeare once put it, "Our lives are such stuff as dreams are made of!"

The action-packed way this truism made itself known on the day Alta-Dena burst into view, revealed the real, ordinary magic that is behind the stuff of our dreams.

– A NEW CONJURING OF THE OPEN ROAD –

Madly honking Blue's horn in a futile attempt to flag down the ever-increasing, speeding driver of the strange truck, we sped together – up, over and down San Francisco's steep hills – like two swallows gripped in a frenzied, fever-pitched mating dance.

We continued to career over several more hills before Blue was able to pull alongside Alta-Dena and cut her off at an intersection, forcing her surprised driver to come to an abrupt, screeching halt.

Thinking that I was a motorist suffering from road rage or some whacked-out 'druggie' who finally had lost it; the long-haired, bearded driver threw open the DIVCO's accordion-like folding door and jumped from its cab.

Assuming a defensive stance in the middle of the intersection, with a wild, "What the fuck's your story, Mac!" look in his eyes; the hippie began menacingly waving in my direction a huge monkey wrench he held clenched in both hands like a baseball bat.

Profusely apologizing for having unduly rattled the poor guy, I quickly pleaded, "Hey, Dude! Hold On! Be Cool! Everything's Cool, Alright? I just want to buy your truck!"

I'd just cashed my paycheck and, as if to parry the man's monkey wrench, pulled out a thick wad of money from my pocket and began waving it back and forth in front of the bulging eyes of the hippie and his wife, who, by then, had also jumped from Alta-Dena's cab. She, herself, armed with a nasty-looking rusty tire-iron, poised at the ready, anxiously wondering what in the hell this crazed breed in the brilliantly-polished blue Comet Caliente hardtop convertible, with a fat roll of dough in his hand, wanted of them.

They both just stood there, flumoxed, staring dumbfounded at one another for several long moments of pregnant silence, before the hippie exclaimed with a broad smile, "Like, Man! This whole thing is too fuckin' much! Me an' the ol' lady just decided, not more 'an ten minutes ago, tah sell our truck, but we ain't even talked yet about no price."

"No problem!", I assuredly snapped back, "Just name your price!"

With that, I continued to tantalizingly wave the wad of cash back and forth in front of the two of them who, by now, had relaxed, the monkey wrench and tire iron slack in their hands by their side.

They continued for a time to follow the movements of the folded bills I held in both hands as if they were a pair of ricocheting tennis balls in a heated doubles match.

"Hold it!", the man shouted, breaking their trance. "Wait just a sec!", whereupon the two of them quickly pulled off to the curb for several, intense minutes of pow-wowing, At one point, the man spun around and hesitantly queried, "How 'bout five big ones?"

"You got it!", I declared, as I licked my fingers and began to peel off five one hundred dollar bills right there in the middle of the intersection.

Bewildered by the speed with which the whole transaction was taking place, the hippie pleaded, "Hey, Man! Like this is far-out an'all, but we ain't got no way of gettin' home from here an' we live way 'cross town. Let's do this right. Follow us back to our place on Cortland, in the Bayview, an' we can settle the deal right over a few tokes of some real good shit we got back at the house."

I did, and in a few short, stoned hours later found myself toasting Alta-Dena's bill of sale over a couple of tightly-rolled 'nails' that become part of a makeshift ceremony held in the street as the three of us stood beside Alta-Dena and Blue.

Before I knew it, Blue sat securely locked at the curbside, waiting for me to pick her up the next day; while I, ecstatic beyond words, waving my goodbyes to the hippie couple like some giddy mad man, drove off in Alta-Dena, back to the Castro and a soon-to-be love affair between her and Blewett. Quickly scribbled upon a note-pad enroute, were the words:

Happy Am I
To Be Or Not To Be
In Alta-Dena.
Visionary chariot –
Carry Me Forward.

Lead me to Many
High Places
Within Myself.

The Voice says,
"Happy Are They
Who Remain As If Children
Throughout Their Lives."

Running into the house, I beckoned to Dave and Sago, "Hey, you two! Come see who's parked next to Blewett! You'll never, in a million years, guess who it is!"

Minutes later, in a light-hearted moment of yet another impromptu ceremony, we wedded Alta-Dena and Blewett; formalized over a lot of puffs of Tibetan hash and drafts of *ZOOM*, a wicked coffee and milk home-brew with a rush worthy of its name. Dancing gaily 'round them with mock-serious pomp, we graced their hoods and panoramic windows with garlands of fresh-cut flowers hastily gathered from our garden.

– A NEW DREAM-MYSTERY OF THE OPEN ROAD IS BORN –

As Dave and Sago drove off in Blewett, still roaring with laughter from all our ceremony's crazy antics, I sat alone in Alta-Dena, sensing that some more serious ceremonial work with her was still to be done.

Looking around at her drab, bare walls, I wondered what colors, images, symbols and words should grace her interior to reflect what all I imagined our coming together represented, spiritually.

It was then that I heard The Voice challenge, "How, Lad, as a trail-blazer of your people, can you rebuild the road – the Medicine Wheel – upon which your people can humbly travel as they follow the Great Turtle's good old ways? How can you help Red, White, Black, Brown and Yellow peoples travel this same good road as true brothers and sisters?"

I sensed Alta-Dena to be some kind of mammoth *tabula rosa* that the spirit world had given me to help address the Voice's questions. As I sat blankly staring out Alta-Dena's huge windows, wondering what kind of ceremony needed to be done to acknowledge all this, I recalled my hanbleceya with Joe Thunder Hawk.

What Joe said to me, during the Medicine Man's Sun Dance at Wounded Knee, about not dancing with the others in the ceremony, kept ringing in my ears. "Look ta' the meaning of your spirit's name for why I tell ya not ta' do this."

A Four Wheeled Holy Chariot of a New Age

Turtle Island Pilgrims Plying Across the Great Desert

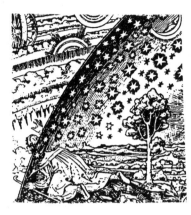

I instantly recalled the visionary woodcut image of the prophet Ezekiel that I mounted on Blue's sun vizor on the day we first came together. I knew that ceremony had to be repeated in Alta Dena.

A lot of time had passed in Blue, thinking about that old medieval monk and what he saw as he thrust himself from the sphere of material reality, up through the starry edge of the physical universe into that place of higher understanding called infinity.

Ezekiel, with his hand upraised, staring out at the Akashic wheels and all their glorious cosmic records extending far back beyond time itself. He the first human to see God encircled by a rainbow, one half immersed within the earth and the other reaching afar into the heavens.

Below the image of Ezekiel, mounted above Alta-Dena's huge windows, I wrote the affirmation, "As a New Fronteir trailblazer, help me, Alta-Dena, to realize that which I seek through the chrysalis of a dream. Help me **TO GO – BEYOND ACCEPTED WISDOM, AGAINST THE MADDENING CROWD, OFF THE BEATEN PATH!**"

Next, I placed near the etching and affirmation an ode, rolled up and tied like a scroll, that I composed in Alta-Dena's honor. It began:

(1)
In Honor of YOU –
Oh, outer reflection
Of an inner voice.
Spirit power set into motion.
Secret language of the heart,
Bypassing the failing of words,
Flowering within hidden chambers
Of mind and thought,
Now enshrined within your walls.

(3)
I take firm hold now –
Of your Grateful Dead-inspired
American Beauty Rose-painted
Steering Wheel.
Bright red gas pedal,
Joyfully pressed to the floor.
Accordion door folded open
My face thrust in the wind.

(2)
YOU –
Oh, mechanical music
Of the spheres.
Purring through
Inner & outer roads
Of many levels
All pulsating together.
Pregnant
With great import.

(4)
Our journey ahead –
Full of expectant moments,
Of birth and rebirth,
Arrested in time and space,
Allowing a glance back
At where I've been.
Presaging a glimpse forward
Towards where I would go.

The final ritual of the ceremony culminated with the placement of a poster on one of Alta-Dena's knotty-pine panelled, sleeping berth walls. It was a declaration by poet Allen Ginsburg that boldly asserted:

> We're in science fiction now. all the revolutions and the methods and techniques for changing consciousness are bankrupt. we're back to magic, to psychic life. Don't you know that power's an hallucination? The Civil Rights Movement, Sheriff Rainey, Time Magazine, McNamara, Mao – it's all an hallucination. No one can get away with saying that's real. All public reality's a script, and anybody can write the script the way he or she wants. The warfare's psychic now. Whoever controls the language, the images, controls the race.

With the ceremony completed, Alta-Dena was about to teach me that the discovery of that which Ginsburg spoke, first comes with learning how to listen well to all the truths to be found in one spot and all the stories these truths will naturally kindle or rekindle within our lives.

The kind of *Remembrance Stories* that will liberate us and so give back to us a dream – a new myth – for being alive. A myth that declares, "From the beginning, a powerful dream was born atop Turtle's back. For all who can feel that power there is hope. Within that hope lies the seed of the destiny the Great Mystery holds for each of us. A destiny that will bring about yet a new epic stage in human story and song."

– A MYSTERY STONE'S DREAM-VISION OF THE FUTURE –

The honeymoon between Alta-Dena and Blewett hadn't even had a chance to cool off when Dave and Sago came to the decision to return to the Benson farm in Minnesota and assume a simple, rural, Quaker way of life as organic farmers.

Inspired by the legendary 19th century words, "Go West! Young Man! Go West!" immortalized by Horace Greeley, one of Sago's illustrious ancestors, Dave and Sago came to the infamous 'City-By-The-Bay' to *see the elephant*, had experienced its fast, crazy pace of life, and at once recognized that it wasn't a healthy way to live nor a wholesome place in which to raise a family. Before leaving, they made me promise to visit them before Spring's end.

Traveling to their farm that Spring, I soon found myself harnessing Alta-Dena alongside Blewett, where Dave and I worked them like a couple of draft horses, hauling about the Benson's farm machinery.

One day, while driving Alta-Dena across a freshly-tilled field, an overwhelming urge all at once arose in me to stop and look for a special stone that seemed to be calling out.

Alta-Dena's Dreaming Place

Soul Memories of the Dream Time

The summer before, David's Swedish-born father, a big brute of a man whose hands engulfed mine twice over, had brought in a huge earthmover and dug down some fifteen feet into the virgin Minnesota prairie to create a dam to water his stock. Consequently, the banks of the large dam and its surrounds were littered with thousands of unearthed rocks, amongst which I began to wander.

Finally approaching a state of near total frustration from the nigh impossibility of the ludicrous task before me, I was just about to give up the search when Dave called out from atop the edge of the earthen dam.

"Hey, Jerry!", he shouted, "C'mon over an' see how much water's already in the dam."

Turning and walking towards Dave in the opposite direction from where my search for the 'magic stone' had been leading, I hadn't taken ten steps when there on the ground, lying directly in front of my path, was a most unusual-looking, round black stone. The stone virtually leapt out from all the rest as if it were glowing with light.

I just stood there for several long minutes, doing nothing more than stare at the stone in the same disbelieving way that I stared at the black, French-cut bead that, just the year before, revealed itself in the wall of the ant people's village near Wounded Knee.

At one point, I reverently bent down, picked up the stone and began rolling it from hand to hand, enjoying the feel of its smooth round surface slide against my skin.

All of a sudden I heard a voice speak out as if it simultaneously came from both inside me and the stone itself. Like it did on the day I found the French-cut bead in South Dakota, the same voice softly whispered, "Lad! Did I find you or did you find me?"

With that, the small, yet heavy for its size, stone fell perfectly between my curled thumb and forefinger, as if it had been custom-tumbled to fit the empty space between them.

I gasped with amazement as my eyes saw inside the center of the stone a distinctly-carved circle with another fainter image in relief inside it. Depending upon the angle at which the stone was held to catch the light, the image in the center of the raised circle took on the appearance of an Indian wearing an eagle headdress or the head of a black buffalo bull. How old the stone was or how long it had been buried there, deep within the virgin Minnesota prairie, was a mystery.

Rushing to mind were the memories of my time spent with the Hunkpatina people of Crow Creek, who originally came from these same Minnesota prairie lands before they were driven out during the hostilities betweeen the white farmers and First Nation people.

As Lucy Sargent-Swift Hawk's face came into view, I knew at once that this stone was meant to be kept in Maġa Bobdu's medicine bundle alongside his Sun Dance stick and the pouch of ceremonial red earth that Lucy had placed in my care.

– A WHITE BUFFALO MEDICINE STONE DREAM COMES –

That night, after having sat in silent meditation for several hours on the rim of the earth dam with my new-found medicine stone, watching the sun's movement through the sky 'til it sank into the West, I felt compelled to take the stone to bed and ask it for a dream.

Preparing to enter into the dreamtime inside Alta-Dena's cozy, sleeping berth, I glanced about, admiring all the hand-painted images, incantations and symbols upon Alta Dena's chambered walls that reflected my New Frontier native mind's eye.

It was always so nurturing and empowering to visually drink up, to fill my soul, with all the spirits who resided within: the surrealistic, light and dark forms of M.C. Escher mounted side-by-side sepia-toned, romantic Edward Curtis impressions of The Good Old Life; the red, white and blue psychdelic stars and comets of Peter Max that complimented the Batik Rainbow Man mural that hung from the ceiling; the ancient visages of First Nation elders, so old that they had become half tree and half human; a Coleman lantern that hissed away, casting a warm glow upon the whole wondrous nighttime encampment scene.

Once I received all the visual nourishment I needed for my dream-time journey, I again cupped the black stone between thumb and forefinger and rested it upon the heart chakra area of my upper chest. Before I knew it, I drifted off into a deep sleep.

Feeling at one stage the stone beginning to roll off my chest, I awoke with a startle. Jerking the hand holding the stone up to my forehead, I smacked myself with it right between the eyes in what, metaphysically, is referred to as "the third eye".

So hard did I whack my third eye that I momentarily saw nothing but rainbow-colored stars of all sizes and shapes. It wasn't until several dazed minutes later that I finally came fully to and realized I'd had a most powefrul dream.

The dream's imagery spoke of a time yet to come when many New Frontier Breeds and metis exiles of all races, colors and creeds will be called upon to serve as the much-needed spiritual elders and guides of their people.

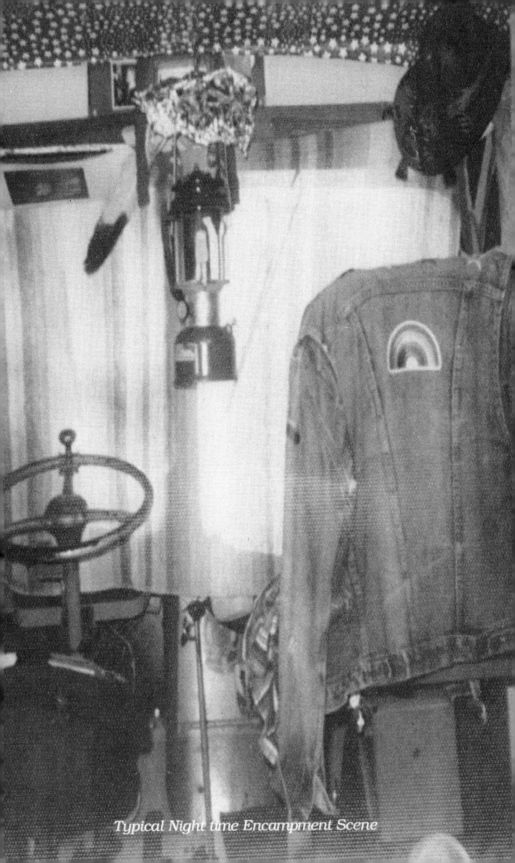

Typical Night time Encampment Scene

Camp out in Alta-Dena

The dream's 'Black Medicine Stone Story', as I came to think of it, encouraged all those who feel such a calling to at once begin to purify and ready themselves for the day when the Great Mysterious One that moves all will call them forward to lead their lost, confused people to places of safety.

In the dreamtime story there appeared a monumental scene of all the natural spiritual leaders of the Black, White, Yellow and Red races who ever were, gathered in a huge encampment that stretched beyond the horizon. Scattered about were their various culture's different historical conveyances by which they once explored the reality of their own living time. Indian scout ponies, Red River Carts, Hippie wagons, Irish lorries and Dolomiten haycarts stood at the ready, close by their owners.

The Holy Black Stone's dream account concluded with a funeral scene of Dave Benson and me standing beside his father's open casket. His father's ghost, in the company of my own grandfather's ghosts – Grandpa William and John from Ireland and Grandpoppa Louie from the Tyrolean Alps – appeared alongside us. These ghosts laughed in unison at how humorous it was to witness their funerals with Dave and I standing close-by their former bodies, crying over the loss of them.

Speaking together, as if there was only one great voice issuing between them, these spirits eerily whispered, "Fret not, Lads! We haven't died a'tall. Did you ever think we had? You see, lads. We live through you now and forever, from dream to medicine stone to all of life."

– THE DREAM SLOWLY UNFOLDS –

Several years after the Medicine Stone Dream made itself known, the occasion arose to travel through the Pacific Northwest in Alta-Dena. I'd gone there to seek out one old, blind, Salish Indian woman that some referred to as "A Sensitive One", and presented her with the black stone. My hope was that she might be able to peel back, like an onion skin, yet one more layer of the stone's connection to the odyssey.

As I slipped the stone into the out-stretched hand of the old Salish mystic, she nodded and held it in her palm for the longest time without saying a word.

Finally, she cryptically remarked, "Yah didn't fine dis' stone, is what I'm gettin'. An ol' man give dis' t' yah'."

"No!", I said, "I really did find it in...." "Yah didn't", she tersely interjected as she cut me off. "An' ol man's given dis' stone t' yah. He means fer ya' t' one day come back an' fine somethin' else dhat waits fer ya' dere in dah ground."

Strangely, though, many years would follow that brief meeting with the old sensitive Salish woman and yet the odyssey never returned me back to Minnesota to find out what that 'somethin' else' was.

Each time her long ago prophecy is recalled, and I get to wondering again why I've not yet returned, The Voice counsels, "Worry not, lad. It may be some distant exit or entrance way cycle still to be made across the Turtle's back. In due time, you will know."

Once, after growing impatient, waiting for this new cycle to manifest itself, I was about to arbitrarily jump into Alta-Dena and head back to the Benson Farm to find out, when something strange happened.

The night before setting out, I again took up my medicine stone, lay inside Alta-Dena's dreamtime chamber as I did so many times before, and meditated with the stone resting against my heart chakra.

I dropped into a deep sleep before I realized the stone was once more about to roll off my chest and involuntarily cracked my third eye with it.

As I lay dazed, the 'grandfather ghost dream' returned and several ghosts chided, "Naughty boy. Know ye will be directed – through dream, animal voice or tree – when the time is right and no sooner!"

Whenever another spiritual foray north or south of The Medicine Line was made – stopping to camp near some old-time Indian healing spring or medicine spot – this dream stone ritual was repeated anew.

One night, as I lay inside Alta-Dena's sleeping berth with my 'philosopher stone', a poem planted itself so powerfully in my conscious memory that it startled me awake so I could jot it down. It declared:

SACRED STONE
Head of a Buffalo Spirit,
Body of a Salmon Spirit
Earthdiver Migration Compass,
Through Endless Worlds
Above and Below.

You, Oh
– Eye of Pisko –
Thunder Hawk Soaring
Above a Dream-vision.
Day & Night'time Eye,

Of Sun & Moon,
Look Into My Soul.
Speak To Me

Of The Great Mystery
That moves All Things.

Each Day –
I Go In Many Directions,
Looking & Listening,
For The Gift
Of Yet Another
Beautiful Spirit Day
You Give Me
To Find.

Each Night –
You Lead Me
On a Different Journey
To Learn
Of The Gift's
Other Side.

I Thank You
White Buffalo Medicine Stone
And You
Whomever Gave You To Me.

I Pledge
Hear & Now
To Bear Your Essence
As A Gift
To Others
In Return.

So, Pilgrim! It's time to realize another living-out-of-every-cell-in-your body experience in your own natural place of retreat. While there, reflect upon some human-made object that has come to symbolize what you would call an outer extension of your wild, gentle voice's image of itself. What thrilling journeys, mysteries or extraordinary moments has this object led you to have? What gifts have you received from it? **GO!**

WELCOME BACK! Driving to the Four Directions *of* The Great Turtle in Alta-Dena – taking long periods *of* time to reflect upon the many Grandfather and Grandmother gifts received along the way from the invisible realm – I continued down the open road.

As Alta-Dena and I went, Ezekiel's vision (Chapter 1, verses 15-21) came to mind. Just as in his vision, Alta-Dena's four wheels had rims and spokes *of* a sort, the hubs *of* her rims full *of* metaphysical eyes, as it were. And when I – her living creature-driver at the wheel – went, her four wheels went, too.

With each mile travelled, it was as if she were asking, through the hum *of* her wheels upon the road, "Lad! Recapture some soul memory *of* why it is you and I have come together again here in this incarnational cycle ."

"Hmmm!", I wondered, "Could those first, second, third, fourth and fifth worlds, that so many speak *of* in political terms, actually be other worlds or levels *of* spiritual consciousness that beckon each to their own? I, in Alta Dena, and the man or woman beside me in their Cadillac or Lincoln, here for very different reasons?"

Each reflection *of* this incarnational cycle a marvelment at how this odd white chariot-New Frontier covered wagon had indeed lived up to its intimate name by the high, soulful, mystical experiences it helped me to realize. Alta-Dena's inherent qualities teaching lessons in themselves.

To begin wth, the hippie couple who previously owned Alta-Dena, once used her rear cab as a mobile candle factory, making and selling, as they said, "Rainbow candles for clear vision in the world." The hippie couple duly billed themselves, "The Makers *of* Rainbow Light."

Alta-Dena's earlier incarnation as a genuine milk truck – its gleaming white body once traveling hither and yon, from the hills high above Pasadena, to distant health food stores, delivering pure, nutritious dairy products to nourish the peoples minds, bodies and spirits – also came to symbolize the degree *of* purity I sought to realize upon the odyssey's medicine path she opened up for me.

Contending with Alta-Dena's always tempermental mechanical nature – her original four-banger Hercules engine either threatening to breakdown or run out *of* gas because her fuel gauge never worked – served as a constant encouragment to overcome whatever personal fears I held about finding myself stranded, all alone, on some desolate stretch *of* open road. Her license plate, 'LWS 729', came to symbolize the strange 'Lone White Spirit, double nine' journey I'd set out upon.

Never able to expect to get anywhere in Alta-Dena with any degree of certainty or exactitude of time, she encouraged me to adapt to a schedule – a philosophy – a life rhythm – that ran more on *Natural Time* than it did on White Man's time. Meaning if I arrived somewhere as planned that was fine, but if I didn't that was fine too, because the Great Mystery of things decreed I should instead arrive elsewhere.

Alta-Dena's heavy, lumbering, two-ton body and her small yet powerful Hercules engine demanded that she never be taken for granted or pushed beyond her limits of 55 mph. She therefore enouraged me to take to the slower, less-traveled back roads, discovering in the process an older, quieter, more genteel America and Canada which still exists beyond the freeway madness of the modern, peptic-ulcerated world.

Alta-Dena's large accordion-folding doors inspired me to drive with them wide-open: standing in her cab with one foot on her bright red gas pedal and the other on her flashy yellow running board; one hand on the suicide knob of her Grateful Dead-inspired, American Beauty Rose-painted steering wheel, with the other holding firm to the chrome grip bolted to her thin skin frame; half my body thrust out the door, face flush with the wind so I could experience the subtle, rapid changes of Nature's ecozones, with all their different moods and fragrances, as they rushed by.

Such simple, fleeting, yet profound joys experienced in Alta-Dena symbolized what it truly means to be alive in the moment. These fragile pleasures all but completely missed by most modern-day travelers who rocket through Nature at ever faster speeds; encapsulated as they are in their fancy air-conditioned, hermetically-sealed, GPS-guided, electronic 'prison cell' phone tracked, sensory-deprivation chambers.

Passing slowly across the face of Turtle Island, making new friends along the way, partaking in the sacred life of each new place traveled to, was always the real spiritual journey – the real gift – of the open road.

Making torrid, visual love with each new creek-river-mountain-valley-desert-meadow passed by; scanning the landscapes for new, unknown, wild life forms; jotting down the spiritual notation of hidden stories discovered in unusual cloud formations; psychically noting the changing dispensations of the day, especially at dawn and dusk; all were part of Alta-Dena's natural legacy.

Guiding that hippie Winnebago, ala Ken Kesey's Prankster bus *Further*, across the prairies and plains of the Great Canadian–American West were priceless 'happenings'. Their low, cloud-filled skies and waving oceans of summer grasses conveying the feeling that if I wasn't a God then I surely was at least one of the Lord's anoited, privileged to be able to pass through the rarefied spaces of these earthen pantheons and commune with their resident magical powers.

The sum total of her legacy: a veritable kaleidoscope of naturally-stoned eco-adventures, shared with other wayfarer–hitch hiker–cosmic hobo–Incredible String Band freaks of the road. Our spontaneous, soulful, communal gatherings at pristine places in Nature virtually unknown in today's fear-riddled, alienated, paranoid world where, in many places, it's even illegal to hitch hike let alone pick up such a person.

From the day our paths crossed, Alta-Dena encouraged me to accept her limitations as a talisman within the odyssey and, when the time was right, to let go of her without a backward glance, and pass on her gifts – in the same way that dear, faithful Blue's gifts eventually were passed on – to the next lot of unsuspecting New Frontier pilgrims to come along.

The young wandering dreamer–gypsy hippie who ultimately found himself in possession of Blue was as ecstatic as I once was over her. He just as eager to set off upon his own long-avowed dream-quest to retrace the old pioneer Route 66 track across North America; hoping to gain some sense of the intangibles of a slower, softer, freer, expectant American way of life for which that much-beloved, well-traveled roadway once was such a grand symbol.

Alta-Dena, like Blue, taught me that whatever are the natural or human-made objects that we happen to deem special or sacred in our lives – whether they be a stone, raptor's feather, precious gem or whatever – are only sacred because we empower them as such in the way we use them in our daily lives. Blue and Alta-Dena not unlike the human body itself which acts as nothing more than a vehicle to house the mysterious entity that drives it through life.

An ancient medicine man or woman's sacred stone or feather resting in the glass case of a museum somewhere, therefore no more holy or possessive of special powers than those we ourselves might come by and 'awaken' in the same way that the ancient holy person once did with his or her own intimate personal objects.

In the years that followed, and Alta-Dena and I got that much further down the open road and that much more intimate with one another, my understanding of such things grew and matured.

Yet the farther we traveled, and the more high-places we reached, all the more grew the realization that there still were so many basic Lesson#1's of Turtle Island's indigenous grammar and spiritual lore that I needed to draw upon.

The next big stop on the road to learn more about all this came only a few miles away from where we first met in San Francisco. Because, by then, another one of those big Lesson#1's was already taking shape on nearby Alcatraz Island.

TURCLE ISLAND

ROAD SIGN # 11

**WHERE DID YOU RECEIVE
YOUR LIFE'S
PERSONAL
SERMON ON THE MOUNT**

– The Medicine Wheel –

Finally, it is beautiful to be a Red man or woman!
Finally, it is beautiful to be a White man or woman!
Finally, it is beautiful to be a Black man or woman!
Finally, it is beautiful to be a Yellow man or woman!

The Red Road of Life! The White Road of Life!
The Black Road of Life! The Yellow Road of Life!
All are coming here to the center. The center being
the center within each of us that links us up with
the center of us all, our hearts and our hands
joined together!

(Archie Fire-Lame Deer, Lakota Pipe Carrier)

– The Long Walk Begins –

Music & Lyrics
by Benny "Q"

Walk on Long Walker, You've Got Lots of MIles to Walk On!
Walk on Long Walker, You've Got Lots of MIles to Walk On!

ALCATRAZ ISLAND:

BORN AGAIN INTO TWO WORLDS

"PILGRIM", impatiently implores The Great Voice *of* The Turtle, *"Look closely at the European, Asian and African immigrants upon my back and the many moral and ethical problems they have in the way they exploit all my native life. Look, too, at the paltry few steps they've taken over the past five centuries to see to it that all my native children and their sacred lands are protected and preserved. What you see will be a harsh, unpleasant truth. A truth that says if the medicine roads of the Four Sacred Colors of People who now live upon me are ever to lead towards some good place of healing and bring everything back into balance, they will have to be totally rebuilt. Sadly, this rebuilding may yet take another five centuries or more. IF, that is, your young reckless civilization atop me can last that long. How have you already begun to rebuild your own life's medicine road and medicine wheel? What healing rituals and ceremonies do you use to help bring these things about? What do you know of my native children's traditional practices and teachings that could help your rebuilding work?"*

⟶➤●◖⟶

Before no time a'tall had past, Blue set off across the Turtle's back on Route 66 with yet another new pilgrim, as eager as I to discover his own truths *of* the open road in his new-found spirit wagon.

By now, my Lacotah hanbleceya vision-quest and the Medicine Man's Sun Dance in South Dakota were ancient history. The healing process and rebuilding work I knew I had to do within myself already well underway. The spirit world itself also was moving historical events ever faster, jerking many *of* us around at a breathtaking pace.

This point in the odyssey found me cast in the role *of* a lecturer and research assistant to Sociology Professor Tom Ryther at San Francisco State College. Our work together addressed his classes on 'Traditional & New Age Communities', as well as on a Stanford University study *of* 'Illness Within The Family & Community'.

An instant soul-mate and epitome *of* the wild, gentle man, Tom Ryther spent years learning from the traditional Shoshoni and Northern Cheyenne in the Wind River country *of* Wyoming.

Thrilling tales of our spiritual eco-adventures and encounters with the invisible realms of the Oglala, Hunkpatina, Shoshoni and Northern Cheyenne daily flew 'round the office, classrooms and hallways we shared.

– A MEETING BETWEEN WARRIOR SOUL-MATES –

One day, as we sat quietly working at our desks in Ryther's office, a light knock sounded upon the door.

The door gently pushed open and in strode a big Indian man whose powerful warrior physique filled the doorway.

"Could I speak to you guys for a minute?", he softly muttered. "My name's Richard Oakes. I'm a Mohawk Indian. I'd like to tell you about something very important to Indian people that you might be able to help us with."

Before Oakes said anything more, his eyes glanced up at a poster that hung above Tom's desk. It was a wall-size, sepia-tone of a 19th century Curtis photograph that showed a Lacotah man, simply dressed in mocassins and breechcloth, standing atop a holy hill, a buffalo skull at his feet and in his hands a sacred medicine pipe held aloft, its stem pointed heavenward in a symbolic offering to the universe.

Oakes stared at the poster for a long, lingering moment before declaring, with a wry smile, "Looks like I've come to the right place."

Oakes took to recounting an incredible tale about us all becoming part of the fulfillment of an ancient native prophecy and vision for North America that soon would become known to the world through their *Manifesto* and occupation of Alcatraz Island by *Indians of All Tribes. Inc.*

The longer his tale continued, the more I thought, "This guy looks anything but the stereotyped image of the militant Indian that everyone soon will see wildly staring out at them from behind their T.V. screens."

Neatly dressed – wearing a London Fog raincoat, sport jacket, starched white shirt and tie, brand new pair of Levi's, with an attaché in-hand – Oakes looked more the part of a studious grad student than one of the main grass-roots organizers of a planned military-like occupation of Alcatraz.

My hanbleceya's intense meditative reflections atop Joe's Holy Hill helped me gain a fledgling sense of how our lives can often take a decades-long, circuitous journey in ignorance or denial of what The Voice has been trying to inform us, since day one, is its real purpose.

Oakes, himself, was about to honor his destiny's call by becoming but one among the many inspirational native leaders who've surfaced over the past five centuries since first contact with the White Man.

Like all his many nameless, faceless Mohawk warrior ancestors, who fought hard and died well to preserve the traditional medicine ways of their people, Oakes soon would pay his leadership dues with the supreme price of his own life. His eleven year-old daughter, Yvonne, also about to meet an early tragic death at the bottom of a steep stairwell on Alcatraz.

The supreme price their destiny's call was about to demand of them would serve as a reminder of that which we each must ultimately be prepared to pay if we're serious about leaving behind us something good and lasting for those yet unborn.

– A TURTLE ISLAND MANIFESTO IS REVEALED –

"Do you mind if I sit down?", Oakes asked. "I have a long story to tell you about a dream-vision that is soon going to become a reality. Here, read this Manifesto that we're ready to reveal to the world in a big way."

manifesto

Indians of All Tribes greet our brothers and sisters of all races and tongues upon our Earth Mother. We here on Indian Land, Alcatraz, represent many tribes of Indians.

We are still holding the Island of Alcatraz in the true names of Freedom, Justice and Equality, because our brothers and sisters of this earth have lent support to our just cause. We reach out our hands and hearts and send spirit messages to all Indians.

Our anger at the many injustices forced upon us since the first white men landed on these sacred shores has been transformed into a hope that we be allowed the long-suppressed right of all men to plan and to live their own lives in harmony and cooperation with all fellow creatures and with nature. We have learned that violence breeds only more violence and we therefore have carried on our occupation of Alcatraz in a peaceful manner, hoping that the government will act accordingly.

Be it known, however, that we are quite serious in our demand to be given ownership of this island in the name of Indians of All Tribes. We are here to stay: men, women, and children. We feel that this request is but little to ask from a government which has systematically stolen our lands, destroyed a once-beautiful landscape, killed off the creatures of nature, polluted air and water, ripped open the very bowels of our earth in senseless greed, and instituted a program to annihilate the many Indian Tribes of this land by theft, suppression, prejudice, termination, and so-called relocation and assimilation.

We are a proud people! We are Indians! We have observed and rejected much of what so-called civilization offers. We will preserve our traditions and ways of life by educating our own children. We are Indians! We will join hands in a unity never before put into practice. Our Earth Mother awaits our voices. We are Indians of All Tribes! ! !

Several weeks after our first meeting with Oakes, Prof. Ryther and some of his grad students gathered at Tom's home to help celebrate my upcoming Scorpio-Sagittarius-cusped birthday. A light, cold rain was falling outside but inside the occasion was a warm, festive one.

A toast was offered up in honor of Bessie Swift Hawk – a 104 year old woman I'd once briefly lived with on the Crow Creek Sioux reservation in South Dakota, near the Big Bend of the Missouri. Her own life's destiny, as one of the 'Stolen Generation' among First Nation peoples, had caused her to suffer through many arduous ordeals as she found herself hopelessly caught in-between the two radically-different worlds of her Hunkpatina people and the invading White Man. I'd just concluded the toast when a loud knock sounded on the door.

In strode Richard Oakes, Ed Castillo and several other wild-looking, free-spirited Indian warrior brothers, all excitedly blurting out, in one adrenaline-laced declaration after another, how they felt as they prepared to hold their final staging meeting at the *No Name* bar in Sausalito before implementing their historic occupation of 'The Rock'.

Every fiber of my being desperately wanted to go with them to become part of the Island's takeover. "Can't I go with you guys?", I begged.

"No, sorry!", Oakes firmly replied. "It's important we Indians do this by ourselves. But we're gonna need all the support you white 'wasicu' brothers can give us back on the mainland."

"I understand, Bro", I shot back. On an intellectual level I understood what Oakes was saying, but on a emotional gut level I couldn't. Recalled were all the times when we Irish had been demeaned by the Whie Man as, "Niggers turned inside out!", or disparaged in racist cartoons as gorillas and monkeys dressed in top hats and tails.

For as long as I can remember, I've either felt like being an Indian in a former lifetime or some weird throwback to my native Celtic Irish–Southern Tyrolean ancestral origins. Equally curious is the fact that my given first name, in Spanish, is 'Geronimo'. And every time my spirit's image finds itself caught by another looking glass, flashes of that old Apache mystic-warrior squinting back at me can be seen.

I wanted to say to Oakes, "Hey, Bro! I, too, feel every bit a part of the historic spiritual reclamation of the ancient spirit of Turtle Island now underway. If ever the White Man and Indian are to join together, and heal one another, we must act on such occasions as if one, single native body, mind and spirit!"

It was then that an image of my spiritual mentor, Joe Thunder Hawk, flew into my thoughts like *Pisko ('Pee-shko')*, the Nighthawk, did, years before, during a key moment in my hanbleceya vision-quest. Pisko soaring through the sky, heralding the coming of the Thunderspirits and vital spirit energies that lay beyond the edge of a breaking lightning storm.

"Look ta' the meaning of yer spirit's name", Thunder Hawk once again said in my thoughts, "for why I tell ya' all these things. How many times do I have t' tell ya' that ya' have a different path t' walk, a different dance t' make among yer people. It's gonna be a mighty tough path. You gotta stay strong. Yer gonna have to be real patient, too!"

As Joe's smiling face drifted from view, an empty, sinking feeling welled up in the pit of my stomach. My face pressing itself ever harder against the damp, rain-soaked window as Oakes and the other brothers poured out of the front door and down the steps.

At least one pair of longing eyes passively watched as they clambered into a beat-up, old rez car and sped off down the street through a drizzling rain, disappearing 'round a corner towards their rondezvous with destiny. A destiny which the Mohawk poet, Peter Blue Cloud, one of the Island's occupiers, said would reveal itself:

AS LIGHTNING STRIKES THE GOLDEN GATE
AND FIRE DANCES THE CITY'S STREETS –
A NAVAHO CHILD WHIMPERS THE TIDE'S PULL,
AND SIOUX AND CHEYENNE DANCE LOWLY
ON THE GROUND.
TOMORROW IS BREATHING MY SHADOW'S HEART
AND A TRIBE IS AN ISLAND
AND A TRIBE IS AN ISLAND.

– BROTHERS & SISTERS OF ALL COLORS COME TOGETHER –

We New Frontier Breeds of the *Wasicu Tribe* weren't allowed to be part of the actual physical takeover of Alcatraz, but we did become the main back-up support arm of 'The Occupation'.

Alta-Dena worked as a pack horse-supply wagon, collecting everything imaginable – food stuffs, bedding, cooking utensils – for the occupational forces. We Wasicu's, and our African-Asian brothers and sisters, likewise ran everything from hot-air balloons and small marine crafts to large fishing boats which, like pirate ships, craftily slipped through the tight blockade of Coast Guard cutters, S.F.P.D. harbor patrols and hovering U.S. Army helicopters that constantly encircled The Rock.

No matter what minor role we each played, it was an epiphanic experience. For we all somehow could sense ourselves to be part of an important historical benchmark on what, in human annals, is an unending spiritual road – a planetary home-coming ceremony – set out upon by many others of different nations, races, religions and cultures long, long before our time. We knew that no matter what any despot, dictator, demagogue might ever do to us, or those who come after, it would never destroy the righteous path we traveled.

Like the historic *Long Walk* First Nation peoples and their allies would make together across the face of America some ten years after The Occupation, those of us who gathered upon The Rock knew it represented but one more tiny step taken by 'old souls' who'd walked together many times before, through time and space, along the same straight medicine road. Our perpetual Long Walk, renewed upon Alcatraz, part of an ever-constant dream-vision to one-day correct all the imbalances of life that ravage the Western Hemisphere, and indeed the world at large.

To the gangster mentality in North America, Alcatraz and its fortress–prison has long symbolized 'the end of the line'. To be imprisoned at Alcatraz was to be sent to the coldest, dampest, furthest-most place on the continent one could be exiled to, with little hope of escape. Spanish hostages, Yankee Civil War deserters, Confederate prisoners, Hopi Indian captives and American convicts all found this out, first-hand, the hard way.

This is why the elders chose Alcatraz to make their stand. By then, Native peoples and their allies also found themselves imprisoned with little hope of escape. The Rock a perfect Turtle Island in minature; a symbol to express the imperative need for the reclamation and release of all our imprisoned roots as naturally free, wild peoples.

Alcatraz became an especially rare opportunity for we New Frontier Breeds to meet and honor, for the first time, the real spiritual elders and resident philosophers of North America and acknowledge what all they were trying to say to the world. The Rock became the place where we first sought to elevate Turtle Island's elders to their long-denied, rightful place as North America's *National Living Treasures.*

– A PROPHECY'S TEACHING UNFOLDS –

The Native Spiritual Renaissance Movement that we set into motion on The Rock was the fulfillment of a prophecy by Black Elk, a Lakota wise man. Decades before, Black Elk often spoke about *The Rooting of The Daybreak Star* which, he prophesized, "One day will grow flowers, four blossoms on one stem – blue, white, red and yellow – that will turn into a new Sacred Tree of Life upon this land."

Medicine Tipi View of The Golden Gate

Alcatraz, with its en-visaged 'Indian Red' painted lighthouse, was meant to serve as a beacon of hope – a First Nation version of the 'Statue of Liberty' – signaling to those awaiting a sign that the rooting of the Day-break Star had begun in earnest.

For we self-professed 'Day-break Star People', Alcatraz became as much a way to celebrate the recovery of a new 21st century spiritual island as it was the takeover of an actual physical one.

Like its Biblical counterpart on 'The Mount', we received many teachings on 'The Rock'. We each were given, as a sacred charge, the task to go out to the Four Directions, spread the subtle understanding of what it means to invoke the words, *"Ho! All My Relations!"* and so bring about a radical paradigm shift in the thought processes and brain patterns of all the people. The 180° shift in world view, invoked by this saying, one that would call to our minds the relatedness of all things in life.

As one elder at the time put it, "Twin Rainbow! If ya' can get yer people t' jus' use this one blessin', they'll know right off who they r' an' what they naturally w'll have t' start doin' t' set things right. That's why we Indians can become militant an' even hostile when it's needed, 'cause nothin' is above doin' when you're protectin' all those things you're related t'."

Or as another elder pointed out, "This is why, Rainbow, th' White Man's afraid of us who do. But all th' White Man needs to do is just follow his own Good Book and it'll tell 'him what to do. Th' one teachin' I'm thinking about is that one outta th' Book of Ecclessiastes in the Old Testament that goes, 'To everythin' there's a season, and a time to every purpose under th' heavens. You know, don't you, Rainbow, th' one I'm a talkin' about? It's th' one that sez there's a time to be born, and a time to die, a time to go to war and a time to live in peace."

On The Rock, we heard one elder after another say, in so many different words, "You must go from this place and teach yourself and your people how to bring all life back into balance. Learn each other's religious teachings and spiritual understandings of our sacred relation-ships to every living thing that is a relation common to us all who we must care for as we would care for our immediate family. The Great Spirit has gathered us together here at this time and place to begin to learn how to do this."

We heard still other elders say, "For the rest of your life, the struggle of indigenous peoples everywhere will be the most important cause you can devote yourself to help resolve. Because this is the best way to protect your own rights as a free people who also one day will be able to reclaim your right to become an indigenous people once again."

Each wise man or woman elder gave us their own explanation for the world-wide historical struggle that has occurred between the White Man and Native peoples. As one put it, "For five hundred years on Turtle Island, the White Man's been actin' like a thief, robbin' Peter to pay Paul, or like a frog, always jumpin' from one pond to the next, never satisfied with the pond they're in. But just like five hundred years ago, no matter how much that frog jumps around, he's still faced with the same problem of how to make his pond a fit place to live, or just keep on a jumpin' into someone else's pond to feed all his greed that never can get enough."

One elder, eager to teach us his peoples traditional ways, eloquently declared, "What I have to say is pretty simple. If all you good folks want to learn about our sacred ceremonies, rituals and the like all you have to do is make your own Medicine Wheel to live by. Just by praying every morning and night to the eight things I'm about to give you, you'll begin to create inside yourself the same kind of mental discipline and a way of seeing that is at the bottom of all our traditions. What I'm suggesting is that you just remember to do eight simple things every day: Pray for your unborn; Pray for your children; Pray for your old people; Pray for all the animals, Mother Earth, the Air, Water and Fire, you depend upon for your life. Make sure they're happy, healthy and holy. If you do all this you can't go wrong. You won't ever have to learn another thing from us or ever meet us again."

So, Pilgrim! It's time to return to your natural place of quiet retreat. Seek out your spirit tree helper. Sit quietly with your back up against its spine and recall what place has acted as 'The Rock' upon which you received your life's most important teaching. Who are the elders who taught you in that place? Recall their words of wisdom. **GO!**

– THE PATH OF THE SACRED PIPE –

WELCOME BACK! Some elders took the opportunity to share with us 'The Way of The Sacred Medicine Pipe', that best symbolized a natural Turtle Island life that they said can be followed by human beings everywhere irregardless of whether or not they ever pick up the Pipe itself.

What they had to say added to what I already had learned from Joe Thunder Hawk, who impressed upon me that The Sacred Pipe, first and foremost, is meant for creating and healing holistic relationships of many different kinds. Just like the function and purpose of the sacred council fire, so, too, is the Medicine Pipe a council fire in miniature.

On The Rock, the elders exposed us to so many, many of the Pipe's mysteries. Those that speak of:

* A total non-violent way of life.
*The sacred life-giving principle that resides within each of us.
* Each sacred direction representative of one of the Four Races of People and the spiritual gifts they bear.
* The union and pathway between the mystical heart and body principles in the universe that exist within our own body.
* The redstone color of the pipebowl a symbol of the peoples blood, mixing with the earth.
*The hollow of the pipebowl representative of the earth's womb, from which all life emerges.
*The pipestem a symbol of the Sacred Tree of Life, and the spine of a man and woman, who act as channels through which all truth flows between Mother Earth & Father Sky.

The Sacred Medicine Pipe also a symbol of:

* The close relationship that exists between the plant and human worlds, as represented by the White Ash wood, said to be the closest plant to human life, from which the pipestem is made.
* An ancient truth that spans all cultures where: the Caduceus & Mystical Rose of the West; the Kundalini Serpent & Lotus Blossom of the East; The Medicine Pipe & Eagle Feather Bonnet of Turtle Island; are one in the same.
* Two realities – one visible and one invisible – one physical, one spiritual – as represented by the two Spotted Eagle feathers that hang from the Sacred Pipe.
* A lofty spiritual condition, an advanced mental attitude and a developed physical state, as represented by the Spotted Eagle feathers and the qualities of the Spotted Eagle who, first and foremost, is a supporter and defender of The Family.
* The Grandfather's breath and spirit of our ancestors represented by the breast plume of the Spotted Eagle, that is tied to a cross and attached to the Pipe's tamper stick.
* The Cross on the Pipe tamper, surrounded by a circle made of red-dyed pocupine quills on a beaded piece of deerskin, representative of the closs connections between human, plant and animal worlds

* The energy of the Sun, the Four Sacred Colors of People, the wetland and dryland peoples represented by the Red Willow,
Bearberry and Red Dogwood roots, leaves and bark that go into
making the ceremonial Kinnikinnik tobacco.
* Kinnikinnik symbolic of the giving of life, rebirth and nourishment of the body and spirit.

We learned, too, about the four songs that are sung with the Sacred
Medicine Pipe. As one elder cautioned, "These songs shouldn't be
replaced by other ones ya' decide tah make up, 'cause they're used for a
reason. They have to do with the old ones who first received these songs,
back in the long, long ago time, with the Pipe ceremony itself and the
sacred spots where these songs first sprang to life. There's a natural
relationship between these things that yah can't mess with."

Another elder added, "Yah better know what yer gettin' into when
yah start usein' these things, because it's not somethin' yah can fool
'round with. It's a whole way of life yah got tah be prepared tah suffer fer.
Once yah pick it up yer life has tah be a giveaway tah yer people, from
that day on. It'll have tah be as straight an' true as the Pipestem, where
nothing of yerself blocks the spirit's path that seeks tah send its gifts
flowing through yah tah the people."

– TURTLE ISLAND VERSION OF THE LORD'S PRAYER –

The elders on The Rock provided us with loads of down-to-earth,
common sense counseling. One Mohawk man said, "You know! The
average person who doesn't know beans about us, our religion, cultures or
political problems doesn't need to look any farther for what we've been
trying to say for the past five hundred years, than to listen closely to the
words in The Lord's Prayer that so many Christians like to repeat a lot."

Continuing his instruction, he said, "Here's what we call The Great
Peacemaker's version of the Lord's Prayer. It goes something like this:
When the White Man asks the Lord to *give us our daily bread and forgive
us our trespasses*, we Indians say they should remember that everything
they receive comes from their Mother, the Earth. So they should include in
their prayer how they're going to give something back to Mother Earth,
each day, for the daily bread she gives them. The simplest way for the
White Man to remember to do this is if they add to their prayer *thy will be
done* **ON OUR MOTHER EARTH** *as it is in heaven.* They also need to
remember that everything on our Mother Earth, including herself, has
rights that no human has the authority to trespass against."

PEACE AND FREEDOM WELCOME
HOME OF THE FREE INDIAN

Stopping to rest for a moment and think in silence, the elder added, "When the White Man asks the Lord to *deliver us from evil* they should add the words *deliver us* **FROM THE EVIL WE DO IN THE NAME OF OUR CHRISTIAN GOD**. Or when they say, *Thy kingdom come, thy will be done on our Mother Earth* they need to also add the Turtle Island phrase *thy will be done* **THROUGH ALL MY RELATIONS** *on our Mother Earth.*"

The elder ended by saying, "If the White Man really wants to think of themselves as good Christian sons and daughters, all they have to do is live our version of the Lord's Prayer everyday the way Jesus tried to teach their ancestors before they killed him. But we Indians already know all this and have been living the words of Jesus for thousands of years. This is what it means to live the Indian way of life."

We heard other elders add that the main problem with those Christians who say they follow the teachings of Jesus is that they focus too much on the after-life time they hope to spend in heaven than they do upon their life on Earth and the many practical things that go into making this world a real 'Garden of Eden' as the Lord's Prayer implies. Another problem being that many of the teachings of different Christian beliefs relate to our Mother Earth as a lowly place, where once upon a time fallen angel spirits were cast for their misdeeds.

As one Indian on the Island put it, "Is it any wonder our Mother Earth is in the sad shape she's in? What other kind of world do Christian people expect to find, than the violent one they've created for themselves. A world where they believe they're filled with original sin 'stead of original grace. A world filled with nothing but trials and misery, where people are always being so tempted by devils to do evil, that they can't wait 'til they make their heavenly flight *to be raptured*, as they say, into *a better world.* So we Indians always worry a lot when we hear you White guys talk about crazy things like *Tribulations, The Last Days* or how the only thing that's gonna *purify this evil world is the second coming of Jesus Christ.*"

A different elder added to this train of thought with the observation that, "All the preachers we hear on the radio or see on T.V. always talk about *The Good Land* they'll find once they enter the pearly gates of their heaven, where all the gold and silver is. That's where they make their big mistake. Now, here on our Mother Earth, is where we should try to make heaven. Our religion doesn't worry about some after-life but what we do here, to-day, about real problems. Like why are the young people so bored? Why do they join gangs? Why is there so much violence, mental illness, poverty and homelessness? Why are so many people in jail?

What is it that we must change in ourselves before we can answer all these questions?"

– A FIRST NATION PEOPLES WAY OF LOOKING CONTINUES –

For almost two years, different elders and their followers came and went on The Rock, bringing the teachings of their people to bear upon the sacred circle or council fire.

They all spoke a great deal to us about our responsibilities for the seven generations ahead of us. They likened the world to a bed and often said to us, "Ask yourself what kind of bed you're making for your children, your children's children and those beyond them."

One elder anguished, "I don't know what to say to convince the Americans, Canadians or any other people that they have a responsibility for the yet unborn ones among them. They either know it or they don't know it. It's common sense. But I hear too many of them say, 'I worked hard for what I have, and when my kids grow up they'll have to do the same thing, on their own'. That's why so many young white people don't care if they throw their parents in an old age home, because they know their parents never really cared about them when they were growing up. Not really! I guess this is why we now see so many New Age people coming to us in Indian Country rather than seek out the spiritual teachers and traditions among their own people."

The vast differences between *Indian Time* and *White Man's Time* was another big lesson we learned over the nearly two years that Indians of All Tribes held The Rock.

As one elder put it, "I never know where I'm gonna be from day to day. I knew I was supposed to be here on The Island, but I didn't know what I was gonna be doing or talking about once I got here. And after I finish talking about spiritual things, I mostly don't remember what I said. I just allow The Great Spirit to talk through me or guide me to where I next have to go. Sometimes it takes only a few minutes for the spirit to talk through me, sometimes hours or days. If I say I'm gonna talk for five minutes, I might speak for maybe an hour or more. Then I might say I'm just going to speak for a minute or two and then talk for over two hours. Or I might say I'm only gonna talk for a couple seconds and then go for a whole day."

Yet another elder remarked, "The way we Indians see it is that Creator makes a natural time for everything. It's not fixed to things like appointments and plans. It's more a life experience of our feelings and

emotions, spiritually connected to a natural movement of real happenings and realities in the world inside and around us. Indian Time has a spiritual value that doesn't move in straight lines, from 8 AM to 9AM or from A to B, but in circles. The White Man instead gives time a money value. You always hear them saying 'Gotta go! Time's money.' They're out of balance because this affects the whole way they see life."

Those of us lucky enough to be exposed to the wealth of traditional wisdom that was shared on Alcatraz, learned a great deal about how connected politics and spirituality are in traditional Indian life.

We often heard the elders speak out against the way the White Man hypocritically preaches about the separation of church and state and then deceitfully combines them anyway. They cautioned us about trying to separate politics and spirituality into neat, compartmentalized, isolated boxes. As one First Nation woman put it, "Those of you who don't think politics has anything to do with our traditional medicine ways don't know what the real healing process is all about. 'Cause politics is every bit a part of our traditional healing proactices, the use of herbs, our own native forms of psychotherapy, rituals and ceremonies. All these things, including politics, is part of a spiritual way of seeing the world as it is."

Young and old native people on The Rock expressed how difficult it is for them to share with outsiders their traditional understanding of life. Over the course of the Occupation it was clear that far too much fear, rage, malice, jealousy and lust for power exists on both sides of the cultural coin, often making communications awkward if not impossible.

– A POIGNANT WALKING WOUNDED MEMORY ON THE ROCK –

Many cross-cultural issues arose over the eighteen months that Indians of All Tribes held The Rock. Towards the end of the Occupation one especially ugly incident occurred.

It was Thanksgiving Day 1970. At that point, many Johnny-come-lately native peoples had taken over from Oakes and the other original visionary occupiers. These new power-grabbing 'Lords of The Rings', as some referred to them, invited the three other Sacred Colors of People – Eúropeans, Africans and Asians – to gather with them 'round the sacred council fire and partake in a huge celebration feast and pow-wow.

Yet by the end of the day – which saw much joyful cross-cultural sharing and good-will – an ugly scene arose as Black, Yellow, Brown, White, Red peoples began to mass together on the landing dock for the return ride back to the mainland.

As a tug approached the landing, to begin the ferrying, a young American Indian Movement 'Dog Soldier' suddenly announced, "Everyone 'cept Indians step aside. Indians will board first and then all the rest of you can board, if there's room, or wait for the next tug."

Some of the non-Indians already had been standing for an hour or more on that cold, wet, blustery dock, waiting to catch the first tug back.

In the crowd, were many venerated African-Americans who had long since paid more than their dues in the fight for justice and equality as they struggled against White racism centuries before even the Civil Rights Movement of the '60's. They weren't about to put up with Indian racism.

There was one old, dignified, grey-haired, ebony-faced couple in particular who stood at the head of the line. When it came time for them to step aside for the Dog Soldiers, who already had begun to clear an aisle through the crowd, they resolutely stood their ground.

"This isn't fair", they both pleaded. "We've been waiting a long, cold time and should be allowed to board first."

But when the two venerable elders attempted to board, they were physically bared by a group of Dog Soldiers.

Several young, tough-looking, Black Turks at once rushed forward to defend their elders. A lot of pushing and shoving soon ensued while the rest of us looked on in utter horror.

Gazing around at all the non-verbal expressions on the faces in the crowd, one could sense what was running through everyone's mind. We'd just spent the day together, listening to each other's voices recount the magnitude of pain and injustice, trials and tribulations our people had similarly experienced at the hands of the White Man.

In so doing, new tentative relationships between the race-spirits of our peoples had been made. Budding good-will was everywhere in evidence. But in that instant, the panged look on all our faces, the anguished cries of outrage that erupted from all our throats, instantly soured the mood.

Forever burned into memory is the look of betrayal – of violation – in the eyes of that Black elder and his wife as they cried out, "Oh, No! Not Here, Too! Not On A Day And Place As This!"

It was as if the Great Spirit sought to remind us that true sharing between our people has never been easy. It was an early wake-up call that we still had a very long, very painful row to hoe together.

At that point, many of us began to chant in unison, "LET 'EM BOARD! LET 'EM BOARD!" The chant quickly morphed into, "LET US BOARD! LET US BOARD! LET'S ALL BOARD AS ONE PEOPLE!", and board we

did by virtue of our sheer volume and mass that moved forward as one body, past the startled Dog Soldiers, who were helpless to do anything about it.

As the over-crowded tug fought its way back to The City through the heavy, wind-swept waves of the Bay, an agitated silence hung in the air as we each were left alone with our thoughts to ponder what this meant for us and the kind of medicine ways it would take to close such deep wounds and mend the massive build-up of scar tissue between us.

I began to wonder how much of this renaissance of Native spirituality eventually would do nothing more than lead to the same old dead-ends of cultural superiority, violence and hatred that tribalism and nationalism, the world over, has shown to be the case down through time. I wondered, too, how elusive would be my search, beyond that which I experienced within myself, for some sense of true spirituality with others.

– FLUNG TO THE FOUR WINDS –

The Rock served we born again Turtle Island human beings well! Immersed within both the most dynamic social laboratory and challenging crucible of emotions imaginable, we were given a rare chance to learn the basics of The Great Turtle's ancient philosophy, and especially the Six Nation peoples teachings of 'The Peacemaker' and how to win over the evil Tadodaho's of the world. It set the stage for future dialogues between the Good Red, White, Black & Yellow Roads of our people.

Those of us who took up the calling, spread ourselves, like the wind, to the Four Directions to do the work. In the years that were to follow, a multitude of symbolic rituals, gatherings, council fires, celebrations and pow-wows would ensue in the wake of our spiritual awakening on Alcatraz.

One symbolic act occured at 3:15PM on July 20th 1978. Tom Birch, a professor at the University of Montana, and two companions, climbed atop a peak called *Triple Divide Peak*, located in Glacier National Park.

Triple Divide Peak is where the three greatest divides of the North American continent converge at its summit; the Continental Divide running north–south and the Laurentian Shield running east–west.

It's from this peak that waters either flow: to Hudson's Bay and the Arctic Ocean; to the Gulf of Mexico and the Atlantic Ocean; or to the Pacific Ocean. Three of the continent's greatest watersheds – the Columbia, the Missouri, Mississippi and the Saskatchewan – all touch at this peak.

Prof. Birch stated at the time of their memorial climb that:

As a general rule, one does not publicize the powerful and sacred places or one's doing in such places. We only share such things with those who are close to us and whom we trust to respect them..........As a culture, responding to what for us was the wildness of Turtle Island, we discovered that the respect mandated by such places can also be appropriately shown by leaving them essentially wild by building nothing there, by keeping our human impact minimal. Thus, we publicize Triple Divide Peak in trust that all who may travel there will seek to minimize their impact on this sacred center....Our thought in doing this was that if the conquistadors could begin the enslavement of the continent by waving their flags on the beaches, then we could reverse the process and liberate the continent by flying the Turtle Island flag at the life-center of the land...Flying the Turtle Island flag from the summit of this sacred mountain was a symbolic disclaimer of any human conquest, and possession towards the continent; an act intended to abrogate our culture's possessiveness towards the land, in order that we might come to live together with the land, in order that we might find remedy for our dispossession.

When first I learned of Professor Birch's moving ceremony atop Triple Divide Peak, I thought of how many times in history conquerors have done just the opposite, arrogantly claiming, in toto, entire continents and all their life forms for some distant monarch.

Some of their symbolic acts proved meaningless and are lost to history. Others – like Christopher Columbus' landing in the New World – took many years, decades or even centuries before their planting of a flag in the soil, and haughty declaration of ownership, took on epic proportions.

"Hmmm!", I thought to myself outloud at the time, "I wonder if, some day, in the distant future, historians will finally look back and acknowledge the profoundness of Professor Birch's simple act? Will he, in turn, someday become Turtle Island's new Christopher Columbus?"

Another symbolic act, that ocurred in San Francisco ten months after Professor Birch's visionary pilgrimage, sought to honor the important spiritual work that Richard Oakes set into motion with the Occupation.

The San Francisco Ballet Company, under the choreographer Michael Smuin, another Alcatraz celebrant of the Occupation, and conductor Charles Fox – with the assistance of the well-known traditional

Indian singers from the Tootoosis Family of Alberta, Canada – presented the world premiere performance of *A Song For Dead Warriors*. The Smuin & Fox Opera House production was a series of vignettes which traced the life and death of Richard Oakes and paid tribute as well to all those Turtle Island spiritual leaders who came before him and died fighting for their ancient ways. Opening night was a veritable Who's Who among First Nation peoples spiritual renaissance movement.

– A NEW PERSPECTIVE OF TIME & SPACE –

Much has happened since those early days on Alcatraz. We now know what our Earth Mother visually looks like from space. We know, too, on a deeper level than ever before, how finite we are in the universe.

The renewed threat of nuclear–chemical–biological warfare – the human idiocies that have brought about a rapid decline in the Earth's life support systems – has already called to most peoples minds the questionable continuation of life on the planet as we now know it.

One political, economic, moral, ethical scandal after another has captured the world's attention, as if the Creator is purposely offering up to us the most wonderfully succinct teaching lessons of what we all need to do to bring life into some kind of balance.

Finally cast like a seed in the wind, away from Alcatraz's foggy surrounds, I pulled back Alta-Dena's folding accordion door, leapt into her cab, seized hold of the suicide knob on her steering wheel and set out across the San Francisco Bay Bridge.

As we sped off the Bay Bridge, our intent was to seek out yet another historic gathering of Indians of All Tribes. This time it was to be in the distant northlands of British Columbia, Canada, at a sacred place of the Musqueam Indian Nation called Eyalmox. As we went, I thought of how many times before Blue or Alta-Dena and I had passed this same way enroute to yet another of the odyssey's spiritual adventures.

Craning my neck once more to catch a final glimpse of the always awe-inspiring silhouette of San Francisco's Twin Peaks, I cried out my fond adieu to those ancient twin sentinels who've always overseen and blessed my comings and goings.

"**PECHAS AZUL! PECHAS AZZUUULLL! I SEE YOU! PECHAS AZZZUUULLL**" I cried out, "**BLESS MY JOURNEY NORTH!**"

Twin Rainbow-Irwin on the Rock
"Pondering the Journey North"

CIRCLE ISLAND

ROAD SIGN # 12

HOW HAVE THE POWERS
OF THE SACRED CIRCLE
RENEWED YOUR LIFE?

– The Sacred Circle –

A Circle,
Wherein energy is brought
As a gift to Mother Earth –
Focused as a spinning wheel!

Gyrations of Love & Vulnerability.
The growth of people
In an ever-expanding circle.

The greenness of all the land,
The colors of the Rainbow,
The brightness of fire,
Smoky gray of burning wood,
All mixing together
With the good feelings
Of those standing and watching:
Living memories
Of those
Who have stood in sacred circles before.

A hope sparks in the memory
Of those yet to come.
The bearer that carries this message –
A soft feather's touch.

(S. Bridges, Jericho Beach 1976)

We are a circle, Within a circle,
With no beginning, and never ending.
We are a circle, Within a circle,
With no beginning, and never ending!

Hey ana, Hey ana, Hey ana-m!

HEALING THE EARTH
AT EYALMOX

"*PILGRIM*", scolds The Great Voice Of The Turtle, "*The defense your North American immigrant society still uses today against its own ignorance of me is arrogance. It's an arrogance based on the belief that the parts of me you can't readily understand with your White Man's mind aren't worth knowing. Or those parts of me that can't easily be turned into money, aren't worth having. When you and your people begin to leave behind all this arrogance you will start to understand what I really am all about. Understanding my ancient ways is the beginning of real sharing, and sharing is the only way to rebuild the Sacred Circle for all you Earth Peoples who live upon my back. My Hopi native children understand this and so follow The Way of The Open Hand of Peace rather than the White Man's Way of the Clenched Fist. Which way do you follow in your daily life with yourself, your family, friends, neighbors, me and all the non-human species who share my body with you? If you do not now follow The Open Hand of Peace, without even knowing anything more about what that means, what changes do you imagine you might immediately have to start making?*"

– FLEEING ACROSS THE MEDICINE LINE –

It was in November of '72, on the day Richard Milhous Nixon was elected to a second term as President of the United States of America, that I began packing Alta-Dena in disgust; readying her to drive North across 'The Medicine Line', as traditional First Nation peoples refer to the 48th parallel between the U.S. and Canada.

By the time we crossed the border that separates those two great nations, it was still looked upon as a 'magic line' that the White Man long ago created to try to heal the great differences that exist between those who follow the Way of The Clenched Fist and those who follow The Way of The Open Hand. Hence the old expression *The Medicine Line.*

'72 proved to be a major fork in the road between these two ways of looking at life. As history since has shown, the U.S., at that moment, by electing Nixon and his ilk, headed down a dark, morally-evil, wilderness track from which it has yet to emerge.

While Nixon grinningly beamed to the world his infamous 'V' for victory, I couldn't throw all my worldly possessions fast enough back into that leather-bound, wicker steamer I found so long ago, abandoned in a storage warehouse on the edge of the San Bruno Mountains.

My Turtle Island journal once more wrapped in that same, old, red thermal nightshirt and tied with the very strands of red-dyed buckskin that the wicker trunk's original Irish pilgrim-immigrant-refugee owner used, a century or more ago, to secure the sacred record of his own odyssean wanderings in the New World.

As I slammed shut the wicker's steel-hard, bone-dry parfleche lid, and latched its two strong, hand-forged, black metal hasps, I wondered, as I did on the day I first was drawn to that old steamer, what caused that mysterious Irishman to leave his ancestral Isle of Mann birthplace and migrate all the way to the Metis peoples Red River Colony in Manitoba.

"Did you, too", I rhetorically asked him, wherever he was in the universe, "finally decide to leave your homeland because of a similar disdain for your government's vicious politics and economics? Or did you, by traveling to the wilds of Canada, hope that you too might, once and for all, find a place and a people, bearing the open hand, somewhere far beyond the reaches of the arrogant Nixon's of your own day?"

With the United States presidential election now a done deal, and the political aspirations of California's Governor Ronald Reagan ('Ronnie Ray-Gun', as we mockingly called him) already gathering steam in the wings, I knew the Peace & Freedom Party ideals, for which I consistently voted, were all but lost.

The beautiful dream-visions of those like Dick Gregory, who ran as the Peace & Freedom Party's candidate for the presidency, perhaps nigh impossible to ever realize, given the hopelessly clenched-fisted, militaristic, mean-spirited nature of the White Man's culture in the United States.

As Alta-Dena lumbered North on I-5, with a distant view of the magnificent Marysville Buttes, the world's smallest mountain range, looming on the horizon, I began to talk to her like I always did, each time we passed her way, as if she were a real person.

"If I can't ever discover, old girl", I said, "some of these Peace & Freedom ideals within the more socialistically-minded country of Canada, then at least you and I can leave behind the concretized, over-crowded, polluted, violent world of the South and experience the tranquillity and peace of the vast Canadian bush and its wildlife in the Far North."

In my mind was a vision of the Canadian flag and the three segments of the Red Canadian Maple Leaf on it that stand for *Safety, Dependability* and *Reliability*. "Sounds good to me!", hummed Alta-Dena's engine.

We weren't just saying all this to one another though because, by this time, we weren't alone on our journey North. For sitting shotgun in Alta-Dena's cab – on a deluxe air-cushioned throne-of-a-passenger seat I'd stripped from a Mack truck, and welded onto Alta-Dena's frame in her honor – was a new-found Aussie soul-mate, medicine-helper, personal spiritual guru from Sydney who'd just deigned to become my wife.

Though her given Christian name was Beverly Ann, to me – from the day we first met in San Francisco through my 4th Grade 'Organic Classroom' at McKinley Elementary, and I looked into her spirit and caught my first fleeting glimpse of her radiant essence – she would forever after be known by her intimate name, *Crystal Freesia*.

Typical of her Aussie heritage, at her core Crystal Freesia was a cheery, fun-loving human being. A brilliant listener and communicator, she already was well on her way to becoming the greatest psychotherapist and most compassionate, empathetic, wisest women I would ever know.

As dense as most men are to the higher qualities their women naturally embody, having the great good fortune to find Crystal Freesia in the first place, and then somehow be lucky enough to even talk her into being my soul-mate through life was the greatest boon imaginable.

But then I couldn't yet know all this, because it would take many years before I suddenly would wake up one morning and realize that the spiritual teacher I'd endlessly searched hither and yon to find amongst First Nation peoples, and anywhere else my wild goose chase could think to look, was all the time lying right there beside me. She waiting for me to finally wake up to the fact and take heed of the many feminine, Earth Mother wisdoms she was ever ready and willing to offer.

With my *two girls*, one made of flesh and blood and the other of steel and oil, I continued to flee northward towards Canada. Like a Hippie-Druid 'Sitting Bull' on his favorite Indian pony, with wife and travois in tow, I wondered what healing the other side of The Medicine Line would have for all my troubled political thoughts.

It was still far too early in the odyssey to know that the three of us had just set out upon but the first of many nomadic wanderings between British Columbia and California that would last for more than two decades.

The quest of each nomadic wander: the hoped for discovery of some new, mysterious part of myself that continually beckoned from both sides of The Medicine Line. Its sound like a strange, exotic singing bird or faerie's song which always seemed a great distance away yet ever distinct, as if close by.

Before we knew it, we'd made it through Oregon, cut across The Dalles into Washington and onto the Wanatchee and Okanagan Valleys.

Soon passed through were the same 'underground railroad stations' that so many young, idealistic, draft-dodger–refugees from the 'Nam War used to seek political asylum as they cried out, "Hell, No! We Won't Go!". With that, Alta-Dena, Crystal Freesia and I slipped quietly across the sleepy border-crossing at Nighthawk.

It wasn't long before we, too, found ourselves receiving the same moral 'Kool-aid & Comfort' as those 'Nam protestors from a fiery, freedom-loving Czech immigrant fruit farmer in the Okanagan Valley. His family, years before, had similarly helped countless Jews, Catholics, Gypsies and other oppressed peoples flee from the Nazi's during W.W. II.

That wonderful old Czech patriot passionately loved Smetana's *Moldau* because as he put it, "With each note, I can see in my mind's eye, as if I were there again, every twist and turn of the music's journey down my dear, beloved, old Danube upon whose banks I once was raised."

It was such a joy to watch him gather every afternoon with his wife, son and daughter in their music parlor – violin, viola, cello and clarinet in-hand – and so passionately breath new life back into Old World masters like Smetana, Mozart, Bach and Handel.

Sitting in their parlor, as the watery musical notes of the Danube floated through the air, Crystal Freesia and I winked at each other. For we knew we'd found a far gentler land than the aggressive one we left behind us in the South. A good place, admired 'round the world for its aid to the afflicted and efforts to promote human rights and build non-exploitative relationships of mutual respect and co-operation. An honorable place with less colonial baggage and no long list of enemies – guided by great statesmen like Prime Minister Pierre Elliott Trudeau and his Deputy P. M. Paul Hellyer.

– THE DREAM OF A NEW WORLD TAKES ROOT –

British Columbia in those days was a mecca for humanistic New Frontier peoples who heard good things about Premier Dave Barrett's compassionate, socialistically-minded New Democratic Party (NDP), and so flocked to it from all over Canada and the rest of the world.

Some retreated to places like the Okanagan Valley and Kootenay Mountains with a desire to recreate, for themselves and their families, a new wholesome, peaceful way of life.

For a time, the Okanagan and the Kootenay's became exciting, tumultuous, halcyon 'Left Banks' and 'Greenich Villages' where we gathered 'round the dinner tables of those like George Ryga, the Canadian playwright. Ryga's play, *The Ecstatsy of Rita Joe*, was a major, early landmark in opening up the world to First Nation peoples indigenous, aboriginal consciousness.

Ryga's nightly soireé's were like a box of Cracker-Jacks, because you never knew what surprises you would find inside. A smorgasbord of fascinating characters in attendance always was an absolute guarantee, among whom were those like: Hyemeyhost Storm, the Northern Cheyenne writer whose book, *Seven Arrows*, was heralded as a Turtle Island version of Aesop's Fables, or; Bill Barlee, a true-blue Canadian patriot–historian–Western writer– NDP politician. Barlee, for years, like a tiny voice in the wilderness, valiantly sought public office in the midst of Premier W.A.C. 'Wacky' Bennett and his successor son's hostile sea of rabid, right-wing fundamentalism and rapacious, unbridled free market capitalism.

Then there were the hosts of up-and-coming Canadian, American, European and First Nation poets, writers, musicians and artisans of all stripes and shades who, on any given night, could be found gathering in Ryga's living room. Each one passing through on their way to bringing their lofty, avant garde ideas to the attention of distant world hubs like Toronto, New York, London and Paris.

These encounters with so many soul-mates on the new frontier of the North, became the harbinger of yet another one of life's seven year cycles. A cycle so bold that even then I could sense it was about to be the intense, vibrant, halcyon days of another most rare moment in time and space.

– THE MYSTERY OF A NEW CYCLE UNFOLDS –

I couldn't believe that it had been just seven, short years since I'd left the CIA and other DIA-Pentagon witches of the American Empire to learn more about Turtle Island's Open Hand of Peace. Yet in terms of the exponential rate of personal growth and consciousness I underwent in the interim, the cycle seemed more like ten times seven years.

So many mysteries of '7' had already begun to be learned: the Cheyenne's 'Way of The Seven Arrows Bundles'; the Sioux Nation's

'Seven Council Fires'; the Dene Nation's 'Tale of the Great Moose', spread over the land seven times to make the earth more beautiful.

My body's muscle tissue, skeletal structure and seven major openings, that mirrored Mother Earth's seven great seas and continents within herself, had, by then, also experienced its own set of cyclical mysteries.

Seven years after having been drawn like a magnet to the Missouri river and lands of the Hunkpatina, the irresistible pull of another one of the Great Turtle's magnets drew me to a new seminal gathering in the Native Renaissance Spiritual Movement. This time it was to be held in the city of Vancouver, B.C., where the world's seven major religions were planning to come together to try to heal the earth.

– THE SACRED COUNCIL FIRE IS AGAIN LIT –

A MESSAGE TO ALL PEOPLE
WHO SHARE A LOVE AND CONCERN FOR OUR MOTHER EARTH

EARTH HEALING CEREMONY

We, the undersigned, gathered at the General Assembly of the International Cooperation Council, this 13th day of January, 1976, at Santa Monica, California, United States of America, hereby request that the United Nations Habitat Forum, to be held the 27th of May through the 13th of June, 1976, in Vancouver, British Columbia, Canada, be established as the site for a healing ceremony for the planet earth, to be led by the spiritual leaders of the Native American Peoples, including representatives of all world religions and faiths, and their spiritual leaders.

It was shortly after a group of Hopi Elders came and went from Vancouver that I first became aware of the Earth Healing Ceremony they were planning to conduct upon the ancient site of the Musqueam Nation's village of *Eyalmox* (Aye-YAL-mough).

The oral history of the Musqueam, or "Peoples of The Grass", as they still call themselves, recounts how Eyalmox, which means "a good camping ground", existed upon that spot for some 3,000 years prior to the coming of the White Man. Since time beyond mind, Eyalmox similarly was used for great gatherings and potlatches between First Nation peoples from different areas.

Yet by the time our Earth Healing Ceremony was held on its grounds, Eyalmox had long since disappeared a century before.

`The story behind how it disappeared is as humorous as it is tragic. On the one hand, the tale has a tragic conclusion for the Musqueam people because it was they who lost their entire village. But, on the other hand, the tale itself so simply underscores the White Man's arrogance and smug sense of cultural superiority as to be rather funny.

The way the story goes, during the early days of first contact, a fleet of British Naval ships, exploring the Pacific coastline, happened upon Eyalmox while it was completely deserted. Its giant Longhouse, some 300 feet in length, and all the village's belongings intact therein.

Why the British Fleet's commander thought for a moment that such a village would have been permanently abandoned, or why he felt he had the right to do what he did, is a curious question in itself but not surprising, given the impertience of those early 'explorers'.

Completely ignorant of the cultural activities of the Musqueam people, he couldn't know they all had simply temporarily moved to their annual fish camps. One might say they more or less just left the house unlocked and the door open, because they never even gave it a thought that they had to worry about burglars since they were the only people in town.

In the end, the Fleet commander decided to dismantle the village and cart it off – lock-stock and barrel – to be reassembled in England as an historical curiosity for the Victoria & Albert Royal Museum.

Imagine, though, the look of absolute incredulity on the faces of all the Musqueam when they finally returned from their fish camps. One of them might have been overheard to say something like, "Hey! Where in the hell are all our homes? Our village? All our possessions?" Imagine, too, all the wild myths of monstors, evil witches, black magic or alien invaders from outer space that at once sprang to life among them to try and explain away this earth-shattering phenomenon.

Our modern-day Earth Healing Ceremony, however, was about to do just the opposite. Overnight, a huge village would instead spring up, as if by a magic far greater than that of the British Fleet Commander's, on the old Eyalmox site.

The international gathering set to convene there was about to become part of what the White people referred to as *Hope Village,* but what First Nation peoples and their natural allies would instead refer to as *Hopi Village,* in honor of the Hopi Elders who would conduct the Earth Healing Ceremony.

The Hopi, themselves, were responding to their own ancient prophecies that they felt obligated to make known to the world at this historic time and place. The spirit world duly sending out to the Four Directions, like at Alcatraz, an invitation, for all those who could hear its other-worldly directive, to come, listen and learn of the great undertaking that had begun in ernest atop the Turtle's back.

Like on Alcatraz during the Occupation, a traditional council fire soon would be prepared and lit by appointed 'Sacred Keepers of The Fire' for the purpose of conducting a high-level spiritual conference; with much pow-wowing, around which the traditional peoples of the world could gather to share their religious instructions, prophecies and warnings.

As at Alcatraz, First Nation Native caravans – comprised of traditional leaders from such distant places as the Hopi Independent Nation, Six Nations Confederacy, Salish, Stoney, Blood, Cree, Chumash, Ute, Yurok, MicMac, Metis, Shuswap, Shoshoni, Cheyenne, Lil'Wat, to name but a few – were already winding their way through Indian Country, picking up steam as they went. Columns of New Frontier hippie wagons also about to make their own pilgrimages to this as yet still nondescript, open meadow by a natural, spring-fed pond near Jericho Beach, a short few miles from downtown Vancouver.

The humble, make-shift 'Village of Hope' that was about to spring up on those grounds, and become a temporary enclave of grass-roots people from around the world, was part of an unofficially-sanctioned 'Alternative Peoples Conference'. The Conference materialized in response to a United Nations 'Habitat Conference' that was planned to convene in downtown Vancouver to examine the deplorable conditions of human settlements everywhere on the planet, but was choosing to ignore the desperate plight of all the non-humans and Mother Earth herself.

The U.N. Council refused to allow any other representatives, save for its own official delegations, to speak to their world body. Thus, a 'Peoples Habitat Forum' spontaneously sprang into being.

– HOPE VILLAGE IS BORN –

Once Hope Village became a reality, it drew through its rustic log-beamed, carved eagle totem entranceway important world personages. Those like: the great humanitarian Mother Theresa; Buckminister Fuller of Geodesic Dome fame; renowned anthropologist Margaret Mead, writer-philosopher-revolutionary thinker Ivan Illich; New Age Spiritualist David Spangler; and world-class, First Nation architect Harold Cardinal; were among those who mingled and conversed with the masses gathered.

The Habitat Forum, that took up residency in Hope Village, was an early pioneering version of the numerous 'Earth Summits' and 'Human Rights' conferences that were to one day follow in its wake. Its grass-roots collective a rich gathering of New Frontier visionary groups, alternate technology experts, scientists and humanists of all description.

The Forum was created to raise the international community's awareness of not only the problems of the displaced, disenfranchised, 'little people' of the world, but also their own unique solutions to the deplorable life conditions they and others suffer.

The simultaneous spiritual grass-roots gathering of Turtle Island's First Nations came about without even being formally sanctioned by the Habitat Forum organizers themselves.

Wild rumors and speculations constantly flew through Hope Village at the time about some kind of 'Native wagon train' that was supposedly on its way there. But beyond all the gossip and conjecture, what was about to occur was a mysterious, unknown quantity to all.

The First Nation Sacred Circle–Earth Healing Ceremony that, in fact, magically came about did so because neither the U.N. Habitat Conference nor the Peoples Habitat Forum were predisposed to discuss not only the horrendous conditions in the habitats of humans but also the equally critical, deteriorating condition of the habitats of all life forms on Earth, including the desperate state of Mother Earth herself.

– LIFE BETWEEN THE VISIBLE & INVISIBLE REALMS –

Prior to the arrival of the Independent Hopi Nation's caravan, a few select Hopi elders had made the long trek from their Arizona mesa homelands to the old Eyalmox site. They'd met with the Musqueam elders and asked them for permission to hold a ceremony in their territory; blessed the ground where the sacred council fire would be lit; consecrated the area as a holy site; and then returned to Arizona to continue their spiritual preparations.

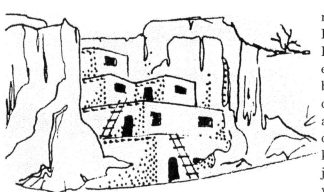The Hopi, for months before the U. N. Habitat Conference and Peoples Habitat Forum ever came to be, had been quietly conducting certain ancient rituals and ceremonies in their distant underground kiva's, spiritually conjuring up what all they wanted to see happen.

By the time the Sacred Circle Ceremony finally got underway, there were those of us present who had already become emphatic believers that some invisible power, greater than we could conceive, had mysteriously moved us to overcome whatever obstacle to make sure we were there. We sensed that everything – the U.N. Conference, Peoples Forum, the thousands who gathered together – all had somehow come about because of the Hopi elder's high-level spiritual work.

The way I became involved in the creation of the Sacred Circle–Earth Healing Ceremony is but one noteworthy account of the many kinds of strange events in the invisible realm that each participant, in different ways, somehow felt led up to the ceremony's culmination.

As things turned out, shortly after the Hopi elders had completed their initial preparations at Eyalmox and departed, I was having dinner with George Abbott, a Medicine Pipe Carrier of the Lil'Wat Nation, and some of the organizers of the Peoples Habitat Forum.

Suddenly, as our discussion turned towards what we each could do to ensure that the consecrated grounds at Jericho Beach would remain protected until the Hopi returned, I heard The Voice bellow in my ear, "Lad! It's up to you, in their absence, to care for the Sacred Circle."

Sitting there stunned by the intensity of The Voice's directive, as if I'd been zapped by a bolt-from-the-blue, I wondered what I could do.

At the time, I held a lucrative, full-time teaching post as an Outdoor Educational Therapist in Alma House, a Vancouver group home originally begun by the old Children's Aid Society of Canada.

Alma House, by then, was legendary in Vancouver's Lower Mainland for its demonstrated success with the most severely disturbed, acting out, incorrigible teenage youth in the region. 'Alma', as it was simply known, was considered by many social workers, probation and

Hope Village

correctional officers to be the ultimate 'last stop' in group homes before doing 'hard time'.

The way I got my job at Alma is almost as strange and magical as how I felt drawn to the Hopi Village at Jericho.

Alone and isolated in a new country, without friends or a job, all but broke; Crystal Freesia and I were just about to pack up Alta-Dena again and head back South, across The Medicine Line, to California when R.D. Laing, a radical Scottish psychiatrist, came to Vancouver as part of his maiden tour of North America.

R.D. Laing, who was then doing amazing, ground-breaking work in the field of schizophrenia, offered to give an intimate workshop-seminar for twenty-select people.

At once, The Voice commanded, "Lad! Make damn sure you're among those twenty. Because there, in the circle with Laing, you will meet an old-soul, soul-mate on your wave-length who will direct you to where you next need to go."

As things turned out, there, in the healing circle we eventually formed together with R.D. Laing, I met up with Megan Monkman, whose surname-lineage is steeped in early prairie Manitoba Metis history. The Monkman's part of the Metis Nation's revolutionary 19th century 'Exovedate' government with their leader-visionary – Louis Riel.

Always flamboyant in her manner and dress – draped in a flowing cape, rakish-feathered hat, musketeer-like, knee-length boots or some other outlandish outfit – Megan Monkman was a real new frontier *coureur de bois* in her own right. She and her husband among the first river-rafters to ever have successfully navigated the treacherous Hell Gate-stretch of the Fraser River.

In an instant, after only a few words of conversation and a quick visit to Alma House where she was the Director, Monkman snapped, in her usual, frank, brusque manner, "I like you and I like your style, Mr. Rainbow Man. I just hired someone else for a position but I don't like him. I'm going to fire him and if you want the job, it's yours."

Several intense, rewarding years spent at Alma House soon came to pass – using Nature's wilds to heal disturbed Native and non-Native youth caught in-between their warring cultures, their heritage lost, exiled to the streets, with drugs, prostitution and crime their basic modes of employment – before I found myself sharing a meal with George Abbott, discussing the upcoming Sacred Circle Ceremony.

The whole time we spoke, I could hear the Voice trumpet in my ears, as before on Alcatraz, the words, as if they'd come down from The Mount,

"Rainbow Bridge Man! There is another sacred circle you must go to. Live upon its holy grounds. Protect them from being violated."

Questioning my Lil'Wat brother as to what he thought about my proposed undertaking, Abbott replied, "Rainbow! No one can tell you yes or no. If it came to you there's a reason. Maybe it came to no one else. It's up to you to decide if this is to be the Creator's wish for you."

So strong was this feeling of being directed, that the rational, practical White Man's side of my brain was told to hold its tongue, while the creative, spontaneous, Turtle Island side said, "Just do it!"

I paid my respects to my Lil'Wat brother for his wise words, jumped into Alta-Dena and rushed home to the tiny cottage my Aussie soul-mate and I occupied in the tiny coastal hamlet of Horseshoe Bay to tell Crystal Freesia of my intent.

"Love!", I began, "I know what I'm about to say is going to sound absolutely mad and idiotic, but I'm going to have to leave you and Alma House for at least two weeks to do what The Voice has directed me to do. I can't even rationally explain all this to myself. I only know I must. For to not do so would be to allow some unfathomable, sacrosanct part of me to wither and die. You'll simply have to trust my decision to do this."

Crystal Freesia indeed thought I was crackers. However, by then, she knew me well enough to know that whenever I started talking about the directives or communiques I was receiving from 'The Voice', I was, as she said, "beyond the pale". To her, Alta-Dena, San Bruno Mountain and my ever-expanding Turtle Island journal were all mistresses and, as such, competitors, vying for my undivided attention, who constantly sought to steal me away from her.

The next day, I went to Alma House and told the staff and youth what my intentions were, explaining to them as best I could the basis of this deep-felt 'religious' responsibility.

"Look at it this way", I said to them, as they gathered in Alma's large living room, "Think of this as if it were my Turtle Island Thanksgiving, Christmas and Easter devotional holidays all rolled-into-one." "But hey!", I added, "If you can't accept all this, I'll understand completely if you instead choose to fire me right here on the spot."

As things turned out, though totally dismayed by my bizarre plan, and also feeling a bit jilted, they heard my heart.

George Simmers – Alma's new director who took over for Megan Monkman when she decided to follow the calling of her own wild-hearted Metis spirit, and let her life's odyssey lead her off in an entirely different direction – reassuringly-declared, "Jerome! Jerome! Jerome!

You're going to drive us all nuts yet with your crazy Twin Rainbow–Turtle Island ways. But if you say you absolutely have to do this, don't worry. Go do what you need to do and we'll cover for you, somehow."

As I hopped back into Alta-Dena and prepared to make the short five-minute drive from Alma House to the old Eyalmox site, I leaned out of her cab and shouted, "Hey, George! From time to time, bring all our kids down to visit me. Look for me somewhere around the pond at Jericho. Maybe by seeing and being with somehone who's doing not what their pocketbook is telling them to do but what their heart and spirit is saying they must do, they'll receive the best possible therapy they could get."

A few minutes later, Alta-Dena and I found ourselves parked in the woods of Jericho, a short distance from the grounds of the Sacred Circle, pondering what all to do next. I couldn't stay in Alta-Dena because if I was to guard the ceremonial grounds against any violation I would have to live in the open, close by the consecrated sacred council fire pit.

So after I'd lit a braid of SweetGrass, and spiritually 'smoked' myself inside Alta-Dena's meditative chamber – seeking to purify my thoughts, words and deeds for what all needed to be undertaken – I said goodbye to Alta-Dena, padlocked shut her accordian-door and headed out.

From that moment on, the events that swiftly unfolded upon the Sacred Circle grounds over the next two weeks proved, beyond any shadow of a doubt, that what was happening there, in the visible and invisible realms, was in the hands of The Great Mystery. As if by magic, one thing after another fell neatly into place.

Standing there, in the natural wide-open spaces that surrounded the site, I took stock of the magnificent scenery that presented itself: Jericho Beach's white sands; Howe Sound's wild waters; spectacular mountains to the East of the Sound, with a view of twin-spired sentinels the local Whites call 'The Lions', but which First Nations peoples and New Frontier Breeds call 'The Twin Sisters'. Awed by the view, I thought outloud, "Okay, Spirits! And you, too, Lolum, Waimatha! Dear Twin-Spired Sister spirit-helpers who've always faithfully acted as the

Northern counterparts of those dear, old Pechas Azul twin sentinels in the South. So now where do I work, eat and sleep?"

Crazy as it seems, I hadn't even thought to bring a tent or sleeping bag, pot or pan. Yet virtually within minutes of asking the invisible realm for help, a young, hippie woman emerged from the nearby bush.

"Hello!", she beamed. "My name's Dove. I've just come all the way from the Kootenay's with a special medicine tipi that my people have blessed. I heard a rumor, through the Mocassin Telegraph, that an important spiritual gathering is supposed to be happening here real soon. Do you know anything about it? 'Cuz I want to donate my tipi, cooking utensils and bedding to whoever will get the best use out of it."

"**AHO!** Indeed I do!", was my reply.

At once, my fully-equipped domicile materialized itself. "Could this just be a coincidence?", wondered the White Man side of my brain. "NO WAY!", laughed my brain's opposing Turtle Island-side, "Don't you know! Its spiritual synchronicity ahappenin' yet again!"

Once Dove and I raised up her brilliant white canvas tipi – with the painted symbol of a soaring dove, surrounded by a shock of blue sky, emblazoned high atop one side – we hugged and she quietly departed, leaving me alone inside its vibrantly-white interior.

I built a small spiritual fire in its center and then sat beside it in quiet reflection. After several hours, the thought arose, "Okay, Geronimo! So now what in the heck are you going to help me do for the next two weeks before the Hopi return?"

Staring into the fire's red-hot coals, I heard The Voice suddenly declare, "Find a way, Lad, to attract good energy around the circle."

On the very next morning, and every morning that followed, I conducted a sunrise ceremony as a way to further purify the area and myself. But what began as a solitary ceremony quickly mushroomed in size as more and more people – drawn by the sight of my lone white tipi, the mocassin telegraph and spirit world's pull on them – responded to the call.

– COMING HOME CEREMONY –
(Part One)

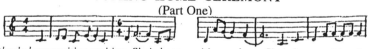

Our Mo-ther's been waiting waiting She's been waiting so long She's been waiting for her white

children to remember to return

Here comes the dawning of a new day hey

Here comes the dawning of a new day

hey   My life in circles

round me, hey ya he-y ya hey ya hey hey

Each ensuing morn – as words spread like pebbles thrown into a deep, still pool – more and more came. Like bee's drawn to nectar, all the while cross-pollinating everything they touched, they came bearing food offerings, poems, songs, chants and incense. These gifts shared, at the end of our sunrise ceremony, in yet another impromptu celebration feast of a new dawning in each of our lives.

Local poets, sculptors, writers, painters and spiritual artisans of all types – each one a self-proclaimed 'Planetary Citizen of Hope Village' – began to spend quiet, introspective time upon the Sacred Circle's grounds, creating their art while sharing intimate thoughts about the creative spiritual process.

Many others came to the Circle in search of solace to their disturb-ed, displaced lives. Sal Brown, a teenage resident of Alma House, was one.

Sal was typical of those who came to help and be helped in return. A member of a hereditary chieftain clan from the Bella Bella Nation of Northern B.C., Sal would have eventually assumed his rightful title had he been born and raised in an earlier, less-turbulent time.

But Sal never would assume his chiefly duties because, in spite of the many good things he received in places like Alma House and on the Sacred Circle, it wasn't enough for him. His life cut short far too early. Yet one more tragic, fatal statistic in the annals of First Nation culture since first contact. Like too many other faceless, nameless 'Sal Brown's of the world', he was too deeply stuck between two civilizations – two world views – unable to ever fully call one or the other 'Home'.

Banished by his own people from their homelands because of unresolved, inner frustrations that he violently took out upon himself and his own people; Sal found himself set adrift upon the drug-infested, inner-city streets of Vancouver before arriving at Alma House.

Sal came to the Sacred Circle one early morning, hoping to find some lost piece of himself. And he did. Feeling an ancient pathway of his people suddenly stir wthin himself – as I ceremonially presented him with his first-ever sacred red, cloth-wrapped kinikinnick medicine bundle – Sal would make a valiant attempt to turn his life around.

It was because of those early healing powers of the Sacred Circle that Sal would eventually be welcomed back amongst his people again and undergo yet an even more severe traditional Bella Bella disciplinary-introspective tribal law test. A test that would require him to remain alone, for long periods of time at a stretch, upon a remote, uninhabitated island of his homelands to see if he truly possessed the courage of his convictions.

Before I knew it, a burgeoning extended family of many other 'Sal Brown's' and an inter-cultural, inter-racial support community had begun to form itself.

There soon arose one need after another. First, a huge pine arbor had to be built around the sacred fire. Many cords of firewood needed to be cut, gathered and hauled to the site. Numerous latrines dug. The grounds and nearby pond, that for years prior were used as a dumpsite, cleared of all the trash. But no formal organization, or logistical wherewithal, to see to it that everything was done existed. Yet, miraculously, the right people, equipment and supplies somehow always showed up when needed.

The dominant feeling was as if we'd all become actors within some kind of ancient Passion Play, assuming the same characters and roles played so many times before down through the ages. This gathering at Jericho, but Act 1 in a play whose final scene one day would culminate in Hopi Land.

Far from being lackluster, this cosmic play of ours was filled with constant suspense and high drama.

Before committing myself to care for the Sacred Circle's grounds, I sought out the counsel of local native spiritual leaders.

One counselled, "Twin Rainbow, you're gonna have to *watch out*. 'Cause there's gonna be a lot of dark forces gather there on account of all the forces for good that'll be there." Another warned, "Be careful, 'cause you're gonna see th' world as it really is and it ain't gonna be pretty. So if ya' go there, keep your eyes wide open and be ready for anything that might come." A third elder advised, "No matter what happens, *Don't Run! Don't Show No Fear!*. Jus' stand up to whatever shows itself, no matter if it's a human, animal or spirit. These things'll test the strength of the Circle and anyone who tries to protect it. But they'll only be able to hurt ya' if ya' run."

Listening to their words of wisdom instantly brought back the memory of almost the exact same sagely words that Joe Thunder Hawk used, seven years before, as he prepared me for what to expect during my hanbleceya vision quest atop Holy Hill.

– DARK FORCES UPON THE SACRED CIRCLE –

The dark forces first manifested themselves in the form of a young hippie man and woman who came one morning to our sunrise ceremony and said they were members of "The Rainbow Tribe".

Before returning to their undrground kiva's, to prepare for the great native passion play that was forming in the wings, the Hopi ceremonially staked and roped off the Sacred Circle area with red twine. The red twine was part of an invisible spiritual wall the Hopi constructed to keep out all negative energy.

However, the dawn of a new morn broke to find the newly-arrived Rainbow Tribe couple in their sleeping bags inside the red-twine-cordoned area, practically on top of the Hopi markers that designated where the council fire pit was soon to be dug.

My intuition said these Rainbow Triber's purposely put themselves there, in spite of my previous warnings to them the night before, so they could selfishly suck up all the good energy without any thought or consideration for the feelings of the Hopi, ourselves or the sanctity of the grounds themselves.

As I stood staring down at the sleeping couple, wrapped up tightly in their mummy bags with the hoods pulled over their heads, I could literally feel, in their silent presence, the embodiment of the ominous dark forces the elders warned me about.

Such a huge, thick, ponderous, invisible mass of black energy filled ever inch of the sourrounding area, that the thought of gently nudging the hippie couple awake, and politely ask them to remove themselves, filled me with a sense of dread that wasn't without foundation. For the vehement, seething response my meek request elicited from the bearded, bedraggled long-hair and his lady would have weakened the stoutest of hearts.

Still, I stood my ground. Once they recognized my resoluteness, which turned into a stern demand to "either get up and move willingly or be dragged off", the two slunk off in a whirlwind of invective abuse. Yet the positive and negative energy dance between us wasn't yet over, because they later reappeared during our sunrise ceremony.

One of the communal acts that occurred in our daily ritual involved everyone linking hands to form an enormous human chain around the outer edge of the roped-off Sacred Circle. The intent was to create an electro-magnetic chain of human current, through which each person, as a link – as a capacitator – could draw from while simultaneously recharging everyone else. Each morning, this ritualistic act proved to be a most successful one which left everyone feeling totally energized.

Yet on this morning, our human 'force-field' wasn't working. The current was being blocked or siphoned off somewhere along its length.

Since I was the leader of the ritual, it fell to me to spiritually rectify what I knew was becoming an increasingly-uneasy common feeling, as witnessed by the growing amount of restless, non-verbal body language that had begun to ripple 'round the circle.

Once again, I called upon The Voice within for guidance.

Suddenly, without even questioning why I was doing it, I began to slowly peel off one layer of clothing after another.

It was an exceptionally-cold, blustery morning, and by the time I peeled off everything from above my waist, everyone on the circle was staring at me, aghast. I could see by all their eyes that they thought I'd gone stark-raving mad.

Yet even though it was freezing-cold outside, on the inside I felt as if my body all at once was a huge open vent, through which red-hot air was fierecely-blowing like a blast furnace.

I hadn't begun to strip below the waist when something curious started to happen on the opposite side of the circle from where I stood. The Rainbow Tribe couple had become extremely agitated and were restlessly-fidgeting back and forth, as if they were standing atop a red-hot griddle.

All at once, they abruptly dropped the hands of those who stood beside them, and angrily stormed away, never to be seen again.

Instantly, upon rejoining our hands on the circle, a surge of positive energy rushed through us as if a floodgate had been opened.

Later, during the ceremony's feast, we all spoke of these over-powering feelings and how each of us, in different ways, were made aware of the interplay – the struggle – between two powerful opposing forces.

The face-off with the Rainbow Tribe couple would prove to be only the first of many hostile encounters that would have to be dealt with, in years to come, in my encounters with certain New Age peoples, who some First Nation peoples refer to as "spiritual energy suckers". Especially those writers, healers and artists of shamanic phantasmagoria who, consciously or unconsciously, rip off aboriginal cultures, worldwide, misportraying or misappropriating the cultural identity and spiritual powers of native peoples for their own aggrandizement.

This New Age cultural-spiritual imperialism would become all the clearer the farther Alta-Dena and I would travel down the odyssey's hard, spiritual road.

Yet still other confrontations manifested during that spiritual preparatory time upon those Hopi-consecrated Sacred Circle grounds. Rowdy Native drunkards who, with cases of beer in-hand, tried to bust into my tipi at 3 A.M. to start a beer-swilling party; a White hippie 'Shaman' carver, who brought to the Circle one morning a bizarre-looking wooden idol, obssesed with the idea of ceremonially burning it, before the Hopi arrived, on the very spot where the sacred fire pit was to be; were but a few of the strange occurrences that manifested.

Then there was that major cultural *faux pas* that nearly caused an insurmountable rift to occur between local and out of province First Nation peoples when the Sacred Circle's pine arbor – which had been ceremonially-built and consecrated with much love by the Lil'Wat Nation – was rudely torn down by those insensitive ones who deemed it too small for the gathering's purpose.

Each new confrontation added to the dynamic tension that was building as the time drew nearer for the Earth Healing Ceremony to begin.

– THE FORCES OF LIGHT STRUGGLE TO BREAK THROUGH –

Once the Hopi finally showed up, and the long lines of Native Caravans began streaming in from every corner of Turtle Island, I sensed that the highs and lows of all the human dynamics we felt over the previous two weeks were nothing compared to what we could next expect.

The same four, distinct, critical stages of the healing process we went through in those initial two weeks was something that we again would have to work through on a much larger scale. Like at Alcatraz, these stages part of the same cross-cultural healing process that all those who desire to affect within themselves, and between First Nation and New Frontier peoples, must be prepared to constantly undergo.

– STAGE ONE: A GIFT OF THE EARTH SPIRITS –

As the Earth Healing Ceremony got underway – and a number of new cross-cultural incidents occurred to underscore the widespread racial tensions, anger, guilt, cultural stereotyping and misunderstandings that always are at play in any given human exchange – I was reminded of what the local Musqueam spiritual leaders previously said about the complex nature of the forces that I could expect to see.

The first day of the Ceremony culminated with an ugly confrontation that arose between some of the aggressive, militant American Indian Movement ("A.I.M.") people present and a few equally strong-willed New Age, 'Rainbow Nation' types.

The New Agers took it upon themselves, in spite of the Ceremony's strict "No Drugs, Of Any Kind, On The Grounds!" declaration, to smoke some marijuana during a Friendship Pow-Wow that was held on the opening night to honor all the elders present.

Both sides were woefully ignorant of the other's radically different cultural morés. The New Agers chose to ignore the First Nation directive because they looked upon their use of marijuana not as a drug but as a 'sacrament'. Whereas the A.I.M. militants simply dismissed the New Agers as ignorant, rude, white druggies.

Like the pushing and pulling tussle that occurred between the young Black Turks and A.I.M. Dog Soldiers during the Occupation of Alcatraz, the embarassing scene left some Fourth & Fifth World peoples weeping, while others chose to at once leave the Sacred Circle, never to return.

As unfortunate as all this way, it seemingly was a necessary stage our gathering had to go through to clear the air befor everyone could move on to explore other, higher, more sensitive spiritual matters.

It was as if, once again, The Great Spirit was reminding us all that this is the real world in which we live, that we constantly need to work through to evolve – to refine – our relationships with one another before we can ever hope to tap into our higher, spiritual nature as human beings.

– STAGE TWO: A GIFT OF THE AIR SPIRITS –

By the ceremony's second day, one could sense events in the invisible realm were speeding up the healing process in the physical realm. Though some issues between our peoples were on their way to being resolved, feelings were still at the tender, awkward stage. Our different cultures mostly still only able to deal with one another on a mental, intellectual plane, using our heads rather than our hearts.

Following the second sunrise ceremony, a significant incident did take place that provided us with the spiritual direction we sought.

As the gathering joined together for breakfast, several Asians, Africans, Indians and Europeans were standing around talking with Thomas Banyacya, interpreter for the Independent Hopi Nation, when a

Thomas Banyacya addresses The Sacred Circle

tiny, young sparrow suddenly flew into the Elder's 'medicine camp' *of* tipi's that were formed on the West side *of* the Sacred Circle, opposite from where my lone medicine tipi stood in the East.

As we spoke and walked about the elder's camp, the sparrow hopped in-between our feet, not the least bit concerned or fearful for its safety.

While everyone looked on in amazement, I attempted to feed the strange sparrow, throwing it bits *of* bread, which it completely ignored.

Instead, the little sparow continued to hop from tipi to tipi, stopping momentarily in front *of* each tipi's entrance, as if it were ceremonially paying its respect to the Elder's inside.

Banyacya, noting that the sparrow wouldn't take anything offered to it, remarked, "Twin Rainbow! Watch closely. This is the way things need to be in the future. You're going to have to tell your people that they're going to have to learn how to give rather than take all the time."

For many *of* us, Banyacya's simple comment set the tone for the rest *of* the Earth Healing Ceremony

– STAGE THREE: A GIFT OF THE WATER SPIRITS –

The sunrise ceremony *of* the third day saw the dawning *of* yet a new level *of* relationship between the diverse world cultures that were represented upon The Sacred Circle.

For two days, the gathering's participants met 'round the sacred council fire, and listened to one another speak their minds and hearts.

Gradually, much *of* the anger and suspicion subsided. Some new understandings and respect for each another as human beings had slowly been realized. By the third day, our spirit's were beginning to soar together around the fire, desiring to fly ever higher.

Yet there were those casual onlookers present, who floated in and out *of* the U.N. Habitat Conference in downtown Vancouver or the nearby Peoples Habitat Forum, who couldn't see any *of* this. Unaware *of* the subtle stages *of* human relationship we were undergoing on the Sacred Circle, they quickly dismissed us as, "Nothing more than a bunch *of* crazy, hallucinating nuts or well-meaning, but simpleton, elders."

To the unaware, outsider-observer, the only significant thing that ever happened during the three day Earth Healing Ceremony was that it rained heavily and a lot *of* people got soaked clear to the bone.

Though it did pour buckets, that in the end had us all looking like a pack *of* drowned rats, we were actually joyful for our spiritual dousing in ways that an outsider could not even begin to fathom.

"The rain", as the Hopi elder, Thomas Banyacya, simply pointed out to us at the time, as it sometimes lightly and other times cascaded down upon us, "is the most natural way that Mother Earth has to ground our attention to her. It's the most natural way she can encourage us to focus our minds and hearts together as One Mind & One Heart, and so bring our artificial, man-made things down to her to be healed."

Throughout the gathering's proceedings, we discovered that the more it rained, the more we concentrated upon what the elders were saying, and the more we concentrated the more we understood who and what they are about.

With each new natural element or invisible force that grounded us, we grew to enjoy, all the more, the rare privilege we were given to come together, for one brief moment in time, as 'One World Order People', to reflect upon how the human spirit not only will survive but flourish if, as the Hopi told us, "You and your people will just take up, wherever you are, your sacred responsibilities as the protectors and guardians of Turtle Island."

Gathered 'round the sacred council fire, we were given the added opportunity to learn that, irrespective of whatever our Asian, African, European or Aboriginal viewpoint, and the severe hurt our often diametrically-different views have inflicted upon one another's culture's over the centuries, we still were human beings who were able to spiritually communicate, on a one-to-one, you-to-me, us-together basis.

In the process, we learned, too, how our Mother Earth, second-by-second, spiritually communicates with us in so many different ways. That no matter how far away we may stray from her higher purpose for us, it is still possible for we humans to communicate back to her, if we can but first learn how to listen well in one place, as the Hopi and other First Nation elders taught us to do upon these ceremonial grounds.

Yet so much of what we had to relearn from the elders was of still such a rudimentary nature that the listening experience often seemed more like re-entering kindergarten.

As the cold, bone-soaking drizzle continued throughout the Ceremony, there were those who choose to do nothing but grumble and grizzle about the idiocy of sitting drenched in the mud. But the Hopi instead kept patiently encouraging them not to run for shelter but to come back to the pine-bough arbor that encircled the council fire.

"Put away all your umbrellas, waterproof mats and rain-gear.", said the Hopi. "Just try to be in the rain with us and feel the soft underbelly of our Mother's body move beneath you."

Sitting there in the mud for three days – listening to countless First Nation peoples stand up before the council fire and, for the first time in their lives, risk baring their souls before non-natives – was as humbling an experience as it was a rare honor that goes beyond words.

– STAGE FOUR: GIFT OF THE FIRE SPIRITS –

Two experiences stand out amongst the many that occurred around the council fire. One came through the ancient song of an old Yurok elder from the Klamath River area of Northern California, and the other came through the almighty, wise words spoken by a Shoshoni warrior from Northwestern Nevada.

Raising themselves up from the soaking-wet body of pilgrims who sat huddled 'round the council fire, an old Yurok elder and his young native companion walked up to the fire's blazing edge, stopped and stood in silence as they reverently stared into the red-hot coals for a time.

The young man finally took a deep, audibly-loud breath and looked up at us. "Just yesterday", he began in a low, soft tone, his chin quivering with emotion, his eyes once more staring into the coals, "early in the mornin', not more than 24 hours ago, I was drivin' through my people's rancheria in Northern California when th' urge came over me to stop by my uncle's place an' see if there was anythin' he needed."

For several days the old Yurok had desperately wanted to attend the Earth Healing Ceremony he'd heard about on the mocassin telegraph, but he had neither the physical nor financial means to do so.

So there he sat, rocking back and forth on the front porch of his old, isolated mountain cabin, praying to the Great Spirit that he might somehow be provided with the means to attend.

The young Yurok continued with his tale, "When I pulled up in front of Unc's cabin an' asked him if there was anythin' I could do for him, he looked at me kinda funny and then smiled. 'Yeh, Nephew!', he said. 'Yah can drive me up ta' Canada right this here minute.'"

By now looking much more relaxed and confident than when he first began to speak, the young Yurok added, "Unc's a good man. I mean a real good man who never asks for nothin', 'less it's mighty important. I didn't have hardly no money, an' my car's what ya' could call a 'rez special' an' so not too dependable. But I just said to him, 'OK, Unc! Let's get her done.' I didn't even have no toothpaste or change of clothes. Unc' blessed me an' ol' Bettsy an' we just headed right on out. An', ya' know, we got here without no problems a'tall."

Tired and bleary-eyed from their long, non-stop journey, the Yurok elder and his nephew only managed to make the tail-end of the ceremony. They drove all that way just so the elder could take a few minutes to give to us the highest, most precious gift he had to offer.

Before he divulged his gift, the grey-haired Yurok, still staring into the fire's coals, deigned to speak in his ancient Yurok tongue. With bowed legs and crooked arms held aloft like huge paws, his aged, bent frame slowly began to resonate, to pulsate, to the Bear rhythm that already was gathering force within him .

His nephew again stepped forward to act as an interpreter, "Thank yah for lettin' me stand before yah," he said. "It's a great honor for me to be here, thanks to my nephew. He's a good boy. Now I want to sing a Bear song. It's a song I've only sung a few times in public. This is th' first time in front of White folks."

As it turned out, we couldn't understand a word of the old Yurok's song, but we didn't have to. For the grunts and animated, Bear-like movements he made conjured up his 'Bear Spirit' who entered into each of us and made us feel that much more stronger and richer for his gift.

As the last low grunt of the old Yurok bear trailed off into a barely-audible murmur, the look of fullfillment, of empowerment, on the old elder's face was still another priceless gift in itself.

Though none of us were able to recall that Yurok Bear Chant, the sense we had at the time was as if we'd received a legacy of immense timeless, intangible power, of intrepid courage and big-heartedness, too, that we knew we would be able to recall, forever.

Even now, while attempting to write about it many years later, the same tears of joy rush back, causing a huge, warm feeling to well up again from somewhere deep inside me as goose bumps and shivers ripple, like the Northern Lights, across my arms and back.

No sooner did those two Yuroks meld back into the crowd, settling back down upon their muddy resting place beneath the pine arbor, when a powerfully-built, swarthy, dark-skinned, Levi-clad Shoshoni warrior boldly stepped up to the fire.

He began, in a deep, bellowing voice to give us several gripping, modern-day accounts of the trench warfare, life-and-death struggles with the White Man that he and his people were daily forced to endure.

The Shoshoni's words of passionate love for his Nation and Nevada homelands, and the angst in his voice over the losses they continued to suffer, were those that could have been uttered down through time by any number of indigenous peoples in the world, as testified to by the loud

"**AHO's**" from us all that interspersed his every sentence. His words spoken with more eloquence, clarity and wisdom than any of the world's so-called leaders I've ever heard speak, before or since.

Afterwards, I approached the Shoshoni to shake his hand and thank him for his gift of fine words. But when I asked him what his name was, the Shoshoni humbly declared, "You don't need to know who I am. But if you hang around Indian Country long enough, you'll hear many native peoples speak far more strongly and with more power than me."

Standing there, talking with that Shoshoni was like being in the presence of a Crazy Horse or Wovoka, a Big Bear or Poundmaker. His intense, penetrating, cobalt-black eyes those of one who is supremely-resolute and confident about the ground upon which he stands.

The gifts the Yurok elder and Shoshoni both freely gave, caused me to wonder how many other similar gatherings and gift-giving like our Earth Healing Ceremony, have been occurring for decades – lo, for centuries – before and ever since the arrival of my people on Turtle Island.

Once one is plugged into The Great Turtle's spiritual circuitry, the rich complexity, and yet utter simplicity, of these gatherings embodies some of the most real, profound, life experiences one can ever hope to have. Yet, once one is unplugged from that circuitry, these gatherings seem as unreal and invisible as anything possibly could get. It's a bit like stepping through a time-space warp. Whichever side one happens to be on seemingly the only reality, while the other side takes on a totally illusory quality.

As time went by, and the Earth Healing Ceremony continued to unfold, we listened to still others speak. Their words like the wind and rain, through which came the power of Turtle Island's living spirit. Their purifying talks, blowing-seeping into all our private thoughts, made us each that much more stronger within ourselves.

Each speaker who rose up made us that much more aware of, as Thomas Banyacya put it, "From this point forward in your lives, you each now know the way you should live and how you should conduct yourself with your people. We're not necessarily asking you to join us. But what we are asking is that you try to understand and respect our ancient ways of life. And if you don't, from here on out, you now know that your conscience will bother you for the rest of your days."

Banyacya's comments struck at the heart of what all those who spoke attempted to share about what they hoped would happen in their future contacts with the world's other races and cultures.

As one Cree elder stated, "What we're tryin' to say to you folks is that the liver in our body shouldn't ever want to be like the heart anymore than the heart should ever want to be or do everthin' the liver's doing. 'Cause the heart, liver, lungs, an' blood in our bodies each has their own gift to share so the whole body stays alive an' can heal itself. Each part should understand that an' respect what it an' all the other parts are doin' together, without them ever havin' to see or be with one another."

Listening to that old Cree wise man, I couldn't help but wonder and ponder about the countless years, decades and centuries of similar such wise elders, from every aboriginal culture and continent upon our Mother Earth who have been trying to say, to whatever new agressor-invader-occupier, the very same things. And yet, because of an insane split that exists within the human brain's left and right hemisphere's, nothing has significantly changed in the dialogue between them. Thus we true human beings, who already know of such things, are forced to endure anew the same stupidity, ignorance and avoidance of these higher truths with each new dawning century or millennium. Each of us forced to start first from within ourselves, and then slowly spread this healing conscious-ness anew to all those sick, ignorant ones around us.

– REVELATIONS OF THE HOPI PROPHECY –

The healing the Hopi sought to bring about within us was meant to conjure up, with our help, the spiritual power of that ancient Musqueam meeting place to heal something far beyond ourselves.

For even though all the Asian, African and European parts of the collective human body were gathered together in the nearby U.N. Habitat Conference, the First Nation parts of the body were excluded.

The Hopi, as if by magic, sought to gain admittance to the U.N.'s inner sanctums. Once inside, it was their intent to issue their warning prophecy that declared the *Bahanna's* (White Man's) world was continuing to move ever dangerously close to the point of destroying all the natural life patterns upon our Mother Earth.

Within the Hopi Prophecy itself is a directive to the elders to attempt four times to formally give their religious warnings to the world about what will happen if certain imbalances are not corrected in time.

"Our prophecy tells us," said Banyacya, "that if we fail, after four attempts, to get the world to listen, it will be too late to avoid the violent catastrophes it must face for the imbalances it has caused within all of Creation's patterns. It will then be time for us to begin making other plans to prepare ourselves for *The Great Day of Purification*, or *Time of The Mystery Egg*, as we Hopi call it, that will come as sure as I'm standing here."

The Hopi had attempted twice before to gain the world's ear, and speak to them of "The Crooked Path of the White Man", but failed on both occasions. The Earth Healing Ceremony at Eyalmox was their third attempt.

This uncertain 'Time of The Mystery Egg', as its referred to within their prophecy, addresses the unknown fate in the destiny of humankind, yet to be hatched, that will lead to either the birth of a new dawn or the death of an old one.

The Hopi Prophecy, while exceedingly long to tell in its entirety, sought to once again try to warn us that greed, ignorance, arrogance and a lust for power would

Pictograph depicts Two Paths in Life:
* The Upper Crooked Path of the White Man traveled by many.
* The Lower Straight Path of Turtle Island traveled by few.

not only continue to destroy the harmony and balance of our own bodies, and that of our Mother Earth, but of our Father Universe, as well.

The elders suggested to us that to follow the Hopi 'Way of The Land', or straight path of Turtle Island, as the foundation of all life, is to become a sacred caretaker who has the power to affect the delicate balance of Nature to such a degree that our actions can determine whether Nature's great cycles bring prosperity or disaster.

The Prophecy sought to profess to us a Sacred Circle way of life, based upon the Open Hand of Peace, that is the only truly revolutionary way to bring about real peace in the world. To live this way is to be Hopi no matter what one's religion, race or creed.

"Our present Fourth World", as we heard the Hopi describe the violent world in which we now live, that follows the opposite way of 'The Clenched Fist', "is the weaving of a pattern we, or our ancestors, set into motion a long time ago. Our departure from the Creator's natural patterns for us, said the Hopi, can be traced back to a time, before even our present physical form."

Through their telling of the Prophecy's revelations, we learned of a long, long ago 'First World' where those, from whom we have sprung, were able to appear and disappear at will. But due to their arrogance, they took their procreative powers for granted and neglected The Creator's *Great Infinite Plan*.

The Hopi spoke to us of how, in the present Fourth World, we've become trapped in our present human form, while remaining caught up in an unending life-and-death struggle between the two sides of our brain.

Our Left Side creative and wise, but too naive and lacksadasical. Our Right Side clever and powerful, but too ignorant and forgetful of The Creator's original purpose for us. This suicidal split indeed one that has governed the entire course of human history through each of the three previous worlds in which we've existed.

We heard the Hopi say that as each previous world reached the brink of annihilation, there always has remained a small minority of 'Faithful Ones' who have managed to live in almost complete accord with The Creator's Great Infinite Plan and the original instructions passed down for eons, from generation to generation, as to how to maintain that accord.

As part of this small minority, the Hopi's have attempted to recall, through their ceremonies, their knowledge and wisdom of these previous three worlds, the reason for our emergence into the present Fourth World as well as our purpose beyond, as we prepare to enter into yet a Fifth World.

Since time beyond mind, the esoteric knowledge of all this has been duly handed down to those like the Hopi who have kept a close watch as each successive stage in their prophecy has revealed itself.

The Hopi Prophecy, which predicted the coming of 'The False White Brother' (i.e. European conquerors and missionaries) to Turtle Island, also speaks of the eventual coming of 'The True White Brother', otherwise referred to as "A Hopi of light complexion", who will have in their possession the matching set of sacred stone tablets that will fit together with those presently held by the Hopi Independent Nation.

The Prophecy foretells, as well, of a future time when a great spiritual gathering in Hopi Land will bring together all the traditional spiritual leaders of the world to reveal more about all this. This prophetic time will come to pass, "When the whole world has begun to shake and turn red against those who are hindering the Hopi."

In the Prophecy, *The First Great Shaking of The World* (W.W. I) was foretold by the "Appearance of black bugs (automobiles) that will travel all across the land." *The Second Great Shaking of The World* (W.W. II) was foretold by the "Black bugs flying through the sky (airplanes) that would leave great trails (bombs) that cause much sickness and death below." *The Third Great Shaking of The World* (W.W. III) is foretold as occurring "When a great house is thrown into the sky (space station) and a war will engulf the whole world, destroying much of it, leading to the end of life as we know it."

So, PILGRIM. You are called upon to once more close these covers and go off for a time to ponder alone in nature what all has been said here. How has what you have thus far witnessed in the world, during your lifetime, agreed or disagreed with what the Hopi speak of in their prophecy? How much of your life is spent practicing either the Open Hand of Peace or Way of The Clenched Fist? How have you felt the ancient struggle between the Left and Right sides of the human brain play out in your life? Do you sense where the world is heading, at this juncture in history, that another great shaking is on its way? But enough talk. **Be Off With Ye! Go!**

WELCOME BACK! The Hopi's Time of The Mystery Egg is what Western prophets have long referred to as "The Apocalypse" or "Time of Armageddon". For those of us who assembled at this time and place with the Hopi, what was otherwise offically referred to as Hope Village quickly became know to us as Hopi Village. We *itinerant Hopi's* who gathered there, as visionaries of planetary peace, knew we needed to try to stave off this dreaded time contained within all the prophecies of the world.

– THE THIRD KNOCK SOUNDS UPON THE WORLD'S DOOR –

Our unassuming, grass-roots gathering at Eyalmox was the Hopi's third attempt to issue their warning that the third, and final, terrible shaking of the world soon would manifest itself, unless everything was turned around 180 degrees.

Their first attempt to bring their prophecy to the attention of the world was tried at the U.N. headquarters in New York in 1948, following the atomic bombing of Hiroshima and Nagasaki. To the Hopi, the

"Dropping of a gourd full of ashes" passage in their prophecy, that speaks to the destruction of these two cities, was one of the major, late warning signs of their Prophecy's more horrendous final predictions. A second unsuccessful attempt was tried in Stockholm in '54, following the renewed threat of nuclear holocaust during the Korean Conflict.

Observing the tense, solemn faces of the Hopi when their caravan first arrived, conveyed to us the serious nature of their presence and the spiritual work they had set out to do. Like the alien in the movie *The Day The Earth Stood Still*, the Hopi knew they were about to face a near impossible challenge to try and almost get the world to stand still long enough to hear their essential message.

At a critical point in the Earth Healing Ceremony, when we had reached Stage Four in the healing process between ourselves, something curious happened. Suddenly there was a great flurry of action amongst the elders. Rumor had it that the Hopi decided the time had come to try to breach the barriers and enter the U.N.'s General Assembly in downtown Vancouver.

We gathered together to hold hands, form a huge prayer circle and put our minds together as One to help the Hopi accomplish their sacred work. With that, a large caravan was quickly assembled to accompany the Hopi to the Queen Elizabeth Centre, where the U.N. Habitat Conference was being conducted. A dozen or more pilgrims piled into Alta-Dena and away we went.

As events turned out in the real world of politics, the Hopi failed in their third attempt to gain direct admittance into the General Assembly. But they did accomplish the next best thing, which was to get a Hopi delegation admitted into the U.N.'s outer chambers.

There they formally meet with, and presented to, Barney Danson, the Canadian Secretariat-General, a traditional symbolic offering of an eagle's plume – symbol of the wild spirit of life and breath of our ancestors, who are with us always – and a handful of sacred Hopi cornmeal and pollen – symbols of the eternal bountifulness and beauty of life.

In return, the Secretariat-General promised the Hopi delegation that he would speak on their behalf to the Assembly.

The joy that flashed amongst the faces of the Hopi as they emerged, semi-victorious, from the Queen Elizabeth was an amazing sight.

Piling back into Alta-Dena, we drove through Vancouver's downtown streets, honking and cheering as if we'd just won the Stanley Cup, all the way back to Jericho and the Sacred Circle grounds.

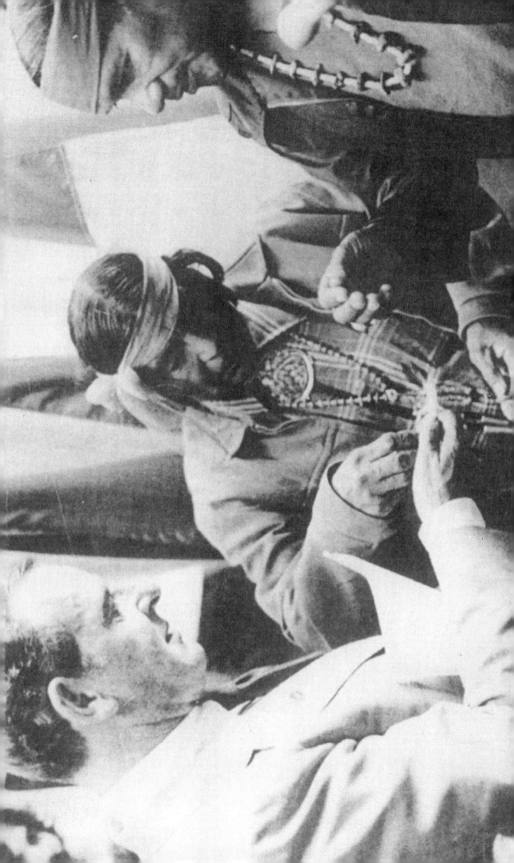

The world's door, while still not open, at least had been pushed open a tiny bit, so that there was still room to hope that perhaps one day the Hopi, on their fourth attempt, might gain admittance into the very *House of Mica* (U.N. headquarters in New York) to deliver their blessings of love and hope contained within the Hopi Declaration of Peace.

Our Ceremony accomplished a great deal. Held on the eve of the Summer Solstice, it became part of a major worldwide solidarity movement and link-in-consciousness with those like the Tibetan's 'Festival of Humanity' healing celebration. Other sacred council fires had been lit in solidarity with the Hopi at: Mount Shasta, California; Mt. Yamnuska, Alberta; Findhorn, Scotland, and; Mt Kilimanjaro, Tanzania. Each council fire serving as yet another channel of healing for the earth.

As on Alcatraz, though much factual head knowldege needed to be transmitted, the real intent of the Hopi ceremony at Eyalmox was to bring about the creation of a planetary ceremony of heart knowledge.

The Hopi were trying to alert the world to the real dangers that, as Frank Waters states in *The Book of The Hopi*:

> Great tremors of unrest and resentment against the imposition of Western rational materialism are shaking the Sierra Madres and the Andes. The psychic chasm separating us from all Red America, Black Africa, Yellow Asia and the Brown Middle East grows ever wider. Who can doubt the signs that a transition to another great new age has begun.

At the very least, the first stirrings of what potentially could become a great new age of peace had, in our minds, began at the Earth Healing Ceremony. Though we knew it might still take many lifetimes to complete, it was, like Alcatraz, one of Turtle Island's early wake-up calls. It came at a time when The Great Spirit was saying to us all, "Okay, my children! You can do this the easy way or the hard way. You can go with the Open Hand of Peace now or deal with the Closed Fist of the AK-47 later. It's your call." To those of us present, if nothing else ever came of all this, we felt a budding sense of a new age – a new frontier – a new opening out of consciousness – within ourselves.

– A SYMBOLIC UNION OF A PLANETARY TRUTH –

The celebration of the Hopi's modest victory, and the symbolic coming together of the world's spiritual traditions and medicine ways, crystallized during the traditional wedding of a young Lil'Wat Nation couple from the Williams Clan.

Beman Logan, the spiritual leader of the Six Nations Confederacy, conducted the wedding ceremony while we looked on from wherever we stood on the edge of the Sacred Circle.

Logan, his medicine assistants and the LIl'Wat couple beside him slowly began to move along the rim of the Sacred Circle, stopping from time to time to speak with one of us.

Beman Logan's assistants would hand the person a shiny, new silver coin, Logan would ask them their name and then announce for all to hear, "You, Twin Rainbow, are called upon today to bear witness to the sacred union that is taking place here."

Many shiny new coins were passed out that day to those who were not only over-joyed to partake in the beautiful marriage of the Lil'Wat couple but to also bear witness to the symbolic union of a universal, planetary truth within each of their lives.

As the long procession of witnesses filed slowly past the honored couple, their proud clan members, and all the revered First Nation elders present – shaking hands as they passed along the line – a group of singers took up a slow, honoring chant on the drum.

Soon, a snake dance of unity, involving hundreds of chanting, laughing, beaming Black, White, Yellow, Brown and Red faces, led by Allen Van Every, a young Mohawk hereditary chief with drum in-hand, began coiling all about in endless, writhing spirals 'round the sacred council drum.

Allan Van Every chanted each verse, while the rest of us responded in-kind. Six times Van Emery called out and six times we answered back:

Way   hey yah hah hey Verse (Repeated) 6x's   Ho   nah, We yah Hey yah Verse (Repeated) 4x's

Over and over echoed Van Every's answer and our response as the giant serpent body that we humans had become, coiled 'round itself, ever tighter and tighter.

As the three day – or was it three years, or maybe three centuries or perhaps even three worlds – Earth Healing Ceremony drew to a close, Banyacya called everyone together one last time to join hands upon the Sacred Circle.

A Hopi elder placed beside the council fire a large open bag of cornmeal. One by one, those who felt so moved approached the fire, took up a handful of cornmeal and made a prayer offering: to the fire which remained lit night and day throughout the ceremony; to the Keepers-of-The-Fire who faithfully maintained it; and to the five eagles who unexpectedly, had appeared overhead and began to soar around the grounds as we made our final offerings.

Five eagles, soaring overhead, at that precise moment, in a modern metropolitan area where, even on the rarest of occasions, seldom no more than one or two were ever known to have been seen before. Yet at that exact moment, five all at once. Coincidence or Synchronicity? A random communique from the universe or our Great Mother Earth's way of expressing her pleasure with what we all had just done there?

The gathering ended on a full moon in June, with the coming of the first Thunder Beings and their eagle emissaries.

As everyone prepared to break camp and return to their respective homelands, five sacred, flowering corn plants, which originally were transplanted in front of my lone medicine tipi for the duration of the ceremony, were dug up and placed in large pots beside the council fire. Each corn plant was ceremonially presented to a First Nation medicine person whose people represented each of the Four Sacred Directions.

Beman Logan spoke of the symbolic message these corn plans were meant to convey. "They represent", he said, "the life-giving spiritual work done here that will continue to grow and feed the people."

– TEACHINGS OF THE SACRED CIRCLE –

Grandfather & Grandmother teachings too numerous to mention were generously offered to whomever found their way to the Sacred Circle.

The Hopi provided more instruction than anyone could ever hope to absorb in a lifetime. Their Declaration of Peace was offered as a blueprint of how each of us could live a peaceful life and so bring about the peaceful seachange that needed to occur.

The Hopi left us to ponder, for the rest of our lives, the simple words of Dan Katchongva, one of their senior spiritual leaders, who said, "You must continue to lead your people on the road that The Great Spirit made for you to travel. You will meet many obstacles along the way. The road will be hard, but the peaceful way of life can only be accomplished by those with strong courage and by the purification of all living things."

We each also received a primary lesson on how to use the Sacred Circle and Hopi Declaration of Peace as conceptual models to reach a consensus between all the warring opposites we encountered in life, forever calling to our minds that which joins all things together in equal manner and how to hold firm to these truths.

We learned from First Nation peoples to be mindful of the many lessons the sacred council fire has to offer. First and foremost, to always remember that whenever we decide to light a spiritual fire, we need to recall that it transmutes, from the denser to the finer states of reality, the essence of the tree people along with whatever thoughts, prayers or songs we choose to send with them into the universe. That the Pine arbor that gave us shelter during the ceremony represents the daily sacrifice the plant people make in order that we may live.

Without any public fanfare during the Sacred Circle Ceremony, a Hopi woman elder, who was Chief-Keeper-of-the-Fire,had instructed four new native Fire-Keepers; teaching them how to use the power of Fire as a medicine way as well as enter into a lifetime of committments and responsibliities that go with this teaching.

During the ceremony, several Carriers-of-The-Sacred Medicine Pipe also quietly received their mystical initiations and a lifetime charge to willingly go wherever in the world a sacred council fire was needed, be it in a fire pit or the bowl of a medicine pipe.

As many Turtle Island prophecies foretold would happen in our times, the takeover of Alcatraz became the first major, modern gathering for those traditional First Nation peoples starved for spiritual unification and political solidarity.

The Lakota Nation's infamous 'Defense of Wounded Knee' had served as the violent assertion of Native peoples frustrated spiritual will, out of which had finally come the consummate lesson that to walk the true path of Turtle Island one must forever follow 'The Way of The Medicine Pipe' rather than 'The Way of The Gun'. The Hopi Declaration of Peace Ceremony at Eyalmox but one more strong link among a long, historic, Turtle Island chain of consciousness in this direction.

For some First Nation peoples and New Frontier Breeds, the Sacred Circle's earth healing ceremonies helped them to recognize and accept, for the first time, one another as true brothers and sisters. For many displaced European, Asian and African people who were there, it was the first time they were ever able to consciously open their hearts to Mother Earth and feel her touch them in ways they never before knew.

Hopi Declaration of Peace

It is in the Power of the True Hopi People to unify the minds and spirits of all true peace seeking peoples of the earth . . .

"Hopi" means "Peaceful People" . . . and the truest and greatest power is the strength of Peace . . . because Peace is the Will Of The Great Spirit . . .

But do not think that just because the True Hopi People have been told by the Great Spirit never to take up arms . . . that the True Hopi People will not fight . . . even die for what we know to be the right way of Life

The True Hopi People Know how to fight without killing or hurting . . .

The True Hopi People Know how to fight with Truth and Positive Force In The Light Of The Great Spirit .

The True Hopi People Know how to Educate by clear thoughts . . . good pictures . . . and by carefully chosen words . . .

The True Hopi People Know how to show to all the world's Children the True Way of Life by setting an example . . . by working and communicating in a way that reaches the minds and hearts of all people who are truly seeking the methods of a simple and spiritual Life which is the only Life that will survive . . .

THE TRUE HOPI PEOPLE PRESERVE THE SACRED KNOWLEDGE ABOUT THE WAY OF THE EARTH BECAUSE THE TRUE HOPI PEOPLE KNOW THAT THE EARTH IS A LIVING . . . GROWING PERSON . . . AND ALL THINGS ON IT ARE HER CHILDREN . . .

The True Hopi People Know how to show the Right Way of Life to all the world's people who have ears to listen . . . who have eyes to see . . . and who have hearts to understand these things . . .

The True Hopi People Know how to generate enough Power to link up the forces of the Minds and Spirits of all the True Children of the Earth . . . and to Unify them with the Positive Force of the Great Spirit so that they may put an end to affliction and persecution in all afflicted places in this world . . .

THE TRUE HOPI PEOPLE DECLARE THAT HOPI POWER BE A FORCE WHICH WILL BRING ABOUT WORLD CHANGE.

Though the Sacred Circle was within full-view of the man-made skyline of metropolitan Vancouver, a nearby pond and its wild surrounds gave one the feeling of total immersion within a natural setting of grass, trees, clouds and sky.

Yet where once Musqueam men gathered upon nearby beaches to cast their nets for surf smelt – while the women collected sedge grass for baskets, rushes for string and cattails for food – we found only the flotsam and jetsam of the resident European culture that had long since driven the Musqueam from the area. The hostile culture of these new occupiers of the land aptly represented by an abandoned tire that floated, half-submerged within the pond's marshy, oil-slick.

Now – where once giant cedars thrived in the pond's surrounding marshy swamps, and vast schools of spawning salmon once swam up Jerry's Cove to reach its feeder streams and rivulets, into which young Musqueam boys paddled their dugout canoes at high-tide to trap muskrats – there only remained a rough, bulldozed ditch.

But in spite of the dramatic changes that took place between the time Eyalmox vanished and Hopi Village appeared, resident magic continued to flourish.

The ancestral stream of the marsh, refusing to kow-tow to the will of the White Man's ugly landfill, continued to defiantly seep fresh water into it, every which way it could. Blue-winged teals and Canadian geese continued to use the refuge of the pond's rushes to build anew their nests and raise their young. Convoys of ducklings, religiously following their mothers in single-file procession amongst the cattails and floating duck-weed, still could be seen on the quiet marshes as Red-wing Blackbirds nestled snugly into their sedge grass beds.

Each morning and evening the frogs of the pond still defiantly sang their ancient life songs for us as they did for those long ago 'Peoples of The Grass' of Eyalmox. A lone pheasant, adept at hiding from the starving hordes of feral cats and dogs gone wild, remained hidden and invisible to all save for its loud, squawking voice that sounded more like two jagged tin cans being angrily rubbed across one another than the call of a wild bird.

When a Cree elder at the gathering first heard the grating squawk of that pheasant one early morning, he smiled and said, "Yah know, don't yah, Rainbow, that this is a real good sign for us here. 'Cause Pheasant was given his voice by The Creator as a special gift to scare away any evil spirits that might be hangin' 'round."

Sitting upon the Sacred Circle, surrounded by all these natural sounds and sights, one could feel this sense of protection. It was as if we were in a sanctuary, safe from the wildly-careening-out-of-control White Man's world that lay just across the inlet. A world which, by contrast, seemed as alien to this simple place and our presence in it as if it were some far-off space station which had temporarily crash-landed near our natural temple but in due time would disappear, forever.

To this gentle setting upon a flat meadow, surrounded by young stands of poplar and alders, we came together at the behest of the Great Spirit. So special was this time that among the Hopi who came were those who never before ever left their remote mesa villages for any reason before they traveled the long, arduous distance to reach this far Northern place.

By the end of the Sacred Circle's ceremonies, it was clear, after listening to so many different visions, warnings and prophecies, that we were entering into a new cycle of life when the purification of the world would dramatically escalate.

"Watch closely!", warned one elder, "Because from here on out, Mother Earth is gonna be warning us more and more about what's comin' through the big changes in her life-cycles. She's gonna be holdin' herself back in some places, making it too dry or too wet, causing drought and famine where once there was plenty. She's gonna be creating energy crises and social chaos where before there was balance and harmony And she's gonna threaten all us with one deadly virus after another."

"Some of you", declared another elder, "will find yourselves retreating deeper and deeper into your fears and ignorance, trying to avoid the changes The Great Spirit wants to make inside you. Some of you will hear The Voice inside you that will take you on a path in life to constantly join together with others of the Spirit, as we've done here on the Sacred Circle, to try to heal all this."

As the last native caravans prepared to pull out of the ceremonial grounds, Janet McCloud, a Tulalip spiritual woman, gave us our last instructions. "Wherever you may go from here on out", she said, "keep asking yourself and your people these questions we've raised here. Ask them about the changes they've felt in themselves and the world ever since this point in time. Ask them what they've done about these feelings. Tell them what happened here. Tell them how you earned to shut up for a change and just listen. No, I mean it. It's really good that you all learned to shut up and listen instead of always wanting to talk."

– A FRAGMENTARY MOMENT IS CAPTURED ON FILM –

At the outset of the Earth Healing Ceremony, the Hopi were approached by local film-makers from the University of British Columbia to record something of the gathering for posterity.

However, as is true with every traditional First Nation gathering where matters of the spirit are the focus, the elders would allow neither cameras nor recorders to operate during the actual ceremonies.

"Any attempt to do so", they told the film-makers, "would be disrespectful of our medicine ways and beliefs. Such sacred moments are meant only for the eyes and ears of those who are present."

Yet on the ceremony's last day, after the main spiritual business had been completed, and the Lil'Wat wedding ceremony was underway, the Hopi said, "Twin Rainbow, help the film-makers capture what they can of the good-will and spirit that still lives among the people."

Scrambling all about, we managed to record flashes of the wedding, the Mohawk snake dance of unity and aspects of the Hopi's address to the People's Habitat Forum and U.N. Conference.

The Sacred Circle, a 16mm documentary, narrated by Thomas Banyacya, Beman Logan and this writer, was produced as a result and since has traveled the world over, delivering the essential hope and love of the Hopi's message that was rekindled upon that spot.

As the last elder was about to depart from the circle, he stopped to speak to the few pilgrims who still stood by the council fire with a lone Fire Keeper, whose spiritual responsibility it was to stay with the fire 'til it naturally went out of its own accord.

"Keep comin' back to this place", said the elder to the group, "whenever you want to lite another spiritual fire, make an offerin' to Mother

Earth, pray for someone in need or maybe just to practice your listenin' skills again and see what this holy place still has to say to you."

– SOUL TALK WITH A SOUL-MATE –

With Dove's medicine tipi finally down and packed away, ready for her to retrieve, I broke camp.

Making my way back to dear Alta-Dena – who all the while stood so quietly in the nearby woods, patiently awaiting my return – I eagerly removed the padlock from her accordion door, folded it back, leapt onto her pedestal seat, and cried out, "Let's go home, old girl!"

As we drove away, I thought how fleeting life's moments really are, no matter how vivid or dramatic their recall. Once they're over, it's as if they were ancient history that could have happened a hundred, thousand or more years ago.

As Alta-Dena crossed the Lion's Gate Bridge and climbed an Upper Level Highway on the way to Horsehsoe Bay, I craned my neck to look back across the Sound and try to catch a distant glimpse of Jericho Beach.

Dim, yet still faintly visible, was the shape of the old W.W. II seaplane hanger at Jericho. Now deserted and empty, during the week that had just passed it had served as the bustling heart of Hope Village, where the world's thronging multitudes daily gathered for drinks and good cheer at the Village's temporary, hand-fashioned bar. A bar that might have even broken the Guinness Records for once being the longest bar in the world.

The hanger's outside wall covered by a huge mural of First Nation West Coast art work that we painted on by taking a transparency of a piece of art, threw it onto the walls with a special projector, far enough away that the image cov-ered the entire face of the hanger, traced its outline and then set up scaffolds to fill in the appropriate spaces with the black, white and red colors of traditional West Coast design. In my mind's eye, I still could see on the inside face of the sea-plane hanger's huge bay door, that fantastic, full color mural that the artist Stark Raven and others meticulously painted of a bucolic nature scene that showed Eyalmox, as it once was at Jericho Beach, with Bears, Eagles and other animals in the foreground, foraging along the beach, while pods of Killer Whales surfaced off-shore.

"Skana's Release" Jericho Stephane Hanger Door Mural
Artists: Ne Chi Zu Muralists (Stewart Marshall & Chi "Stark Raven" Hamilton)

"What a waste!", I shouted aloud to Alta-Dena, "All that beauty lost, once the authorities decide to tear down the old hanger. That wondrous, once-in-a-lifetime scene of artists and artisans, wise men and women, nothing more than a specter of a rendezvous' passing, held in the minds of ere a few. And when we all die, that'll be that!"

Hopi Village, like its Eyalmox predecessor, already was fast fading into the mists of time, growing dimmer with each passing second and mile that Alta-Dena and I sped further away.

As Alta-Dena continued onward, I reflected upon how wise the elders are never to let cameras and recorders capture their spiritual activities. Because they know that, in real time, there always are many more subtle dimensions at play than just the gross dimensions of physical reality. They know these subtler dimensions can never be captured on film nor do they want to be, because they're part and parcel of the living moment, and so meant only for the six senses of those present within that moment and so an integral part of the universe at that point in time and space.

The elders in all their wisdom, that only comes from eons spent in one place pondering such realities, know that someone else from another point in time and space – idly looking at a photo or watching a movie, that is but a semblance of what all is really going on – have no business trying to be part of, or partake in, what no longer exists.

As I craned my mind's eye around again to look upon that magnificent view of the Twin Sisters, I caught another glorious glimpse of those mountain sentinels that always faithfully acted as the Northern counterparts of Pechas Azul in the South.

"Lolum! Waimatha!", I cried out. "Thank you for this journey! Thank you for all your guidance and inspiration! For all your feelings of goodness and gladness! **AHO!**"

Hours later, while sitting with Crystal Freesia in our matching Victorian Grandpa and Grandma wicker lounge chairs, sipping on a pot of fresh-brewed tea, I struggled to put into words what went on during this most momentous gathering. An ever so brief moment that was one of the most moving experiences ever known in life.

Yet Crystal Freesia was still having a tough time hearing what all I was trying to say because she remained fiercely angry and dismayed every time she had to play second fiddle to my odyssey's crazy quest.

She'd heard it all, too many times before, about The Voice directing me to do this or that, guiding me to go here or there. To her, it was as if The Voice, and all the ruminations in my Turtle Island journal, was my secret mistress, constantly luring me away from her. No different, albeit a spiritual pursuit, than the CEO corporate husband who was never home.

I didn't see it that way, because I felt I had no choice but to listen to The Voice and her directives that spoke to the very core of my being and why I was here on Earth, one last and final time. To ignore or deny her more like flaunting life itself.

"Love, you and I are soul-mates. Pure and simple!", I said. "Nothing ever will change that. I have absolutely no doubt that just as we are together now, so, too, were we together in the ancient past and will be in the distant future, in this world or whatever world lies beyond."

Though Crystal Freesia continued to listen in silence, I could see she was slowly coming around. "The bottom-line, Dinkory Donk", as I so affectionaly called her sometimes, "is that we each come into this world alone and go out alone. In the meantime, we each must decide to either follow The Voice that resides within our core, or listen to someone else's voice and follow its dictates. So if The Voice ever directs me to instead stay with you rather than go off to the next big ceremony or whatever comes next, so be it. I have no problem with that. I don't ever think there is anything I will miss out on, one way or the other! But if, on the other hand, The Voice suddenly directs me tomorrow to go back to California to some spiritual gathering or holy place, like San Bruno Mountain, then this is what I also must do. If that means I must leave you for a time, than I hope you can understand why."

The two of us talked long into the night about things like: love, relationship, committment, responsibility, compromise, compassion and personal freedom.

Begrudgingly, through all our soul-talk, Crystal Freesia heard my heart even though, down deep, she still preferred not to, as she put it, "Have to constantly deal with all your Indian Time–Natural Time, spirit voices, Turtle Island mojo, mumbo jumbo. I'd rather just like to know that you're always going to be there for me, 100 percent of the time. Then I would be happy to support you in whatever you decide to do."

In truth, as the years have revealed, the odyssey's trek primarily has been made possible, precisely because of Crystal Freesia's ever-abiding love and forebearance that has always kept the door open between us.

As the true, star-crossed, cosmic soul-mate that she is, it has been her constant encouragement *To Forever Go, But Forever Stay True* that this odyssey has unfolded the way it has.

– THE VOICE & OPEN ROAD CALLS YET AGAIN –

Like the sacred corn seeds that originally were planted in all our minds and hearts on Alcatraz, the Sacred Circle at Eyalmox brought that seed to its next stage of germination – to its next sacred cycle.

As the flowering corn plants were dispersed from Hopi Village, many felt their inner voice goading them to disperse and light still other council fire's around which to gather with others, plant more seeds of dialogue and speak of the many good things we thus far have learned.

Before I knew it, and much to Crystal Freeshia's chagrin, I was saying goodbye again to her as Alta-Dena and I prepared to pass back across The Medicine Line, to journey for a time amongst the people of the South.

There was yet so much to learn, so many holy spots that beckoned forward the next pilgrimage. So many elders – Chumash, Pomo, Tulalip, Lakota – met during the Earth Healing Ceremony, who had extended a standing invitation to visit with them in their own homelands and learn more of their medicine ways, struggles, visions, warnings and prophecies.

"LOLUM! WAIMATHA! LOOLLUUMM! WAIIIMAATHAA! I SEE YOU! DO YOU SEE ME, TOO?", I cried out as Alta-Dena's engine revved itself up "BLESS MY JOURNEY SOUTH!"

CURCLE ISLAND

ROAD SIGN # 13

HOW HAS YOUR LIFE TAKEN
TO THE OPEN ROAD?

The great home of the soul is the open road. Not heaven, paradise. Not 'above'. Not even 'within'. It is a wayfarer down the open road. Not by meditating. Not by fasting. Not by exploring heaven after heaven, inwardly, in the manner of the great mystics. Not exhalation. Not by ecstasy. Not by any of these ways does the soul come into her own. Only by taking to the open road. Not through charity. Not through sacrifice. Not even through love. Not through good works. Not through these does the soul accomplish herself. Only through the journey down the open road. Exposed to full contact. On two slow feet. Meeting whatever comes down the open road. In company with those that drift in the same measure along the same way. Towards no goal. Always the open road. Having no known direction even. Only the soul remaining true to herself in her going.

(D.H. Lawrence)

– The Long Walk Continues –

Music & Lyrics
by Benny "Q"

Walk on Long Walker, You've Got Lots of MIles To Walk On.
Walk on Long Walker, You've Got Lots of MIles To Walk On.

SOUTH OF THE MEDICINE LINE:
THE
INDIAN & NEW FRONTIER BREED MEET

"PILGRIM", cautions The Great Voice Of The Turtle, *"It has never been easy for my native and immigrant children to become allies and support one another, politically or spiritually. I have seen many good-hearted ones from both sides try. A few have successfully created an honest dialogue but too many more have failed and 'gotten scalped', emotionally or spiritually. As your journey has taken you across my body, how have you sought to become a bridge between your people's world and whatever new world of mine you hoped to enter into? When you tried to cross-over into this new world, did you get scalped or caught in the dangerous quicksands that lie hidden in the no man's land between them? What was it like? How did you survive? What lessons did these experiences teach you?"*

—————⟫●⟪—————

Turtle Island's dream-vision – reborn on Alcatraz and nurtured at Eyalmox – imaged the ten thousand thousand sacred council fires that one day would encircle North America.

In those days, fires were lit from the farthest northern reaches of Canada to the distant, southernmost borders of the U.S.. Like that other great flurry of council fires that spread through Indian Country in the 1890's – when Wovoka, a Paiute seer, first spoke of a vision he received, that became known as 'The Ghost Dance' – we, too, in our time, felt the same intense excitement and great expectations.

For many Pipe Carriers, Fire-Keepers and other traditional spiritual practitioners, the dominant feeling not unlike the same religious fervor that spread like wildfire in Wovoka's time. We, too, fancing ourselves as new 'Ghost Dancers', who were also trying to honor all our ancestors by renewing their traditional ways within ourselves and our diverse communities all across Turtle Island.

Yet just as those Dancer–visionaries of another century also discovered: the dream-vision and reality are always two entirely different matters.

– 322 –

The singlemost, sobering lesson gained, as we traveled from camp to camp, was that the spiritual unity and higher relationships with life we sought, were as elusive as ever. Whatever small gains we made, only came after much self-discovery and self-less, hard-slogging work between the good Black, Yellow, Red and White Roads.

Our task was, "To do the real work", as the 'Road Chief' puts it at the end of every sunrise celebration of a Native American Church Meeting, "that begins when you lift back the door-flap of the medicine tipi and face a new day. For only when you pass through its opening into the tough world that awaits, will you discover how strong and true your commitment must be as you seek to apply the spiritual truths and wisdoms that The Great Peyote Counsellor helped you to learn in this holy place."

– WHERE THE FANTASY & REALITY MEET –

For the next seven years, Alta-Dena and I crossed back and forth across The Medicine Line many times, sharing much soul-talk with Crystal Freesia before once more moving on to yet the next First Nations– New Frontier encampment.

This zigzagging, forwards and backwards, odyssey soon became a far-reaching probe. Discovered along the way was: a personal 'Medicine Way' healing process that works; how far apart the spiritual fantasy is from the real world, and; what cultural truths or lies exist between First Nation–New Frontier peoples and their different world movements.

With each zig and zag taken, a remark D.H. Lawrence once made, about what he himself learned as a traveler upon life's open road, slowly grew into something of a thesis that I sought to prove or disprove.

D.H. Lawrence, or 'Truth Seeker' as he is still known to some, once said, "Malice is the basic feeling in the Indian heart towards the White."

Drawing upon his life's hard lessons, Lawrence held serious doubts that any real reconciliation, in the flesh, ever would be possible between the White and Red Races, that no real mystic connection can ever exist between their race-spirits. Lawrence further declared:

> You can't make two streams that flow in opposite directions meet and mingle soothingly...But the spirit can change. The White Man's spirit can never become as the Red Man's spirit. It doesn't want to. But it can cease to be the opposite and negative of the Red Man's spirit. It can open out a new wide area of consciousness, in which there is room for the Red Spirit, too...To open out a new wide area of consciousness means to slough off the old consciousnesss. For the old consciousness has become a tight-fitting prison to us, in which we are going rotten.

What D.H. Lawrence meant became clearer the day Alta-Dena and I pulled into the McCloud compound near Yelm, Washington.

– A JOURNEY INTO THE SALMON PEOPLE'S COUNTRY –

I never forgot what Janet McCloud said to all us non-Indians, as we prepared to depart from the Sacred Circle grounds at Eyalmox, when she encouraged us to, "Shut up for a change and just listen to what we First Nations peoples have to tell you about the real world we live in."

I knew then that Janet McCloud and her people had something more to teach me, and that one day I would venture into Tulalip-Puyallup Indian Country to find out what exactly that something was.

The time had once more come to spiritually purify Alta-Dena and myself with the holy smoke of another braid of smoldering Sweet Grass. Alta-Dena also received a fresh change of 20W-50 oil in her crankcase. This was how we always prepared for yet another trek into the vast no man's lands that lie in-beween the White and Red Races's spirits.

Blessing Crystal Freesia with one final fan of Sweet Grass smoke, Alta-Dena and I quietly drove southward through the Okanagan Valley and once again slipped back across the Medicine Line at Nighthawk.

It wasn't long after passing through the Wanatchee Valley that we reached Yelm and the home of Nisqually spiritual man, Don McCloud.

By then, McCloud, his wife Janet and their large clan, were highly regarded, far and wide, for their tireless work as seasoned activists within the First Nation–Fourth World Spiritual Movement.

The McCloud's weren't the showy, lime-lighting Indians one often sees in the media, hobnobbing and posturing with politicians and CEO's. They were the trench workers on the front lines who, without any fanfare, did the unheralded grunt-work that needed to be done.

For starts, they were among the founders of the Indian Fishing Rights Movement in Washington, whose influence has long since swept across the U.S. and Canada, where fishing rights battles still rage.

When 'The Fishing Wars' erupted, the McCloud's were among the first in their boats. When there was an important spiritual gathering, political meeting or council fire to attend in North America, the McCloud's were among the first caravans to hit the blacktop.

They were the ones who slept in their cars on the shoulders of lonely roads, ate stale baloney sandwiches on the run and took brief respites in grimy gas station lavatories; with just enough gas and little else other than the will of The Great Spirit in their hearts to drive them ever onward.

In short, the McCloud's lifestyle put them at the top of the list of those selfless ones who've ever sought to live in-keeping with the highest traditions of their people.

– A TRADITIONAL TEACHING LESSON –

It was a hot, muggy summer's day when Alta-Dena and I rolled into the McCloud compound.

Don immediately invited me – in his typically-loud, joyous, playful tone of voice – "Hey, Mr. Rainbow! C'mon back of the house where we can sit a spell under the arbor."

As we spoke, Don and I gazed upon a mystical scene of his people's sacred Mount Rainier, shrouded in clouds, afar off to the East. At our feet, thick chunks of fresh-caught Salmon and just-picked ears of corn, still in their husks, sizzling and spitting, slowly roasted in the red-hot coals of an open fire.

Like the time before with my Lakota brothers at Pine Ridge, as we carved those eagle wingbone whistles for the dancers to use during the Medicine Man's Sun Dance at Wounded Knee, the two of us soon got down to some serious heart-talk.

McCloud began with a short anecdote his father told to him when he was just a small boy. "A story", he said "that's affected my whole life. It's not so much to tell, Rainbow, but it's somethin' I've never forgot."

Don stopped for a minute in silence, as if he once again was conjuring up that long ago time, returning to the place where he sat with his father, recreating every nuance of that singular moment.

"One muggy, still day", he softly whispered, "just about like this one we're havin' right now, Dad and me was sittin', quiet-like, on a boat dock at Frank's Landin'.That's my Dad's first name, by the way. They named that landin' after him."

Don stopped there and got up to turn the husked corn and salmon so they would cook evenly.

Settling down beside me, Don continued, "So, anyways!", he said, as he reached out and latched a firm hold of my hand, "We was starin' at the slow-movin' Nisqually passin' under our feet, when Dad grabbed hold'uv my hand, like I'm grabbin' yours now, looked me straight in the eye like I'm doin' with you, and said 'Son! I want ya' t' remember somethin' real important. Always 'member that ya' was put here on this Earth to do somethin' more with your life than just make money or work fer a livin'. We're all put here t' somehow follow the ways of our ancestors. This is yer only reason fer bein' here. Don't ever ferget it."

As Don related his boyhood tale, I recalled the mood of another soft, gentle moment, long gone, when me own Da', Francis Joseph, spoke to me with that same beauty and simplicity resonating in his voice.

It was the same affinity so often felt with other First Nation and New Frontier people who, in truth, are North America's native-born philosophers. Name-ly, those who, traditionally, have been brought up in a close relationship with the Earth and so are naturally taught, early on, to constantly reflect upon their role and place within the greater scheme of things, always remaining mindful of the real purpose and meaning of life.

Don's words also caused me to reflect upon how many other North Americans seemingly have been taught just the opposite, and so learned from a young age to shun all philosophical reflection as if it were the plague.

The two of us continued to sit there, staring into the red-hot coals as we listened to the fire give its own crackling, spattering insights as to what all goes into the essence of such soul-talk moments. The fire called to our minds that it's not so much all the fine words, intimate non-verbal asides or communal drinking and eating, as it is the *gestalt* of the experience that's always greater than the sum of its parts.

Still in silence, we watched and listened as an ancient wind rustled through the trees, brushing against our faces as it passed by. Popping corn kernals and sizzling drops of fat began mixing with the screeches of birds and buzz of irritating insects. Our militant plots of resistance against the White Man's insidiousness, interrupted by a McCloud child's more immediate need of solace. Our plots interrupted again by the frantic screams of a neighbor in dire want. Each happening part and parcel of that same indigenous gestalt between us.

The McCloud's way of life a teaching, where everything – spirituality, politics, economics, sociology, psychology – are intermingled rather than compartmentalized, where *LOVE* translates into: **L**ife **O**mnipresent **V**ictoriously **E**xperienced.

Don's simple tale of this indigenous philosophy that his father, Frank, once imparted to him led me to recall a similar passage from Ecclesiastes (3:9-11) which asks:

What gain hath the worker for his toil? I have seen the business God has given to the sons of men and daughters of women to be busy with. He hath made everything beautiful in his time; also he hath set the world in their hearts so that no man can find the word that god maketh from the beginning to the end.

– ANOTHER SIMPLE TEACHING OF THE OPEN ROAD –

The time had come to continue the odyssey's meanderings south-ward. Half-sitting, half-standing again on the edge of Alta-Dena's flop-down pedestal driver's seat, I revved up her Hercules four-banger and tapped each of her gauges to make sure they all were working.

Suddenly my attention was drawn to the sound of a loud, husky voice coming from behind a closed screen door of the McCloud home. "Wait a minute!", bellowed the voice. Emerging through the dark doorway came Don, waving a small, thin book. "Here!", he barked, as he reached inside Alta-Dena's cab and thrust it into my hands. It was a copy of **The Shape of Events To Come** *(Out of The Inferno Power–Lust Builds Apace – Will Rise A Chastened And United Race)*, by Gopi Krishna.

"Here!", he repeated again. "I want to give you somethin' more to think about as you head South. A Hopi elder gave us this book at the Sacred Circle gathering at Eyalmox."

Don said when he and the other elders read it, they thought it was the closest thing to their ancient prophecy they'd ever seen written by an outsider. "Share it, Mr. Rainbow, with your people", he added, "or whoever else you meet up with along the way."

As McCloud passed over the book, it fell open to a passage which I took as a sign to read aloud to Don and all the other McCloud's who'd started to gather 'round Alta-Dena to see us off. The passage read:

This highly gifted being is not born,
To work himself to death for earthly things,
But to irradiate, like the sun at morn,
The light of love, which cheer and warmth brings.

What after all, is thought men here for?
To toil and sweat for wealth or seat of power?
And lose them both at death or war,
Living in dread of this to the last hour?

Remember, Life can be a fairy tale,
A dancing sunbeam when it bathes in light,
Some charming landscape, a blooming hill or dale,
And makes all that it touches alive and bright.

"Sounds pretty good to me, Mr Rainbow!", chimed Don. "Have a safe journey to wherever it is you're going!", he added, as he waved goodbye.

"Thanks for everything", I shouted as Alta-Dena rolled away.

Alta-Dena's huge panoramic side view mirror – with its round, convex magnifying glass insert – caught a different, heart-warming close-up of all the McCloud's as they waved their goodbyes. Alta-Dena's rusty, screw-worn, loose mirror waving back its own fond adieu as it flashed at them, in thanksgiving, one last blinding, dancing sunbeam of reflected sunlight.

As we drove away, The Voice chanted as we went, "Heya, heh! Heya hey ahey, hey, hey, hey! Hear me, Lad! A part of you and me will forever remain seated under that pine arbor with the McCloud's and their Mt. Rainier spirit ancestors, shucking corn and filleting Salmon."

As Alta-Dena plied her way southward – along quiet, winding, serene back roads through Washington and Oregon – I continued to pour over the words of Gopi Krishna and D.H. Lawrence.

Especially Gopi Krishna teachings that speak of life's path as a fairy tale meant to, "cause the shrunken hearts of others to expand with joy and hope and return to light their darkened lives...to ease their pain and grief or destroy their fear until the ebbing strength revives."

Or those words of Lawrence that speak to the need for each of us to assist the evolution of human development by "opening out a new, wider area of consciousness within ourselves that will slough off the old."

What all had to be done became even clearer as Alta-Dena pulled into a Southern California encampment of the Chumash Nation.

– A CONFRONTATION IN THE NO MAN'S LAND –

Before entering into Chumash territory, Alta-Dena and I stopped to rest along the Russian River in Northern California.

One day we met up with a wild-eyed, hot-tempered, six foot-two Irishman, with flaming red hair, who lived in a tent with his mangy runt of a dog in the woods on the edge of Guernieville, an old, time-honored California resort town.

This self-proclaimed 'Irish warrior', described himself as the black sheep of an internationally-renowned family, he cared not to name, who amasssed a fabulous fortune in the cosmetic industry.

Rejecting all the comforts and privileges his family's wealth, power and prestige afforded him, he chose instead to become, in his youth, a drug dealer and strong arm enforcer.

His life of crime on the streets of L.A. eventually got him enmeshed in the criminal justice system. This, in turn, led him to become part of a unique Department of Corrections rehabilitation program known as *The Vision Quest Wagon Train*, that was based in Tucson, Arizona.

"How odd", I thought, as I stared at this strange guy, "that while we vision-questing hippies, in our lone covered wagons, were freely travelling every which way through Indian Country, there was an actual wagon train of captive European-African-Asian-Hispanic Americans, who were being forced to search for whatever visions along the same lonely trails as us."

Though this feral Irishman tried several times to run away from the Vision Quest Wagon Train, as it plodded across the West towards points unknown, its wagon master – a real-life 'Billy Jack' type character, black cowboy hat and all – tracked him down each time and brought him back to the Train to complete its novel rehabilitation program.

After he was released from the wagon train, this Irish renegade entered the military and soon became a crack 'Green Beret' in Vietnam. "Where", as he put it, "I was trained to kill with my bare hands."

After 'Nam, this complex Irishman, who chose to only go by the first name 'John', later became a member, and then president, of a Hell's Angel club in the San Francisco Bay Area.

When 'Big John', as I quickly nicknamed him, learned that Alta-Dena and I were on our way to a Chumash Indian healing encampment near Santa Barbara, he asked, "Can I come, too? I've never met any real Indians and so don't know much about 'em. But I've always dreamt about someday spending time with 'em in Nature. 'Cause to me they're the real spiritual people of the earth." So away we went the next morn.

By nightfall, the four of us – Alta-Dena, Big John, his scraggly Heinz 57 mutt, and I – found ourselves parked at a spot, close to Point Concepcion, that the local Chumash refer to as *The Western Gate*.

To traverse the scrub coastline that surrounds 'The Western Gate' required the permission of armed guards who restricted access past a gated-community of some of Hollywood's most famous movie stars.

Once inside, we learned from a traditional Chumash spokesperson who greeted us, that, "The Western Gate is a spiritual opening that lies along the Pacific Ocean. For centuries upon centuries, The Gate has acted like a narrow, invisible highway or path along which the spirit's of our ancestors, and the newborn of each 'Living Time', travel back and forth. We Chumash are the Keepers of this sacred place."

This revelation didn't come as a complete surprise since I'd heard it said before that traditional Six Nations peoples on the East Coast also see themselves as the Keepers of a similar 'Eastern Gate'.

The Chumash encampment, set out in a desolate stretch of Pacific coastal scrub, came about to protest the proposed construction of a large liquid-degasification energy plant on the site of what the Chumash elders referred to as *The Doorway* of The Western Gate.

The elders told us that the spiritual and physical balance of the whole area was so delicate that the presence of this plant on that spot would for-ever disrupt it, causing The Doorway to close or react in some unknown, violent, calamitous way. They graciously thanked us for coming to join with them to create a sacred healing circle and council fire to gather around and try to stop the plant from being built.

As the mocassin telegraph spread the word of what was happening, concerned people from all races and walks of life began streaming towards the camp to give whatever moral and spiritual strength they could to assist the Chumash.

Like at the Hopi-led gathering at Eyalmox, a sunrise prayer ceremony, each morning before dawn, was convened by the Chumash.

Once formed into a large circle, around a ceremonial fire, we were each invited to give, silently or out-loud, whatever testament, prayer, song or chant spoke to the intent of our spiritual work there.

However, by the end of the first day, one could sense that, like the heated dispute that erupted during the opening pow-wow at Eyalmox over the use of marijuana as a sacrament, the mutual cultural ignorance between First Nation and New Age people was still widespread as ever.

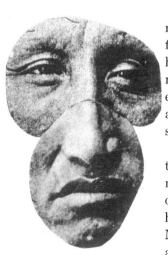

The rage that many Indians hold towards non-Indians, grew more obvious, throughout the first day's activities, with each hard stare or hostile reaction by the angry, militant A.I.M. members who began to gather at the Chumash encampment. The racism that those New Age and New Frontier people present were being subjected to was already all too palpable.

By day's end, it was clear to Big John and I that the Chumash still suffer from the same magnitude of pain and loss that we Irish and other dispossessed native peoples, historically, have felt and still feel because of the White Man's destruction of our traditional way of life and the illegal occupation of our homelands.

Before arriving at the camp, Big John and I took the opportunity to visit Santa Barbara which, following the White Man's occupation, sprang up in the heart of what once was the ancient territory of the Chumash.

Glancing at all the glossy promotional flyers and travel brochures that hyped Santa Barbara's many attributes, the one most commonly-used phrase that glaringly jumped out at us was, "Come to Santa Barbara, *America's Eden.*"

Big John and I lingered long upon what it must feel like to be a modern-day Chumash, who, every day of their life, is reminded again and again of the personal 'Garden of Eden' their ancestors, not so very long ago, once had all to themselves. A legacy to be forever denied them, their children and their children's children.

We both agreed that any dispossessed native would forever feel the same enormous disconsolation over whatever 'paradise' of their ancestors – Tahiti, Hawaii, Australia, Ireland – was stolen from them.

We also went with Alta-Dena into the mountains, on the edge of Santa Barbara, to visit the 'Painted Cave' where Chumash youth once made a pilgrimage in search of a dream-vision to guide them through life.

We remained there an even longer time to try to experience the same mystical presence the Chumash once intimately knew, that still pervades the cave and its surrounds. A presence that remains undiminished, though this holy place has been savagely vandalized to the point where local authorities have had to place a locked steel grate across its entrance to save what little remains of the ancient, pictographic Chumash legends.

Before arriving at the encampment, Big John and I stopped as well along the coast of Big Sur, in search of those Chumash whose ancestors we heard once had fled north to Salmon Creek and beyond to escape the wrath of the White Man's invasion–occupation of their sacred lands.

We wanted to talk with these full-blood and mixed-blood descendants to find out what it now means to be a traditional Chumash in an occupied land as densely populated by invading immigrants as is California.

By the time the first day of the encampment drew to a close, the two of us pulled aside to discuss what all we learned at these different places before coming to the invisible doorway of the Western Gate.

A heated discussion ensued between us over whether or not the phrase 'reverse racism' was too strong a term to use to describe the cause of the unsavory treatment we and others had received from different Chumash and Indians from other tribes present in the camp.

As two dispossessed Irishmen, we both intellectually and emotionally understood the indiscriminate rage and 'us vs them', 'siege mentality' that has gripped First Nation peoples since the days of early contact. As displaced Irishmen who'd lost so much, we also knew, all too well, what it means to still suffer from the rageful effects of eight centuries of English racism and genocide. We also could acknowledge that it's never ever easy for any culture to work through all the pain when it remains imprisoned within its own private Auschwitz. Yet all this awareness still didn't make it any easier for the two of us to deal with the same blind rage when we felt it turned around and directed towards ourselves.

Big John ended our discussion by saying, "Well, as far as this Mick is concerned, I don't have any original sin a'tall that I have to pay for on account of what's happened to Indian people. The way I see it is that all the spiritual, cultural and psychic pain that Indians feel, comes in many colors, shapes and sizes. What sometimes feels like reverse racism is exactly that, 'cause Indians are no more exempt than any other race or culture when it comes to expressing bigotry and intolerance."

– IF THE SHOE FITS, WEAR IT –

As the sun slowly sank into the Pacific, at the conclusion of the opening day of the Chumash healing ceremony, and the last notes of my 'End of Day' chant passed from my lips, a most disconcerting thought crossed my mind.

I woundered aloud, "How, indeed, has your life, as a self-proclaimed Druid–Hippie–New Frontier Breed, grown richer from all the hatred and rage you've experienced in your travels upon the open road?"

Big John had less patience and forebearance than I, and already was inconsolably distraught over some of the ugly behavior he'd thus far seen manifested in the camp.

After travelling with Alta-Dena and me for several days, he'd heard all my stories about: the hanbleceya in South Dakota with Joe Thunder Hawk and Wanagi Wacipi; the high and low points of the Occupation of Alcatraz; the Earth Healing Ceremony at Eyalmox; and sundry encounters with Metis and other mixed-blood teachers like the McCloud's, the Kruger's and others.

Big John heard my spirit and knew my heart was true. He was furious that he accompanied me the long way from the Bay Area only so he and I could be subjected to such rude treatment.

"HAH! A Healing Ceremony For The Earth and All Earth Peoples!", he mocked. "What A Joke! These Indians wouldn't know how to heal a cut on my little pinkie."

This fiery-tempered Irish warrior was not one to trifle with. He didn't suffer fools well. Whatever he lacked in tact, he more than made up for with absolute candor.

By the time night fell, I was emotionally and physically drained from having struggled, throughout the day, to convince Big John to keep his cool, when he would have otherwise rather just drilled some of the Indians with whom he'd come in contact.

"SHIT! DOG SOLDIERS, MY ASS!", is all he kept barking that day about the native policemen who were in charge of running the encampment. "I'll even tie one hand behind my back and still kick the fuckin' shit out of the whole goddamn lot."

I lay awake in Alta-Dena through the night, unable to sleep a wink as I stared through her panoramic window at the cold, starlit night. As the Milky Way's brilliant light show passed before my eyes, I tried to rationalize away the reasons for the unfriendly vibes of that Western Gate.

Suddenly the Voice cried out, "Lad, hear me well! Tomorrow morning, during the sunrise ceremony, I will help you bring about a healing for this unhappy place."

– THE HEALING COMES THROUGH AN ULTIMATUM –

During the sunrise ceremony the next morning, prayers made 'To the Four Elements', 'To the Four Sacred Directions', 'To Universal Brotherhood & Sisterhood', soon began to travel clockwise 'round the Sacred Circle's edge.

What caught my attention most amongst all the lofty sentiments was a prayer that was offered up by one of the angry, racist 'Dog Soldier's' that Big John and I had a run-in with the morning before.

"Oh, Great Spirit", he began, "May we find spiritual unity this day and continue the good feelings we have begun here."

Hearing his sanctimonious, holier-than-thou words, I found myself muttering under my breath to Big John, who stood next to me, nodding, "Actions speak louder than words, my friend."

As the prayers moved 'round the circle, drawing ever closer to where we stood, I continued to wonder what kind of healing prayer, song, chant or words I could offer up that would address the widespread spiritual dis-ease that was in evidence among those gathered.

Yet the more my conscious mind tried 'to think' of the right thing to say or do, the more I drew a blank.

"Surrender up to me, in your heart", commanded The Voice, "and simply allow me to pass what I will through you – like the smoke of the sacred kinikinnick that you inhale into your body and then exhale, through the medicine pipe, back into the universe."

When it came my turn to speak, I did as The Voice suggested.

After I finished, though, I discovered that I couldn't recall anything that had issued forth.

I took this to be a good sign that what all I said and did, without any interference from my head, was the truth.

The reaction I received from different Indians and non-Indians on the circle – who either came over to shake my hand, smile and nod affirmatively, or give me a soft pat on the back as they passed by – suggested that what all was given voice to deeply moved many who were present.

After the sunrise ceremony's conclusion, I remained standing beside the council fire, alone in my thoughts, peering intently at the glowing embers; looking for whatever reactions the fire itself might care to give about what all just happened.

Suddenly, as the fire spat sparks in my direction, I felt a hard, unfriendly jab on my back.

I turned to identify the source of this rude intrusion upon my spiritual meditation, and came face-to-face with the stern, angry stares of two young Indian men.

Because of their bright-red berets and stiff military demeanor, I immediately took them to be A.I.M. members or some local Chumash version of a Plains Dog Soldier.

– A QUICKSAND TALE IN THE NO MAN'S LAND –

"Someone wants to talk with you", snapped one of the militants, in a brusque, military tone of voice. "You're to come with us, NOW!"
The minute I turned to follow them, they closed ranks on either side of me. Like two stone-faced Death-Row guards, accompanying a 'Dead Man Walking', we proceeded towards the encampment..
The whole time, we walked in stony silence, passing by all the gathering's participants as they breakfasted together, 'til we reached a point along the camp's distant-most edge.
Standing fifty yards out in the sparse, barren Southern Californian coastal scrub-brush, was a lone Indian who had the authoritative look of the two militant's leader.
With a brisk, angry wave of his hand, the middle-aged Indian, whose chest-length grey hair was wrapped in two long braids, motioned us to come forward.
One of the young camp policeman contemptuously barked, "Move it, Hippie!"
After taking a dozen steps, I glanced over my shoulder and saw the two young men hadn't moved from their position on the edge of the scrub. They just glared at me as they stood at parade rest, ready to spring into action, at the drop-of-a-hat, if their leader so ordered.
As I continued to walk towards the old, enraged Indian, who stood so rigidly-still, the whole thing took on classic dimensions.

"You Are the Man I Want to Talk With."

It was like the stock scene from some Western movie, where the half-breed interpreter walks out alone, into hostile territory, to parlay with the Indian chief.
Each step I took, both figuratively and literally, was like walking ever-deeper into the no man's land that's exist-ed, since day one, between the two great civilization's of Turtle Island and the Western World.

My every step seemingly covered a multitude of years filled with the ignorance, fear, hatred and misunderstanding that has accrued between their two Race-spirits.

Walking up to where the old 'chief' stood, I stopped directly in front of him and said, "HI! You wanted to speak with me?" I held out my hand to him in friendship, but he refused to reciprocate.

We stared intently at one another for the longest time, as if our eyes were scanning the many centuries which had passed between our people, before finally bringing the two of us down to this seminal historic moment in time and space.

The elder's hard-looking eyes narrowed and turned deathly-cold as he angrily queried, "Who are you?"

His hard eyes and blunt question instantly called to mind another scene from a movie I'd just seen, three times in a row, a few days prior to coming to this Chumash gathering, which profoundly moved me.

In the Australian-made, Peter Weir-directed film, *The Last Wave*, a White Man suddenly finds himself sitting before an old aboriginal tribal headman, who begins asking him, over and over again, in varying haunt-ing intensities of voice, the same question, "Who are you? Who are you? Who are you? Who are you? Who are you?"

Just like the White Man in the film, who at that critical moment of truth, senses himself to be fatefully wedded to the destiny of the aboriginal man and his people, I, too, sensed a similar connection in this Chumash elder's question."

"I'm Twin Rainbow!", I answered, in a proud yet gentle way.

Hearing my name, the Indian's hard eyes briefly-flashed wide, with a look of surprised recognition, before they turned into an even harder, narrower squint.

"I've heard that name before", he muttered through clenched teeth.

Pausing for a long awkward moment, as if he were recalling what all he'd ever heard about the name, he then asked, in a combative tone, "So, tell me, Twin Rainbow! Who gave you permission to say that prayer and song you made this morning on the circle?"

Instinctively pointing to the sky, I meekly answered, "The Great Spirit spoke them through me."

"NO! The Great Spirit did not!", spat back the elder. "Besides, It doesn't make any difference. You had no right to say what you did without prior permission."

"Why?", I innocently queried. "There were many others on the circle, Indians especially, who also gave lengthy prayers and songs."

"Yes, that's true.", he snapped back. "But they're Indians. They've a right to say those prayers. But people like you need permission. This is Chumash land and this is a Chumash gathering. So you must do as we tell you. DO YOU UNDERSTAND?"

Perplexed and irritated, I responded, "Hey, hold on a minute. It's my understanding, the way I've been traditionally taught, probably just like you, that each of us standing upon the sacred circle of life, is free to give whatever Spirit directs them to say or do. That's what a sacred circle means, doesn't it, where everyone on it is equal?"

The elder, almost beside himself – even more enraged than before that this upstart of a White hippie in front of him dared to stand his ground and question him in return – barked, "Yes! That WAS a powerful prayer and song you gave. It affected a lot of people who spoke to me after the ceremony. That's why I brought you here to me. There's some things we're gonna have to get straight."

"Tell me", I asked, "Were the upset ones just Indians or did they also include some of the non-Indians in the camp? 'Cause I can tell you that a lot of 'em liked what I said."

"Never mind!", he snapped, "Just don't do anything like that again, if you know what's good for you. DO YOU UNDERSTAND?"

"Listen here!", I objected, "If this is truly a sacred circle and a spiritual gathering, then I have the same right to pray as one who also receives his inspiration from the same Great Mystery that moves through us all. Right?"

The Chumash man, by now so livid he could spit, just glowered. The non-verbal message he gave out with his whole being was that the one thing he wanted most in life to do at that moment was to strangle to death, on the spot, the impudent Twin Rainbow-White Druid-Hippie-New Frontier Breed who stood in front of him.

Slowly, he seethed through clenched teeth, "Well, okay then! If you want to pray that way, then go start your own tribe. Make up your own ceremonies, rituals and circle gatherings somewhere else."

Pointing over my shoulder, towards the encampment's entrance behind me, he hissed, icily, "You know the way in, so you know the way out if you don't like the way we run things around here."

Nodding back at him, I resolutely declared, "Maybe what you say IS right! Maybe I WILL, one day, have to do as you suggest."

At that moment, I felt as strong and confidant as the day I stood atop Joe Thunder Hawk's Holy Hill and received my vision, that *Pisko* acknowledged by soaring above my head and hovering in mid-flight to stare directly into my eyes and heart.

I knew who I was, and at once recognized this gathering to be what it was: a sad place, full of anger, unhappiness and disparate souls.

My mind and heart could readily acknowledge what all the White Man, historically, has done to native peoples everywhere. But, like Big John, I wasn't about to don the mighty burden of White guilt, which too many liberal-types perpetually wear like a 'crown of thorns' or 'hair shirt'.

The thought arose, as I stood there staring into the Chumash man's eyes, "Hey, I know the goodness and purity that lives in my heart, even if you don't."

I knew then, as never before, that any relationship – whether it be between two people, two nations or two races – is always a give-and-take dance on both sides, with both partners accountable for the dance between themselves. Neither partner ever totally responsible for what transpires between them.

In a similar vein, the 19th century's mythic portrayal of Indians as *Noble Savages* is as preposterous a concept as the 20th century's portrayal of females, collectively, as *Noble Women*.

The White Man and Indian, as well as the Male and Female genders of whatever race, in truth, possess the same feet of clay, of which they need to make themselves and one another constantly aware.

The instant all these thoughts flashed through my mind, the Sun, from behind where the Chumash elder stood, suddenly broke through, what up 'til then, had been several enormous black storm clouds. Its bright, happy rays dispelling the menacing thunderclaps and violent bolts of lightning which, somewhere in the invisible realm, occurred there between us.

Much to the elder's surprise, before turning to leave, I again extended my hand to him. But the vehement, non-verbal response I received, as he recoiled back, suggested that the idea of shaking my hand was about the last thing in the world he wanted to do.

Yet after a couple of awkward seconds – while still glaring at my outstretched hand, as he nervously shifted his weight from foot to foot – he weakly clasped my hand in a half-hearted shake.

With that, I spun around on my heels and proudly retraced the fifty yards I'd come through the scrub, back towards the encampment's edge and the two young miltants who still stood rigidly, at parade rest, glaring at me like two gargoyles.

A short time later, a camp crier began moving amongst us, crying out as he went, "ALL SPIRITUAL LEADERS! MEET AT THE BIG TIPI!"

Without any hesitation, I proceeded towards the twenty-five foot-high ceremonial tipi because, even though I've never gone through a particular bible school or seminary training program, nor ever received any kind of license or permit to practice, I've always considered myself to be a spiritual leader of my people.

Long before this moment in time, I'd received traditional teachings from many different First Nation spiritual leaders like Don McCloud.

"Always remember one thing, Mr. Rainbow!", Don counseled. "Remembr that no one can ever tell you that you are or are not a spiritual leader of your people, 'cause that's a personal thing just between you and The Creator. If someone ever tries to tell you that you aren't, you'll know right away that they're not real spiritual people themselves."

However, no sooner did I arrive at the tipi when I was stopped by the same two young Dog Soldiers who marched me back into the scrub.

"Hey, it's the hippie again!", one shouted to their leader, as they waved to him to come over to where we stood.

Another heated discussion between the elder and I again ensued. This time the issue was over allowing me to enter into the tipi to partake in the spiritual leadership discussions that were being held.

"You can't go in there!", said the elder. "'Cause, from my point of view, you're not a legitimate spiritual leader. Tell me, anyway. Who are your people? What's their name? Where are your traditional homelands?"

It was then that I, along with Big John and several other New Frontier Breeds who were standing within earshot, knew this encampment to be a place in which we no longer desired to stay a minute longer.

So, the two of us wasted no time hopping into Alta-Dena, while the others jumped into their rigs, and we quietly left the same way we'd come.

As Alta-Dena bumped and jolted across the open scrub, Big John and I discussed how strange it was to have travelled so far to get to this place only to abruptly leave it and yet feel so strong that we could leave content, because we knew we'd received exactly the lesson we'd come to learn.

We took special note of the mythic origins of this powerful place, where the ancient ancestral spirits of the land pass to and fro – and where the Chumash Earth Goddess *Hutash* is said to once have created a Rainbow Bridge, across which all the people could safely pass over the dark, foreboding Pacific Ocean depths to populate their Santa Barbara *Garden of Eden*. How curiously odd, we both thought, that this place was where we, too, gained safe passage over our own rainbow bridge. We, too, the recipients of a new ancestral spirit awareness of who we are as New Frontier Breeds.

When Alta-Dena reached a rise in the scrub-brush, I pulled her to a halt so Big John and I could break open a special bottle of wine he'd been saving for a special moment.

"A toast!", I said, as the two of us clinked glasses, "To that Chumash elder, to the Chumash people and to all the good ancestor spirits who can hear us. Thank you, Hutash, for the rainbow bridge you've created between our heads and our hearts upon this most sacred doorway into the world beyond. AHO! "

Staring at our last view of the Chumash encampment, away off in the distance, I sat down on the ground, to get closer to Mother Earth, and put into words what my heart longed to express. What came out was:

– The Dream & The Voice –

My respects to you, oh Wild, Gentle Voice. My secret dreaming self survives, thanks to you. You who look into my soul with eyes that go back beyond time. You Grandfather Sky, Grandmother Hutash, have planted your wise seeds inside me which I now seek to grow ever closer towards.

I, The Wild, Gentle One within you now speaks:

"There is a dream dreaming us both, Lad. It's enough for you to know this and navigate your life by its charted course. For a man is what he dreams! You're a storyteller who must speak of this to all the people. Like the barred Painted Cave of the Chumash, the visions and vision-questing places of the people now are mostly imprisoned behind the invisible bars of the White Man's world. The whole nation a giant Alcatraz Island with phantom bars, whose shadows cast much darkness and confusion. This is why so many flock to Alcatraz like awed lemmings in search of what they know not! Help them to see in their waking, daylight selves that which is begun in the darkness of their nighttime reveries. This is your path. You, and those like you, must live the problem of it out alone. You must learn to cope with the split that exists between your dream pattern and the scattered nightmarish ones of the world around you. Live your life pattern of peace no matter what. Don't ever punish this natural archetype within you. Don't ever fear to tell the truth of that issuing from your deepest being, like starlight streaking through the heavens. To ignore these truths is to bring about a fearsome dis-ease within yourself. The terrible healer then will become manifest and seek to correct these imbalances. Do not draw to yourself the harsh demands that it will exact. I give you this certainty of promise: that you will meet many other isolated, lonely spirits along the way. Know that you are members of a new nation which as yet has no institutions to express itself, yet cannot be prevented from coming forth, though it still may take many decades or even centuries. Console yourself and those kindred spirits you meet along the way with this truth. Say to them, 'Brothers! Sisters! I bid you welcome as new frontiersmen and frontierswomen upon this last great landscape of the human experience. Learn to live happily in the no man's lands. Remember, we're all still but children in a nursery rhyme of time and space. Tell them, too, Lad, to rememeber to always keep intact the first laugh of that authentic child within themselves. You, yourself, as a child of Nature, must forever nurture your deep, warm, caring, instinctual self. Allow the archaic rhythms of your spirit to move you naturally from place to place through sacred song and dance. Dialogue often with your White Buffalo Medicine Stone – through stone to self, to all of life, history and time. Your 'Coming Home' work is to discover your own personal myth and then live it out-of-very-cell-in-your-body. Whatever you find, it must answer these questions:

How will you do all these things through the renewal of your peoples ancient values?
How will you walk this hard, dangerous way in the purest way possible?

When the people ask, 'Twin Rainbow, convince us that the rewards are good enough', say back to them "The path I offer isn't a safe, smooth, concrete one but a rough, untrodden one that each of you must blaze alone."

– THE SEARCH FOR THE NEW FRONTIER'S PATH CONTINUES –

Hurrying off in search of my true kinsmen and women, Alta-Dena, my wild Irish Warrior brother and I roared away from the Western Gate.

At this point, Big John wanted to visit some old biker buddies in L.A.. "HEY,Twin Rainbow", he said. "I hope you don't mind, but I need to head South on my own. I've had my fill of Indians for a while. I'll just hitch from here on, and you go do what you gotta do."

We embraced in a big bear hug, gave thanks for the many wonderful things each of us taught the other, and parted company.

I watched Big John and his little mixed-breed mongrel saunter down the shoulder of the road, 'til they disappeared 'round a bend, without so much as a backward glance my way as they went.

For a time I sat parked in Alta-Dena, wondering if our paths ever would cross again. Or if they were just two more wayfarers, like so many others Alta-Dena and I had picked up or met along the way, and shared a brief moment of soul time together, never to see one another again.

The angry, scowling face of that Chumash elder kept floating back and forth, before my mind's eye, changing into Don McCloud's happy, friendly countenance. I wondered which face would most typify the First Nation peoples I could expect to met up with in the future.

"Can I expect", I shouted aloud to the spirit world, "a face-off with one Chumash elder for every Don McCloud I have the good fortune to meet? "

"How bizarre it is", I thought, "that two virtual 'strangers' can suddenly come together for an instant – have such a powerful, all-encompassing life experience – and then, blip, like two passing ships in the night, veer off as they continue onward along their different, mysterious courses. Each one going somewhere, but where? Our life's ultimate meaning and purpose as unfathomable as the journey we call 'death'. "

So, PILGRIM. You're called upon to once more close these covers and head off to some place *of* solitude where you can be alone with your thoughts. Ponder what similar encounters you've had with those 'strangers' encountered along the path your life has taken. What truths were revealed? What lessons were learned? What gifts were received? **Be Off With Ye!**

WELCOME BACK! While among the Chumash, I heard *of* a Native Media Conference that was soon set to convene in San Francisco. It was to be a gathering *of* traditionals and progressives from among a wide-array *of* First Nations who desired to explore how to meld together old and new forms *of* communication to reach out to each other and the rest *of* the world and so share the many gifts The Creator has given them.

"AHO!", I shouted to Alta-Dena, as I lit another braid *of* Sweet Grass and smoked ourselves with a blessing, "Take us back, old girl, to that 'Baghdad-By-The-Bay' place where you and I first met."

Heading North in my hippie prairie schooner, we traced the twisting, winding way we'd come along the Big Sur coastline. Alta-Dena, poking along at her usual snail's pace, encouraged me, as always, to stay in 'The Now' and enjoy every pleasurable nuance and natural happening *of* the journey as much or more than the anticipated destination itself.

Rushing back into view, with each drawn-out mile *of* our return, were so many fond memories *of* that wondrous cosmopolitan place that those *of* my day simply called 'The City', but who, once-upon-a-time, was heralded as "The Paris *of* The West" by those other immigrant pilgrims who long before us passed through her glorious Golden Gate.

So many memories flooded back into conscious thought: those early childhood expeditions into the San Bruno Mountains; the mystical boyhood connections with Indian Head Cave, that were the source *of* my own 'Painted Cave' mysteries; the many fun-filled escapades through the City's back alleys and hidden lanes with Dave and Sago in Blewitt; all those expectant cries of hello and goodbye to Pechas Azul, asking them for their twin blessings of the odyssey's next phase; the tumultuously-thrilling times spent during the Occupation of Alcatraz.

**Let us Join together
for
Understanding & Respect**

NATIVE

NEW

DAWN

EARTH

STAR

PEOPLES

So Be It Our Mind

We participants of the Native Media Conference soon were introduced to representatives of NASA who put before us a dream they had for a 'Native Communications RCA satellite' demonstration project.

The NASA people were prepared to offer, free of cost, to First Nations peoples the use of a satellite to experment with various forms of communication between themselves and the world.

The goal of this two year project was to solicit the cooperation of at least three First Nations, located at great distances from one another, who would be willing to link-up in a series of three-way video conferences. NASA's intent was to demonstrate the superiorty of space-age technology over older, more conventional modes of communications.

When first we heard of this, many Indians and non-Indians present became greatly excited by the prospect of such a native satellite, that they immediately dubbed it, *A New Dawn Medicine Drum*. Some wondered if this was to be the predicted coming of 'The Blue Star Kachina', that the Hopi prophecize one day will appear in the heavens at a critical moment in the world's history.

I told the NASA officials that I would commit to make informal contact with some of the tradtional native peoples in the Far North and seek out their opinion on this project.

I now sensed this leg of the odyssey South of The Medicine Line to be complete. It was time to return to 'Grandmothers Land', as Canada once was known to the old-timers.

I longed to be back with Crystal Freesia, and share what all had transpired in each of our separate, yet eternally together, lives since last we were together. Our reunion always was like a second honeymoon with an added Twilight-Zone flavor to it. Each coming and going between us tinged with an etherealness, as if it were simultaneously playing itself out in a number of different dimensions all at once.

"PECHAS AZUL! I SEE YOU!", I cried out, as Alta-Dena and I passed by those magical Twin Peaks of San Francisco. "Protect, once again, my journey north, until next we meet."

Pulling onto I-5, Alta-Dena began the long, hot, arduous journey through the San Joaquin Valley interior of California. After half a day of plodding onward, we passed those much beloved Marysville Buttes, *Histum Yani* ('Spirit Mountain') as the local Maidu call their one-time island refuge. After fording the mighty Sacramento River, we came to a spot where we pulled off the road to seek out the renewing strength of yet another one of the Great Turtle's sacred sites.

It was time to pay our respects to an even grander pair of sacred twin spires who always stood for us as *The Keepers of The Door To The North*. To many First Nation and New Frontier peoples, Mts. Shasta & Shastina, and their seven sacred glaciers, are looked upon as America's 'Mount Fuji', or as the natural 'Heart Chakra' of Turtle Island. Still others call them the 'Magic Mountains' or 'Spirit Stairway to Heaven'.

Some traditional native people speak of Mt. Shasta as "The Northern Chief" of California's mountains, which they describe as so many turtle's who stand parallel with the Pacific Coast.

One can gain some sense of the prominent place this chief among all the mountains holds, if they will envisage two giant, imaginary-cupped hands to have emerged from the Pacific Ocean and come to rest across the State. The thumb of the left hand, or northern-most mountain's, are Mts. Shasta & Shastina. The remaining fingers of both hands are the other 'turtle mountains' that lead southward, 'til they reach the thumb of the right hand in the San Gabriel Mountains.

Whenever traditional people from Shasta Nation address Shasta & Shastina they chant, says Mary Carpelan, a Karuk medicine women, "*Waka Nuni! Tucki Wuckie!*" (Wahkah-Noonee! Tookey-Wookey!), which translates to, "All around the Mountain, but never on top!" This Karuk chant meant to call to the people's minds that they might climb all over the Mountain's slopes but never scale to its top, because it's a sacred place, forever reserved for the Creator's resident spirit forces.

The hearts of traditional Karuk, Wintu, Shasta natives, and their New Frontier allies, forever ache over all those who, out of ignorance or arrogance, ignore the subtle wisdom embodied within this simple chant and choose to violate, by their physical presence upon their summits, Mts. Shasta & Shastina's 'sanctuary of the spirit'.

We traditionals who do respect this holy sanctuary often wonder if the average Californian or North American will ever come to realize how great the gift of humility is that can come to one by honoring the spiritual directives of the Great Turtle's native stewards in such matters. To realize, at the same time, the great inner peace and humility that can come from always stopping short of the sacred summits of the Turtle's great mountains, so as to pay homage to the invisble realm and the lofty magnificence of some thing's in life which must, by their nature, forever remain mysterious and unattainable to we humans.

"*Waka Nuni! Tucki Wuckie!*", I chanted as Alta-Dena continued our travels past them. "Heya, hey! Heya hey, ahey! hey, hey, hey! Thank you Grandfather Shasta! Grandmother Shastina! Protect my journey northward to find out something good for my people. So many hungry souls upon the open road again. I look towards you Grandfather, Grandmother – Powers of the North – for your direction. Give me the hardening strength and purity of your snowy mantles to assist me as I go this way – Humbly! Happily! Holy!"

– A HEALING PLACE OF THE NORTH –\

Passing back across The Medicine Line through Nighthawk, Alta-Dena lumbered a short distance further, climbing into the hills above the town of Osoyoos, 'til we reached the edge of a lake the local Okanagan natives refer to as *Ha K⚛ Lilx* (Hah-Kli-Luk).

Ha K⚛ Lilx, or 'Spotted Lake', as the White Man calls it, is where I arranged to meet up with Napoleon Kruger, an Okanagan medicine man who was the uncle of Jack Spotted Lake, who received his name when he became the 'Keeper-of-The Lake'.

Napoleon and I planned to lite a private council fire, around which we could do some spiritual pow-wowing and, as the old Lenape 'pow-wow' word implies, "allow us to see through one another and know the thoughts of each other's hearts." I especially wanted to tell him about what all I'd learned from my travels in the South and seek his counsel regarding what he thought of NASA's proposal for a Native-run communications satellite.

Ha K⚛ Lilx seemed the most appropriate place to do our pow-wowing because it's a story in itself of the historical relationships which have taken place between: the Okanagan Indians and the natural world; those Indian Nations hostile towards the Okanagan's, and the European immigrant-invader-occupiers who took over the whole area.

If nothing else, Hah-Kli-Luk's surrounding timeless desert land-scapes, shimmering winter Northern Light-lit nights and summery shooting star-filled skies make it one of Turtle Island's most dramatic natural settings in which to delve into the world of the spirit.

Grandfather Shasta and Grandmother Shastina

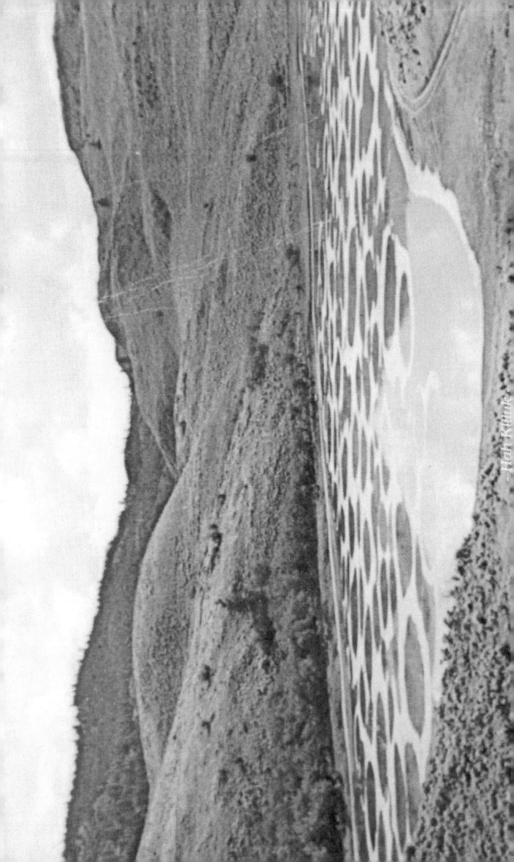

If one sits long enough upon one of the lake's surrounding ridges, they will note more than one strange occurrence. For starts, on a sunny day, one can watch as its 365 individual pools, one for every day of the year, visibly change colors, like sparkling gems slowly turning in the light. One pool that is emerald green in the morning may be ruby red by noon or turquoise blue by evening.

Strange natural rock formations, assuming the shapes of eagles, bears and other animals can also be seen all along its edge, each one raising its own puzzling question of what unique legend or tale might account for their having come to be.

Local oral tradition has it that at another, earlier time in history, medicine men and women, from all over the region, once regularly gathered there to collect the lake's special healing clays and conduct their healing ceremonies in its therapeutic pools. One can still see, all along the lake's edge overgrown mounds of rock cairns, some so old and huge that only their tips protrude above ground, which contain rock samples from many distant geologic areas, left there by unknown hands as prayer offerings.

Even when the lake and its surrounds were owned by local White entrepreneurs, one could still find signs of fresh tobacco offerings, made upon tiny earth-mound altars, or the remnants of red, white, black and yellow-cloth prayer flags, left tied to the branches of pine trees, high above the lake, as reminders of some traditional person's vision-questing.

New, unusual rock offerings continue to appear upon the old, over-grown rock cairns as a sign that these mounds still are vitally-alive. These offerings sometimes made so surreptitiously, that one can visit one place on the lake and return only a short time later to discover that some 'pilgrim' quietly came and went, while symbolically leaving behind a piece of themselves.

Local Native prophecy has it that at some future time, when the human world reaches a most precarious stage in its evolution, medicine men and women from many nations will once more return to Hah-Kli-Lik to renew the spirit of the land and life of the people through the powers of the lake's many healing pools.

Located at the northern-most tip of the Great Sonoran Desert, Hah-Kl-Luk is where healers from all over the world make pilgrimages to collect its rich mineral clays for their healing practices. Local First Nation peoples know to go there to collect their sage, said to be amongst the strongest-smelling, most medicinally-potent sage found in the region.

It's also said that in pre-contact times, pregnant women once traveled there to have their babies; immersing their new-born and themselves in the lake's saline waters, which Western scientists since have determined has a saline content even greater than that of the Dead Sea. Thus Indian mothers and their babies once bobbed up and down like corks in the lake's pools as they ritualistically passed from one pool to the next in a clockwise manner. The mother pushing her baby before her while chanting to it 'til all the pools were ceremonially visited. Hah-Kli-Lik's waters acting as the amniotic fluid of the mother's womb, thereby becoming the infant's first nurturing experience with its larger Earth Mother.

Yet for all its potential to heal the physical, mental and spiritual wounds that still plague the lives of the European immigrants and First Nations people of the area, the lake has assumed a darker, sadder role. It serving as a veritable albatross around the necks of all those who've ever tried to misuse its powers for their own personal gain.

The White owners, for example, who once sought to commercially develop the lake and its surrounds – by turning it into a fancy, European-style, resort & health spa – suffered gravely as a result of the opposing forces that gathered there. Endless litigation, physical-mental-spiritual disease and death forever plagued their personal lives.

It was to this place that Napoleon, his wife, daughter and I choose to come to hold a beautiful, all-night ceremony to talk about the many things that still separate our peoples different worlds and impede our ability to communicate with one another.

– THE MASTERY OF THE OLD WAYS OVER THE SPACE AGE –

Seated beside our spiritual pow-wow fire, the four of us spoke throughout the night of the White Man's NASA satellite proposal. The whole time, orbiting satellites and shooting stars, as if they were entering into a similar dialogue between themselves, vied with another for our attention as they raced through the black void.

Huddled beside the flickering flames of the fire, that warmed us against the Northern Sonoran desert night's bitter-cold air, I watched as Napoleon's sharp Mongoloid features – softened by a wispy, Metis-style mustache and goatee – reflected the play of dark shadows against the orange-red glow of the fire's hot coals.

As he stared heavenward, at one point, watching the trail taken by a lone, slow-moving satellite as it passed overhead, I asked, "So Napoleon, tell me, truthfully, what're your thoughts about this space-age satellite for Natives? Do you think it's a good idea or not?"

In that instant, as if Nature itself sought to answer my question with its own reply, Napolean's answer was interrupted by a shooting star, that rocketed past the satellite as if it were standing still.

Hesitating before responding, as he once more stared intently back into the fire's red-hot coals, that Okanagan mystic continued to peer into the coals a goodly while as if he were searching for their own answer to my question.

Finally, he looked up at me from across the fire, his blazing eyes seeming to pass straight through mine. With a slight smile curling at the edge of his lips, he replied, "Let me answer you, my brother, with a story." Picking up another log and thoughtfully tossing it on the fire, Napoleon warned, "This story's gonna take awhile, so we might as well get comfortable."

Taking a moment to meditate again in silence, he continued:

Earlier this year I was sittin' 'round a spiritual fire like this one, quietly thinkin' to myself, when a powerful thought came over me. The thought directed me to immediately make plans to visit an old medicine friend. The feelin' I had was that I should do so without delay. Now my medicine friend lives nearly a thousand miles away from here so it ain't easy to see him. But without questionin' the thought, I made plans to leave the very next day. When I finally arrived at his place, I discovered that a lot of others also was beginin' to arrive at his place, 'cause of similar powerful thoughts that also came to 'em from that same nowhere place inside themselves."

Stopping to put another log on the fire, to ward off the frigid desert night air that was getting colder by the minute, Napoleon quipped, "Boy, it's gonna be a mighty cold one tonight in'it."

Picking up where he left off, he said:

Well, anyway, you see, none of us ever received a phone call, letter, telegram, message or nothin' from any one. Yet I was always taught to recognize and honor these powerful thoughts when they come.

He had to stop again for or a minute, to stretch his legs that were going to sleep on him, before continuing:

Well, yah know for the four days that we all pow-wowed together, I can tell you that few words passed between us, yet before we'd left much had been communicated. When it finally came time for us all to leave, I decided to drive straight through so I could gather with my wife and family to tell 'em what all had taken place. But on the way home, I became sleepy and started dozin' at the wheel. Finally, I guess I went sound asleep. But all of a sudden, I heard my wife's voice shoutin' at me, scoldin' me, sayin' 'Napoleon! Wake Up! You're too tired to drive. Pull over and rest for a while.

As Napoleon got to this part of the story, his wife became very animated. Smiling and nodding her head, over and over again, she said, "I got some things to add to this. But I'll wait for my husband to finish."
Napoleon giggled, and continued where he left off:

So I quickly opened up my eyes and seen I was drivin' off the road, headin' right for a steel bridge I was about to cross over. Well, I jerked the wheel hard and managed to bring the car to a safe stop on the shoulder of the road. Thankin' my wife, who came to me in my dreams, I curled up on the front seat and went sound asleep. After several hours, I woke up feelin' fresh and continued on my way home without a problem.

With that, his wife couldn't contain herself any longer and begged him to let her finish the story. "Okay!", he said with a broad smile, "You take her over from here!" She continued:

Well, it's just like Napoleon says. The minute I saw him pull up, I went running outside to see if he was alright. 'Cause that night I had an awful dream that was just like he said what happened. Because of the dream I couldn't sleep for the rest of the night and was worrying about him all day. When I saw him in my dream about to crash into that bridge I screamed so loud for him to wake up and stop that I woke up in a fright.

With that, the two of them just sat in silence, smiling and nodding at one another before Napoleon finally summed up the meaning of it all:

So, brother Rainbow, I guess this story is my way of sayin' to you that for centuries we Native peoples have had our own natural ways of communicatin' between ourselves over long distances. Over the years, with each new fast-food convenience of the White Man's world, our natural skills in these things have been gettin' weaker and weaker. These White Man's space age toys are just crutches that encourage us not to rely on our own natural powers and the discipline to walk the hard traditional road our ancestors left to us to follow. This road and these old skills are still available to us today. But we gotta be prepared to work hard for 'em.

His tale at once caused my thoughts to wander back for a moment to an earlier encounter with George Abbott, a Medicine Pipe Carrier from the Lil'Wat Nation, who, himself, had dedicated his life to follow Turtle Island's hard, traditional path. Abbott similarly helped me to discover another side of these natural, disciplined ways.

Months after the historic Hopi-conducted Earth Healing Ceremony at Eyalmox had ended, I found myself making a return pilgrimage to the site with George Abbott. For several hours, Abbott and I sat quietly beside one another upon the stilled, council fire pit, without saying a word to one another, while our thoughts communicated together somewhere else in another realm.

After a time, Abbott slowly bent over and, as he touched his forehead to one of the sacred stones that lined the edge of the cold fire pit, began sobbing, uncontrollably. There was no need to ask this warrior brother the source of his deep sorrow for I, intutively, knew his tears were being offered up for all those who continue to lose their natural powers because of all the White Man's many violent oppressions and intrusions into their lives.

As Abbott raised himself back up, I leaned over and whispered, "I appreciate what your tears have taught me, Bro. I only hope that one day I, too, will be able to cry with as much depth of feeling and healing for these things."

The massive losses that Mother Earth and all her Earth Peoples continue to everywhere endure, as we head even deeper into the darkness of what some refer to as 'The New World Order', is what can cause even the strongest and bravest of warriors to weep, unabashedly.

Abbott and I sat there together for some time longer before he uttered:

Thank you, for your fine words, Rainbow. To give completely of yourself is what it really means to be a traditional person. It's a rugged path to follow that will constantly have you leaving your loved ones to go off and do the work you know you have to do. So you should know what you're getting into when you walk this way. You should know also, Rainbow, that there aren't any simple answers we Indians can give to people like you. There aren't even any questions. You must raise them both within yourself. But if you do, the rewards you'll get will be as rich as the risks you're willing to take. If you can do it, it's really a great life."

– AN UNEXPECTED GIFT OF A DREAM AND A VISION –

It was just before early twilight, when Napoleon and I noticed something unusual about the tall grass that lay behind us, not more than ten feet away from our spiritual fire. Once we really looked at it, we realized it was all matted down, as if some large animal or animals had rested in it throughout the night.

As we stared into the darkness, trying to adjust our eyes to make out if there was still anything in the tall grass, we detected a slight movement. Suddenly we saw a doe and her fawn quietly get up and slowly saunter off.

Napoleon just smiled at me and quipped, "That doe and her baby wanted to come in close so they could listen to what all we were saying, Rainbow. That's a real good sign for the work you have to do. I'll pray for you, Brother Rainbow, that in your spiritual travels from here on out to find your own balance, in-between our peoples ways, that you don't go crazy or lose yourself."

Pointing to a high ridge above Hah-Kli-Luk, he added, "Before we leave this good place, and before the sun comes up, I want yah to climb up there, high on the hill, and find a special tree I want yah to sit under for a time. I want yah to think about what all we've talked about this night, while yah watch the dawning of a new day. When yah finish, come on back down, tell me yer thoughts, and we'll talk some more."

Glancing up at all the pines on the top of the ridge he was talking about, I implored, "What tree are you taking about? I don't...." "DON'T YOU WORRY ABOUT WHICH ONE!", he interjected, "Just let yer own spirit find the one I mean."

It was early twilight by the time I reached the summit of the ridge. Far below, I could see Napoleon standing beside the fire, his large, plump, Santa Claus-shaped body flickering in its glow, his outstretched arms held high above his head that was bent back, as if he were commiserating in silence with the spirit world.

The top of the ridge provided a commanding view of the whole region. To the North I could see the distant Osoyoos Lake with the Inkaneep Indian Reserve and dry desert terrain on its eastern banks and the White Man's irrigated, lush-green, orchard country on its western banks. To the East, I could make out Anarchist Pass, rising abruptly skyward from the Okanagan Valley floor, while to the South was a clear view into the dry, arid Wanatchee Valley system that extended far across The Medicine Line into Washington State.

Not knowing what tree Napoleon meant for me to find, I seemingly forgot everything I'd traditionally been taught about such things. Instead of just allowing the spirit tree to find me rather than the other way around, I ended up wandering for a time, like a 'boob', trying to 'rationally' find the tree he intended I should sit beneath.

I don't know why I began wandering from tree to tree. Maybe it was because I was punch-drunk tired from having talked with Napoleon non-stop throughout the long night.

I continued to wander aimlessly all over the ridge, at first picking out the most magnificent-looking specimens I could find. But each time I found what I 'thought' was the 'special tree', I restlessly moved on to yet the next one and then another and then another, 'til I was bouncing all 'round the ridge like a ping-pong ball.

Finally I stopped and frustratedly blurted out-loud to myself, "Hey, Geronimo. HOLD IT! THIS IS BLOODLY INSANE! You know better than this. Napoleon said to you, 'Just let the spirit direct you'. Okay?"

I immediately sat down where I was and remained still for a time while practicing some disciplined, deep-nasal breathing to tame my mind so I could go ever-deeper into thought.

Suddenly, a puny, stunted pine, unlike the grander ones I earlier sought out, caught my eye. Looking hardly like what one might expect a so-called 'special tree' to look like, I nevertheless walked over to it and said, "Hello, Charlie Brown! Mind if I sit with you for awhile?"

Settling myself up against its twisted spine, it wasn't long before I began noticing all 'round its base, various 'spirit signs'. For on a flat rock, beside the tree, were four small pebbles which had been mindfully positioned at each of the four directions, around which someone had recently sprinkled a fresh tobacco offering. While high above, in the tree's branches, were tied colored prayer flags, one for each of the four great powers in the universe.

I knew at once that this had been someone's 'holy hill', upon which they underwent a rigorous prayer-fasting vigil. "YEAH! DIS IS DAH PLACE, ALRIGHT!", I squealed with glee.

The spot overlooked one of the most peaceful, tranquil scenes I'd ever know in life. Far below, Napoleon still could be seen standing with his outstretched arms held high, while everywhere above Hah-Kli-Luk, a score of Nighthawk's, swooping and banking in chase of swarms of mosquitos, made their signature 'Ommm' sound as the wind rushed through their wing feathers each time they broke their plummeting descents with quick, darting ascents skyward.

Before I knew it, I nodded off. The reverie or deep sleep I fell into seemed like hours-long but may have only been for a few minutes when a great, bellowing voice – like the one I heard years before in my dream-vision, while atop Thunder Hawk's holy hill – bellowed, "TWIN RAINBOW! WAKE UP! SING A SONG!"

Startled awake, I jumped to my feet thinking I missed the sunrise. Yet I discovered my timing was perfect since the distant-most edge of the eastern sky above Anarchist Pass had only just begun to become a faint, warm crimson glow against the dark-purple, twilight night overhead.

Elated that I hadn't missed the dawn, I vigorously began chanting aloud my New Dawn Song, that originally came to me, years before, during my hanbleceya prayer-fast in South Dakota.

Here comes the dawning of a new day hey

Gazing all about at Nature's magnificent symphony, that already was slowly tuning itself up in preparation for another triumphant day – listening intently as its Concerto *of* 'Life in Balance' in E Major grew ever louder – brought back the intensity *of* my hanbleceya's original dream-vision that once spoke to me *of* finding balance within myself.

On the day that dream-vision manifested atop Thunder Hawk's Holy Hill, I knew I was henceforth obligated to direct its healing gifts to all those who've ever found themselves caught in the same cross-cultural quicksands as I, in-between the good Red, Black, Yellow or White Roads *of* their people. Such travels through those no man's lands always a potentially crazy-making path to take, and one that is certainly not for those faint *of* heart.

Like so many other drifting soul's met up with along the way, I've often come close to becoming lost, but never completely, thanks to the guidance and prayers *of* those like Napoleon, who, in some other dimension, forever stands there on the edge *of* Hah-Kli-Luk, commisserating on my behalf with the spirit world.

That special, puny, stunted tree Napolean encouraged me to find also forever after serving as one *of* life's metaphors for all those who've ever lost their way, and so been swallowd up by the quicksand or forced to join the legions *of* walking wounded among all our peoples. That simple, unpretentious tree forever more acting as a constant reminder to always carry myself among my people in as humble and unadorned way as possible.

As I sat there resting up against the spine *of* my Charley Brown mentor, pondering the whole wondrous scene, I realized another important dream had come to me in my momentary slumber.

In the dream, I'm sleeping beside Hah-Kli-Luk where a large sacred circle and council fire has been formed. Some *of* the young Indians present are suspicious *of* my presence. They suddenly turn hostile. I stand on the Eastern side *of* the circle, talking with their chief who sits on the Western side.

All at once I rise up and walk 'round, in a clockwise direction, to leave, knowing I'm not really wanted there. Before leaving, the presence *of* a small lizard, looking like a carved African or Celtic totem, is noticed lying on the ground, trapped within a block of ice. At first it appears to be a frozen, lifeless form. Yet upon picking it up, I realize that under all that ice it's quite warm and alive.

Ecstatic by my find, I keep saying, over and over, to the Indians present, "This is an important sign! Remember the story of the lizard in the dreamtime? DO YOU?"

The dream lizard is brightly-colored, with a black head which looks more like that of a snake, with large electric yellow circles around its deep, black eyes. Its upper body is a lighter blackish-grey, set within a white checkerboard design. Its belly, hands and feet have a mystical, silvery-yellow, bright-pinkish, iridescent hue to them.

The lizard telepathically announces itself to be a symbol of the authority of we New Frontier Breeds. The Indians nod as I say, "It's high time those like myself begin our own tribes! Our own circles! Establish our own traditional homelands! But how to do that is the question."

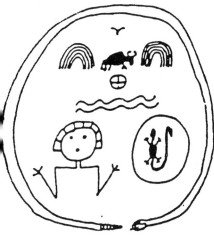

With that, the lizard all at once is surrounded by Rattlesnake, who forms himself into a circle with the opening between his face and tail facing South.

At this point in the dream, Rattlesnake and all his symbols fly into the air, like a sky-writing plane releasing a long trailing plume of coloured smoke, and paint themselves all across the sky over-looking Hah-Kli-Luk.

The dreamtime drama ends with me shouting from my resting place against my spirit tree-helper, "HEAR ME! SPIRITS!"

Following the guidance of dreams and those like Napoleon, Don McCloud and others has helped to plot the way through the many human and cultural storms in which the White and Red Race spirits still remain so embroiled. Weathering all the storms has led to the realization that those like myself have become, in the process, solitary free lancers and lone wolves, out along the razor's edge between the White and Red Roads of our people.

– A DREAM'S POIGNANT MORAL –

The imagery-feeling of that razor's edge in the dream is like walking all alone down the hard cobblestone street of an old hamlet. It's the eve of Winter Solstice. The setting is a piercingly-cold, pitch-black night with the stars massed above in a wondrously-blazing, twinkling profusion. The stilled mood a deeply mystical one.

Each shop window along either side of the hamlet's narrow, empty streets and the cozy residences above them, all are gaily lit. The warm radiance of light beaming through their leaded, stained-glass windows, piercing the heavy mantle of darkness, beckons the cold and hungry wayfarer to enter. At that moment, the dry, fresh-fallen snow, crunching underfoot, gives off an exquisite sense of purity and rebirth.

The discipline of this new razor's edge asks of the wayfarer, with each step taken on two slow feet, to make as faint a track and as little sound as possible, so as not to disturb the holy silence of the moment.

The wayfarer looks longingly through each window at the rich panorama of life that lies within. But as his hand touches the doorknob, a twinge of pain stabs at his heart and stomach. It's the pain of a spiritual hunger, a deep homesickness, which only the open road can feed.

Above, in the cold, star-lit night, the magic interplay of the Aurora Borealis veils through the heavens, and it is then that the wayfarer knows where home to be.

Ever so gently releasing his grip from the knob, he happily throws the thick wool scarf an extra turn 'round his neck, and bend forwards into the shrill wind that forever challenges the way forward. Contentment to be found in an inner-knowingess that his life's odyssey is truly his own.

The eventual destination for each lone New Frontier Breed's odyssey forever remains an unknown. As strange and vague a place as it often-times has left each Breed standing, it also has given each an exciting opportunity to see all sides of their people's relationships with one another.

In the end, each Breed realizing that wherever he or she may happen to fall in-between their peoples race-spirits, they each possess distinctly unique and valuable gifts with which to share. Each of them aware that they have yet another exciting side of this Turtle Island tale to tell.

– THE DREAM WITHIN A DREAM JOURNEY CONTINUES –

Napoleon was pleased by what all he heard about my dream and the many visionary wayfarer thoughts that came to me while atop the ridge. "That's pretty much the way I see it, too, Brother Rainbow."

He laughed, heartedly, when he heard me recount how I bounced around the ridge like a ping-pong ball. Still laughing loudly, he said, with that sly wink *of* his, "Heh! Heh! I knew alla time you'd find that tree I was thinkin' about. Spirit's funny, in'it, the way it shows us what we need."

With that, we paid our respects with some tobacco offerings to the now still fire pit, to the doe and her fawn who secretly listened in on our conversation throughout the night, and to the whole sacred moment *of* the time we spent together in the wild. After sharing a lot *of* bear hugs all 'round, we broke camp and went our separate ways.

Once again, I couldn't wait to get back to Crystal Freesia and our cozy cottage in Horseshoe Bay we called *Pacem en Terris*. That tiny dwelling, like so many *of* its one-time counterparts, once was the much sought-after destination *of* summer holidayers and honeymooners who also saw it as a place where peace reigned on earth.

Growing ever stronger, with each mile travelled, was the dream *of* reaching Pacem en Terris and quaffing down yet another large Brown Betty brew *of* Irish Breakfast tea with a half-dozen home-made Aussie pikelets, smothered in butter and jam, amidst Crystal Freesia's ribald laughter and love. The two *of* us once more sharing, as so many times before, the exquisite mysteries *of* our alone but eternally together odyssey's.

TURTLE ISLAND

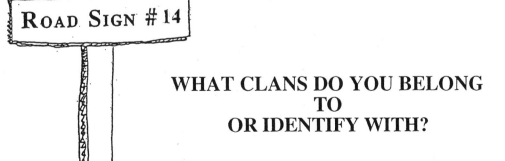

ROAD SIGN # 14

WHAT CLANS DO YOU BELONG
TO
OR IDENTIFY WITH?

– MT. TS'ZIL –

Wintertime Forests....Pristine....
Waters Cascading....Downward....
Powerfully Young Mountain....Nature In Her Youth....
Dark Prehistoric Swamps....Primeval....
Moist Wet Fogs....Deep Gray Galactic Skies....
Electro-Magnetic Earth Forces....Raw Elements....
Crucibles of Time & Space....
Youth....Side By Side....Old Age....
Salish....Hopi....Mayan....Egyptian....
Visitors From Other Worlds.... Worlds Within Worlds....
In Flux....In Unending Change....

(Jerome Twin Rainbow-Irwin)

– Today Is A Good Day –

(Lil'Wat Song To Reclaim The Good In The Day)

LILWATUL CLAN LIFE:

A TURTLE ISLAND MODEL

"PILGRIM", militantly challenges The Great Voice Of The Turtle, *"The pledge of the Indian Liberation Movement of Canada declares that Creator put you humans atop my back to respect and protect every part of me and all things that look to me for their survival. Some of my native children honor this responsibility by pledging their total loyalty, convictions and life's energy to whatever 'The Movement' would have them do. To what great movement on my behalf do you pledge your allegiance?"*

———————⟶⟩●⟨————————

It was several years before the Earth Healing Ceremony at Eyalmox that I first met up with the Williams Clan of Lil'Wat Nation.

The occasion was an historic one for the Lil'Wat ('LEEL-wat'), because they'd just formed their own school board and were about to make their village of *Lilwatul* the first native community in British Columbia to take complete control of their reserve's public school system.

The first bold step the Lil'Wat School Board took to send a signal to the world that they'd made a psychological break with the past, was to denounce the shadow name – *Mt. Currie* – that, in the mid 1880's, the White Man used to rename them, their village and their sacred mountain – Mt. Ts'Zil ('Ta-ZEEL').

To the arrogant White Man's world, they commonly became known as 'Mt. Currie Indians'. who lived on the 'Mt. Currie Reserve' at the base of a magnificent snow-capped mountain called 'Mt. Currie'.

The only problem was, John Currie was nothing but a screwed-up runaway teenager from Quebec, failed California gold miner and hapless Cariboo cattleman, who just happened to wander into the Lil'Wat's ancient homelands in 1885 and married a Lil'Wat woman before he died penniless in 1910. Hardly the mythic stuff to rename so much! But then the White Man's done this all over North America since day one! Its landforms and human settlements oft renamed after the worst of the worst.

The Lil'Wat's new school board, headed by Mary Williams, who was its founding principal, invited Crystal Freesia and myself to become part of a team to help them take over, from the Catholic Church, the elementary and secondary school system on their reserve.

Crystal Freesia, who formerly taught art to high school students in Australia, was excited by the prospect of developing an enriched creative arts curriculum that brought together the best of Western and Lil'Wat art. For my part, I was eager to help the people develop a Lil'Wat-based, interdisciplinary curriculum for their experimental Ts'Zil High School. A curriculum that would integrate the core subjects with an outdoor wilder-ness component that held its classes in the Lil'Wat peoples homes, in their fish camps, on their trap lines or wherever else to expose their children to the rich complexities of the Lil'Wat world.

In those days, what the Lil'Wat sought to do was typical of what First Nations all over Turtle Island were doing to try to wrest back control over the destiny of their lives as free, sovereign peoples.

Upon our arrival, the Williams Clan said we could either live in a replica of an *s7estkin* ('Esh-kin') – a traditional underground cedar house their people once used as a winter residence, that the Williams built as part of a 'Rediscovery' cultural youth camp – or in an old, historic, two-storey log cabin that once was home to some of their elders.

The problem was that neither the s7estkin nor the cabin had been used for human habitation for some time and thus had become the domain and private reserve of sundry barnyard and other wild critters.

My first impulse was to move into the s7estkin, situated near the meandering Lillooet River with a sterling view of Mt. Ts'Zil. But Crystal Freesia would have none of it.

"Love!", she said, "You can't be serious! If you think I will bloody well climb up one ladder and down another every time I have to go to the bathroom in some outhouse, or enter or leave for whatever reason, say in the dead of winter, you're a complete drongo. If you think, in your wildest dreams, that I could live for one minute in such a humpi, open to the elements, that would act as a magnet for every Wolf spider, lizard, bug, insect or snake to take up residency with us, then you are the biggest Galah there ever was. Cricky! Where would I ever put all my china, lace, linens, Edwardian clothes and fine things in one big circular, underground room with earthen walls and floors? You must be joking!"

I wasn't. I was intrigued by the idea of problem-solving how to architecturally adapt one of the Lil'Wat peoples traditional underground cedar houses to meet the needs of modern-day life. But I could see that no amount of persuasion would make even the slightest headway with Crystal Freesia, and so we opted for the log cabin.

Yet even once all the broken hay, rat droppings, cow pies and horse manure were removed from its rooms and surrounds – all the bird and roof rat nests eliminated from the nooks and crannies of its walls and attic bedroom, the floors scrubbed back 'til they were spotlessly clean – it still took some doing to convince the last of the critters to give up asserting their right of entitlement to its estate by virtue of inheritance.

As if to heap one more challenge onto our already overloaded plate, the log cabin was located on the opposite bank of the Lilloett River, from where the nearest gravel road passed. Which meant the only way to access it was to find a safe off-road place to park Alta-Dena, padlock her up tight, climb down the river's embankment to a place where a leaky row boat was kept tied, row across to the other side, tether the boat to a tree branch, and then scale the opposite bank to where the cabin sat on a ridge.

What a crazy scene it was to ever get to and from that log cabin. What with us having to: pull Alta-Dena off the road late at night, in the pitch-black dead of winter, in the middle of a blinding snow storm; slipping and sliding down an icy bank while juggling bags of groceries, briefcases and sundry items; Crystal Freesia holding fast to the boat's slippery gunnel while trying to balance on the seat what all we carried so as not to let herself or her load fall into the ice-filled river or land in the deep slush that lined the bottom of the boat; her other hand struggling to hold steady a flashlight beam so I could see where I was rowing; the two of us finally scrambling up the river's opposite bank,

sometimes loosing control of the groceries that broke through their soggy bags and slid, helter-skelter, back down to the river's edge and floated away; plowing through waist-high snowdrifts to reach the cabin's porch; grappling to lite damp kindling in an air-tight stove to try to bring some warmth and cheer back to the cabin's interior that looked and felt like Dr. Zhivago's frozen ice palace. Such experiences meant life was never ever boring. Each still has the same vital immediacy as on that day when it first made its indelible imprint upon our memory.

We spent but a short time among the Lil'Wat, however, because to be an out-sider on any reservation or reserve, and try to introduce or implement whatever new program or idea, is never easy.

The outsider always the one who gets caught between complex, confusing clan feuds or vendettas, of which they know next to nothing about, that may have raged for hundreds of years and since the coming of the White Man have become all the more aggravated.

The outsider always the one who both sides of the rift, consciously or unconsciously, use as a scapegoat–whipping post–tar baby, upon which to project whatever pent-up, unresolved animosities and frustrations.

The outsider, if he or she learns this lesson well, quick to realize that it's nothing they should ever take personally. Because this is simply the way of things and how tribal peoples throughout the world, since time im-memorial, have learned to keep all their rage within tolerable limits and, at the same time, ensure their survival as a people.

Realizing the sheer futility of the awkward position we were in, Crystal Freesia and I finally were left with no other choice but to move on like every other outsider who, ultimately, must also place their own well-being and survival above all else.

– MEMORABLE MOMENTS SPENT AMONG THE LIL'WAT –

As our brief stay amongst the Lil'Wat came to an end, it seemed more than happenstance that fate brought us together in this way. It was like what Native American Church members mean when they part company after a meeting and say, "Now that our path's have crossed upon the Good Medicine Road, we know we will meet each other again and again somewhere farther along the way."

I sensed this initial 'touching' between us somehow involved a survival relationship together in the distant future.

An ancient prophecy of the Lil'Wat warns of a time when the not too distant urban area of Vancouver, to the southeast, will dry up and blow away like so many leaves in the fall. The prophecy warns that when this happens waves of desperate urban refugees, in search of a safe haven, will seek out the protection of their northern mountain valleys.

Their prophecy says this isn't the first time nor the last that the human beings in that part of the world will be compelled to seek safety in their homelands after a great calamity has occurred.

Local oral tradition has it that Mt. Ts'Zil, the sacred mountain of the Lil'Wat, where the young men still go for their vision-quests, was one of the places where the original peoples sought refuge at the time of The Great Flood. As with Noah and his people on Mt. Ararat, Ts'Zil is one of the world's sacred spots where it's said some of the survivors reconstituted a new way of life.

The oral traditions of the Lil'Wat also speak of a time when extra-terrestrials stopped for brief sojourns among their ancestors.

Chills went up and down my spine the first time I heard the Lil'Wat speak of their contacts with travelers from other worlds. Those same chills rush back again every time I stare into yet another crisp, starlit, Aurora Borealis-filled, winter's night, and recall those early days spent on horseback with the Lil'Wat: riding through Boulder Valley and listening to stories of its mysterious A7xA7 ('A'huh'ah') spiritual powers; tracing my  fingertips over pictographs that recounted the Lil'Wat's ancient contacts with extra-terrestrials and where their ancestral spirits are said to still welcome the souls of the newly-departed into the after-life.

One memorable moment recalled is the time Alvin Nelson, a Williams Clan member, and I set off on horseback – on another bitter-cold, moon-lit night, in the dead of winter – to check his traplines.

As our horses leapt and plowed through deep snow drifts, the two of us shared still other prophecies and warnings of our people. But we spoke only in the most hushed of whispers, so as not to disturb the still mood cast by a full moon's light upon the tranquil wintery scene that surrounded us.

Alvin and I pushed our mounts ever-deeper still into the mountains 'til we reached a lofty point where we could stare off into the heavens. Once there, we shared many secret thoughts. Thoughts about: the spirit world, UFO's and 'the little people of the forest'; and how we sensed that Ts'Zil and its valley's, one day, will again become one of the normal meeting places between we humans and time-space pilgrims from other dimensions.

– MORE TOUCHINGS BETWEEN OUR SPIRITS –

The next time the Williams Clan and I met up was at the Earth Healing Ceremony at Eyalmox. They came to the Sacred Circle grounds with a special cedar arbor they'd ceremonially made and their elders had blessed. Their clan's entourage bursting with pride because not only were they able to make this important contribution to the international spiritual gathering but they planned to also use it for the setting where a couple from their clan were to get married at the conclusion of the ceremony.

This was the same arbor that when the Hopi arrived and saw it, they deigned it to be far too small for the gathering and, in a moment of surprising cultural insensitivity, tore it down without thinking beforehand of the impropriety of their actions or its potentially disastrous political and spiritual repercussions.

By then, Alta-Dena and I had already visited the McCloud compound in Washington State but still had a long list of elders met at the Earth Healing Ceremony who we planned to visit in the future. The Williams Clan of Lil'Wat Nation were high atop the list.

So preparations were immediately undertaken to get Alta-Dena and myself ready to make the short jaunt into Lil'Wat Territory from our tiny *Pacem En Terris* cottage in Horseshoe Bay.

Once again going through my *Holy Rituals of The Road* checklist, I topped Alta-Dena's crankcase with another quart of 20W-50 oil, smoked Crystal Freesia, Alta-Dena and myself with another braid of smoldering Sweet Grass, placed my medicine bundle of sacred feathers and herbs on Alta-Dena's dash and bid Crystal Freesia a fond adieu.

After only a few hours journey along the Sea to Sky Highway – past Squamish, Rainbow Lake, Whistler and the Green River – Alta-Dena was once more retracing her tracks back along that old gravel road that paralleled the Lillooett River. She and I waving as we passed within view of our old log cabin that now stood abandoned again, once more the reclaimed domicile of a host of denizens from the non-human world.

Pulling into the Williams compound was always a time-warp experience that was like being caught in-between this century and some earlier one; what with Western architecture, tools, and sundry art-ifacts jumbled together with their traditional Lil'Wat counterparts; kids and adults dressed in a strange mixture of store-bought Western garb and hand-made, old-time Lil'Wat cedar hats and bark clothing; fish and meat-drying racks beside an old-beat-up freezer, loaded to the top with the foods from two civilization's, that still worked as it noisely rattled away.

Stackwall house in Williams compound that blends Western & Lil'Wat design

– A MODEL OF TURTLE ISLAND LIFE IN ACTION –

By the time we arrived, the Williams compound had long since been a mecca place of sorts for those native and non-native peoples who've sought to learn how to integrate the old, traditional ways with the realities of the modern-day world.

As the heads of their clan, John and Mary Williams gladly accept the role they play as the consummate teachers and ambassadors of Turtle Island's ancient teachings. As such, they are the living embodiment of Canada's Indian Liberation Movement and those of Lil'Wat Nation.

John Williams
('ucwalmicw')
with grandchildren

Like their counterparts among the McCloud Clan in the South, their's is not a flashy, window-dressing way of life, but rather a simple ancient way of being, involving many natural processes that encompass everything from birth to death and all points in-between.

Besides providing for the on-going welfare and survival of their own clan, their expressed ultimate goal is not to seek acclaim for themselves but to call the world's attention to the fact that North America has yet to totally recognize a single, sovereign Red Nation, or their hereditary political and economic systems, which the Williams, collectively, work towards re-establishing once again amongst themselves.

The daily struggles they grapple with to realize their lofty vision could be said to be, perhaps, the most important metaphor for today's disenfranchised, alienated modern world. Their clan a living metaphor of the tumultuous times in which we live that calls to mind the extent to which even the average North American is being held hostage to, and victim of, the same bureaucratic, fascist systems that equally enslave them, although in ways that are less immediately apparent.

As John Williams bluntly states the problem, "The truth is, that most North Americans today live a life we call being imprisoned by a Totalitarian Democracy. Since they've never known the kind of freedom we native peoples have enjoyed, they think the totalitarian one they've got is the best one that's ever come down the road."

To spend whatever length of time with the Williams Clan, thereby becoming an integral part of their interactions with one another and the natural world around them, is to experience, first-hand, what Turtle Island's sovereign, indigenous, clan way of life means in personal terms on a human scale

It isn't any one particular sacred ritual, chant or ceremony the Williams do that makes their day-to-day life so, unless one considers every second of every minute of the day a sacred ritual time, sung within the holy communion of all that life is. Family life! Clan life! Spirit life! All lived fully in both the external and internal world's of each member.

As one clan member, _NicNekWilWat_, (Attsie Williams) puts it:

> Although we have never elected John as such, I still consider him to be my chief. He is a tower of strength that keeps us all going. Whenever this traditional path gets too hard and I'm just about to throw in the towel, John is there with his quiet strength, encourag-ing me to hang in there. Why I stay is because I know that he and the rest of the clan are always there for one another. We never let each other down but back one another up no matter what the situation. I've pushed to earn the big bucks in the past and been sucessessful in the _sáma7_ ('shama', meaning 'white man') world. In that world, though, I neglected my little girl as well as my own spiritual life. Now I'm really happy, my kids are really happy and nice to be around. We all stay close together now within our clan and it feels real good. Real natural! I feel so sorry or those in both the _sáma7_ and native world who don't have the kind of close personal backup system we in our clan have. Because all anyone ever wants in life is to be stroked and shown that someone unconditionally loves them and is totally there for them.

However, to live amongst the Williams for a time is to realize that, local Indian politics always being the cauldron that it everywhere is in North America, there are more than a few clans among the Lil'Wat who go out of their way to bad mouth the Williams clan.

The more traditional purists among them are quick to argue that the Williams, as consummate entrepreneurs, focus too much on economic issues rather than spiritual ones. While the progressives argue that the Williams are too doctrinaire in their rejection of the White Man's world and their refusal to accept any monies at all from the government.

The Williams, in a sense, act as a painful mirror that both philosophical persuasions among the Lil'Wat care not to look into, because it calls to their minds too many realities missing in their lives, of which they would rather not be reminded.

Yet though, at first glance, the spiritual element may seem lacking in the daily life of the Williams Clan, one soon senses, while spending some time among them, that all the rituals (the sweat lodges, tobacco offerings, council fires, holy prayers and chants), and all the ceremonies (the potlatches, pow-wow's, vision-seeking quests and sacred circle gatherings), while vitally important, are but the final 'icing on the cake'.

One realizes, as well, that life's rituals and ceremonies are never ends in themseles but only the means by which aboriginal and non-aboriginal people, the world over, re-charge their spiritual batteries to prepare themselves to go back into the real world and do the hard, slogging work that goes into making a traditional way of life a reality, not only in spiritual terms but in economic, political and social terms.

By this definition, one could say that the Williams Clan are, indeed, one of Turtle Island's role models of how to accomplish this in the 21st century.

One especially can see how this manifests in the Williams Clan's through their wholesome child-rearing practices. John and Mary the proponents of an indigenous form of education many thousands of years old.

While the White Man's public school systems and its leading thinkers rush from one ideological fad or pedagogical theory to another, grasping for existential straws in yet some new strategy – vouchers, charter schools, home schools, new math, old math, phonics, whole word reading, scripted lessons – the Williams Clan chooses a much simpler, time-honored course of action.

They place their faith in the ways of their ancestors and an organic process of learning that, in Western academic terms, one might refer to as a "School Without Walls" or "University of Life". Their pedagogical style the ultimate in "Free School" settings that states, in a nutshell:

We are the First People of this land. We strive to encourage our children to preserve our own way of life. We teach them that we have our own laws and governments and that we have our own well-defined territories within which we have lived and sustained ourselves from time immemorial. We teach them our own curriculum which includes our language, culture and religion which have been passed down through history. We teach our children that this ancient educational process extends 24 hours a day from birth to death, based upon the teachings passed down to us from our elders. We call to their attention that the onslaught of the colonists and th missionaries have not broken the spirit of the First Peoples of this land and that we continue to survive. We teach them that survival is a right for all peoples and that as an eternal people, we will continue to successfully survive whatever harships befall us.

On the day we first met, the Williams already were actively infusing their philosophy into the local Catholic-run educational system that they were about to take over and so set the standard for First Nation-run schools throughout the province.

Their clan's visionary efforts to develop a summer cultural camp for Lil'Wat Nation youth, preceded, by six years, even Haida Nation's own *Rediscovery of Ancient Pathways & New Directions* summer camp project. A concept, originally blazed by those like the Williams, that since has led to the creation of an international network of indigenous cultural camps and stimulated a province-wide resurgence of First Nation-based wilderness encampments for youth, adults and families.

By then, the Williams Clan, cognizant of their peoples ancient prophecies, already were busy mapping out an ambitious five, ten, twenty year plan to ensure the long-term survival of their clan.

Their plan included many lofty goals, such as how to: develop an educational alternative for youth-at-risk; find a way to bridge the generation gap between their children and the elders; promote their clan's personal health and fitness within an alcohol/drug-free environment; develop individual and clan social responsibilities through community and tribal cooperative activities; retrain their people in survival–outdoor skills and traditional native technologies; encourage within each clan member a greater sense of pride for Lil'Wat culture and one's own accomplishments within it; provide maximum opportunities for cross-cultural sharing, and finally; assist their young peoples transition into adulthood through culturally-relevant rites of passage experiences.

To accomplish their goals, the Williams simply applied to each a healthy dose of native pragmatism.

If the young people were to learn about how their ancestor's once caught and dried salmon in the old fish camps, they didn't simply read about it from a book, draw cute pictures, make models of how a traditional camp once looked, smelled, felt and tasted, or maybe take the odd, random field trip to actually visit a modern fish camp.

No way! John and Mary's philosophy is that if the children are to really taste, touch, feel and see what a fish camp, trap line, or any other aspect of traditional Lil'Wat life really is like, then they should become an integral part of it, from the ground up.

"This", says John, "is the only way that our children will learn that these ancient practices of ours aren't just quaint cultural curiosities of the past but vital living aspects of a sovereign way of life that still continues to work well. They have to be shown by the elders that these things matter enough for all of us to do them not just in some 50 minute classroom lesson plan or for a few hours a week but all week long, with all of us totally immersed in every aspect of it."

– SELF-EDUCATION IS ALWAYS THE BEST KIND –

John, like most Indian's in their youth, was forced to matriculate through the White Man's residential boarding school system and thus wasn't taught any of the old ways of his people.

But years later, as a grown man and a young father, rather than moan about how he was ripped off, he willed his life's odyssey towards the direction of educating himself in the traditional ways of his people.

If the challenge was to learn how to fish in the old way; cut up salmon the traditional Salish way to prepare them to be dried upon the racks and turned into *tswan*; or simply learn how to make camp bread (bannock); John took it upon himself to seek out elders among his people, like *Momma Plas* (Momma 'Pay-lah-she'), who he encouraged to start teaching the rest of the adults and children among his clan.

Following the self-taught example of their father, as John's children grew up, they took it upon themselves to visit the elders, read books, visit museums or do whatever they had to do to learn how to recreate the old split-cedar root

basketwork, hats and buck-ancestors. One day their would lead them to great skill of their artistry and cottage industry for their

Finally, after years their ownTs-Zil Board of of these ways – the Board of the White Man's more classroom box and narrow Mary withdrew their child-school system and formally Lil'Wat way of learning.

Today, whenever the Indian school come down to visit our each week, the kids act like fish

skin clothing of their tenacity and dedication acclaim for the great a lucrative First Nation art work.

of trying to convince Education of the wisdom intstead opted in favor regimented, constrictive curriculum. John and ren from the Ts'Zil began anew an old-time As John put it:

kids from the regular band fish camp for a few hours out of water themselves.

The little girls and boys are actually afraid to take hold of a salmon for fear of getting their hands all slimy. They have not been made a part of it and so they act as squeamish as most non-native kids would around such a foreign setting. Yet with all my own kids, from the time they could walk they were in the fish camps and I would give each of them a little fish to hold in their hands and carry around with them until they had become completely familiar with it. If a fish camp was being set up, they helped in setting it up. If ti was repairing a dip-net or gaff hook, they did it. If the elder's were there, they were right beside them, listening to their many teaching stories.

Listening to all the feverish excitement and playful pitch among the Williams Clan's elders and children at one of their fish camps – watching them turn into a well-oiled, delicately-syncopated, highly-efficient human machine during an annual salmon run – caused me to recall the similar ways I once heard the old Lakota and Dakota people describe how it felt in the old days to be with their people during an annual buffalo hunt.

The dominant feeling both embody is what native peoples of all races and cultures still experience because they know how essential it is to work, play and share life's struggles together as an extended family unit.

By contrast, the White Man's dominant culture of the isolated nuclear family: where both parents work two, three or more jobs to make ends meet; separated from each other and their children for most of the day and night; their children raised by foreign-born nannies, teenage baby-sitters, or by themselves while playing violent video games or watching decadent, pornographic T.V. programs; is the sorry counterpart of the modern world. But a dim twilight memory of a civilization whose greatness has long since passed.

In juxtaposition to this pathetic excuse for the White Man culture's raison d'état, is the intensity and personal involvement of everything the Williams Clan do together, whether it's the way they: make their snow-shoes; pick their boxwood to sell to the florists; gather wild pine mushrooms to sell to the Japanese haute cuisine market; gather xysum ('ho shem', juice squeezed from soapberries, out of which they make 'Indian ice cream'); or prepare their xysumatkwa7 ('ho shem atquah', a soapberry herbal drink rich in Vitamin C, commonly referred to as 'Indian Kool-Aid', that they sell to the health food stores).

This same joyful attitude can be seen, as well, in the way they carry out life's more mundane task, such as repairing their vans and farm equipment, tending to their livestock, doing household repairs or equipment, tending to their livestock, doing household repairs or whatever else the clan may have to do in the course of their combined efforts.

No matter how young or old they may be in actual years, the Williams simply have learned how important it is that everyone can depend on each other when things need to get done. As John recounts:

When my son Joey was only seven years old, we happened to have needed to dig a trench over 1/4 mile long in which to bury our water pipes. I was by myself and so I naturally taught Joey how to operate the tractor by himself. Together we dug that trench and layed down the pipes in no time at all and as neat as you could expect. Joey handled the tractdor as expertly and responsibly as any adult could possibly have done. Another example of our ways was something that happened once when our people had established a protest blockade across the local road running through the reserve. We learned that over 60 men from Gold River, some five hours hard drive through the mountains, were immediately coming to join our blockade. I simply turned to my daughter Gay, who was only thirteen at the time, and said to her, 'They'll be tired and hungry from their long drive. See to it that they've something to eat when they arrive.' Because of the traditional way Mary and I have taught all our kids to be self-sufficient, Gay took command and by the time the men arrived, enough salmon, rice and potatoes had been provided to feed them many times over. I said to the men, 'Go on and eat all you want! Try to eat me out of house and home if you can!' But they couldn't, 'cause Gay provided more than enough for their needs.

John's face beamed with pride in the telling of this tale. It was the same beaming glow of self-assurance, dignity and pride that one sees in all the faces of the Williams children. This same self-respect, and a natural acceptance of others in their midst, is what twinkles foremost in all their eyes.

– STANDING UPON THEIR OWN GROUND –

The Williams Clan are representative of so many Indian people who, historically, when confronted by the White Man's alien ways, have diligently struggled to break through, and grow beyond, those cultural traits of theirs that may have proven to be self-defeating to themselves and their people. As a result, they demonstrate a remarkable ability to constantly adapt and creatively adjust their lifestyle to cope with whatever outside force impinges upon their way of life.

Especially those cultural traits that, among tribal peoples at large, often can cause them, if they're not alert, to: become an isolated, closed communication system; deal with outsiders, especially non-native ones, on a purely racial rather than a human basis or; avoid sharing feelings and instead let issues smolder until the rage turns into acts of passive aggression, thinly-disguised malice or violent self-destruction through alcoholism, drug addiction, family abuse or suicide.

Similarly, the Williams Clan applies their pragmatic educational philosophy on a community-wide, societal level in such a way that no real separation exists between the two as they grapple with whatever angry, bigoted, sometimes even racist, feelings that they experience at the hands of many of their own people. Whenever the need arises, they're not afraid to call a spade a spade, whether it's among their own clan or in their dealings with other clans among the Lil'Wat.

Unlike many so-called traditional Indians who talk a good game but don't walk the talk, the Williams strive to act as living examples of the tried and true ways of their ancestors. They never miss an opportunity to encourage others around them, as well, to follow their example in-kind, in spite of the fact that the vast percentage of the rest of the village of Lilwatul no longer are interested in following the old ways and many even resent the Williams attempts to do so.

John's own take on what true spirituality means, in the indigenous sense of the word, is not simply to look the part of the medicine person but to actually 'be it' to the best of one's abilities

John thus gives short shift to many of the so-called 'medicine men' or 'pipe carriers' one can find in Indian Country who have the spiritual gift of gab down pat, but who then may proceed to drink, womanize, carouse about, and generally abuse their families in the process, while drawing their welfare checks from a system they despise.

As one of John's daughter's, Attsie Williams, puts it, "I know two pipe-carriers in our community who I wouldn't leave my children with for even one minute. Yet I leave them with Dad and Mom all day long and think nothing of it 'cause I know they'll be honored and respected."

One day, while observing the way John and Mary conduct themselves, I was reminded of something John Lame Deer, a Lakota wise man, once said to me regarding how to recognize the real spiritual leaders in Indian Country from the 'make-believes', as he put it. Lame Deer suggested:

Jerry Vista. When you're at a gatherin' an' a fancy dan up front is gettin' all the attention, maybe 'cause of his braids, Indian jewelry, feathers and everythin', just ignore him. Instead look 'round the gatherin', maybe even somewhere way in the back, fer a plain simple-lookin' man or woman. This man or woman might even have short hair or maybe dressed in a ragged ol' sweater or worn-out dress that's full of holes. When yah see such a person look at their eyes. Their eyes'll be real clear an/ strong-lookin', but they'll be gentle lookin', too. When yah finally see such a person then yah can petty well figure you've found the real power behind the fancy dan up front. They're the one's yah want to pay yer respects to later on.

John and Mary Williams are the kind of real power houses in Indian Country that Lame Deer was speaking about. Yet, for all the gentle, quiet strength to be seen in their eyes, instead of it earning them the respect and admiration that is their due, they too often receive the unearned envy, jealousy and even the hatred of more than a few.

Their's seemingly the fate common to so many highly-conscious, free-thinking human beings, from many different races and cultures down through time, who've ever sought to wake their people up and encourage them to think through certain fundamental issues of life.

Undaunted by all the criticism, the Williams simply persist in doing what they know to be right and true. They continue to speak out to anyone who will listen to warn them that the White Man's systems are slowly, inexorably collapsing and, in the process, take little of anyone's best interests to heart except their own.

They work tirelessly to make those around them more conscious of the fact that the real fundamental changes they need will never come from those leaders within the White Man's system – be they at the federal, provincial, band or tribal council level – but instead will only ever come from the grass-roots people themselves.

John's basic political philosophy is contained within a one-liner that one will often hear him use, which is also, he says, to be the title of a book he hopes to one-day write. Taking the lead of a well-known Zimbabwe book *Nobody Excepting Ourselves*, John simply declares, *"Nobody But Us!"* Meaning nobody but us is ever going to turn things around 180 degrees.

This simple philosophy has often led the Williams Clan to be summarily dismissed, as "Those damn ILM radicals!"

– AN INDIAN LIBERATION MOVEMENT OF CANADA DREAM –

As "The Mouse That Roared" within the native world, the Williams began this 180 degree 'nobody but us' turn-around, by becoming the founding members of a loose confederation of traditional native peoples that called itself the Indian Liberation Movement (ILM).

'The Movement' or 'ILM', as it's variously referred to, became part of a Canada-wide coalition of similar grass-roots groups who, in 1981, in an effort to make themselves heard, traveled to Ottawa from all parts of the country in a series of native caravans that become known as 'The Constitutional Express'.

The ILM, initially formed by traditionals among the Lil'Wat and Bella Coola Indian Nations, joined 'The Express' to protest the repatriation of the Constitution to Canada from England without the prior consent of Canada's First Nations.

As their official manifesto, the ILM simply reiterated the Sovereign Declaration, made in 1911, by the 16 hereditary chiefs of the greater Stl'atl'mx Nation that declared, in part:

– DECLARATION OF THE LILLOOET TRIBE –

We, the underwritten chiefs of the Lillooet tribe declare as follows:
We speak the truth, and we speak for our whole tribe, numbering about 1400
people
We claim that we are the rightful owners of our tribal territory, and everything pertaining thereto. We have always lived in our country, at no time have we ever deserted it, or left it to others. We have retained it from the invasion of other tribes at the cost of our blood. Our ancestors were in possession of our country centuries before the whites cam. It is the same as yesterday when the latter came, and like the day before when the first fur trader came. We are aware the B.C. government claims our country, like all other Indian territories in B.C. **But we deny their right to it. We never gave it nor sold it to them.** They certainly never got the title to the country from us, neither by agreement nor conquest, and none other than us could have any right to give them title. In early days we considered white chiefs like a superior race that never lied nor stole, and always acted wisely, and honorably. We expected they would lay claim to what belonged to themselves only. In these considerations we have been mistaken, and gradually have learned how cunning, cruel, untruthful and thieving some of them can be. We have felt keenly the stealing of our lands by the B.C. government, but we could never learn how to get redress. We felt helpless and dejected, but lately we begin to hope. We think that perhaps after all we may get redress from the greater white chiefs away in the King's country, or in Ottawa. It seemed to us all white chiefs and governments were against us, but now we commence to think we may get a measure of justice.

(signed)

James NRAITESKEL, Chief Lillooet Band	James STAGER, Chief,Pemberton Band
Peter CHALAL, Chief Mission Band	James JAMES, Chief Seaton Lake Band
John KOIUSTCHEN, Chief Pasulko Band	David EKSIEPALUS, Lillooet Chief #2
Charles NEKAULA, Chief Nkempts Band	James SMITH, Chief Tenas Lake Band
Harry NKASUSA, Chief Samakwa Band	KOITELAMUGH, Chief SkookumChuck
August AKSTONDAIL, Chief Port Douglas	Jean BAPTISTE, Chief Cayuse Creek
SWINSTWAUGH, Chief Bridge River	Thomas BULL, Chief Slahoos Band
Thomas JACK, Chief Anderson Lake	Francois ADOLPH, Chief LaFountain

Other Canadian native organizations, like the Assembly of First Nations, chose to enter into negotiations with the Canadian government concerning the entrenchment of Indian Rights into the Canadian

Constitution. The ILM, however, assumed the more traditional position that the issue was and is not a multitude of legal questions concerning land claims, and other native legal rights, but the single question that addresses the simple, straighforward matter of *Native Sovereignty*.

One prominent land claim issue that the ILM took special issue with was over the preservation of the Stein Valley. Located within the territorial boundaries of their ancestral homelands, which the Lil'Wat and Nlaka'pumox Nations have sought to preserve since time beyond mind, the Stein Valley represents within their ancient life systems of values and heritage what the human heart is to the body.

Yet, as John Williams points out, "The Stein cannot exist in isolation to every part of Mother Earth's body that makes up our homelands. All her parts are important to preserve, just like all the parts of our own bodies must be preserved if we want to live a full, healthy, happy life."

John and the ILM are critical of those outsider environ-mental groups who fail to grasp the holistic relationships that exist among the many parts of First Nation peoples homelands, and instead only focus their attention upon preserving the more 'glamorous' Stein Valley's of the world. They rail against those who enter into land claims issues with their own preconceived New Age environmental agenda or philosophy.

Over time, the Williams Clan have tended to look much more askance at their 'white environmental friends' who express an interest in aligning themselves with their work. John once characterized them as:

> Part of the same alien world view that still seeks to compromise us to the point of eventually eliminating us as a sovereign people. Many of these white environmentalists come into our lands saying they want to help us carry out our sovereign wishes, but they really don't listen very well to us. They have their own fixed hidden agenda for the way they think we should or shouldn't live in the future that hasn't anything to do with our own agenda as natives. Many of them have good hearts, but they always come to us carrying the seeds of a way of thinking that is deadly to our sovereignty. They try to impose upon us their own ideas about how we should or shouldn't log, how we should or shouldn't fish and trap, or how we should or shouldn't develop industry, tourism, parks or whatever else in our homelands. It always seems that whether we're dealing with the cultural imperialism of the White Man or these New Age environmentalists, we Natives always end up getting the short end of the stick in the long run. What we're simply trying to say about all this is that real sovereignty means just that – to be free of all such outside influences, PERIOD!

Talking like a Dutch-uncle, John cajoled me to:

> Tell all this to your people wherever Alta-Dena and you go. Keep reminding them that each race of people has been given their own task and medicine ways

to maintain the earth in balance where they live. Keep reminding them that real First Nation sovereignty is something they know nothing about and must learn from us. Tell them we need their support, but we don't really need them meddling in our business. We're trying like hell to take care of the ground we stand on with the help of our own people. The whites and other races need to do the same thing with their people in their own way.

Mike Arnose, A Shuswap Nation member with The Movement, more pointedly suggested:

Jerry! Tell your people that The Hopi tried four times to warn them to take care of their own world, but now they've gone back home to wait what they know is comin'. Our traditions tell us that we also are to try three times to tell you people the same things. We have one more warnin' to give and then we're gonna go home and wait like the Hopi. But if your world doesn't stop messin' with our sovereignty, it's gonna be too late for our world to share with you. It's really too late already. When your world finally goes down the tubes all the way, and you guys come into our valleys looking for refuge, we're not gonna help you. Or if we do, you're gonna be our slaves for a change.

From its inception, The Movement sought to call the world's attention to the simple fact that true, unadulterated, native sovereignty is the one issue the Canadian Government, in all its many negotiations with native peoples, from the time of first contact up to the Constitutional repatriation talks, has deemed to be a *Non-Starter* point of discussion. Whereas the formal position of the ILM assumes the opposite tack that this is EXACTLY the one point of discussion that is non-negotiable – Period!

Like a broken record, the ILM constantly points to the historical fact that the British Crown confirmed through its Royal Proclamation of 1763, and reconfirmed in the Canadian Constitutional Act of 1982, that the territories of First Nation people have been reserved for them unless, and until, through their consent, they ever cede them over to the Crown.

The Movement persists, as well, in calling attention to the Indian Act of 1954 – which, without the consent of First Nations people, conferred upon them the status of naturalized citizens of Canada – as yet one more underhanded way to illegally dispossess them of their sovereign territories and further subjugate them against their expressed will to the contrary.

It wasn't long after its inception that the ILM became a warning beacon to all that the Canadian government had every intention of effectively terminating the previous international agreements they entered into with First Nation peoples, under the guise of offering them a variety of diluted forms of self-governmnt.

As proof, they pointed to the Canadian Bar Association's Governing Council who, after spending three years wrestling with the issue, balked at supporting the native sovereign concept of self-government. The ILM pointed to a particularly damning comment made by one of the Governing Council's lawyers who noted, "If we let native peoples govern themselves, it could lead to an aboriginal state within a state or virtually an autonomous kingdom within Canada. So let's steer away from all that and instead support the idea of self-determination."

But true determination from a native sovereign point of view, as the ILM quickly pointed out, carries even much more weight than the White Man's illusionary notion of 'self-government'.

The Movement saw through this latest bit of White Man-talking-with-forked-tongue-deceit, and warned that the government's attempt to force native peoples to *enshrine*, or more truthfully *freeze*, their so-called rights within the Canadian Constitution was nothing more than a ploy to once and for all eliminate the native sovereign meaning of self-determination

As the philosophical–semantical debates raged, the ILM continued to hammer away at the Canadian Government's choice of the word 'determination', which, to the ILM, really suggested 'de-TERMINATION'.

According to John Williams, "The government knows if they simply move the prison bars, which have always surrounded us on the reserves, back far enough, to where we won't be able to see them as well, it will give us a sense of new freedom. But it will be a false sense of freedom that will be nothing more than the larger prison cell that all the dispossesed immigrants who've come to our homelands also now occupy."

Williams sagely words speak to the monstrous sham that the corporate governments of Canada and the U.S. have perpetrated upon their citizens. The citizenry blithely going about their daily life, convinced that they indeed live in democratically-run countries who tell the truth in their schools, courtrooms and a free and independent press.

The ILM encouraged First Nation peoples to address still another critical sovereignty issue. "If we truly are a free people", it posed, "and never willing became citizens of Canada, then can Canada impose its immigration laws on Indian Territory?"

As one of the major think-tanks within The Movement, the Williams Clan was instrumental in encouraging Indian Nations like the Nuxalt ('Nu-hault') to begin re-enacting their own national laws for immigration into their territorial homelands. This sovereign right to control their own immigration was put to the acid test in early 1984.

- AN ILM VISIONARY OR COMMON CROOK -

Satiacum, said by some to have been an hereditary chief of the Puyallup Nation in Washington State, and a direct descendent of Chief Seattle, fled to Canada from the U.S. in 1982 to evade a 300 year prison term conviction.

As the ILM contended, the criminal charges that the U.S. Government brought against Satiacum were trumped-up because of the economic activities he engaged in on behalf of his people, that threatened to seriously cut into the profits of the corporate big-boys.

The ILM dismissed as ludicrous the idea that Satiacum received three consecutive life sentences in an otherwise corrupt, lawless country where even serial killers seldom receive as lengthy a sentence, not to mention the virtual slap-on-the-wrist sentences that are given to the mogul racketerring Malkin's, Trump's and Boetsky's of North America.

This stance taken by the ILM put them at odds with some First Nations people South of the Medicine Line.

Various traditionals among the Puyallup, and even a few from Satiacum's own family, contended that Satiacum never was a chief, other than a self-styled one, and never was for his people, excepting when it led to his own self-aggrandizement. Some even said that, in his own small way, Satiacum was a dictator every bit as much as a Bush, a Yeltsin or your average, everyday, Banana-Republic leader who only maintains his power base through devious, illegal means.

Among Satiacum's detractors were those who went so far as to suggest that the sexual molestation charges that were originally brought against him in the U.S. were true to the extent that he even transmitted commun-icable diseases to some of his young victims.

As is always true, however, with every issue or controversial figure in Indian Country, there usually ends up as many opinions and sides to each story as there are factions to put them forth.

From the perspective of the ILM, the real reason that Satiacum received such a punitive sentence in the U.S. was because, to begin with, his voice was a powerful, if not annoying, force in the decades-long debate that swirled around the legal struggle of the Puyallup Nation to regain their traditional lands and fishing rights.

Satiacum, with Frank McCloud and others, was an early point man in the Fishing War's that erupted in Washington State. Satiacum also was a pioneer in the establishment on reservations of highly-successful, venture capital enterprises – such as smoke-shops, fireworks stands, mega bingo–gambling casinos and lotteries – which all since have swept through North America's non-native communities, as well.

Whether he was a chief or no chief at all, Satiacum possessed a far-reaching economic vision for First Nation peoples, as manifested in the radical strategems he put forth, that were intended to effectively make their nation's truly sovereign once again.

In those days, his brilliant economic tactics caused a great many native peoples to rightly think of him as a modern-day corporate 'Sitting Bull' or 'Wovoka', and, as such, was indeed a force who was rightly to be feared by both the U.S. and Canada's transnational corporate powers.

Satiacum's brilliantly-conceived strategems for tax-free money making enterprises went from what, at first, were only irritations until finally his revolutionary ideas were decried, by the movers and shakers among the monied classes, as economic heresy.

Thus, the ILM perceived Satiacum to be the victim of a criminal conspiracy by the U.S. Government who was going to eliminate him, one way or the other, once it realized what the next radical stage was in his master economic plan for the cause of Native Sovereignty.

Satiacum's next stage was a proposal that hereditary leaders all over Turtle Island take advantage of their unique 'Hong-Kong' tax and duty-free status on reservations and reserves.

His plan called for the immediate establishment of such economic entities as: international oil cartels; tariff-free marine ports; mini-'Liechtenstein'-incorporated industrial centre's, and; a host of other duty-free economic enclaves.

His bold strategies most certainly would have totally revolutionized Indian reserves and reservations, turning them into powerful economic and political power brokers in their own right.

But, as the world since has learned, through the ugly realities of the illegal invasions of Iraq, Afghanistan and attempted coup in Venezuela, the United States, as the world's self-appointed super-cop and front for the Western world's oil and drug cartels, will never ever tolerate any 'upstart' Third or Fourth World power messing with its critical monopolies.

Any world leader who dares to try, will find him or herself, overnight, turned into an odious, vile Hitlerian figure.

Satiacum became one so demonized, early on in the emergence of the new American Empire-building process, who had to be silenced before he became too powerful and well-known to be easily controlled.

Well aware of Satiacum's shortcomings, the ILM choose to look beyond Satiacum the man to what 'Satiacum the chief-maker' symbolized for native peoples ultimate liberation from the White Man's oppressive systems. Mary Williams said:

> Our efforts on Satiacum's behalf aren't necessarily for him, but for the principles of sovereignty that he represents. The day we met him and told him of our work for The Movement, the first thing he asked us was, 'Okay! Sounds good to me. But what's the economic basis of your movement?

– NATIVE SOVEREIGNTY PUT TO THE ACID TEST –

First Nation people decided it now was time to exercise their right of sovereign jurisdiction over the laws that govern immigration and political asylum within Indian Country.

Chief Leonard George, son of the late Chief Dan George, did his part by adopting Satiacum into his Burrard band of the Squamish Nation. The Nuxalt Nation next followed suite.

In 1984, Chief Nuximlyc, one of their hereditary leaders, bestowed the name *Uniquak* upon Satiacum, thereby giving him the same rights and privileges as those enjoyed by every Nuxalt person.

However, by this time, Uniquak had languished in a B.C. prison cell for two years, pending a hearing before a Canadian immigration board of revue, because the government chose, yet again, to flagrantly deny the inherent right of native sovereignty.

It wasn't until three years later that Uniquak's extradition case finally was heard by the Supreme Court of Canada. In the end, though Uniquak won his battle to remain in Canada, he ultimately lost the war because of the intense pressure that the U.S. continued to put on the Canadian Government to over throw its Supreme Court ruling by alleging that the decision was "factually and legally flawed."

Uniquak was again arrested, speedily tried, found guilty of yet another trumped-up sexual molestation charge, and was scheduled to be deported back to the U.S. when he fled into Lil'Wat Nation territory, hoping that the Williams Clan could help him obtain political asylum.

Though the subject of an intense R.C.M.P. and FBI manhunt, Uniquak, with the Williams help, successfully hid out for over three years until he was captured.

He died shortly before he was deported of what some, at the time, said was a, "broken heart caused by a life that had become a broken dream."

Uniquak – a 'chief among chief's' or no chief at all – once said to have been worth 80 million dollars in his role as economic counsel for the Puyallup Nation – ended up becoming, like Sitting Bull a century before, yet another native visionary who fled north to Canada to escape the American White Man's wrath.

Yet the dishonest way his native refugee status was eventually compromised, and the woefully inadequate medical care he received at the time of his capture, immediately prior to his death, succinctly bore out the one point that Uniquak often sought to make during his lifetime.

That point, as Uniquak said with his last dying breath, was that, "There's no justice ever for Indian people anywhere. When our people are brought into the White Man's jails, or if we go into one of their hospitals or wherever, we are always treated differently than others."

Those First Nations who sought to help Uniquak, gathered after his death to make a joint declaration. "What we have done for Unquak", they said, "has now been recorded for posterity and those who would take the time to question Canada's honor on the matter." Chief Nuximlyc added:

> He suffered in a Canadian jail because Canada called him an illegal immigrant. But the border that divides our land belongs to the White Man, and the laws that condemned our brother are White Man's laws not ours.

– A GENUINE TURTLE ISLAND CLAN MOTHER –

John Williams strength and determination with the Indian Liberation Movement is matched only by that of his wife, Mary, as a founding member of *Concerned Aboriginal Women* (CAW).

Mary and CAW were not only active on behalf of Uniquak, but for years miltantly spoke out in favor of better housing for native peoples throughout the province of British Columbia; a basic need that has been denied them since the day the White Man seized control of their lives.

Mary's efforts to call the world's attention to this shameful historical reality eventually led to her arrest, with over a hundred other Indian women and children, for the landmark sit-in they staged, in 1982, at the Department of Indian Affairs (DIA) headquarters in Vancouver, that became known as *The Black Tower Occupation*.

The position she took after The Black Tower Occupation was that she, like so many First Nation peoples in B.C., were sick and tired of the constant embarassment of always having to beg the government for monies for everything.

"The band council system of government on our reserves", she says, "is a living contradiction. It tries to have its feet between two cultures but ends up being nothing more than a puppet of the DIA's bureaucratic mess that we Indian people find ourselves hopelessly caught up in, no matter which way we turn. The band council gives us little more help than the DIA, and is just as out of touch with our sovereign needs as anyone."

The Black Tower's Occupation, The Constitutional Express, the endless legal maneuvers on behalf of Uniquak, their many road blockade disputes over sovereignty and land use issues, forced CAW, the ILM and the Williams Clan to address several basic, critical questions that affect traditional First Nation peoples all over Turtle Island.

"The questions we asked ourselves", said Mary, "was, 'What do we do now? Where do we go from here? We need a new form of indigenous politics! But what should it be? And where do we start?'"

For twenty years, Mary and her clan faithfully went to one DIA, Lil'Wat Band Council or Union of B.C. Indian Chief's meeting after another. But as Mary puts it, "After meetings on top of meetings on top of meetings, the very same things that were said at those early meetings are still being said 20 years later with little or no real changes ever taking place in our lives on the reserves."

The ILM & CAW, instinctively, knew the only answer was to create a new-old form of traditional Indian government to supplant the decadent, inefficient, unresponsive band council system.

Mary and John Williams envisioned a new kind of government in which counselors would be chosen to represent each clan. These clan representatives would join together with the nation's clan mothers to form a way of governing based upon the consensual agreement–proportional representation model of their ancestors.

"To this day", Mary says, "we are still trying to liberate ourselves from the White Man's band council system. We don't exactly have a formula for where we're goin', or how to get there yet, but we have a goal, and have made our pledge to reach this goal."

John, as his clan's *Head Man*, strikes at the heart of the real problem within First Nation peoples lives, when he says, "The band council system is continually looking for government handouts. The band council leaders and heads of different native organizations allow themselves to become side-tracked away from the sovereignty question because of their constant concern for 'programmes' and 'programme funds'. *Programme talk* has become an addictive fix that keeps native peoples forever dependent upon those bureaucratic systems which seek to keep us away from becoming a free people once again."

Mary, speaking about her own evolutionary process in consciousness, and how it personally liberated her, rephrases it this way:

I also went through the residential boarding school system like John, and it wasn't until 15 years later that I returned back home. Yet the strength of the old ways helped me to retain my native language and some of what I learned, before I was forced to go away, from the old people who taught me the ancient values and traditions of my people. My mom always wanted me just to have a nice house and a steady job, like my brothers and sisters, and remain a Catholic instead of following the ancient religion of my people. I really tried to do so for a number of years, but the feeling I was continually left with was that it was goin' nowhere. Since we have begun to pick up some of the old ways again, we have less money but we are rich in other ways. Today, I would not say we are poor. It's just that we don't have much money. I recognize that one has to have some money to exist, but we see its use now as a necessity in an altogether different way than we did before. We see it not as an end in itself, or even as the main focus. It is only incidental to our goal which is the survival and continuation of our ancient ways as a legacy, because becoming a leader is not really where it is at either. Both John and I could become leaders overnight and have all the monetary benefits and importance that goes with it. We have done it in the past so we know we could do it again. I've taken the expensive band council trips to Ottawa and been wined and dined at the expense of 'programme funds'. I remember one dinner where four of us were served the best wines and foods which came to over $135.00. I thought to myself at the time, 'I could feed my whole family on that for two weeks!' It all seemed so hollow and empty to me. The present bureaucratic native leadership system is also a hollow illusion.

– SOVEREIGNTY IN ACTION –

The Williams sovereign lifestyle isn't like that of many of today's high-profile First Nation leaders; who spend more time rubbing elbows with corporate muck-a-mucks and silky-tongued lobbyists – or scheming with venture capitalists to promote yet another glitzy gambling casino or tourist resort – than with their own people. The Williams instead draw their strength from simply staying put at home and carrying out the same sacred responsibilities as their ancestors before them.

The "proof is always in the pudding", as the old saying goes. And the pudding of the Williams Clan is indeed a rich one by the way they manage to generate enough income and resources to maintain their way of life without any government help.

Yet as is so typical with the feuds and vendettas that rage throughout Indian Country, when a clan like the Williams is successful at anything there always is some clan or clans who will make it their business to tear them down. Deep within the core of this resentment, that fuels these age-old feuds, lies the same old issues of power, envy and control that have plagued every race and culture since time began.

Many prominent First Nation political leaders in B.C., and elsewhere in North America, gladly accept their roles as puppets of the Canadian and U.S. governments because they know their own tenuous positions of power and control will be eliminated if the kinds of traditional political, economic, cultural, spiritual ways that the Williams Clan represents are ever reinstated.

Acting out of self-interest, they refuse to acknowledge organizations like the ILM and CAW, denigrating them as, "Fly-by-nights". Some barely give them passing notice. Others ignore them altogether. But a small handful have begun to see the handwriting on the wall. They realize that such grass-roots people hold the native vision for the future, whose time will surely come to pass some day.

Meanwhile, the Williams, like voices in the wilderness, continue to take their first faltering steps towards sovereignty, on a small scale, by creating and maintaining their own independent economic bases.

Besides all the wild food stuffs and natural products they gather and sell commercially – the boxwood for the florists; the 'matsutake' pine mushrooms for the gourmet restaurants; indigenous fruits, vegetables, berries, herbs, honey and pollen for the health food stores; or fresh willow saplings for the twig furniture industry – they continue to initiate other collective business ventures as well.

One big, as yet unrealized, dream of their's is to one day even be able to divert profits from their ventures to fund an official ILM office in Vancouver, with a Telex system linked to organizations like Amnesty International, the indigenous NGO's in the United Nations in Geneva as well as other international native communication networks.

But as John Williams is quick to admit:

Our master plan isn't dependent upon any of our economic enterprises. Because we know that if we're ever going to really be sovereign again, we can't be dependent upon any economic market we don't have control over. It doesn't worry us if the pine mushrooms, boxwood or twig furniture markets dry up tomorrow, 'cause we can always rely on our fishing, hunting, gathering and farming. But we'll do these things as long as there's money to be made. We'll just keep on adapting to new things when we need to. That's the way our ancestors done it for thousands of years, and that's the way we need to do it again to honor our pledge to The Movement.

Yet, over the years, the bought-and-sold Canadian media and legal system of B.C., like their counterparts among the province's puppet native band councils, have refused to validate or promote the significance of The Movement's work and the simplicity of its pledge that states:

Since The Creator put us here to respect and protect our Mother Earth, I PLEDGE:

* ***MY HONOR*** *to that responsibility*

* ***MY LOYALTY*** *to the efforts of the ILM*

*****MY DISCIPLINE*** *to reflect the integrity of First Nation Sovereignty*

* ***MY ENERGIES*** *to publicize the history of colonialism from which our Indian Nations struggle to free themselves*

In July 1990, the invasion of the sovereign Mohawk Nation at Oka, Quebec, ignited the ILM's sense of solidarity with their eastern brothers and sisters. Like what happened to the Mohawk people of Oka, the insensitive White Man also built a golf course and airport over the Lil'Wat people's sacred ancestral burial grounds. Logging companies, as well – operating under illegal licenses, issued by a B.C. provincial government that had no real legal jurisdiction over their lands – had long since been sending upwards of 124 logging trucks to daily stream through their unceded traditional territory. Not to mention the loss of their sacred burial ground and pictographic sites of Boulder Valley or *Mkwal'ts*, as it's called, where their *Scwenaxem* (medicine people) have trained since time immemorial; fasting and living in isolation for up to seven years, learning to know their spirits, control their spirits, even touch their spirits before returning there, at the end of their life, to be buried in that place. This spiritual site so sacred that most Lil'Wat's are forbidden to even go into the area so as not to disturb the spirits who reside there; and yet which also was blown up by the logging companies for the roadways they needed so they could steal ever more of the Lil'Wat Nation's timbered resources.

– THE LIL'WAT PEOPLES MOVEMENT EMERGES –

The devastation of their lands from insensitive clear-cut logging methods; the irresponsible use of pesticides and herbicides aimed at quick-fix reforestation practices that created cancerous growths in the wild plant and animal life the traditional Lil'Wat depended upon for their survival; the contamination of their sacred river's salmon spawning grounds by a local PCP storage station; were the final straws that broke the Lil'Wat's back.

Many of those who had ignored or resented the example set by the ILM, began to wake up to the realities of their lives. The Williams Clan quickly became the moral nucleus around which the revived traditional LIl'Wat spirit took its stand.

Now it wasn't just an 'Indian Liberation', but the *Lil'Wat Peoples Movement.*

This parallel grass-roots movement gathered its forces until, in the summer of '90, 63 native men, women and children were arrested for blockading a key 'Duffy-Lillooet Road' that runs through their territory.

The William knew they had little time left. Their earlier false arrests, in 1975, by the Government of Canada for a similar road blockade, at the same place and for the same reasons, taught the Lil'Wat many things about the White Man's legal systems and its often bizarre, twisted sense of justice.

They knew that each new legal battle they took on to call the world's attention to the abuse of their national sovereignty, no matter what its ultmate success or failure within the Canadian Courts, only served to further steel their resolve and raise the ante for the next legal go-around.

They also were well aware of how Mother Earth, herself, would also continue to up the ante of her struggle the less she, too, was able to sustain the wholesale abuse she was taking. A truly dangerous situation that, if not peacefully resolved, one day would disintegrate into a desperate, panicked, chaotic, violent struggle for basic survival.

By 1990, the criminal charges brought against the Williams Clan in the Law Courts of Vancouver, for their role in what was a peaceful road blockade, set a precedent for all of Canadian jurisprudence.

As their federal lawyer, Dr. Bruce Clark, put it:

For the first time in the history of the British Empire, and Canadian legal system, the issue of Indian spirituality and sovereignty has been put squarely before the courts. Standing in the way of materialistic progress and tyranny, the Lil'Wat court case turns upon the very concept of the supremacy of God and the role of Canadian Constitutional Law.

Yet like so many other well-intended outsiders also have painfully learned the hard way, Bruce Clark soon found that his lofty attempts to unravel the legal complexities of Indian life quickly earned him more ridicule than accolades from quarters within both the native and non-native world.

Indian politics always the hot-bed of discontent that they are, the shifting allegiances and volatile political positions of the Lil'Wat Peoples Movement, that verily seemed to change with every nuance in the human weather – with sisters often pitted against sisters, brothers against brothers, not to mention husbands, wives, families and clans – challenged Clark at ever turn.

Even the stance taken by the Williams Clan led to their own internal divisions over the legal arguments that Dr. Clark chose to put forth.

Clark found himself bombarded by accusations that, "You didn't really listen well to the directions our elders gave you about their unequivocal position on Native Sovereignty!" While others declared, "We already are sovereign and so don't have to ever try to prove it within the White Man's courts or any other foreign country's courts!"

As one Lil'Wat brother put it, "All Clark should do is find a way to fit into Canada's legal system a basic rule of law that supports the straight-forward fact that our sovereignty never has been terminated. What's been goin' on with white peoples independence movements in places like Quebec, Russia, Ireland or wherever, proves our liberation movement is part of the natural way of things. I'd say our chiefs way back in 1911, who made their Declaration of Sovereignty known, were real prophets!"

Whatever will be the final historical outcome of such legal subtleties, in places like Lil'Wat Country, still remains an unknown. A time-honored saying that seems to hold true anywhere one goes in Indian Country is, "Stay tuned for the latest up-to-the-minute breaks in this real-life harrowing hell of an _As The World Turns_ drama."

– ONE OUTSIDER'S BAPTISM IN THE FIRES OF RESERVE LIFE –

At every turn in his legal efforts on behalf of the Lil'Wat Peoples Movement and Robert Satiacum, Bruce Clark was forced to grapple with this most quintessential lesson about modern Indian life under the shadow of Western culture.

This lesson deeply affected Clark, personally and professionally, the further he probed into the fundamental imperialism of the English-Canadian jurisprudence system as it applies to those (women, natives, minorities) who aren't already part of the closed, corrupt, Machiavellian 'old boys club' notion of truth, justice, morality and ethics.

By the summer of '91, Clark – a distinguished Ontario lawyer – already had liquidated a lucrative law practice, sold his home and moved his family to B.C. to be nearer to the Lil'Wat. As Clark set off on a veritable one-man crusade to argue their nation's sovereign position before the Supreme Court of Canada, he soon discovered that he'd begun to lose many one-time allies within both the legal world and among those he sought to represent.

Touted by many to be, perhaps, the most knowledgable, acerbic, legal mind regarding the Indian land claim issue in Canada, yet vilified by others as a complete nut case, Clark found himself effectively snubbed and isolated by his legal peers within British Columbia as they closed ranks against him.

A provincial court judge finally told Clark he could not continue to represent the Lil'Wat in B.C., because its Law Society was no longer will-ing to give him permission to practice.

At one point, while he defiantly threatened in return to lay a charge of treason against the preciding judge in question, and indeed against Canada's Prime Minister Brian Mulroney himself, Clark was un-ceremoniously dragged from a courtroom by two burly deputy sheriffs and placed under arrest.

As Clark was being bodily dragged away, screaming in protest, a stunned courtroom gallery heard him vow, "The Law Society of British Columbia will never get away with this, even if I have to go all the way to Geneva and the World Court!"

Later, once all the heated emotions had calmed down, from the solitude of a cell, he simply declared, "At the very least, the Law Society and Court of British Columbia should contritely apologize to the Lil'Wat people and to me for what they have done."

Be he a genius, madman or a little bit of both, Dr. Clark learned, first-hand, what one old Salish elder in the courtroom meant when he leaned over and whispered to me, "Yah know somethin', Jerry. When white folks start tah wake up an' deal with the real genocide stuff they're doin' tah us Indians, they're gonna find out, real quick, that our friends an' enemies are the same as their's."

To find myself standing in that courtroom, in solidarity with those 63 criminally-charged Lil'Wat men, women and teenage warriors – shackled like dangerous menaces to society, because they meekly yet resolutely dared to assert the supremacy of Indian Law, and so stand in the way of the White Man's imperious exercise of abusive power – was an honor beyond words.

To have been one who stood up with the Lil'Wat when the presiding judge first entered the court room – and boomingly chanted with them their Bear, Eagle and Deer power songs, set to the beat of seven Lil'Wat drums, against a back drop of glaring baliffs and Crown prosecutors angrily look-ing on as the judge impotently hammered for silence with his gavil – was to feel and know a solidarity with the human spirit that transcends all races, colors, creeds, time and space.

– TEACHINGS OF THE DIFFERENT FLAGS WE FLY –

The White Man's interpretation of the symbols on the provincial flag of British Columbia are as different as day is to night when compared with those given by the Lil'Wat and other First Nation peoples.

Over the years, each succeeding White Man's government of B.C. officially has maintained its own survival story–meaning of the symbols on its provincial flag.

Taken from its offical seal of 1896 – which originally showed a symbol of the Sun in front of seven blue and white wavering lines and the images of a Wapiti and Rocky Mountain Goat – the 1906 designers of the modern B.C. flag chose not to reflect its early connections with the wildlife of the region and so dispensed with their images, while imposing over the natural symbols of the North those of the Royal Crest and Union Jack of England.

The arrangement of the symbols on the flag meant to serve as a permanent reminder to all of the Western European's colonial sovereignty over whomever the indigenous peoples it has supplanted, as well as the multitudes of non-human nations and the Laws of Nature herself.

Instead, the image of the Sun, as a simile of the British Empire's glory encircling the world, is meant to call to the minds of all, except First Nation peoples, their origins prior to 1871. Hence, B.C.'s motto, as "The Empire's western-most frontier", *Slendor Sine Occasu* or "Brilliance Without Setting!" The White Man there, even officially, remains somewhat vague as to the definitive meaning behind the flags blue and white wavering lines.

First Nation peoples, from the time of first contact, have otherwise construed the symbol of the Sun to mean, "The supreme law of The Creator, which shines down equally upon all the people."

They otherwise suggest that the blue wavering lines mean, "The mutual respect among the people for one another's sovereignty is to be true and lasting for as long as the rivers flow clean and true." The white wavering lines meaning, "This understanding is to be true and lasting for as long as the snow's remain upon the mountain tops."

The traditional Lil'Wat flag, itself, graphically expresses from whence those like the Williams Clan draw their eternal inspiration. The red-rimmed sacred circle in the center of their flag, set against a solid blue background, meant to symbolize, "the eternalness of the sky realm and all the sacred waters that flow through our homelands." The red-rimmed circle further symbolizing, "The blood, passion and heart as the seat of all Red Nations everywhere." The four red arrows around the circle, one at each of the sacred directions, remind the Lil'Wat of, "Our primary responsibilities to all of Creation."

Inside the circle, the images, in the foreground, of a salmon-drying rack, a lone pine tree and the Lillooet River, with Mt. Ts'Zil presiding over them in the background, "Are there to remind us", say the Lil'Wat, "that their survival and ourselves are all one in the same."

– MANY MORE SURVIVAL SHARINGS YET TO COME –

Ever since this odyssey crossed paths with the Williams Clan, an inner sense of knowingness has suggested that native peoples and New Frontier Breeds have so much to give, to share, to learn from one another for our mutual survival.

Over the years, the odyssey has caused me to periodically touch bases with the Williams.

There was that one year when we traveled for several months, like nomads, living and sleeping together in our vans as we wandered to the four directions of the province – from Vancouver Island in the West to the Kootenay Mountains in the East, North to the high-Chilchotin plateaus and Nass River Basin, back South again to the coastal mountain ranges – searching for the ever-elusive wild pine mushroom.

In that brief yet action-packed time, there were so many intimate sharings that occurred as we: bushwhacked, for days on end, through dense, sunless, pristine forests; sat around a campfire at night and swapped wildly funny or hair-raisingly-mystical stories; lay packed like sardines in mummy bags and dreamt together each night; rising here and there for a quick smoke, to share a dream's strange tale, or note a funny aside over the aroma of someone's vile fart or uncovered secret revealed while talking in our sleep.

Though, through the years, we've lived but a few short hours drive from one another, our contact has remained sporadic at best. Yet there always is some brief new touching: a 'chance' meeting, while coming out of a crowded elevator in the Department of Indian Affairs; a 'bumping' into one another during a peace march of 100,000 people; an 'unexpected' passing in a car and hurried wave; an 'accidental' encounter at a pow-wow gathering; to serve as a reminder of a some kind of odd relationship or connections that exists somewhere, if not in this world than in another one for sure.

Each time another touching occurs and we're about to part company, a mighty chuckle erupts as I repeat my standard one-liner, "I'll have to come up to Ts'Zil and spend some time with you guys one of these days." The joke being, of course, that I never do.

This one-liner like the prophecy that that old sensitive Salish woman made on the day she first held my White Buffalo Medicine Stone in her hand and said, "dah ol' man who gave dis' stone t' yah means fer ya' t' one day come back an' fine somethin' else dhat waits fer ya' dere."

Though I often wonder when The Voice will give me some sign that another new cycle of the odyssey will lead Alta-Dena and me back to the Williams compound, to find out what exactly that 'somethin' else' is that yet has to pass between us, the sign still hasn't come.

Whenever such brief encounters similarly take place on the open road, with still many other First Nation peoples and New Frontier Breeds, I can hear, in my mind's ear, the repeating of that tongue-in-cheek one-liner between the Williams and me. Each time, I mightily chuckle again as one of the Williams kibitzs, in my mind's ear,, "Oh, sure! That'll be the day!"

– THE WISDOM OF THE OPEN ROAD BEARS ITS FRUITS –

Upon first learning something of the ancient symbols of the people, animals and lands of the Lil'Wat, my thoughts drifted back to my own Irish-Tyrolean ancestors sacred symbols and time-beyond-mind connections with Salmon, Bear and the Elements of their world. My spirit's mind eye peering once more into those Paleolithic caves in Countae Claire and Tyrol that still bear the ancient, pictographic claw marks and footprints of Bear and bones of Salmon in their middens.

"Lad! Do you still think it curious", bellowed The Voice at that moment, "that I should once have caused you to travel far and wide, before coming to the mystic lands of the Lil'Wat, to remember these same things of your distant past? Do you not know by now that there is nothing peculiar about all this? That it's simply the destiny I've given to those New Frontier Breeds like yourself to realize?"

As Alta-Dena sped back to Pacem en Terris and another long overdue reunion with Crystal Freesia, I wondered how many more places like Lilwatul would serve as the spawning rivers of a fate that forever flowed through some unfathomable, always homeward-bound part of me.

I, like Salmon, no matter how miles we might swim afar to explore what lies beyond, pulled back again, with the same fierce, resolute determination, to the sacred spawning place of our origins. All the while jumping and hurdling up and over whatever obstacle ever gets in the way of our life's primary task. Overcoming, as well, whatever other duties the great mysterious source of our being first gave us to complete before returning to continue the cycle through those young fingerlings who one day will follow in our stead.

The Voice directed me to meet up with the Indian Liberation Movement of Canada to learn of such things. Yet though the ILM one day may cease to be – like so many once vibrant, visionary First Nation causes that have long since come and gone and are all but forgotten – British Columbia itself had still so many other gifts to bear. Its Greater Vancouver bioregion one of the White Man's finest modern urban models that enjoys a well-earned, widespread reputation for being one of the leading anti-war, anti-nuclear, pro-union, pro-environment, pro-native, least-violent areas of the world, that some call "The Peace Centre of North America".

So, PILGRIM. We've covered a great deal of ground together, since last you were called upon to close these covers and retire again to some quiet, still place where you can be alone with your thoughts. Once there, ponder the timeless, quintessential lessons you've learned from the clans you belong to or identify with. What turns and bends in your life have they caused you to make? **Be Off With Ye! Go!**

WELCOME BACK! As a self-styled 'Ambassador of Turtle Island's New Frontier Thoughts', I knew it was time to head back South, across The Medicine Line.

I'd heard, on the moccasin telegraph, about a lot of different New Age White Shamans, intentional communities, medicine societies and cults, that were springing up all over California and elsewhere in the South, who were causing quite a ruckus amongst traditional First Nation peoples. Especially by the way they were rushing into native communities, like bulls in a china shop, desperately searching for whatever new rituals, ceremonies, chants, songs and medicine ways they could find to make their own.

I wanted to see for myself, first-hand, what all the commotion was about and see if these New Frontier pioneers were rebuilding their Medicine Wheels in respectful ways, that would enhance their relationships with First Nation peoples, or in disrespectful ways, that would only drive First Nation peoples to renew those old feelings of malice towards the White Man that so many were trying so hard to move beyond.

So with that, I once again went through my *Holy Rituals of The Road* checklist: topped Alta-Dena's crankcase with another quart of 20W-50 oil; smoked Crystal Freesia, Alta-Dena and myself with another braid of smoldering SweetGrass; placed my medicine bundle of sacred feathers and herbs on Alta-Dena's dash; and bid Crystal Freesia another one of my bittersweet adieu's.

CURCLE ISLAND

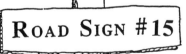

ROAD SIGN #15

WHAT HAVE YOU LEARNED ABOUT
WHO YOU ARE,
FROM TRAVELING UPON
THE GOOD RED, YELLOW, WHITE
OR BLACK ROAD OF LIFE?

In California there's all this groping around., people getting intoevery kind of ar-out thing: previous lives, evrything that goes with the New Age *Mojo*, but it's a spiritual hunger; we're all born with a hunger to know God.

(Singer/Actress Maria Muldaur)

– On The Road To Find Out –

Words & Music
By Cat Stevens

So on and on you go,
the seconds tick the time out,
there's so much left t'know,
and I'm on the road to find out.
Ohhhh! Ohhhh!

IN THE LAND OF THE GREAT WHITE FATHER: ENCOUNTERS WITH METIS & WHITE SHAMANS

"PILGRIM", probes The Great Voice Of The Turtle, *"Many of you, who call yourselves Canadians and Americans, have begun to take a strong interest in things that have to do with my Rainbow Serpent Spirit. Many of you also are eager to learn whatever you can about what you call Shamanism. But do you really know how hard you must work to reach the level of relationship, belonging, harmony, peace and unity with all that I am before you ever will be able to truly understand who my Rainbow Serpent Spirit is, or what my own kind of shamanism is about, even though my native children and I don't call it that? Can you even imagine what you first would have to begin doing every day – for the rest of your life – with yourself, your family, your community and all my life forms where you live? To start, you must ask yourself what level of relationship – of communications – it is that you want with me and all my two-legged, four-legged, winged, finned and rooted children! Then you must ask yourself what you are prepared to sacrifice to get it! "*

———⊃●⊂———

For years after the Earth Healing Gathering at Eyalmox, Alta-Dena and I kept saying hello or goodbye to Crystal Freesia in British Columbia as we set out upon yet another foray South. The two of us passing into *The Land of the Great White Father* before once more returning North again to *Grandmother's Lands*, as the old-timers once referred to the U.S. and Canada.

Each time, Alta-Dena and I followed the song of the open road as we went – like two wild, white geese – migrating one way or the other with each great, changing cycle in Mother Earth's body. Year after year, adding yet more branches and spokes to the odyssey's Family Tree and Medicine Wheel. Each new branch or spoke burgeoning with a multitude of Turtle Island tales and yarns.

– A WINTER COUNT TEACHING –

As the opening and closing of another epic cycle of the odyssey came and went, so, too, did another entry find its way into this Turtle Island journal.

The sum total of each new lot of experiences recorded in the journal by a single pictographic symbol tacked onto the end of a large, ever-evolving spiral. This spiral like what the old tribal historians among the Plains Indians, back in the days, once set down on their buffalo hide 'Winter Counts' to chronicle their peoples lives. The tribal 'Keeper-of-The-Talking Sticks' using each symbol as a mnemonic device to conjure up, and breath new life into, the old stories of their relationships with all of Creation.

At the center of my own Winter Count spiral lay an open, vulnerable heart, with a multi-coloured bouquet of Freesias resting across it. Heart and Freesia's wrapped in a swath of the sheerest gossamer silk.

The heart symbol, that lay at the core of the odyssey's account, followed by a rainbow bridge in the shape of a serpent, one half engulfed in a thunder and lightning storm with the other half bathed in radiant sunshine. The bridge connected either side by an eaglebone whistle on one side and a fetus on the other. The fetus – part white, red, yellow and black – slowly gestating inside Mother Earth's womb, surrounded by a birthsack in the shape of a lotus flower.

Spiraling outward from the rainbow serpent bridge, flows: a sacred circle, surounded by coloured dots, representing the Four Sacred Races of People; a heart and medicine pipe, encircled by a ring of fire; a white cloud in the shape of a buffalo bull head; a frolicking Grey Fox and Mission Blue Butterfly atop a mountain; a red lighthouse upon an island; a smiling Calico cat; a fairy ring of wild, pine mushrooms; a Red River Metis cart, parked beside a white milk truck; a Tolkien-like cottage with leaded glass windows and stone chimney with smoke lazily drifting skyward.

On and on, at each coil's turn, appear still other pictographs that recount the odyssey's key benchmarks. At each First Nation–New Age–New Frontier encampment, gathering or conference Alta-Dena and I traveled to, the answers received, the lessons learned, about Turtle Island's mysteries, one in the same.

The Voice declaring at each Spiral's turn of the Winter Count:

Lad! The answers you seek on the open road forever lie 'a head' and 'a heart' of you. Some must remain in one spot to do the difficult homework this road demands. Some, like you, as natural 'Ambassadors of the Great Turtle', must travel to many different places to speak to others of this good road. But no matter where your journey may lead, remember always that this sacred road really is only eighteen inches long yet, at the same time, is an interminably long one that will take you back and forth, between your head and your heart, for the rest of your life. The most direct route between them is the one that cuts straight through the unexplored territories of whatever secret, dishonest communications you may hold between yourself and the false mythology you've contrived about your life and the world around you. Cutting through these unexplored territories is the best way to renew an honest, healthy, holy relationship with your own body, mind and spirit. This is the real meaning behind the *All My Relations* consciousness I first exposed you to so many years ago. Without this foundation, you can never hope to do the kind of spiritual bridgework between the Red, Black, Yellow and White Roads that will truly make this world a better place in which to live.

"So on and on I go!", as Cat Stevens sings in *On The Road To Find Out*, "the seconds tick the time off! There's so much left to know, and I'm on the road to find out. Ohhhh! Ohhhh!"

Down the road, came one benchmark gathering after another that underscored the vast amount of false mythology that drives peoples lives and the rampant crisis in relationship that everywhere exists in the world between individuals and their own body, mind and spirit. This same crisis manifested, in turn, between couples, families, neighborhoods, cultures, races, nations and all their relations with Mother Earth herself. Nothing new! Same ol', Same ol' that hasn't changed in 5,000 years of human history.

In those days, everywhere Alta-Dena and I went, we heard First Nation peoples crying out about this crisis in relationship. Before heading South one year, we traveled to Port Alberni, British Columbia where we heard the World Council of Indigenous Peoples bare their hearts in:

– A SOLEMN DECLARATION –

WE, the Indigenous Peoples of the world, united in this corner of our Mother the Earth, in a great assembly of men and women of wisdom, so declare to all nations that:

WE glory in our proud past:
When the earth was our nurturing mother.
When the night sky formed our common roof.
When Sun and Moon were our parents.
When all were brothers and sisters.
When our great civilizations grew under the Sun.
When our chiefs and elders were great leaders.

When justice ruled the Law and its execution.
Then other people arrived:
Thirsting for blood, for gold, for land and all its wealth.
Carrying the cross and the sword, one in each hand.
Without knowing or waiting to learn the ways of our worlds.
They considered us to be lower than all the animals.
They stole our lands from us and took us from our lands.
They made slaves of the Sons & Daughters of the Sun.

However:
They have never been able to eliminate us.
Nor to erase our memories of what we are.
For we are the culture of the earth and sky.
We are the ancient descent and we are the millions.
Though our whole universe may be ravaged,
Our people will live on – For longer than even the kingdom of death.

Now:
We come fom the four corners of the earth.
We protest before the concert of nations, to say,
WE are the Indigenous Peoples.
We are a people with a consciousness of culture and race,
Who live on the edge of each country's borders,
Marginal to each country's citizenship.

And:
Rising up after centuries of oppression,
Evoking the greatness of our ancestors,
In memory of our Indigenous martyrs,
We still live in homage to the counsel of our wise elders.

We Thus Vow Here:
To Control again our own destiny!
To Recover our complete humanity!
To Renew our pride in being Indigenous people!

In those days, this Declaration was but one jewel among the many that sparkled in the Native Renaissance crown. Yet each one Alta-Dena and I discovered, was also somehow tarnished by the historical tensions that have existed between the Indian and non-Indian. Each jewel flawed by too much negative cultural baggage on all sides that continues to keep our relationships with one another too distant.

Still to come were the many other jewels in the crown of First Nation and New Frontier peoples separate spiritual renaissance movements. Each jewel, though glistening, yet tarnished in its own way.

Several years after the World Council Gathering in British Columbia, Alta-Dena and I were pulled back across The Medicine Line to Spokane and an intentional community run by Sun Bear, a Chippewa Indian, and his New Age 'Bear Tribe' followers. After that there was another return to the San Francisco Bay Area with other veterans for the 10th Anniversary of the Occupation of Alcatraz. Alta-Dena and I next drawn to a Southern California *Medicine Drum* Gathering of New Age 'NAMA' (North American Metis Association) people, held at a seaside encampment near San Luis Obispo, to protest the operation of the Diablo Canyon nuclear plant. Only to be drawn back North again to Washington State and a Puyallup Indian-hosted *Medicine Talk for Mother Earth & All Earth Peoples* encampment. Followed, in turn, by Alta-Dena rocketing still farther North, into Grandmother's Lands, to Batoche, Saskatchewan and the Metis peoples Centenary Celebration of the *Northwest Resistance Movement.* Alta-Dena and I later migrating back to the Bay Area and a New Age *'Save The Mountain'* gathering on San Bruno Mountain by the local defenders of The Mountain's endangered species and their habitats.

At every gathering, there always was some type of confrontation, like the ugly incident with the Chumash elder, that ensued between Indians and non-Indians, or full-bloods and mixed-bloods, to reflect the wide divide in our relationships that constantly bedevils us all.

By the time each gathering concluded, we were reminded, too, how much not only men in general, but also many women, need to learn what most women already know, at a gut level, about what the hard work of relationship really means, on an intimate level, with all things.

– A WATERSHED ULTIMATUM CREATES A CRISIS –

Crystal Freesia tried time and time again to make me more aware of what all I needed to do about the relationships in my own life – with my own body, spirit and emotions – in order to realize, on a day-to-day gut level, what as a woman she naturally knew had to be done.

By this time, she'd grown increasingly tired of my North–South 'wild-goose chases' in Alta-Dena, searching everywhere for the intimate relationships that all the while were right under my nose, waiting for my simple acknowledgement.

When Crystal Freesia heard I was planning to go off to Sun Bear's compound near Spokane, to spend some time with his Bear Tribe, it became a watershed moment of crisis between us.

"This time, Love," she warned, "if you decide to rush off to Sun Bear, it will be the last straw for me. I'm tired of you always running off, hoping to join this or that tribe or intentional community when you and I both know I can't follow you there because it isn't my path in life. So if you feel this is the path you must follow, don't expect me to be here when you return."

I didn't know what exactly to say, because it had all been said many times before, and I could see how it looked from her side. But I also could see that I was dealing with some very deep, complex emotional-cultural-karmic stuff in my heritage that went back to many other lives and beyond, that I knew, as I've always known, that I have no other choice but to finish with, this time around. To not do so would be to set back, perhaps for untold more lifetimes, what needs to be completed during the span of this particular lifetime.

"Can't you see, Love", I declared, "that I must follow The Voice's directives, when they come, or allow some as yet unfathomable part within me to shrivel and die. You're absolutely, without a doubt, my primary relationship but, as irrational as it may seem, I must go, no matter what. Please try to understand what all I'm saying and be here when I return."

Crystal Freesia wasn't one who gladly suffered rude, ignorant people. By this time, she already had her fill of the ill-mannered, uncivil cultural slights and racist acts she became the brunt of through her contacts with different Aboriginal peoples in Australia as well as with First Nation people in Canada.

She felt tribal peoples, in general, carry around far too much negative cultural baggage towards white people, as a whole. She didn't feel any personal guilt for what she herself wasn't responsible for and so wasn't prepared to wear it like a hair shirt. Her life was more about beauty, gentility, joy and elegance, little of which she saw in many tribal peoples lives and so avoided them like the plague.

So off I went in Alta-Dena again, this time hoping Crystal Freesia and I had a long way yet to travel together.

– ON THE ROAD AGAIN –

The brief sojourn at Sun Bear's compound on the outskirts of Spokane proved most revealing because it only took a short time living in his tribe's communal 'longhouse' to realize how far out of balance so many spiritually-starving New Age people are within themselves.

I'd previously traveled to Sun Bear's place with Wally Rupert, a big strapping Cree Indian from the Canadian prairies, who was a Bear Clan brother I worked with at Alma House, that group home for native and non-native teenagers in Vancouver.

Wally and I heard some good and bad things about Sun Bear and read his book, *Walk In Balance*. As two Bear Clan brothers and outsiders among our people, who found ourselves on opposite sides of the cultural no man's lands, searching for some new tribal turf we could call our own, we wanted to check the Bear Tribe out to see if there was anything they had to offer us that we could adapt to our own displaced tribal lives.

Wally and I traveled in Alta-Dena to Sun Bear's compound, lived and worked with the Bear Tribe for a time, helping them redo the roof of their longhouse, tend to their livestock and participate in the daily rituals conducted by their tribe.

Once we finished our quick peek at the Bear Tribe and returned to Vancouver, I immediately started making plans to take a longer leave from Alma House so I could return to take up Sun Bear's invitation to travel with him up and down the West Coast's New Age spiritual circuit, while, at the same time, take an even closer look at the Bear Tribe.

When George Simmers and the Alma House staff heard me say, "Hey, you guys! I think The Voice is once more directing me to go off for a time to do some more Sacred Circle work!", they just rolled their eyes and sighed, "Oh, God! Here we go again! Just go, Jerry! Do what you have to do and we'll cover for you."

– AN INTRODUCTION TO NEW AGE SPIRITUAL CULTS –

My travels with Sun Bear led to many gatherings up and down the West Coast. At each one, there occurred ugly encounters with some militant A.I.M. warrior or elder who knew Sun Bear personally or by reputation.

It was during a guest appearance at an 'Earth Day' gathering on the U.C. Davis campus near Sacramento – one of the earliest celebratory sites of that, by now, world-wide festival – that I heard more than a few angry First Nation peoples publically deride him. To them, he was 'Fun Bear', because he and his Bear Tribe avoided doing the more contentious militant political activism that First Nation peoples everywhere then were doing as an integral part of their spiritual way of life.

A.I.M. members present derided Sun Bear and his followers for their propensity to instead indulge in New Age, airy-fairy, *Mojo* talk of 'shamanic drum circles', 'shaman apprenticeship programs', 'medicine wheels and shields', 'animal totems' and 'vision-quests'.

Others derisively called Sun Bear, 'Chief Iron Crotch', because of his notorious promiscuity with the young female-sycophant-spiritual groupies who were drawn to him.

This disparaging nickname fit with my own earlier observations of how he conducted himself with the 'harem' among his Bear Tribe. I began to wonder if Sun Bear might find it difficult to accept someone like myself among his Tribe because of whatever Alpha Male, two-stallions-in-the-same-corral, reservations he might harbor.

The more time I spent with Sun Bear and his Bear Tribe, the more it seemed Creator intentionally directed Alta-Dena and me to his compound just so I could counsel a few of the lost, confused New Agers who came to him, hoping to join his tribe.

Many of these spiritually-starving, emotionally-needy ones went so far as to sell all of their worldly possessions – homes, cars, boats, furniture – prior to coming to Sun Bear, with little fore knowledge about what to expect once they got there. To make matters worse, they then turned over whatever liquid assets they had to Sun Bear, with no strings attached. I couldn't believe such naiveness, and told them so!

– A LIFE & DEATH STRUGGLE WITH THE DARK FORCES –

A strange thing happened one day as I sought to counsel one particular newly-arrived family of four from Pennsylvania – who recklessly sold everything, left their jobs and burned whatever bridges they had to the outside world – before coming to join up with the Bear Tribe.

All of a sudden, as we spoke, it was as if someone just waved an evil magic wand over me. A fever at once rushed through my body like a tidal wave, my nose started running like an open faucet and I instantly became drained of all my energy.

By the end of the day, I'd grown so weak and feverish that I became bedridden and even had to resort to the use of a chamber pot, I kept handy in Alta-Dena, to relieve my bodily needs. But no one in the Bear Tribe paid any attention to my plight and actually seemed disinterested.

After several days, my condition deteriorated to the point where I knew I needed to get myself to the nearest hospital in Spokane. But I was too weak and delirious to drive Alta-Dena and knew no one else could ever manage her tricky transmission – with her long, wonky, floor-mounted gear shift and a clutch that had to be deftly double-pumped each time, to ease through her gears without grinding off all her teeth or causing her to pitch and lurch like a bucking bronco. I knew, too, that no one possessed the strength required to hold onto her steering wheel's suicide knob and turn her unwieldly two-ton body.

Never once, though, during my illness did Sun Bear, as the head man of his tribe, ever look in on me to see how I was faring. I thought this was very strange and began to sense something was seriously amiss.

But when I pleaded with a number of other Bear Tribe members, "Please! Please! Someone drive me to a hospital!", every one declined. They apparently were too fearful of Sun Bear's wrath of what he might do to them if they ignored their daily assigned duties and had the temerity to borrow one of the tribe's vehicles, without formal permission, to drive me the long distance into Spokane.

Many among the tribe avoided me as I continued to languish in my bed in one of the longhouse's lofts. After several more days passed, and I'd grown all the more weaker and desperate, I knew my only resort was to turn to the invisible realm of the spirit world for help.

Instinctively, I turned to the Great Spirit of the Bear – my totem in the animal world. I began to pray out-loud to my four-legged clan brother, "Oh, Mighty Brother Bear! You who, in the beginning, were the one who taught all us weak, pitiful humans how to doctor ourselves, come to my aid in this dark time. My very life may be at stake! Please come to me now!"

It wasn't long before I heard The Voice warn, "Lad! You're in a most dangerous place at this moment. Someone in the tribe is the source of your illness. They are doctoring against you. You must get yourself at once to a hospital without delay. Fear not, I will see to it."

The Voice had barely trailed off, when one of the tribe's young, newly-arrived males approached my bedside to see how I was doing. "I've been watching you slowly get worse", he said, "and don't think it's right that no one here will take you in to see a doctor. I've finally decided that I don't care what happens to me, or if I get thrown out of the tribe. So I'm going to go downstairs right now, get the keys to one of Sun Bear's vans and drive you in myself."

Helping me out of the loft and into the van, we quickly sped off as other tribal members gauwked at us like we were two escaping prisoners from Alcatraz, who'd just pulled off a 'Mission Impossible'.

Several hours later, I found myself in the emergency ward room of a Spokane hospital, dressed in a white gown, awaiting the arrival of the doctor-on-call.

As I waited behind the closed curtains of a cubicle, a young blond nurse, with a radiant smile, suddenly parted back the curtains. "How are we doing in here? What can I do for you today", she asked, with a broad smile. "The doctor will be in to see you shortly."

Weak and delirious, with my chin quivering from fear, I asked, "Do you know what might be wrong with me? I need some help right away. With that, the pretty nurse gave me another beatific smile, firmly yet gently took hold of my hand in her's, winked and said, "Don't worry. You're in good hands now!"

The instant we touched and I heard her lovely, consoling words, it was as if whatever evil spell had been cast upon me was at once broken. Instantaneously, as she continued to lovingly stroke my hand, all the pain, delirium and weakness vanished as if I'd been exorcised. The relief was so complete and immediate that I was shocked.

Looking up into that nurse's deep blue eyes, was like seeing the most beautiful angel imaginable. "Wow!", I exclaimed. "I don't know what you just did, or what just happened. But I feel totally fine now and light as a feather. Like that old pop R & B song goes, 'Yoooooouuuuuu've got that magic touch! Ohh! Ohh! Ohh!"

She laughed and quipped, "Anytime! Happy to be of service!", as she departed through a break in the curtains.

With that I sprang out of the bed, pulled off my hospital smock, dressed and rushed out to where the young Bear Tribe man sat anxiously waiting for some word of my condition. Dumbfounded, he just sat there for a long moment, gaping up at me and the amazing transformation that had magically taken place. "What in the heck went on in there, anyway?", he queried.

"Hey! I'm absolutely starved", I said. "The treat's on me! Let's go get ourselves a big plate of spaghetti, some garlic bread and a large bottle of wine to celebrate and I'll tell you all about it."

At first, the young man, still feeling intimidated by what might happen to him if he stayed away any longer from his Bear Tribe duties, or dared to indulge himself with some wine, which was one of the express taboo's of Bear Tribe members, declined the offer.

"No!", he said, "I better get back. We're not supposed to drink any alcohol or do any drugs in the tribe."

But when I counseled, "Hey, are you your own man or just some tribal zombie?", he thought about it for a moment and finally snapped, "Yeah! You're right! What the hell. Let's celebrate and drink a whole bottle of wine or maybe even two or three if we feel like it!"

By the time we returned to the tribe's compound it was late and everyone was asleep.

Curiously, the next morning I learned that just as quickly as I had been healed, or exorcised, of whatever ailed me, one of the tribe's females, who was their master herbalist, steeped in the esoteric arts of Native medicine, had suddenly been stricken down by some unexplainable illness.

– A POSITIVE HEALING AFFIRMATION WORKED –

During the whole time of my illness, an affirmation was repeatedly made to my Bear Clan brother in the spirit world. "Oh, Bear!", began the affirmation, "If there is someone out there who is conjuring against me, help me to defend myself."

As part of this positive imagery, I saw Bear standing up in front of me, like a mighty shield, deflecting whatever negative energy was being directed at me back upon whomever was behind the sorcery. "Bear!", continued the affirmation, "Send back to that evil source twice what they are sending to me."

I didn't ever wait around the Bear Tribe compound, though, to find out what eventually happened to that female. The next morning, while everyone was still fast asleep, I hopped into Alta-Dena, lit a braid of Sweet Grass, smudged myself in the holy smoke, symbolically blessed the Bear Tribe encampment and all the good spirits there who had assisted me, placed my medicine bundle back atop Alta-Dena's dash and quietly slipped away.

"So much for following the spiritual guru trip and doing the intentional community thing!", I laughed outloud, as Alta–Dena bumpt and jolted along a dirt track.

When Alta-Dena finally reached the paved open road, my thoughts went out to Crystal Freesia, who I hoped still awaited our return across The Medicine Line in Canada.

The closer we got to our cottage in Horseshoe Bay, the more intensely grew some healthy self-talk. "Twin Rainbow", I said, "This open road odyssey you've chosen is a crazy one for damn sure. Especially when someone as beautiful and loving as Crystal Freesia who, so many times before, has lain there, alone in her bed, while you galavant off to realize some crazy phantasy when the reality of her love for you is the most beautiful thing you will ever find anywhere, at any time, in your life."

With that The Voice answered back, "Yes, indeed, Lad! It does, at times, seem crazy and absurd. But you knew the vision you received atop Holy Hill so many years ago, and the path it set you upon, is a tough one. Perhaps the toughest of all. You know there are sacrifices to be made no matter what path one chooses in life. But The Great Spirit has given you the most beautiful woman in the world to help guide you and keep you on this path, even if it is as hard for her as it is for you. She is your true medicine teacher. Love her, cherish her, nurture her and return to her often for her guidance and help in all this. She will always be there for you."

After spending some time, upon my return, with Crystal Freesia – learning of her own medicine work journey as a counselor and therapist committed to healing so many other lost, confused souls along the way – the open road South again beckoned Alta-Dena and me forth to return to Alcatraz Island.

– RETURNING TO THE ROCK –

"*Lolum! Waimatha! I see you!*", I cried out to those twin-spired Squamish sisters, as Alta-Dena and I passed over the Lion's Gate Bridge. "*Bless my journey South!*", I added, as one last spiritual refrain. "*Make it a prosperous one in, in all ways!*"

"*Waka Nuni! Tucki Wuckie!*", I chanted as Alta-Dena once more came into view of Mount Shasta and Shastina. "Heya, hey! Heya hey, ahey! hey, hey, hey!", I chanted as we continued our travels past them. "Thank you Grandfather Shasta! Thank you Grandmother Shastina! It's good to be in Cal-i-for-ni-a again. Guide my journey to find out something good for my people. So many hungry soul's lie stranded upon the open road now. I look towards you Grandfather, Grandmother for your direction. Renew within me the hardening strength and purity of your snowy mantles to assist me as I go this way – Humbly! Happily! Holy!"

It wasn't long after fording back across the Sacramento River, spiritually saluting as we went those sacred Marysville Buttes, that I was shouting once again, "*Pechas Azul! Pechas Azzuuulll! I see you!*" It was

The Twin Sisters

always so exciting each time Alta-Dena and I caught our first glimpse of the twin-breasted silhouette of those ancient sentinels, who always have watched over and blessed our comings and goings from the Bay Area.

"Pechas Azul! Lolum and Waimatha bring you greetings from Squamish Territory! Grandfather Shasta and Grandmother Shastina extend to you their blessings, as well! Protect my journey in the South, Help me to know when it will be time to head back North again!"

It was good to once more gather on the Rock with Indians of All Tribes to celebrate the 10th anniversary of our historic spiritual undertaking to reclaim Turtle Island for Mother Earth & All Earth Peoples.

It was during an *Elder's Medicine Way Health & Healing Gathering,* that simultaneously took place in Golden Gate Park, that we Veterans of The Occupation heard many spiritual leaders, like Archie Fire Lame Deer, call to all our minds the path we'd set out upon, a decade before, and its significance for the times in which we lived.

Years before, during my sojourn at Crow Creek, I often sat beside Archie's father, John Fire Lame Deer, and heard him speak of the mystical nature of all things. "Never forget, Jerry VISTA", he would say:

> that the meat you eat comes from your four-legged brothers who give themselves so you can live. Remember that the steam from the stew pot you cook with is living breath. It was water, now it goes up to the sky and becomes a cloud again. We Sioux spend a lot of time thinking about everyday things which, in our minds, are mixed up with the spiritual. We see in the world around us many symbols that teach us the meaning of life. To the White Man, symbols are just words. But to us they are part of nature, part of ourselves, part of even little insects like ants. We try to understand them, not with our head but with our hearts.

On the eve of our 10th reunion, we shared where that long journey of some eighteen mere inches, between our head and our hearts, had taken each of us since we left The Rock and scattered to the Four Directions. John Fire's son, Archie, dubbed our symbolic regrouping as, "A drinking together between ourselves as Black-Tailed Deer!" Lame Deer took the opportunity to inform us of what he meant by this, as he shared a small portion of the Lakota Prophecy of where his people came from and where they are going. Archie said:

The 1st World my people lived in was *The World of Herbs.*
The 2nd World my people lived in was *The World of the Buffalo.*
The 3rd World my people lived in was *The World of the White Man.*
The 4th World my people now are entering is *The World of the Black-Tailed Deer.*

This 4th World deals with the question of survival, based upon the old ways.
For the Black-Tailed Deer is a symbol of our times and the part that native
peoples will play in the future. The Black-Tailed Deer is a rare species of deer,
with a line running across its face. It lives on the mountain tops and each
morning, before the Morning Star comes, the Black-Tailed Deer goes down to
the stream and drinks the water and in so drinking, purifies it. It is a symbol of
a journey to pick up the old ways by returning to the place where we dropped
them, to purify ourselves and all things for the survival of our people and a
natural way of life.

With Archie's words, I sensed how absurd and misplaced was all the
New Age talk about shamanism that I heard bantered around by those like
Sun Bear and his Bear Tribe. I knew it was the simplicity of the old ways,
not all the New Age hyperbole, that would direct the medicine way healing
work – whether political, cultural, spiritual, economic or emotional – that
first had to be done with one's own people, on whatever land they hold to be
sacred. The journey that of a humble Black-Tailed Deer rather than some
lime-lighting New Age Shaman–showman.

Yet as Archie spoke of such lofty symbolic world's, how the real
world is between the relationships of Indians and non-Indians, full-bloods
and mixed-bloods, blatantly made itself known.

Once again, like the ugly encounter with the Chumash elder, a
similar incident arose at the Medicine Way's Gathering in Golden Gate
Park's 'Hall of Flowers' meeting place. It served as a reminder, to those of
us present, of the kind of real, basic 'shamanic' healing work that
constantly has to be done from scratch every time our different world's
come together.

The intervening decade's multitude of health and healing gatherings, spiritual pow-wow's and sacred council fires already had bore witness
to the richness of the odyssey's of we Alcatraz Island celebrants who
sought to effect much health and healing among our people.

But during our gathering, many, still unresolved, cross-cultural
communications problems kept cropping up between us. One in particular
manifested in the person of an extremely distraught, elderly, mixed-blood
woman.

– A VOW & DREAM AMONG THE WALKING WOUNDED –

Midway through Hopi elder Thomas Banyacya's revelations of the Hopi Prophecy, the woman abruptly stood up and began incoherently shouting about the hurtful things that had happened to her in her lifetime.

Screaming at the top of her lungs, she cried out, "GODDAMN ALL YOU INDIANS! YOU AREN'T REAL MEDICINE HEALERS! I KNOW THE TRUTH!" Some of us close beside her tried to console her, but to no avail.

"I'm a half-breed!", she screamed. "I've really suffered in my life because all you fuckin' full-bloods haven't ever lifted a finger to help us mixed-bloods. That's why I say, here and now, that you're all a bunch of discriminatin', racist, chauvinistic phony's. All the poor, gullible young white people, who are here with us today, need to know the way it really is about us mixed-bloods and how little health and healing we've received in Indian Country. I sure can tell all you a thing or two if you want to listen."

At first, Banyacya and the other male elders tried to ignore her until it became apparent that her wild rants threatened to unsettle the gathering even more so than the earlier milder protests of yet other discontents present, who, for various other reasons, were also unhappy about what all was being discussed.

Her rants took me back to Alcatraz Island's landing dock, ten years before, during that ugly racist incident that occurred between those A.I.M. 'Dog Soldiers' and the elderly African American couple. I once again could sense all the same thoughts that were running through everyone's minds as before.

– A TURTLE ISLAND MEDICINE WAY PUT INTO PRACTICE –

Two short, husky Native women in the audience finally positioned themselves on either side of the old woman and likewise attempted to calm her. But when even that failed, they gently wrapped their arms around her shoulders and, with the woman still protesting that no one would listen to her, they slowly escorted her out of the Hall of Flowers setting.

As the distraught woman was led off, arm-in-arm in the grasp of the two mute-faced Indian women, one could sense that that poor lady somehow symbolized the personal pain and confusion that many First Nation and New Frontier Breeds present were also experiencing at that moment. Seen in the sad eyes of those around me was all the ugliness we'd experienced in the past because of our own futile attempts to try to simultaneously follow both the road of the White Man and that of The Great Spirit's.

After the women left, an uncomfortable heaviness hung in the air. Something dramatic needed to be done to clear it, but what and by whom?

Without any fanfare, or so much as a single word from anyone to inform us of what was happening, one of the elder's young medicine assistants lit a braid of Sweet Grass and began unobtrusively encircling, in a clockwise direction, the edges of the gathering.

This simple act wasn't a planned 'healing demonstration', conveniently staged to correspond with what the gathering's brochure promised us would happen. Instead, it was an actual holistic Turtle Island healing practice being applied to correct an existing imbalance in our hearts and minds that needed to be brought back together as One Mind & Heart.

With each new inhalation I took of the sweet, fragrant smoke that lazily wafted through the crowd, a subtle healing process began to occur within my own mind and heart.

It was then that I made a vow to myself to henceforth seek out, in every way possible, the opportunity to spiritually pow-wow with others, as I had been taught to do, to reinforce with whomever I am with all the simple, positive, uplifting aspects of Turtle Island's natural, ordinary way of life.

– A WALKING WOUNDED TEACHING –

Before coming to this Medicine Way Gathering, I already knew that the Lenapé Indians, who live on the eastern shores of Turtle Island, traditionally used the word *pow-wow* to refer to 'a dreamer'. The Cree version of the same word – *pawa-miwin* – means 'a dream'. While amongst the Narragansett's, their word *taupowauog* refers to 'a dream counselor'.

In the old days, pow-wow's, in the Lenapé language, referred to the native priests or medicine people who devoted themselves to divination. These Lenapé priests became the interpretors of the dreams of others and claimed for themselves the power to dream truthfully of things in the future or 'of the absent '. It's said that in the visions of the old Lenapé, during their pow-wow's, their guardian-spirits visited them and they became, in their own words, "All light, allowing us to see through men and women and know their minds and hearts."

As the Medicine Way Gathering's spiritual pow-wowing to learn the secrets of one another's minds and hearts continued, Banyacya again picked up where he left off with his telling of the Hopi Prophecy. As I scanned the room, I could sense how that troubled half-breed woman served as an outward reflection of so many outstanding issues that exist between native and non-native peoples – metis, mestizo and mulatto peoples in particular.

She especially mirrored the pain and anguish that we New Frontier Breeds experience whenever we attempt anew the all but nigh impossible task of trying to straddle two worlds at the same time; standing, as it were, with our feet on the running boards of two separate vehicles, traveling at different speeds, in opposite directions from one another.

The old woman also served as a metaphor for those of us close to Mother Earth who deeply feel the pain she and all her wild life daily experience because of the wholesale frontal assault that is constantly waged against them and their habitats.

She recalled for us, too, in different ways, our own bouts with alcoholism, drug addiction and mental confusion that often left us on the brink of totally losing a sense of who we are.

Ever since, that old woman, though anonymous, often still enters into my dreams, causing me to constantly give thanks to her, upon waking, for all the light she provided me with on that long ago day to know the thoughts that lurked in all our minds.

Every time I awaken, and recall another meeting between her in the dreamtime, I declare outloud, "Wherever you are, dear lady, thank you. I hope you now walk in a more balanced, beautiful way!"

Yet the malice that was present in some of the Indians who were present at that Medicine Ways Gathering, which crystallized around the disturbed woman, also dirged up in my mind, still other emotion-laden walking wounded memories of the many New Agers met up with in my travels. All those artists, writers, musicians and wannabe shamans who, in their impatience to provide themselves with instant cultural recognition and acclaim, were, consciously or unconsciously, more than willing to misappropriate the cultural identities of Indian and Metis peoples alike for their own aggrandizement.

In those early days of the native spiritual renaissance movement, the extent of many Indians and Metis peoples animosity towards outsiders, whether native or non-native, who attempted to adopt or adapt their traditional medicine ways for New Age consumption, manifested itself through all manner and form of protest and outrage.

Something euphemistically referred to as *The List of Names* began to circulate amongst certain Elder's Circles throughout Indian Country. One list, which traveled through the Plains and Pacific Northwest, cried out:

WARNING!!   WARNING!!   WARNING!!

THE FOLLOWING PEOPLE HAVE BEEN GOING AROUND TURTLE ISLAND, SELLING INDIAN RELIGION,CEREMONIES, ETCETERAS. THESE PEOPLE ARE USUALLY SELF-PROCLAIMED OR DID HAVE SOME TEACHINGS AT ONE TIME, BUT NOT ENOUGH TO MAKE THEM TEACHERS. THEREFORE THEY HAVE NOT BEEN ENDORSED BY ANY TRIBE OR INDIAN NATIONS TO REPRESENT THEM SPIRITUALLY AT ANY LEVEL. THE GRASS-ROOTS PEOPLE, WE NATIVES OF THIS TURTLE ISLAND, ARE STRUGGLING TO SURVIVE AND WILL NOT TOLERATE SUCH MISREPRESEN-TATIONS. WE FEEL THAT IT TAKES THE EYE AWAY FROM THE REAL ISSUE THAT FACE INDIANS TODAY. THEREFORE TO INSURE THE PROTECTION OF ALL INDIAN RELIGIONS, THE FOLLOWING LIST HAS BEEN MADE TO WARN THE MANY INNOCENT PEOPLE OF THE FACT THAT THE EXPLOITATION AND COMMERCIALIZATION OF INDIAN RELIGION CAN BE HARMFUL TO THEM AS IT IS TO THE IMAGE AND SPIRITUAL WELL-BEING OF GRASS-ROOTS PEOPLE.

BEWARE OF THE FOLLOWING:

Max & John Bear	Rick Two Dog	John Round Him	Joe Tiona
Selo Black Crow	Ruth B.B. Hill	Spotted Eagle	Leonard Crow Dog
Good Horse Nation	Ron Williams	Crazy Bear	Jamake High Water
Jim Hoffman	Sonny Hale	Ella Mae Tao	Dianne Battung, Phd.
Hal Grey Eagle	Bill Turtle	Robert Willson	Archie Fire Lame Deer
(Bordeaux)			
Elaine Hubbard	Two Crows		
Gentle Earth Woman	Phyliss Water Woman (Maloney)		Rev. John Crazy Horse
Sun Bear Tokecdelia	Hyemeyohsts Storm		Brookes Medicine Eagle
Wallace Black Elk	Grace Spotted Eagle		Harley Swift Deer (Regan)
Oliver Eastman &	Phillip Martin (Rolling Thunder)		Mary Grimes (Thunder
Devere Eastman	Milo Yellow Hair		Woman)

In time, some *of* these hit lists turned into spiritual 'Joe McCarthy' witchhunts, and came to symbolize the kind *of* 'circle the wagon' mentality that historically has bedeviled native peoples, *of* whatever color or race, who've ever felt the heavy hand *of* imperialistic colonialism.

A mind-set whose end process, typically: discourages criticism *of* one's own self, culture or race; encourages the bitter projection onto out-siders *of* whatever personal–cultural shortcomings; implodes into self-destructive, color-on-color violence amongst whatever native peoples; stimulates a harkening back to a golden past 'Eden' fantasy; frustrates the ability to adapt or cope well with transitions between eras, and; suppresses or silences altogether whatever creative cultural innovation.

– CHECKING OUT SOME OF THE NAMES ON THE LIST –

The odyssey in Alta-Dena soon turned into a search to discover, for my own personal growth and development, what truths or lies – mysteries or non-mysteries – these 'List of Names' actually represented.

Like an investigative reporter or gumshoe–sleuth, I sought out some of those identified on the lists to determine, first-hand, whether they indeed represented the grass-roots of traditional Turtle Island spirituality or some basterdized, bogus New Age version of shamanic phantasmagoria.

This odyssey-within-an-odyssey led Alta-Dena and I off in all directions to many brief meetings or encounters with those like: Ruth Beebe Hill and Chuska Yuha, her Lakota literary cohort, authors of the controversial book *Hanta Yo*, at a Washington State University writer's conference; Marcellus 'Bearheart' Williams at a Native American Church 'Road Chief's' Meeting in New Mexico; Leonard Crow Dog at a Rosebud pow-wow and later at his 'Crow Dog's Paradise' in South Dakota; Jamake Highwater at a writer's conference in Southern California; Wallace Black Elk at a World Health Expo in San Francisco; Rolling Thunder at a World Humanity Foundation gathering in British Columbia; Rev. John Crazy Horse at a private Sun Dance gathering in South Dakota; Brookes Medicine Eagle at an Intl. Aboriginal Conference in Northern California; Harley Swift Deer and Hyemeyohsts Storm at a Medicine Drum gathering in Southern California.

Some of these encounters proved hostile, while others turned out to be heart-felt sharings between 'old souls' reconnecting once again.

For years, the odyssey's path twisted and careened to avoid all the Indian and non-Indian 'medicine way' entrepreneurs who blithely traveled an international spiritual circuit, like New Age Buffalo Bill's & Billie's performing in their own private Wild West side-shows, taking advantage of the widespread spiritual hunger and cultural confusion that everywhere abounded.

"OK, Twin Rainbow!", said The Voice, each time another encounter was made with a plastic, instant-mix, medicine man or woman, "If, because of the traditional way you've been taught, you don't like the way the old medicine teachings are being diluted by second-rate teachers or basterdized by bogus gurus, what are you prepared to do to right the situation? If you aren't prepared to ride the coattails of these sacred teachings, and reap the instant fame and fortune that's there for the taking, how can you pass on these wisdoms in the time-honored way they were intended?"

The Voice goaded the odyssey ever onward with the *quest*-tion, "How, Twin Rainbow, can mixed-breed, small-case metis like yourself – as the scattered descendants of exiles, refugees and immigrants from many distant native lands – gain a commonwealth land base, or some other prominent platform, from which to make a much needed political-cultural-spiritual statement to the world about all this?"

– SOUL-TALK WITH A METIS WISE MAN ON THE OPEN ROAD –

As the Elder's Medicine Way Gathering in Golden Gate Park drew to a close, and we Veterans of the Occupation prepared to return to wherever we came from to continue our healing work, I met up with Tijo Hatier, a Scottish-French-Cree wise man who then was living in Berkeley, just across the Bay.

Berkeley was the last place in the world I ever expected to bump into a Metis of Hatier's stature. Steeped as he was in the history of his people, he could trace his lineages back to the early days of their military-like organized buffalo hunts with Lord Selkirk's colony in Rupert's Land that later became part of Western Canada.

His presence in Berkeley was a reminder to me that we humans can never fully know, until the end, why The Great Spirit puts us upon the open road to go or do whatever we feel we must in the world before our time runs out. Where we each end up and why, truly part of some 'Great Mystery'.

Hatier had the classic features of a Metis man: a distinctive nose, chin and eyes that proudly represented the rich blend of two great civilizations; a tall, broad-shouldered, muscular body; long, curly black hair and a French 'habitant' moustache, that reminded me of Louis Riel, the 19th century noble leader of the Metis Nation. Hatier seemed, as well, from another time and place: always dressed as he was in a plaid shirt, worn Levi's, black cowboy hat and boots; a large-sheathed hunting knife strapped to his waist; his big, French Cree-named dog constantly by his side.

Louis Riel

Hatier's house, too, set high in the Northern Berkeley hills, also reflected the same rich blend of European and First Nation cultures, what with its: early Californios-Western post and beam ceilings; adobe walls and thick, rough-hewn doors. Upon a primitive brick fireplace and mantle hung a musket, powder horn, medicine pipe, eagle fan, Indian hand-drum and a prairie fiddle; while the surrounding floors were crowded with stacks upon stacks of books and magazines, with boxes atop boxes of everything imaginable occupying the nooks and crannies of every room. Hatier's tiny, heavily lived-in kitchen, was full of pots, pans and cooking implements that hung, helter-skelter, from the ceiling and covered every last inch of wall space. Eating utensils and food stuffs covered, as well, every last inch of counter and table space. Outside, a long corridor of firewood, bottles, cans, shovels, axes, animal traps and rubbish lined either side of the path to the front door, while a sweat lodge and firepit were so well secluded, in a thickly-treed front yard, as to be all but invisible to even the nearby neighbors. A worn red pictographic symbol – identical to one I once saw painted on a rock wall of the ancient Anasazi village of Keet Seel in Arizona – emblazoned upon a facing wall near the front entrance, always was ready to welcome whatever visitor happened upon that spot.

In short, if one was led blind-folded to Hatier's place, and didn't know it was in Berkeley, they would swear it was some old Metis's cabin far out in the bush in Montana, Saskatchewan or some other isolated spot in the West. To leave his house – and walk the 90 feet past his sweat lodge to reach the nearby city street, and 'normal' urban world that lay beyond – was like passing through a time machine from the 19th to the 20th century. The lever that sent the visitor hurtling back into the 20th century tripped each time whenever Hatier's old baling-wire and wood-slat gate, with that large rusty cow bell attached to it, was pulled back and made its distinctive, noisy clang.

Hatier, as I soon learned upon meeting him, was the President of the *Metis-Indian Alliance of North America* (M.I.A.), otherwise commonly referred to as 'The Alliance'. He, along with other Canadian–American Metis and Indians – from such diverse nations as the Mandan-Hidatsa, Blackfeet, Turtle Mountain Chippewa, Hopi, Cherokee, Miwok and Tshimshian – co-founded The Alliance. Their intent was to address the alarming increases of New Age shamanic-type individuals and groups who, intentionally or not, were misappropriating many of the cultural aspects of indigenous peoples.

As a 'Friend of The Alliance', I sought, through my own self-proclaimed role as one of the Turtle's 'Ambassador's', to encourage whomever I met to help bring about some mutual understanding and good-will to bear upon the disruptive, counter-productive conflicts that more and more were occurring between First Nation and New Age peoples.

Hatier, and his Alliance brothers and sisters, created their cultural-political-spiritual body not only to respond to this glaring historical issue but to also encourage a greater respect for the ancient traditions of Turtle Island and those who seek to preserve them. They sought, as well, to raise the general awareness of the blind, rough-and-tumble, mixed-blood vs. full-blood prejudices that, historically, have everywhere raged in Indian Country.

Special emphasis was put upon what the Metis in Canada, or those living in scattered locations throughout the U.S., constantly suffer at the hands of both the Indian and European communities that surround them.

Historically, the emergence of The Alliance was neither the first nor the last time that the need has arisen, or that hopes have been dashed, that some constructive body, once and for all, would act as a vehicle for Turtle Island wisdom and healing practices.

Since the earliest days of contact, many good-hearted, well-intended groups like The Alliance have come together to try to address humankind's 'poverty of the spirit' and inability to share, cross-culturally, in a respectful manner, one another's different ways of seeing life.

However, as history has revealed, many visionaries like Hatier and The Alliance have come and gone without leaving much of a trace outside of the immediate circles within which they once moved. The Alliance's initials – M.I.A. – came to symbolize for me all those non-violent soldiers in the war against humankind's poverty of spirit, who have ever gone *Missing-In-Action*, never to be seen or heard of again.

It never has been easy for the First Nation and Western European civilization's – nor for the Metis, Indian, Dené and Inuit themselves – to reconcile their vast differences. In Canada, the contentious *Nunavut* land negotiations between the Dené and Inuit, to determine the boundaries of their respective homelands, is one recent historical example.

Another example is the equally contentious disagreements which occurred between Metis and Indian people over the 'Native Constitutional Conferences' that were held to negotiate the repatriation of the Canadian Constitution from England. Especially when the Metis simply put forth their *Declaration of Rights* which asserted:

We, the Metis and Non-Status Indians, descendants of the "Original People" of this country declare:

That Metis nationalism is Canadian nationalism. We embody the true spirit of Canada and are the source of Canadian identity.

That we have the right to self-determination and shall continue – in the tradition of Louis Riel – to express this right as equal partners in confederation.

That all Native people must be included in each step of the process leading to changes in the constitution of Canada.

That we have the right to guaranteed representation in *all* legislative Assemblies.

That we have the inalienable right to the land and the natural resources of that land.

That we have the right to determine how and when the land and resources are to be developed for the benefit of our people and in partnership with other Canadians for the benefit of Canada as a whole.

That we have the right to preserve our identity and to flourish as a distinct people with a rich cultural heritage.

That we have the right to educate our children in our Native languages, customs, beliefs, music and other art forms.

That we are a people with a right to special status in confederation.

The National Indian Council was another body, formed like The Alliance, to address the cultural squabbles that, for centuries, have created one factious splinter group after another among Native peoples. The National Indian Council, itself, also couldn't keep its focus intact and eventually split into two different offspring organizations – the Canadian Metis Society and the National Indian Brotherhood.

One could cite many similar visionary organizations in Canada or the United States who've surged onto the cultural scene only to eventually fragment or go 'missing-in-action'. The no man's lands between our respective peoples on Turtle Island littered with the broken dreams and spent visions of those forever caught within the same vast sea of quicksand fraught with unresolved malice, envy and rage.

Those like Hatier and his Alliance – who've ever tried to fundamentally transform the dark side of the human spirit – indeed discovered what it means to become the "divided monstors" that D.H. Lawrence wrote about in his description of a writhing snake that seeks to create the pattern of a new skin for itself. They may know what the new pattern is that they want, but are still forced to nearly thrash themselves to death before the pattern can become fully manifested.

– A NEW TWIST IN THE WRITHING SNAKE'S STRUGGLE –

The time had come for Alta-Dena and I to part company with Tijo Hatier and his Alliance's dreams and once more take to the open road.

As with the beginning and ending of every leg of the odyssey, I lit another braid of Sweet Grass and smudged Alta-Dena and myself with its fragrant smoke.

Encircling Alta-Dena, in a clockwise manner, I blessed her with the same *Prayer For The Open Road* that I use each time we're about to set off together on our next great adventure.

"Oh, Great Spirit!", goes the prayer, "Bless this journey. Bless Alta-Dena's split-rim tires that they get us to where we need to go without any mishap. Bless these bright headlamps, that they cut through all the darkness up ahead. Help them to shed new light on whatever dangers may await us. Let these huge bumpers harm no living thing but instead warn away any and all wrong doers who stand in our way. Help this faithful engine to continue to purr, with all her systems working in harmony and balance with one another. Bless, too, this steering wheel and seat. Let no harm come to anyone who travels within these walls. **AHO!**"

So off we went on our next investigative reporter, gumshoe–sleuth assignment, hoping to find the seaside encampment of a group of New Age 'Metis' that was rumored to be gathering near San Luis Obispo to protest the operation of the Diablo Canyon nuclear plant.

As Alta-Dena's panoramic windows passed beyond view of San Francisco's Twin Peaked-spires, I cried out, as always, "Pechas Azul! Pechas Azzuull! I see you, oh breasts of an Amu maiden, covered in Blue Lupine. Bless the road ahead, that it may be a good one. Spirits of the South! Hear me! I ask you, too, for your guidance and direction."

Half a day's trek later, Alta-Dena and I found ourselves pulling up beside an odd assortment of fancy cars, hippie vans and strange rigs of all shorts that were parked on a bluff overlooking the Pacific Ocean.

It was indeed the camp of Harley 'Swift Deer' Reagan and his New Age followers. Also present was his mentor, Hyemeyohsts Storm, who I hadn't seen since the Earth Healing Ceremony at Eyalmox, and earlier soireé days with Canadian playwright George Ryga.

– A SURREAL GATHERING –

Swift Deer's encampment was unlike any other camp I visited before. The first shock was the number of high-priced luxury cars and vans that many of his obviously well-heeled admirers and followers came in.

Next was the way they dressed. Instead of the simple street clothes or bush gear I was accustomed to seeing at native peoples grass-roots political–spiritual gatherings, many of the women present had that well-manicured, pampered, coiffured, L.A./Hollywood look about them. They decked out in the latest haute couture, Indian-designed fashions, high-top moccasins and all. Their hair adorned with beaded eagle feathers. Their fingers, wrists, ears, necks and waists bedecked in pricey turquoise–silver rings, bracelets, necklaces, ear-rings and concho belts. Elaborately-painted Indian hand-drums, rattles, peace pipes, smudge sticks and medicine bundles were everywhere in evidence.

The way they acted, too, felt alien. Unlike the normal, down-to-earth behavior one experiences among grass-roots native people, those gathered in Swift Deer's camp seemed more like subservient devotees to a guru than they did free-thinking supporters of some leader or cause.

Also at opposite ends of the poles was the way they conducted themselves, running all about like over-excited children – playing Indian, dancing and chanting – in a way that had more of an unreal air of show business about it than genuine spiritual business.

Another bizarre thing was the hierarchical, military-like structure to the encampment and the way Swift Deer, Hyemeyhosts Storm and their inner circles of devotees communicated with one another. Swift Deer's and Storm's followers addressing them as "General this or General that", "Yes, Sir! No, Sir! By your leave, Sir!" Swift Deer and Storm, in turn, referring to them according to their rank, "Carry on Lieutenant!", "As you were, Private!"

Then there were the guns present in the camp. Lots of them. Strapped to Swift Deer's waist was a fancy-blued .45 caliber pistol that he often took out of the holster and toyed with, while his followers brandished, as well, a wide assortment of hand guns and rifles.

All the virulent, ultra-right patriot talk and kinky sexual admissions that were uttered throughout the camp soon caused me to wonder if, instead of coming to a New Age Spiritual gathering, I might have accidentally stumbled onto a local assembly of New Age Minute Men or congregation of some new weird sexual cult.

"Christ!", I thought to myself. "This is California, and Southern California to boot! So I suppose anything is possible!"

To say the whole scene was surreal would be a gross understatement. Once I had a good look, I couldn't get out of there fast enough.

– GURU OR SLICK CON ARTIST –

By the time Alta-Dena and I found our way to Swift Deer's seaside encampment, he already had come under intense criticism from many First Nation peoples who called him, "a fraud and a pervert."

Though he claimed to be a Cherokee Medicine Man, who grew up on a reservation in Texas, a number of reputable leaders in the Cherokee Nation said such claims were completely bogus because the Cherokee never had a reservation in Texas.

To hear Swift Deer tell it, he learned to become a sorceror from Tom 'Two Bears' Wilson, a Navajo medicine man, who taught him to shape-shift back and forth from a deer to a man. Yet many Navajo publicly said his allegations were an utter hoax.

Swift Deer also told us that he practiced an ancient indigenous form of balancing spiritual and sexual energies that he called *Chulaqui Quodoushka* and identified it as half-Cherokee and half-Mayan. He also spoke of certain sacred sexual practices that he said his Cherokee grand-mother 'Spotted Fawn' once arranged for him, at age 14, to be sexually initiated into with the help of a Cherokee 'Phoenix Fire Woman'.

This Phoenix Fire Woman allegedly taught Swift Deer the art of love making and something about the nine different kinds of vaginas and penises that women and men possess as well as the five levels of orgasm they experience. By this time, however, many voices within the Cherokee Nation already had gone on record to say that there existed no such sexual initiation rites within their nation nor did they know of any person called 'Spotted Fawn' or 'Phoenix Fire Woman'. Yet, like Sun Bear, Swift Deer, by then, already had established among his followers a reputation as a 'sex guru' who talked a lot about 'sacred sexual living' meditations that they regularly did with him.

He bragged a lot, too, as was his want, in camp about his teachers, who, as he said, "Are the *Twisted Hair Elders of Turtle Island.* These elders are from North, Central and South America, as well as Australia, who have been meeting every four years, since 1254 B.C., sometimes in this dimension, other times in the fifth dimension, and represent a tradition that goes back 128,000 years." Yet for all this braggadocio and smooth spiel, First Nation people, early on, typed him as a, "charlatan and a snake oil vendor."

In spite of the many encounters he had with A.I.M. warriors and elders, who vociferously challenged him every chance they got, Swift Deer remained undaunted in his practices. "Assholes in Moccasins!", is how he contemptuously characterized his detractors, while adding, "Their bigoted, prejudiced, socialist and communist radicals! Cowards in heart, spirit and body! Only four conditions of human life exist: living heroes, dead heroes, dead cowards and living cowards. They're all the last and worst kind of human condition. Fuck 'em!"

With that, Swift Deer would sit back, lite up yet another one of his chain-smoked cigarettes and take a moment to relish the verbal grenade he'd just lobed into whatever ears could hear them and didn't give a damn who got hit by the shrapnel. "Wow!", I thought, "This Swift Deer cat is one strange dude to type."

To his detractors, he was everything from another Jim Jones cultist leader to a classic con-artist, who was part of a much detested international network of people who were ripping off First Nation Medicine Ways. But to his followers within the *Deer Tribe Medicine Society*, who walked the *Sweet Medicine Sundance Path*, he was either a sex guru, a semi-messiah or just a simple, honest, sincere leader with over-powering charisma and magnetism. "His steely blue eyes and piercing stare", as they said, "can look straight into our hearts and minds."

To himself, he was a master story-teller who loved to spin tall tales. "The first thing I always tell my students", he said," is don't believe anything I say. You'd be a fool to. You have to feel it."

Swift Deer, who preferred the nick-name 'Gunnie' or 'Shooting Shaman', proudly claimed to be a life member of the NRA, *Gun Owners of America, Citizens Who Support The Right to Bear Arms* and instructor of the *Deer Tribe Gun Club.*

Concerning his association with the Twisted Hair Society, he said, "I meet with the secret society once a year in the flesh and almost every night in the astral plane."

He enjoyed recounting how he once was an alternate to the 1964 U.S. Olympic Judo Team, even though, as it turns out, there apparently exists no record of proof that he ever was on that team. He also proudly stated that he was a decorated Marine who served four tours in Vietnam, before being blown out of a helicopter and falling 300 feet to the ground, even though again there apparently is no record of him ever receiving the bronze and silver stars that he claims he received. He even claims that he once was a CIA agent, though that is a hard fact to prove and must be taken at face-value along with his assertion that he is the reincarnation of Billy The Kid.

Swift Deer was quick to admit that he was in the process of readying himself and his followers for the, "Time of the Razor's Edge", which, as he prophesized, "will come in the first decade of the 21st century when the American people will undergo a severe test of their hearts, minds, bodies and spirits. I seek to train my followers as warriors because I see us moving towards a civil war."

At the time, I thought, "No matter how one slices it, this Harley 'Swift Deer' Reagan cat is a real piece of work that defies description. He's gotta be the loudest, most boisterous, unpretentious, cantankerous, riveting, arrogant, blowhard-bull-shitting Texan, or anyone else for that matter from Timbuktu or wherever, that I've yet to come across."

The longer I pondered, the more I thought, "If this guy ever was to become a car salesman, he no doubt could sell a Model T off as a Porsche and still have satisfied customers return every year." The scariest thing of all about him was his super-patriot, 'We The People' rhetoric, which was laced with disturbing undertones of white supremacy.

In those days, there was so much desperate spiritual, physical, emotional and sexual hunger that it was easy for phony con-men, con-women and half-truth teachers to materialize upon the scene, spin whatever tall tales about their powers, invent a tiny 'Bear Tribe', 'Deer Tribe', 'Turtle Tribe' or whatever, and then gain, overnight, something of a local, national and even an international following.

Before leaving the Swift Deer encampment, I was approached by Hyemeyohsts Storm, or "General Storm" as he was referred to among the Deer Tribe. Storm wanted to feel me out about playing a pivotal role with him in realizing his grand dream-vision to found a national–international organization of mixed-blooded people of all races he wanted to call *The National American Metis Association* (NAMA).

– THE REAL GENERAL BEHIND THE SCENES –

If Swift Deer was a two-star general in the world of the Deer Tribe's Medicine Society, Hyemeyohsts Storm was a four-star general. For he was the real power behind the throne of so many would-be New Age shamans and writers like Swift Deer, Sun Bear, Evelyn Eaton and Lynn Andrews.

However, Storm preferred to remain in the shadows or, as he once put it, "Listen carefully to my first name – Hyemeyohsts. Say it very slowly and you will hear and understand that, 'I am a Ghost', who desires to move about, invisible, like a ghost."

Storm, who wrote *Seven Arrows*, a controversial book that the Cheyenne Nation disavows as having anything to do with their beliefs, claimed, in addition to his Sioux-Crow-German heritage, to be part Cheyenne. But, as apparently is true to his avowed ghost-like nature, the Cheyenne say they have no one by his name on their rolls.

After Seven Arrows came out, Joe Little Coyote Sr., Sweet Medicine Chief of the Northern Cheyenne Dsi'sti'stahs and Suh'dio Nations said:

Seven Arrows is not conducive to the beliefs and tenets of the Northern Cheyenne, and is a false and inaccurate account done for his own personal gain and exploitative purposes.

Storm, in his later books, *Song of Heyoehkah* and *Lightningbolt*, would further claim that certain earth wisdoms have been passed onto him through a direct lineage of Zero Chiefs, of which Storm is one such 'Zero'.

According to Storm, "The disciplines of the Zero Chiefs extend back thousands of years in The America's, to the Mayan culture and beyond. These dedicated Zero Chiefs are responsible for the discovery of the earth science and spiritual philosophy called 'The Way of the Medicine Wheels'. The Circle of the Earth Temple, CETI Institute, and the international school of Metis art I intend to found will welcome Metis peoples of mixed blood and mixed heritage from all nations."

This partially-blind, yet keenly-observant coyote trickster, of whatever mixed-breed origins, suggested that the two of us join forces for the major undertaking he had in mind. "Twin Rainbow!", he said, while turning his failing eyes into even narrower slit sthan they already were, "That's a pretty good name for the role you see yourself playing between all our people. But the name I'd instead give you is *Medicine Drum.*"

Evincing all the more that typical, inscrutable Chesire Cat, Coyote-Heyoka trickster smile of his, Storm continued, "To me, you're like a fast movin' Prairie Dog or Roadrunner; who pops his head out of one hole somewhere, zings his visionary healing message out to the world, and then – Beep! Beep! ZOOOMMM! – disappears, only to pop out of another hole again, maybe even clear 'cross the country. Your lightnin' voice travelin' like a healing drum, bent along the ground, in all four directions at once. Yah, Medicine Drum, you're what I'd call a classic example of a 21st century NAMA pioneer."

Tilting his head all the more to one side, so he could more easily see from out of the corner of his better eye, Storm suggested, "I'd like you to consider becoming NAMA's National Director. And if you accept my offer, I'd like you to immediately start by touring university campuses and traditional Native communities all across North America, to inform young and old alike of NAMA's Metis dream-vision for the future."

Flattered by Storm's acerbic perception of the unsung 'Johnny Appleseed' role that many New Frontier Breed's, like myself, everywhere seek to play as Turtle Island's Earth Ambassadors, his offer was nevertheless flatly declined for several crucial reasons.

For starters, NAMA's careless, voguish, if not arrogant, usurpation of the name *Metis* to describe their budding movement, at once set off alarm bells in my head. If Tijo Hatier had been there, a lot more than bells would have gone off inside his head.

The loose bantering about of terms like 'shamans', 'shamanic medicine ways' and 'patriotism', to describe the activities of some of NAMA's associate members, also set off still more disturbing alarms. Storm tried to allay my concerns. "I want to send out", he said, "an invitation to all people of the heart to create a new American dream. A new dream that will become a multi-racial movement of mixed-blooded Metis peoples of whatever racial mixture – Irish-English, French-Polish, Indian-Scottish and so on – that will encourage everyone to think of themselves as Natives of this land regardless of their racial origins."

I knew at once that Storm's zealous desire to quickly weld together a multi-ethnic organization, like NAMA, would instantly send a wave of rage rippling throughout Indian Country, especially among the Metis.

NAMA did have among its founding members a few individuals, possessing varying degrees of Indian blood, who identified themselves as Metis. Yet the vast majority of those attracted to NAMA's vision were displaced peoples, primarily of European descent. Storm's intent was, as he said, "To encourage all displaced, mixed-blood natives to come together and discover for themselves a new North American indigenous identity."

Storm handed me NAMA's first official flyer, that he intended to dessiminate to the general public, that stated, "From the beginning, *The Dream* was born in America. Our forefathers and foremothers discovered the power of The Great Mystery that is destined to heal the world – America!" Which at once sounded an awful lot like the red-white-and blue, 'We The People' rhetoric Swift Deer had earlier espoused.

NAMA's flyer went on to say, "American Indians are part of the larger problem of America's denial of full cultural and spiritual rights to *many* ethnic and racial groups. The healing is needed *for all kinds of Metis peoples* – not merely for those of American Indian descent."

I tried to warn Storm that his dream to create a Pan Indian–New Frontier Breed movement, no matter how much it is needed, would only encourage the wide-spread misuse of first Nation peoples medicine ways. That it also would inadvertently set into motion anew, a process that native peoples everywhere understand, all too well, that inevitably breaks down the local constraints – the time-honored, traditional practices – which hold together the delicate balance between Humanity and Nature.

But Storm wasn't prepared to hear this. He deftly attempted to side-step the controversy by disavowing that NAMA would become a chain of ersatz Medicine Lodges, Women's Earth Lodges or Metis Men's Brotherhood Lodges, that would mix and match First Nation medicine practices.

"No!", said Storm. "NAMA is meant to be a cultural and patriotic organization which, for a variety of spiritualities and cultures in America, will support the availability of a religion of choice to all sincere and caring Americans, whether it be Christianity, Buddhism or *Medicine.*"

What Storm avoided addressing, was a willingness to accept the idea that First Nation medicine ways aren't a religion, like Christianity or Buddhism, that one can simply join or pick up if they so desire. Because First Nation medicine ways are inextricably joined and bonded to a particular people and a particular sacred place, both of whom emerged as part of a long-stand-ing life process together. Storm instead insisted on claiming that, "NAMA's beliefs are over 2,000 years old and so race is not a determining factor."

In those days, Turtle Island's elders began to take cautious note of the burgeoning numbers of such White European, shamanic-oriented groups with whom they more and more were coming in contact. They could see that these people, who were either seceding from or being pushed out of their disenfranchised, alienated parent cultures, though while perhaps well-intended and open-hearted, brought with them a seed of destruction for traditional First Nation communities.

As one elder put it, "Yah know, Twin Rainbow, it's not so much our enemies we got to worry about as it is our friends. 'Cause when we invite our new White, Black and Asian friends into our communities we make ourselves vulnerable. And being vulnerable, we can sometimes get hurt in ways that we'd normally protect ourselves against if we were facing our enemies."

Storm's fatal mistake was that he wanted to make NAMA a passive, non-political, patriotic organization rather than an activist, political-spiritual movement that could align itself with other groups like the American Indian Movement, Indian Liberation Movement of Canada or the Green Party. He was unable to see that NAMA needed to immediately demonstrate some kind of pragmatic, traditional community-building process as those fostered by the Mohawk Nation's 'White Roots of Peace', the Lil'Wat's 'Indian Liberation Economic Strategy', or the Haida's 'Rediscovery Wilderness Encampment' philosophy that set out to relearn the ancient pathways of their people while, at the same time, discover new directions for these ancient pathways to take.

Storm's concept of NAMA couldn't grasp how living solely within one ecosystem, and depending entirely upon the continuing function of that ecosystem for one's survival, implies a sophisticated sense of how one's politics and spiritual practices need to become wedded together as one. Or as Mahatma Gandhi once put it, "Those who say that religion has nothing to do with politics do not know what religion means."

I warned Storm that the *coup de grâce* for NAMA would come from the money-making activities of its associate members and their national–international seminars that mistaught 'Native Medicine Ways', set up 'Metis Men's Brotherhood Lodges' or published, books, magazines and newsletters that identified themselves as Metis works.

"A better way", I said, "is to encourage your followers to practice what the Haudenosaunee 'Six Nations' Confederacy, or 'People of the Long-house', as they call themselves, refer to as *The Silver Chain Covenant*." By that they mean if we are to truly ever link together, as one, the spirits of all our people – and so keep the human chain that links us pure, strong and un-tarnished – we need to find new ways to constantly polish each silver link that bonds nations, races and people without infringing upon their independence. Each one marching to their own drum as they explore their own unique way to sink their roots ever deeper into Turtle Island.

"For NAMA to begin this polishing", I said, "it first will have to understand how the real Metis earned the names *O-tee-paym-soo-wuk* and *Ka-tip-aim-soot-chik* from the Cree. Both names roughly translating into, *'They who are their own selves, beholden to no one!'* NAMA will never earn such a name by taking the easy way out and co-opt what those like the real Metis people have earned the hard way."

My long monologue to Storm concluded with the advice, "Perhaps the best lesson of all NAMA can draw from the Metis Nation's living historical story is to study the record of rage they've been subjected to by Indian and European alike. Maybe NAMA's most important contribution to help polish the Silver Chain will be to encourage your followers, as well, to document their own experiences with prejudice and rage and the ways they've been discriminated against by both the First Nation and White Man's world's."

During my gentle harangue, Storm said little. He just sat there squinting with that inscrutable Chesire Cat smile of his. I could tell, though, that, like so many instant-mix shaman–showmen and women, he couldn't hear me because he was too eager to ride the crest of the cultural wave that he sensed a growing interest in Metis culture represented.

I could also see that, to him, I now already was an 'ex-Metis' who had no further purpose in his grand scheme and so couldn't be used as yet another literary front or mouthpiece for his dubious ends.

– MEMORIES OF THE WALKING WOUNDED RETURN –

Taking leave of Storm and walking beyond the edge of Swift Deer's camp, I searched until I found a responsive tree that invited me to sit up against it, fuse our spines together for a time and gain whatever new insights into this whole issue might come.

Deep in thought, I mentally scanned the some two decades I'd thus far taken to explore what it means to be an outsider in the dominant society in which I was raised.

Revisited, in my mind's eye, were all those long processions of my people in their New Age covered wagons as they made their annual migrations to seek out traditional Indian, Metis, Dené and Inuit communities to try to heal the trama they suffered as outsiders. Recalled were the many times that I saw so many of them enter into Indian Country with so little pride or dignity and in such a spiritually-starved condition that they had no sense of who they were, where they came from or where they were going. As is so typical with starving people, all they could think to do was stuff their own empty stomachs without taking much care for who they might be depriving or abusing in the process.

One part of me could see that the basic instincts of such spiritually-starving people were right to desire higher 'shamanic' relationships with themselves and the world around them. But that their judgment was hopelessly clouded because instead of doing the hard work, because their needs were so great, they opted instead for the more dramatic, quick-fix, superficial elements of pop shamanism and its commercialization. They unable to see how they were embarassing themselves as the unique people that they are, possessing rare gifts to exchange in-kind. Nor could they see how they were opening themselves up to unnecessary humiliation and ridicule by the very people they sought out for help.

"But how", I wondered, as I sat with my back up against my new-found rooted counselor, "can we all gain a greater degree of dis-crimination and not sell ourselves short or put our swelled bellies out in front of those of our own people?"

– TAKING A PAGE OUT OF THE METIS HISTORY BOOK –

As Alta-Dena and I quietly slipped out of Swift Deer's camp, we stopped for a time on a high bluff that overlooked that crazy, mixed-up gathering of lost souls and the dangerous cultural precedent that was incubating there.

Mulled over and over again was the single-most question that has constantly driven this odyssey forward. Namely, how can we solitary free-lancers of the New Frontier – all we lone wolves who run along the razor's edge between the Good Red, Yellow, Black and White Roads – finally coalesce, culturally, politically, economically and spiritually?

From the perspective of where I then stood upon this new Rainbow Road, I could see that we solitary free-lancers and lone wolves were in a similar, historically-awkward, position as once were the early forefather's and mother's of the Metis Race upon North America's rugged physical frontier. They also once-upon-a-time forced to struggle as outsiders, in anonymity and isolation, for many generations before finally coalescing around the Fur Trade and then later around the Buffalo Trade. They only subsequently receiving a very small part of the recognition that was their due, as North America's first truly unique race and culture of people, when they became the West's early 'teamsters'; first as *voyageurs* and *coureur de bois,* travelling upon and through the continent's rivers and forests, and then as the drivers of Red River Carts along the Buffalo Trail and early Indian-White trade routes.

It was while sitting there in Alta-Dena, enjoying the vantage point of that historical high-ground, that I was able to acknowledge how the struggle of we New Frontier Breeds also has to do with coming together around yet another major economic enterprise, a new pivotal geopolitical crossroad, or perhaps just kick up a couple of notches the role we already successfully. play – as tiny, systemic agents of cultural change – in infiltrating and influencing the consciousness of the dominant society that spawned us.

– A NEW SOJOURN UPON THE OPEN ROAD IS REVEALED –

Heading back North to Canada, and a long overdue reconnection with my Aussie soul-mate, Alta-Dena and I stopped to rest in what some New Frontier people refer to as the Sonoma bioregion of *Kuksu Nation* in present-day Northern California. This place the same setting chosen by Ursula LeGuin for her 'Imagine–A–Native–White–Culture' novel *Always Coming Home.*

It wasn't mere chance that also led LeGuin's odyssey to once upon a time stop and choose the Sonoma bioregion as the setting for her futuristic novel. For this one-time heart of Bear Country has long been one of the major hot-houses for the environmental, deep-ecological, shamanic and bioneer movements in North America.

If, as LeGuin fantasizes in her writings about 'The Kesh', some White European Native culture ever is to really emerge upon the North American continent, the Sonoma bioregion remains one of the most likeliest of places for it to first occur.

This temporary respite in the South soon put me in touch with some of the architects who sought to create a real, viable deep-ecological movement within the dominant White Man's culture. One which if, in the coming decades or centuries, it properly does all of its 'Coming Home' work, it will indeed create a real-life 'Kesh' culture of its own.

I knew that once I returned North to spend some quality time with Crystal Freesia, I would have to come back to this place and spend a much longer time to learn more about what was so special about the earth there that desired to bring this about.

So, PILGRIM. How have you felt your life to be part of some great cultural–spiritual movement that, if realized, would greatly change, for the better or worse, humanity's future? What role do you play in whatever is taking place? What or who are some of the forces that seek to block this movement's work? Waste no more time here. Retire to your quiet place. **Be Off With Ye! Go!**

WELCOME BACK! Before I could cross over The Medicine Line, back into Grandmother's Lands to see Crystal Freesia, I felt the need to make contact with some of Turtle Island's elders.

Someone had to tell them that the ever-growing spiritual colonialism of groups like N A M A – and individuals like Swift Deer, Hyemeyohsts Storm, Sun Bear and others – wasn't what every New Frontier Breed was intent upon doing. As an Earth Ambassador of my people, I felt compelled to let the elders know there were those of us who were as outraged as they by all the 'White Indian–Tarzan's', 'Copy-Cat Grey Owls', 'New Age Missionaries' and 'Spiritual Conquistadores' among our people.

These new invaders, this time around, intent upon occupying and stealing the spiritual parts of Indian Country, by cleverly using the argument that in America everyone has the God-given right of freedom of religion. Which to the new Tarzan's, Grey Owl's, Missionary's and Conquistador's means the right to take, without permission, whatever First Nation medicine ways they see fit to use for their own ends, while branding, as racists, all those who object to them and their philosophy.

– A NEW FRONTIER DECLARATION IS PUT FORTH –

Just as First Nation peoples have their own international Fourth World passports and 'Continuing Declaration's of Independence or Interdependence', so, too, do I feel it equally important that we Fifth World pioneers, individually and collectively, draft our own declarations and make First Nation people aware of them.

It wasn't long after Alta-Dena and I left Swift Deer's camp that a bulletin came zinging over the moccasin telegraph to alert everyone that a *Medicine Talk For Mother Earth & All Earth Peoples* gathering of elders and spiritual leaders was preparing to convene in Washington State.

"This is my chance", I thought. "I must get there at once!"

Knowing how important it always is to begin every spiritual journey with a prayer to the higher powers to protect one's self during their travels, I again entered into my ritual smudging ceremony inside and around Alta-Dena and myself, while placing my medicine bundle back atop Alta-Dena's dash.

"*Pechas Azul! Pechas Azzuuulll! I see you!*", I shouted, as Alta-Dena sped past those ancient grandfather and grandmother sentinels again, before turning East onto the San Francisco-Oakland Bay Bridge. "Thank you for the richness of the journey in the South this time around. See you when I see you! Stay well! Pray for me!"

"*Histum Yani!*", I heralded, as we passed those Marysville Buttes the early Spanish once called 'Los Pichachos'. "*Waka Nuni! Tucki Wuckie!*", I chanted as Alta-Dena once more came into view of Mount Shasta & Shastina. "Grandfather! Grandmother! Thank You! The journey is good. I go North now, with your help – Humbly! Happily! Holy!"

Reaching the The Medicine Talk Gathering, held on the lands of the Puyallup Nation, near a former Indian Drug & Alcohol–Mental rehabilitation hospital, I discovered I was one of the first to have arrived.

Yet in a manner similar to the way I was approached by those Dog Soldiers in Chumash Territory, several Puyallup camp policemen abruptly walked out in front of Alta-Dena, forcing me to pull her up short of the gate that led into the grounds of the gathering.

My large Roman nose, square face and high cheekbones often cause Native peoples to mistake me for a Metis or half-breed. This time, with my long auburn hair done up in Cree-designed buckskin wraps, emblazoned with red-beaded lightningbolts set against a white seed-bead background, I looked even more so.

The two camp policemen quickly nodded their approval, and were about to step aside and wave me through the gate, when one of them glanced into Alta-Dena's cab and noticed her psychedelic Celtic–Indian–Hippie interior. "Hey! Hold up just a sec' bro!", he said, in a friendly yet puzzled tone. "What tribe ya from?"

The second I innocently replied, "I'm a Celtic-Druid tribesman!", both their faces turned hard, and the at first friendly one snapped back in a harsh, belligerent tone of voice, "HOLD IT THEN, MAN! If yah ain't Native, yah can't go in yet. Only Native's 'll be allowed to enter the grounds first. Then all you White guys can go in."

"HEY, WHADDAYAH MEAN!", I protested. "THAT'S NOT FAIR! I'VE COME A LONG WAY! BESIDES, I AM, TOO, NATIVE! I can trace my hereditary chieftain clan all the way back to the ancient Druids and our fairy ancestors in Ireland. Besides, I've just come a thousand miles to get here. I'm tired and would like to be able to set up camp and rest. Anyway, I thought it was a traditional custom with Native peoples to always extend themselves to the guest in their homelands."

The whole time I sat in Alta-Dena's cab, looking down at them, the two camp cops just glared back with stony, passive aggression and thinly-veiled malice in their eyes. Like the time before with the Chumash man, I felt as if I were being treated like a second-class citizen.

As I directed Alta-Dena to pull off somewhere closeby, I knew I would not have an easy time getting across to the elders my New Frontier Breed declaration of peace, brotherhood and sisterhood.

Coasting to a stop on the side of the road, I at once undertook the spiritual preparations that I felt were needed to address the serious nature of the work that lay ahead.

Burning this time a wrapped stick of Sage sprigs and Cedar boughs, I bathed in their healing smoke to become sensitized to whatever good spirit forces might hear my silent prayers and make themselves known to me in some way. As the aromatic fragrance of the medicine herbs filled my lungs, infusing into my bloodstream the essence of their powers, my thought processes gradually became more elevated.

Another Lifetime -
Momentarily Relived

Another Remembrance of some Distant Past

Before I knew it, the onerous burden of the task that lay ahead of me drifted off into a blurred reverie of fond remembrances. Recalled were the times spent as an altar boy in Our Lady of Perpetual Help Church, undergoing Christian rites of purification with the help of sacred Myrrh and Frankincense. Those childhood remembrances, and all the Sage, Cedar and Sweetgrass-smudging years that followed, all slowly blended together as I drifted off into a trance-like state of mind. Hours later, the sweet-smelling smoke still hung heavy inside Alta-Dena's walls as I lay in my bunk, suspended in a semi-conscious meditative daze.

Suddenly, a loud rap against the side of my New Frontier Red River Cart jarred me awake, and I heard a gruff, unkind voice bark, "OKAY, HIPPIE! YAH CAN GO IN NOW!"

However, by the time I, and the other New Frontier Breeds present were allowed to enter, the ground's best campsites already were full of Indian's and their campers, tents and tipi's, leaving the rest of us to camp out wherever best we could.

The first thing I did was to dig out the large stack of copies I had of my *Mockingbird Declaration*, as I called it, approach the elder in charge and asked him, "Can you please see to it that this declaration is handed to every elder and spiritual leader at the gathering." It declared:

THIS ONE WISHES TO SPEAK TO YOU
AS A MOCKINGBIRD
OF HIS PEOPLES VOICES

My good wishes to you. May these words find you in good health. I hope in the future to be able to speak with you in person so that we both may come to a higher understanding of the things which concern us.

Many of my people as well as yours are confused, but there are those of us who are becoming increasingly clearer about our mutual medicine ways. We wish to bring these understandings to you now as gifts to exchange.

We are concerned that a bridge of mutual advantage be built between us. Though, at times, this seems a totally hopeless task that may not happen for maybe centuries, we still take it as a personal responsibility to try to build this bridge from our side to yours and offer our services in whatever way you may see fit.

As one who takes this responsibility seriously and, to the best of my ability, act as an interpreter for my people yet, at the same time, representing no one else save for myself, I extend to you the friendship, brotherhood and sisterhood of my people and seek to speak to you of the goodwill and warm hearts among us.

Were we meeting in some long ago time, we might not ask anything more of one another than to let us each safely and freely pass, while paying our mutual respects. We both know, I am sure, that there's much more to it now because of the tiny global village in which we live that grows ever tinier by the day.

Neither of us, perhaps, can ever forget nor forgive what has been done to us in distant, as well as more recent times. You have heard our children crying in the night and we have heard yours.

We both also know, I'm sure, that our peoples ancient pathways   must now lie alongside one another if we are to safeguard the future of our children and their children's children seven generations hence and beyond.

There are those among us who've once again begun to pick up the sacred drum of our respective peoples, and who are trying to listen for new songs, stories and dances to return to the people. We need your counsel and guidance in these matters and look to you for your good-will. We, in turn, expect not to come empty-handed but bear gifts of equal value to bring together the best of both our worlds.

At this time, I'm deeply saddened and distressed by the things I see happening in both our camps. In our encampments, the spiritual starving ones are everywhere and their want is so keen that they are extremely dangerous.

It's not surprising that many of you, as you've seen my people come to you as spiritually-bankrupt, beggar-refugees, have often turned us away with your disgust, indifference or contemptuous rage. It's no wonder that many of you often have felt such intense distrust or suspicion of my people. We both are aware of the many times when my people have reciprocated in-kind.

Because it has been so difficult in the past for us to seek out the legitimate spiritual teachers among your respective Nations, we've often had to seek out whomever was the most visible and accessible. It's simply a question of supply and demand. The more among my people who come forward, the more demand for teachers – any teachers – will increase. Unfortunately, without having anything upon which to compare and contrast what we're learning, some of the more needy or gullible among us tend to accept everything we hear or see, hook-line-and sinker.

The more we delve into your medicine ways, the more we get caught in the middle of long-standing vendettas between your traditionals and progressives, full-bloods and mixed-bloods. This has led to much confusion and disorientation.

Just as you are concerned about all the: Hollywood Indian medicine men and women; spiritual circuit shaman-showmen; traveling vision-questers, marketing their Castanada wares; snake-oil 'vision-in-a-bottle' peddlers; MacDonald hamburger-type Sacred Pipe–Sweat Lodge–Sun Dance franchises; so, too, are we. Rest assured that there are INDEED those among our side who intend to do something about them. This declaration is Step One!

WE need to come together as equals, representing One Face, One Heart & One Race, who intend to formulate a creative, constructive response to this problem.

From our side of the bridge, we can bring our keen mental powers and organizational clarity to accomplish such goals. Yet, when we come to the Sacred Circle you must be willing to accept and acknowledge that we have a different way of thinking, being and doing than you, which isn't better or worse but only different. Just another piece of the human puzzle that longs to put itself back together again and realize what still hidden images await the puzzle's completion.

Many of us already are organizing our encampments and circles upon which to try to rediscover our own small pieces of this great cosmic puzzle. Some of us are becoming oral storytellers again. Some of us, however incorrectly, are calling ourselves shamans. Such people are springing up everywhere in dance, music, literature and the theater. These are but the tip of the iceberg of a spiritual shift that is taking place in the hearts and minds of many ordinary folks among us.

But if we don't like what we're seeing by this explosion of energy and movement in this direction we need to come together and share these thoughts. We don't have any time left to remain focused upon our many differences due to ace, religion or color and use these things as barriers of mutual understanding.

Too many barriers already exist between us. But there are those among us who truly have the spirit of this land in our hearts, perhaps some of us have as much, if not more, of this spirit than even your own people.

I must speak to you of those among us who are wrongly calling themselves Native North Americans and Metis North Americans. But however unwise this is, it speaks to a world-wide rediscovery process of spiritual empowerment that is of pure heart looking for a voice and a body to house it.

This voice is saying that we all are mixed-blood/half-breeds of one sort or another, but first and foremost we all are of the Native Spirit of The Great Turtle.

Though my declaration was received by all the elders and spiritual leaders gathered there, never once, during the course of their Medicine Talk Gathering, was it ever directly addressed. Although a distasteful incident did occur that spoke to a dominant feeling, held by many natives towards white people as a whole, that already was in full evidence.

– MALICE IN THE RED HEART RESURFACES –

One early morning, as we all stood upon the Sacred Circle, sharing our common prayers for unity and healing as we did at the Chumash encampment, a young, blond, White female, standing opposite me on the circle's edge, commiteed a real *faux pas.*

For when it came her turn to share her innermost thoughts, the anorexic-looking hippie soon became carried away by her self-endulged 'shamanic raptures', which she began to endlessly rant on about.

During the entire time she went on, she seemed oblivious to the large number of highly-respected elders and spiritual leaders present, who stood awkwardly fidgeting in place, in the blazing hot sun, trying to calmly await their turn to speak.

The poor, pathetic woman seemed oblivious to the pitiful spectacle she was making of herself, talking about her private visions and dreams. Her starving spiritual condition by far outweighed her ability to intuit what all was going on around the circle. It was as if, from her point of view, we on the circle had willingly become her own private, captive audience that she was going to regal herself before.

As she persisted with her shamanic theater, my eyes scanned, one at a time, the faces and non-verbal body language of the Natives on the circle.

As one who knew better, I stood cringing within myself, wincing and feeling mortified, since I knew all too well what was going on in the minds and hearts of many of the Indians present.

In that moment, the words of the old Duwamish Chief Seathl ('Seattle') flashed into mind when he said of the White Man and Indian, "We are two separate races and must stay separate, there is little in common between us....Day and night cannot dwell together. The red man has always retreated before the advancing white man as the changing mists on the mountain slopes run before the blazing morning sun."

I knew the Natives present were not only thinking about the poor woman but about all us White's on the circle.

Still, I felt a pang of compassion for her. Because I saw this walking-wounded casualty of my people as no different than all those First Nation peoples who lost their own traditional roots, and the balance and harmony it once provided them. The only difference being that, instead of shamanic raptures, they resorted to booze, drugs, violence and passive aggression to mask their despair.

Russell Means, a Lakota warrior – who some say is the most important Sioux leader to come along since Crazy Horse or Sitting Bull – and who years later would became an unsuccess-ful Libertarian Party candidate for The Office of The President of The United States – was also standing on the circle.

No sooner did I finish thinking about what I would've liked to have said to the poor, spaced-out woman and those gathered there, when Means stepped forward into the center of the Sacred Circle and cut her short. It wasn't the fact that he did it but the harsh way in which he did that became an issue in my mind.

One could see by the distressed woman's body language – her head bowed low in humiliating defeat, her crossed arms fitfully clasping and beating themselves defensively at her chest, her legs nervously running in place, as if they couldn't wait to flee the scene – that she was devastated by the heavy-handed way Means chose to berate and demean her.

Throughout the rough dressing down that Means gave her, the look of incredulity upon her face said she was clueless that what she just did was to portray every aspect of the pushy, self-centered, domineering, insensitive White Man that First Nation peoples know only too well.

For her part, she probably thought she'd achieved an 'at oneness' with all the people, plants, animals, Earth, Sky and Universe present upon the circle, with whom she eagerly sought to enjoin with her visions.

Yet the rude, cruel way Russell Means chose to summarily dismiss her became the other side of the age-old Indian-European human equation that D.H. Lawrence referred to when he said, "Malice is the basic feeling in the Indian heart towards the White."

As Means stood beside the disconsolate hippie woman in the center of the Circle, the hard, cold look in his eyes summed up the past five centuries of sheer rage which Indians have felt from the loss of their autonomous, independent way of life.

Means seized the opportunity to look into the eyes of every one of us non-Indians on the circle and admonish us in the way one would chastize ignorant, selfish children.

His fierce stare again caused me to think of something else Chief Seathl meant when he said, "I will not mourn the passing of my people. Nor do I blame our white brother for causing it. We too are partly to blame. When our young men grow angry at some wrong, real or imagined, they make their faces ugly with black paint. They are hard and their cruelty knows no limits. And our old men cannot restrain them."

Means finished his vituperative tirade – which by then had all the elder's present looking red-faced with embarassment – by saying, "There's gonna come a time when you White's better not get in the way of me and my people. 'Cause if you do, we'll crush you like bugs."

Later that evening, at an honoring pow-wow for the elders, Means again took the opportunity to tell a searing racist joke about some Indians and Whites who suddenly found themselves stranded together in a life boat. The up-shot of the joke came when, given a life-and-death struggle, where push-comes-to-shove, the White's are all tossed overboard. The wild, raucous laughter Means joke elicited from the predominantly Indian audience, semed to highlight the underlying tenor of the gathering.

I thought to myself, "Okay, Geronimo! This may be about the right time for you and Alta-Dena to skedaddle on out of here. 'Cause your outnumbered, in hostile territory and there ain't no cavalry acomin'!" So off we quietly went.

– THE ANTICIPATION OF WHAT LAY AHEAD –

I was more anxious than ever to see Crystal Freesia after such a long absence. There was so much we had to renew in our lives together. Yet there was so much, too, that I wanted to do to move beyond all the endless controversies between the First Nation & White Man's worlds, the Metis & White Shamans, the full-bloods & mixed-bloods.

I was equally anxious to return to the Sonoma bioregion of 'Kuksu Nation', because I somehow sensed I would find there my 'Walden Pond' where, like Thoreau, I could pull off from the din of the world for as many years as he did to ponder life's higher principles. Like Whitman, I also needed to find a place to write my 'Leaves of Grass'. Or, like Gandhi, to simply find a *sanctum sanctorum* where I could 'withdraw from everything just to spin some cloth'. A place to 'spin the fabric' of my tales on paper, rather than work, to gain some inner clarity to my life and so adjust my needs, wants and desires accordingly.

I couldn't wait to see Crystal Freesia! But I also couldn't wait to leave to find my Walden Pond.

TURTLE ISLAND

ROAD SIGN # 16

HOW DO YOU DAILY
LISTEN TO THE ANIMALS
AND THE LAND
WHERE YOU LIVE?

The White Man must treat the beasts of this land as his brother. I am a savage and I do not understand the other way. I have seen a thousand rotting buffaloes on the prairies left by the White Man who shot them from a passing train....What is man without the beasts? If all the beasts were gone, men would die from great loneliness of spirit, for whatever happens to the beast also happens to man....One thing we know which the White Man will one day discover. Our God is the same God....This earth is precious to him. And to harm the earth is to heap contempt on its creator.

(Chief Seattle)

– Miwok Kuksu Dance Song –

(Sung When Kuksui Comes To Dance)

(A song so sacred that its sounds must remain a mystery, left to the longings of the imagination)

wila hena (Come On, Spirit) Sung 5X's
kuksui yomigo   .   Sung 2X's
wila hena   Sung 6X's
kuksui yomigo   Sung 2X's
wila hena   Sung 8X's
Ohhhhhhhhhhhhhh!

CHOCUAY BEGINNINGS:
DIALOGUES WITH THE SPIRIT WORLD

"PILGRIM", sadly wonders The Great Voice Of The Turtle, *"Chief Seattle's words have been spoken many times, in many different ways, by my native children over the past five centuries. As ever-growing numbers of my children among the plant, bird, fish and animal nations daily, almost hourly, go extinct, or are in danger of going extinct, Chief Seattle's words fall on deaf ears. Do his words speak to what you have seen in your lifetime? Do you feel as lonely as I do, that most of my native human and non-human children, who once lived where you do, now no longer inhabit that place? What ancient lessons have you learned from those few survivors among my children who are left? What kind of intimate relationships do you have with them or the spirits of those who now are gone? What steps have you taken to awaken those around you to the important roles my surviving native life will play in teaching your children and their children's children of many Living Times yet to come?"*

Crystal Freesia is the most-gifted healer I've ever met. This simple fact became more obvious each time Alta-Dena and I crossed back over The Medicine Line to Grandmother's Lands to be with her.

As great as her healing powers are, all the greater is her humility. For Crystal Freesia would be the last one to call herself a 'medicine person', and yet she's every bit one in the best sense of the meaning. She has that ability of all real healers to empower others to heal themselves, staying as much in the background as possible to allow the healed person to take the bulk of the responsibility and credit for their own healing process.

CRYSTAL FREESIA & TWIN RAINBOW

Each time I came into her presence and left, I felt that much more stronger and confident that I could continue onward towards wherever the odyssey fated I next should go.

"Lolum! Waimatha!", I cried out, "It's a joy to see you once more and move beneath your watchful gaze! It's always too short! Alta-Dena and I seem to leave as quickly as we come!"

"Che-che-yoh-ee! Che-che-yoh-ee!" ('Oh, Power above all others!'), goes the chant each time those snow-capped beauties fill my eyes again with their splendor; tantalizing me with the mystic gifts that those twin sisters, and their nearby twin brother-husband spires – *Swaikaos* and *Smanot* – daily offer up to the human world.

Following my chant, I give thanks to the *Sk wx̱_wú7mesh* ('Squ-ah-mish') people of that place who once introduced me to their own Earthdiver–hero figure – whih-NAHN-kwee-oh – to their twin-headed spirit helper – WHIHCH-ih-TAWL – and to their legend of the twin rainbow as the manifest soul of The Great Thunderbird.

whih-NAHN-kwee-oh
&
WHIHCH-ih-TAWL

The power of my spirit's intimate name constantly moves me to return to this place of twin mountains and twin spirit-helpers in a way that no matter how many times I leave, I'm pulled back again to be renewed.

"Kla-how-ya, tillicum!", I cry each time, in an old Chinook patois greeting or goodbye. "Kla-how-ya, Lolum! Kla-how-ya, Waimatha! Kla-how-ya, whih-NAHN-kwee-oh! Kla-how-ya, WHIHCH-ih-TAWL! Protect the journey South. Protect Crystal Freesia in our absence."

– MY WALDEN POND SOMEWHERE AWAITS –

As Alta-Dena and I went South, I pondered how mysterious every human being's journey is in this life. How we each are directed by unseen hands, minds and hearts in the invisible realm to do what we must, to go where we will, to fulfill some unfathomable longing or desire.

At one point, The Voice spoke out. "Is it not strange, lad!", it said, "that years before, your soul-mate should have received her advanced training as a healer in the very bioregion that I now direct you towards! There are many earth wisdoms that also await you there!" The Voice was right. Crystal Freesia had indeed spent several years at Sonoma State University, whose Department of Psychology, in those days, was one of the cutting-edge leaders in the nation of humanistic psych-ological–spiritual theory and practice.

Now here I was, heading back to that same spot, hoping to find, somewhere in its *Kuksu Nation*, a 'Walden Pond' that was to become my own cutting-edge 'University of the Great Turtle' center of advanced learning, through which I could matriculate.

 Caught once more under the spell of 'The Mountain Chief' and his wife, as some traditionals refer to Mount Shasta and Shastina, I recalled again one of the Wintu-Karuk peoples creation stories about Shasta.

"It was atop The Mountain Chief", say the elders, "that Creator wished into life the first man, woman and bear from three pieces of the same tree branch. Taking up a big stick, Creator broke off one piece, stuck it into the Mountain's side and said 'This shall be a Man'. And the stick turned into a Man. But Creator knew that just as The Mountain Chief has its female mountain-companion to balance himself, so, too, did Man need the other side of his nature for balance. So Creator broke off a second piece of the stick, stuck it into the Mountain's side and said 'This Shall Be a Woman'. And the stick turned into a Woman. But Creator had one piece of the stick left. After a time, Creator said, 'This Man and Woman will need a teacher to show them how to heal themselves and each other'. And with that, Creator stuck the last piece of stick into the Mountain's side and said, 'This Shall be a Bear'. And the stick turned into a Bear."

"WAKA NUNI, TUCKI WUCKIE!", I chanted as Alta-Dena and I passed beyond view of Mount Shasta and Shastina, "Grandfather! Grandmother! as I enter again into your once great territory of the bear, I ask for the Spirit of Bear to heal me and make this journey even stronger. AHO!"

– CHOCUAY TOUCHES MY SPIRIT –

Alta-Dena and I traveled the length of the Pacific Coast – from a warm Southern Californian summer afternoon in Chumash Territory, to a cold British Columbian winter's morning in Lil'Wat Country – returning this time to Northern California to the glorious dawning of a

Pomo-Miwok springtime. Still hot as ever in pursuit of an new-old dream-vision of life to harmoniously balance, within myself, the White Man and First Nation's two worlds, and so heed Chief Seattle's long-ago sagely words of warning.

If our lives are seasons, each a fugue-like variation on a theme, then this important crossroad in the odyssey could be called 'The Indian Summer Keynote' of the odyssey's narrative.

For the time about to be spent in Kuksu Territory would prove to be one of those key passages in life's renewal of winter and rebirth of spring that come together in the mellowness of a harvest moon's ritual of thanksgiving. Its sonorous notes harkening forth the death knell to the programming of the White Man-side of my brain which for years sought to breed within me too many feelings of isolation, greed and ego.

Alta-Dena and I found ourselves immediately drawn to a narrow watercourse that wound itself through the nearby town of Petaluma.

Situated high upon a knoll above that watercourse – that the local White people call 'Willow Brook', but which New Frontier Breeds and the Coast Miwok ('Me-wok') call *Chocuay* ('Pretty Willow') – was an old chicken farmer's house. Like the way Dove's tipi made itself available, during the Earth Healing Ceremony at Eyalmox, this simple ordinary house presented itself as a humble place of sojourn.

Chocuay – located in what some people refer to as 'Shasta Bioregion', or other's say is within 'Kuksu Nation' rather than in California – winds close by the sacred site of *Likatuit*, an ancient Miwok village of the *Lekahtewut*, or 'Crossways Willow' people. Stone grinders, arrowheads, amulets and other artifacts have been found all along her banks and surrounding hillsides.

By the time Alta-Dena and I came upon her, Chocuay, historically, already witnessed many newcomers pass along her way, from: Spanish Conquistadors or Russian explorers plying her narrow waterways, looking for an inland passage to the Pacific Ocean; followed by Mexican soldiers later crossing her on their way to the *El Camino Real*; to Yankee hunters feverishly killing every living thing along her length, to feed the invading hordes of gold-crazed miners who were pouring into the nearby Bay of San Francisco.

In more modern times, Chocuay has been denied her role as the beautiful life-giver and purifier that she once was before the coming of the White Man. Chocuay relegated instead to the indignity of becoming a dried-up, polluted body of water which the local White townspeople seldom, if ever, pay attention to excepting when she over-flows her banks, thereby causing them some temporary inconvenience for which they generally curse and demean her. Once the inconvenience has passed, she's once again is forgotten about and allowed to return back to her place of ignominy within the life of the new immigrant humans who surround her.

Those immigrant hordes unaware or indifferent to the resident life force that still teems within and around her. The life cycles of Turtle, Muskrat, Crayfish and Trout still tenaciously assert themselves there. Turtle, Muskrat, Crayfish and Trout Nation's intent upon surviving in spite of the hordes of cheap thrill-seeking, gun-crazed teenage youth who make regular forays along Chocuay's banks; searching for her peaceful, innocent, unsuspecting denizens to use as idle target practice.

These forayer youth ignorant of the fact that they're the direct descendants, or sorry benefactors, if you will, of a White Man mentality which has continued, non-stop, to do the same thing along her banks for over a century and a half.

But by the time I first met her, Chocuay's spirit was still strong. She patiently awaiting the day when the new native humans around her will reinstate her to her rightful place of respect she once enjoyed among the Miwok.

In a not too distant past of 140 years or so – almost within the lifetime of one very old man or woman – Chocuay felt the movements of the vast numbers of non-human nations who also once came to her in respectful ways, seeking sustenance.

Untold numbers of Antelope, California Tule Elk, Roosevelt Elk, Columbia Black-Tailed Deer, California Grizzly, Cinnamon and Black Bears, Bobcat, Cougar, Bald Eagle, Condors – not to mention the hundreds of thousands of waterfowl and other smaller critters – all once flourished beside her. Their vast numbers, for all intents and purposes, totally wiped off the face of the land in the period of two or three years, during the height of the Gold Rush era, by European hunters and thrill-seekers.

– THE STRANGE TEACHINGS OF ANOTHER FLAG REVEALED –

The California Grizzly, once found in great numbers along Chocuay's banks, only existed in dim memory by the time I arrived.

CALIFORNIA REPUBLIC

Yet, considering that the White Man killed off every last Griizzly with great relish, I thought it a strange introductory commentary that the White Man there has chosen to turn around and so honor the Grizzly, as its most esteemed symbol with which to hold up before the world's eyes, by placing its image upon their State Flag.

From the perspective of indigenous peoples the world over, to so totally destroy something, only to then turn around and revere or hallow it, is not the act of a civilized race of people but of barbarians.

This bizarre contradiction between what's real and fantasy, manifested at the local level, as well. For the origin of *Petaluma*, is a name that comes from the language and traditions of the old Coast Miwok. Yet all the Coast Miwok were either killed-off or run-off before anyone bothered to ask them about the rich legacy behind the name that the White occupiers felt obligated (guilty conscience, perhaps?) or compelled (their own spirit voice's speaking to their higher self?) to use to call their town and themselves. Like Chocuay, the legacy of this ancient Miwok place-name still awaits the higher consciousness of the White Man there to wake up to the many mysteries it still has to offer.

But one could replace the names of Miwok, Petaluma and Grizzly Bear with 10,000 or more names, describing similar historical scenarios all across North America, and the story's outcome would read the same.

Faced with these initial thoughts upon my arrival in Kuksu Nation, a critical question arose that demanded an answer. "OK, THEN!", I found myself shouting aloud, "What really constitutes a civilized person or culture from that of a barbarians?"

According to the White Man's dictionary, to be civilized means to be socially advanced. It's the up-lifting of a person or culture beyond certain barbaric traits. It presupposes that the inherent rights of 'mankind' are recognized and protected. Yet to be a barbarian is to be ruthless and cruel. A barbaric person or culture is one that commits brutal deeds. Its usage stems from a Greek root which means 'foreign' or 'ignorant'. It presupposes a lack of civilized standards and a contempt for knowledge and wisdom.

This enquiry led to the questions, "If the White Man's 'Christian' way of life in places like Petaluma has always been that of a civilization's, how, by eliminating so many human and non-human nations there, has its culture become socially advanced? How has it become culturally uplifted? What barbaric traits or cruel deeds did it lift itself above by replacing its Miwok predecessors? What contempt of knowledge or wisdom must it one day own up to?"

Continuing this enquiry, I wondered, "When the Coast Miwok lived along Chocuay's banks, these now extinct non-human nations flourished. But was it cruel, or even barbaric, to allow these nations to flourish? Did they flourish because the Miwok lacked certain 'civilized, Christian' standards, or was it in spite of the Miwok's 'primitive' religion?"

Given the subsequent destruction of the native landscape and annihilation of so many indigenous life forms in places like Petaluma, I couldn't help but wonder, "What inherent rights of mankind have been duly recognized and protected? If Western Civilization is indeed continually uplifting itself in Petaluma and elsewhere, what will it need to do, in the next one hundred years, to advance itself from where it was in 1840 or in 1940?"

Whether civilized or barbaric, the European, Asian and African ways of life that have rooted themselves in the New World, historically, have not allowed many life forms their natural right to procreate and live as the Creator originally intended. They've been forever deprived of these rights, yet those who now live where they once did also have been deprived of their inalienable rights to know and learn from them.

An ancient sacred spirit drew me to itself in Petaluma to learn its many wisdoms. But the more I tried to settle there, the more I realized how much I've been deprived of. As time passed, I felt that much more personally cheated that I wasn't able to hear what all it was that they, like Mockingbird and the many voices of life it rejoices in sharing with others, would have had to teach me.

For days on end, I wandered along Chocuay, searching through the limbs and branches of every tree along her banks, for the vast numbers of birdlife who once were there. "Chocuay", I cried out, "To what invisible place have all your vast numbers retreated? What can I do to encourage you, my winged relatives, and especially you Condor, wherever you are, to once more return and regal me with your songs, colors and unique, timeless ways?"

Coming upon a clearing of Live Oaks, or cresting a rise in the golden, rolling hills, I wondered anew, "To what invisible place have all you Tule Elk, Antelope and Grizzly's retreated, as well?"

Desiring to reach out to where'er they'd all gone, my wild, gentle, questing spirit struggled in vain pursuit. With each futile mental attempt came the mixed feelings of a child-like eagerness to intimately know these kinfolk and renew our relations, while my cynical adult mind knew, all along, that all this could never be.

As this abject sense of loneliness and aloneness grew more intense, all the deeper became the unconscionable despair, forlorn and defiant rage that kept welling up.

It was then that I began to better understand, to appreciate, how deeply saddened First Nation peoples have become over the centuries, and how much pain they continue to suffer because of the same personal loss to their lives. I could better grasp how horrified their ancestors must have been by their initial contacts with such a crass European mentality that could so wantonly destroy so many levels of consciousness, including its own.

Like Chief Seattle, I was incredulous that this mentality would even ignore the prophetic warnings in its own Christian holy book which declares, "He will bring to ruin those ruining the earth" (Revelation 11:18). Or that willingly denies its own prophecies in: Isaiah 11:6,7,9; Matthew 10:29; Luke 12:6; and even those in Genesis 1:28 & 9:4,5.

"Chief Seattle!", I called out, to wherever he might be in the invisible realm, "For any culture to ignore even its own religious warnings and instructions is nothing less than a calculated, deliberate act of suicide and omnicide by a mentally-deranged culture that has run amuck."

A significant postscript to this line of thought, that underscores the enormity of the gulf which still separates Turtle Island's and North America's mentalities, was offered up through the sad death of a Bear brother.

– TALE OF A DEAD BRUIN WARRIOR –

The bear's death scene, spread across the front page of a local news-paper, sent deep, jabbing pangs through my heart. For it was like seeing a great warrior forced even in death, to suffer outrageous indignities, trussed upside-down and hung like a great stuffed Mexican piñata, while his unworthy human foes *counted coup* beside his mag-nificient, mute spirit. "GRR! RROAR!" growled my own bear clan voice in wild, abandoned fury.

"How many times", cried out The Voice, "has this drama appeared in as many different photographs and paintings? How many times have other anonymous facesvincing those same smug, superior grins – appeared beside another fallen hero-warrior buffalo, elk, wolf or Indian-Metis-Irish-Tyrolean patriot?"

That newspaper headline continued to gnaw away. "*Predator?*", shouted The Voice, "There's a helluva lot more real predators among

Predator Bruin Dispatched

humans than non-humans. *Bruin*? What healing powers – that go back to man, woman and bear's simultaneous creation from the same sacred branch *of* life – once were honored by that old High German-Dutch term? *Dispatched*? In what cold, business-like, off-handed way was that ancient bruin power stilled?"

As Alta-Dena and I drove across the Petaluma River, on our way back to Chocuay, she practically drove herself while I, with the Bear's death scene in one hand and a pen in the other, composed on a pad:

– Requiem For A Warrior –

On Sunday last, a large, proudly-defiant, adult male Black Bear, thought to be one of the two last of his kind known to inhabit the northeast region of Lower Sonoma County, died from a bullet wound to the head because he was a "headache" to the local humans.

His real problem, like that of so many of his/my/our brethren, was that he tried to survive too near humans who feared him and couldn't be bothered with trying to figure out how they might co-exist. He, like so many others among us, was simply considered "expendable". Bear's fatal error was that he misjudged the fact that even though he was legally protected, he was considered of less *economic* importance than the domesticated brethren he took for his sustenance. Brethren who, themselves, were solely kept alive by their human master-predators so they, too, could one day be murdered or, ahem, in human parlance "harvested", so as to realize their predator owner's a handsome profit.

In life, Bear stood seven feet tall, weighed 400 pounds and possessed powerful paws seven inches in width. A loner, he came from the north where he made an annual circuit, with each season, in the Mayacamas mountains east of Sonoma Valley. A natural-born botanist and herbalist, he knew the fruition times and locations of every kind of wild and cultivated vegetation in the natural and man-made world. His keen sense of smell could catch, from great distances away, the scent of a succulent tuber or ripening fruit. He could be miles removed from the human animals who surrounded him and yet still detect subtle changes in their different moods and emotions by the chemical odors they emitted.

For years, he was known to have adroitly avoided the human predator's ever-encroaching civilization, traveling at night while hiding in the daytime. Such a feat might even be considered legendary given the dense human populations in the surrounding urban and rural areas, the countless packs of dogs as well as the many eager trophy hunters and blood-lusting, thrill-seekers who'd heard about him and kept an ever vigilant eye. Yet now all the unwritten, fascinating tales he had to tell of an exiled life in his own native homeland will never be known and can only be imagined.

His real guilt, for which he was summarily condemned to death, was that he was naturally fond of young saplings which made him unwanted by the timber companies and cultured Christmas tree farmers who make money *off of* the tree peoples dead bodies. Bear also naturally fond of the bee peoples honey *off of* which the apiarists make money before killing the hive each winter. Bear's crime not that he wanted to make an excessive profit off of what other's produce, but that he simply desired to survive and propagate his kind like his two-legged brethren.

The stirring events which led to Bear's death underscore his prowess as a hunter and skill as a survivalist in avoiding his pursuers. Before being taken, he skillfully eluded the best efforts of a professional hunter-trapper who resolutely stalked him for twenty days. The agonizing tale of his last futile efforts to outwit the hunter will never be known. Finally cornered, realizing his time of truth had come, he turned and, as any proud warrior would do, valiantly rallied.

The trapper, commenting on his own part in the taking of Bear's life, noted in passing, "If we could, we would have transported it elsewhere and set it free, but once a bear begins serious depredation such as this, you have to assume he'll continue doing it. I think it was a right decision."

BUT WHY, BEAR, must we humans always assume this attitude of depredation about you and your people? What would you have us do about the way we humans now live or could in the future to accomodate in our midst all of the wild nations of humans and non-humans, including the biggest and strongest like yourself?

In the future, will our children and their children's children know only the smallest, weakest, tamest of those few non-human nations who've been allowed co-existence? The trapper candidly expressed the real truth of the matter when he stated, "I don't feel that I killed the bear. I think we all did."

Yet what satirical mockery it is, Bear, that the human animals of the place you once called your homeland should now herald your clan by placing your image on their state flag! Why do they everywhere still proudly wave your brown, hulking form to the world from high atop all their flag poles? Why, on all their blue and gold roadsigns posted along their highways and byways, do they highlight a silhouette of your massive body embedded in an outline of California's borders? What memory of you do they hope to honor, recall or reclaim?

Each time I pass amongst a grove of ancient redwoods, I sense how deeply sad and lonely they are that they no longer can share all the joys of life with you as they once did!

Oh Bear Brother! Were I Creator, I would wish you back to life with the quick thrust of one of your Sister Redwood's branches deep into the soft, receptive, flesh of our mother earth. But it is not to be! Go in peace, My Wild Brother! We humans can only beg our God to forgive us our trespasses!

As Alta-Dena crossed over the Petaluma River, I wondered again about the equally mysterious nature of the name that waterway bears.

Every day, for well over a century, since the first White Europeans seized the area from the Miwok and took for themselves an Indian name they knew little about, the local townspeople have continued to utter, over and over like a mantra, the strange sound and meaning that *'Petaluma'* seeks to raise within their consciousness.

"What lost memory of innocence!", I shouted out in Alta-Dena's cab as the two of us went, "What vital earth connection or secret of life is *Petaluma* trying to elicit within all you humans here? Wake up!"

So, PILGRIM. Return now to your natural mentor to ask it some of the questions raised here. What 'Chocuay' place have you known in your life that has similarly raised your consciousness? Who has served as your 'Bear Spirit' that has caused you to become the Town Crier of a new, deep-ecological, holistic sense of community responsibilities for *All Your*

Relations? How have you sought to become the eulogizer of whatever spirit sings to your own wild, gentle voice? **Be Off With Ye! Go!**

WELCOME **BACK**! Imagine, for a moment, what it would mean to North America if all of us, who recognize ourselves as 'Keepers-of-the-Sacred Place' in which we live, were to take it upon ourselves, as part of our own odyssey, to in some way herald the spiritual uniqueness of where we live or the places we've known.

If just one of us, from every bioregion in North America, did so as a part of our own vision-seeking, imagine the rich collection of Turtle Island images that eventually everywhere would emerge. Just think of the extent of the collective healing power we then could generate for good and so turn everything around 180 degrees.

– A SACRED DOORWAY LEADS INTO MOCKINGBIRD LODGE –

The time spent at Mockingbird Lodge, as I came to know the humble chicken farmer's house that sat high above Chocuay, indeed became the Walden Pond I sought. It quickly became a key benchmark of an inner shift towards an all-encompassing spiritualization process.

A shift towards what William Bridges, psychologist and author, once penetratingly described, in *The Season of Our Lives*, as:

Away from the linear and so, away from the mechanistic; it is towards the cyclical and so towards the organismic. It is away from understanding things by connecting them to their future outcomes. This shift has a particularly great impact upon our view of life's second half, in the great point of passage called *dying*. If these shifts sound familiar, it is because the spiritual tradition of several millenia have established them as the first stages of the turning from the secular to the religious outlook. The move away from the rectilinear shapes of the Western World and toward the watercourse of the East.

If, as the old saying goes, "Life begins at 40", then Mockingbird Lodge was where, after four decades of nomadic wanderings, I stole myself aways from the world to gain a fresh new perspective on life.

It fell to Mockingbird Lodge and Chocuay to be where the odyssey-within-an-odyssey to compile the narrative of these Turtle Island eco-adventures received its genesis.

Like Mahatma Gandhi who "needed to withdraw from everything just to spin some cloth" – or like Henry Thoreau when he said *of* Walden Pond, "I went there because I had got ready to go" – I, too, needed to finally stop and weave together some inner clarity before I got ready to go again.

Life lived on a shoestring became an acceptable exchange for the solitude so eagerly craved. The time taken for quietude, reading, writing and reflection; the intense bonds created in community with friends, the land and its natural life forms that surrounded Mockingbird Lodge; the organic way this holy place *of* withdrawl evolved its name in my consciousness; each became a poignant living reminder *of* the real essence behind Chief Seattle's prophetic vision.

Each day spent away from all the marketplace's glittering tinsel pretensions, smoke-and-mirror deceptions, mind-numbing dis-information and vicious backbiting, served to amplify and affirm Turtle Island's relationship-building process that I desired to make an even more integral part *of* my future life.

In the end, this new cycle within the odyssey simply proved to be a most special time taken just to sit in silent tribute to 'The Coming-Home Ceremony', 'The Great Awakening' that was taking shape within me.

It set into motion the fulfillment *of* a fervent, life-long desire to communicate to others what this coming-home, awakening has felt like in the course *of* growing up and evolving through life.

With the opening and closing *of* each day's narrative that was to follow for the next two years, the sheer physical act *of* writing unexpectedly became a separate process *of* self-realization unto itself.

The intense introspection that followed at once demanded that I begin to slough off aspects *of* my past life like the dead skin *of* a snake.

Every word chosen, possessive *of* its own life-force, served as but an outer reflection *of* an inner movement taken to manifest this new skin pattern *of* the kind *of* Turtle Island human being I longed to become.

The right word, as if with a mind *of* its own, refused to come 'til, somehow, as if by magic, the requisite psychological-spiritual shift first occurred. The recognition *of* when that moment had come announced itself, each time, through the clarity *of* the word, or turn *of* phrase, which heralded, "It is Good! So be it!"

Each word – like a faithful sentinel or skilled guide – led me ever-deeper into an inner frontier that beckoned. Every word as if a therapist, who cajoled me to probe ever-farther beyond the: rat-race 9 to 5; violent nightly TV episode or internet game *of* conquest; offensive lyrics *of* a pop song; escapist Friday night-at-the-movies or saloon swill; frivolous weekend shopping spree in-the-mall or two week summer holiday malaise; that life threatened to become.

The word's collective meditations suggesting that the journey to discover a new Turtle Island skin pattern to clothe myself with, had something more to do with becoming part of *Ordo Vagorum Gyrovagus* than with pursuing one creature comfort after another. To become, as the poet Gary Snyder once put it:

Part of The Brotherhood of The Road. One of those world-walkers – most ancient of elites. Those wandering fools and scholars, peripatetic saints, preaching instreals, itinerant thinkers, rainmakers, back-packing dreamers, tinkers, errant monk-knights, mendicant artists, peregrinating dancers, easy riders, minnesingers, noble hobo's, goliards, bhikkus troubadours, Wander-vogel gypsy-hippies, sannyasins, journey men or journey women, dharma bums of the legendary trip-trap, roving poets, God-made nomads, Eastern wayfarers, staff-bearing sadhus, footloose renouncers, Never-Returners, super-tramps, pilgrimsof the guru-circuit, holy hikers, thousand-faced heroes rambling empty-handed the easier to scale celestial walls. Garbed in ochre robes or folded togas, kimonos, astral-blue jeans, Sufi-patched, cloaked and sporting a Christic cockle-shell or "clothes in space", naked as the way is long. The Boddhisattva at large, wholly engaged in questing for the warm-blooded grail of the sacred self. For love of Lady Poverty or of the irresistable open road, the prince leaves his palace forever in the dead of night, the commonoer his solid state hearth, saying *"No to owning, Yes to being!"*, in total reponse to the call of the mystic adventure. Birds of passage, these vagabonds have always mapped the spiritual routes, migrating from Bamboo Grove to Celtic Cave, across the vast Amerian flats, ever in search of the miraculous, traveling as lightly as possible, the better to be everywhere and no-where at home.

This consciousness-raising process the same as that which D.H. Lawrence meant when he wrote:

You can't have a new, easy skin before you have sloughed the old, tight skin...The slow forming of the new skin underneath is the slow sloughing of the old skin. And sometimes this immortal serpent feels very happy, feeling a golden glow of a strangely-patterned skin envelope him. And sometimes he feels sick, as if his very entrails were being torn out of him, as he wrenches once more at his old skin, to get out of it...He's got to have his new skin on him before ever he can get out. And he's got to get out before his new skin can ever be his own skin. So there he is, a torn, divided monster.

The gift offered up by Mockingbird Lodge was that the ability to acquire such a new skin pattern forever comes through the development of one's natural observational powers to really hear, see, and feel what all of life around one's self is constantly attempting to inform them about. To simply use all the senses to become more consciously aware of the *ingness* – the *isness* – of the world and one's tiny role within it. What exactly this means, first made itself known in a way least expected.

– A SACRED NAME ORGANICALLY EVOLVES ITSELF –

One day, awhile sitting at a secluded garden table-desk, on the red-tiled sun-deck of my Petaluman sanctum sanctorum – preparing to put pen to paper, to set down what spiritual grains of wisdom had been harvested from yet another Indian Summer – my attention was drawn to the sky realm.

It was in that moment that two most unusual gifts were offered forth by the spirit world, seemingly as symbols of the writing's inner and outer quest. One spiritual gift manifested itself in the form of a Red-Tailed Hawk feather and the other came, in the same instant, through the song of a Mockingbird.

The Hawk feather became a symbol of the wild, passionate, native freedom my soaring spirit sought to express upon the blank pages of the open journal. The Mockingbird's song a symbol of the gentle, lyrical beauty of the many spirit voices of Turtle Island, for whom I sought to act as a spokesperson.

With eyes closed, head reverently bowed, the open palm of either hand resting upon the open journal, The Voice began to utter in my ear, "Lad! This great journey of words I am about to set you out upon will become your life's own Iliad. The long-ago vision you received from Pisko, while atop Joe Thunder Hawk's Holy Hill, has been preparing you all along for this most arduous of path's. You must be prepared to sacrifice everything as I call upon you to begin the arduous struggle that is necesary to reduce your life down to words-upon-a-sheet-of-paper. Much will be asked of you. You will be challenged many times to go far beyond the levels of frustration and ambiguity you presently can tolerate. You will be buffeted by many forces that will try to get you to turn and flee or give up. But do not worry! The Great Spirit of the Bear is with you always!"

As my eyes slowly opened – and my hand groped for the pen to begin to jot down something on the journal's fly-leaf about this proverbial first step of the ten thousand mile, two hundred thousand word odyssey that lay ahead – my attention suddenly became riveted to the sky realm.

Curiously, the shadow of some object began to waver upon the journal's stark-white, blank pages. As I stared down at it, the circling shadow grew larger and larger 'til it began to look like a feather.

As I glanced up to see what it was, a Red-Tailed Hawk feather, descending from the vault of clear-blue sky overhead, slowly drifted down.

What seemed like an eternity passed, as the feather's lazy fluttering spirals in the wind carried it ever-closer to where I sat with *Little Meg* – a Calico cat-assistant-soulmate, named in honor of one of Louisa May Alcott's characters in the novel, *Little Women*.

Meanwhile, Little Meg continued her loud, rhthymic, machine-like purr's as she lay beside pen and journal, unaware of the great drama in the spirit world that was slowly unfolding.

Finally, with one last, sudden gush of wind, the hawk feather, incredibly, came to rest upon the very page of the open journal that caused Little Meg to abruptly flinch, take one hard look at the feather and instantly kick into her people's ancient, involuntary, strange-sounding, cat-hunting-bird-mouth-twitching cackle

Half-laughing over Meg's antics, half-dumbfounded by the feather's mysterious appearance, I stared at the pale pinkish-brown, stripped feather 'til my eyes took to frantically searching the sky realm for the bearer of this unbelievably-good omen. But the deep-blue sky was empty, save for a few strange-shaped, wispy, abalone-shell coloured clouds and one lone, faint, rainbow-coloured sun-dog that hung in the sky.

Picking up the Red-Tail feather between thumb and forefinger, I began waving it in a gentle, ceremonial way, as if it was a smudge stick of holy incense, over Little Meg's and my head before everywhere reverently patting our bodies with it as a form of silent supplication.

Meg actually seemed to like this impromptu ritual as she resumed her own purring ritual, while this time sprawling herself out, spreadeagle, across the open journal, as if she desired to absorb every last bit of the words that hadn't yet been written but which she already sensed were set down somewhere in the spirit realm.

"Ho, Little Brother!", telepathically shouted the feather, "I am the Keeper-of-The-Spirit of your journey. Place me within the journal as your soaring spirit's own book marker of progress."

At the same time, while all this was happening, a Mockingbird, sitting atop the upper-most-branch of a nearby pear tree, laden with fruit, trilled a rich medley of his repertoire that included everything from a bull frog and hawk to a jack-hammer. In the days, weeks and months that followed, Mockingbird religiously appeared atop that pear tree, as if he were conducting a ritual. Each dawn and dusk he flitted from branch to branch, while recounting the prolific litany of life of all his relations of both the sky and earth realms.

Every time Mockingbird appeared, my bardic mind would set off a wanderin' through all the amazing tales of his relation's countless exploits.

However, not only did Mockingbird imitate and amplify the songs of others, but he sang his own original compositions and medleys, each one an intricate combination of his ever-expanding repertoire.

But Mockingbird, singing to my spirit's ears, also trilled:

Listen to how many beautiful songs of life already are being sung by my relatives. I relish the chance to repeat them for you, but not just repeat them FOR I AM MOCKINGBIRD! I have the power to sing them in ways never before heard, that will cause you to marvel at the rich bounty and joy of this world that we daily bring to you from on high. We birds, you know, have magical properties. We know the secrets of many things for we can see far and wide. But do no take our word for it. Listen to our morning songs and then listen to your own heart and spirit soar with it. Listen to the wisdom it brings you. Think long upon the spiritual meaning of our feathers. They are symbols of natural, lofty wisdom and inspired thought. Of humility, as well, for even the greatest and most majestic among us must come down to nest within our Mother each night and, in so doing, remind you humans that no one of us, however old or great we may be, can forever live above all other life. HEAR ME WELL, LITTLE BROTHER! For I sing to you from atop this pear tree to remind you of the rich fruit of this life which you have been given as gifts to unselfishly share with your own kind. As you continue to write, do not desire so much the rich songs of others. If you feel them to be out of key, or wish to repeat them in your own special way as I do, then sing them in the key of yourself. Make yourself the keynote of your peoples voices. Pass all their songs onto others so that they may have an opportunity to also hear their beauty.

Mockingbird didn't speak in words as we human use. Although the oral traditions of Turtle Island tell of a time, during Native peoples golden age as hunters and gatherers, when they spoke directly to all living creatures and the creatures, themselves, understood and spoke in whatever dialect the native person understood.

"But", say the oral traditions, "because you humans committed so many violations against the Natural Rights & Spiritual Laws of Life, all the non-human nations now can only be understood by you when they telepathically speak to you through your imagination."

Brave Buffalo, an old-time Lakota spiritual man, once said of such things,:

> I have noticed in my life that all men have a liking for some special animal, tree, plant or spot of earth. If men would pay more attention to these things that speak to their heart, and seek what is best to do to make themselves worthy of that animal, tree, plant or spot to which they are so attracted, they might have dreams that will purify their lives. Let a man decide upon his favorite animal, bird, fish, tree or plant and make a study of it, learning its innocent ways. Let him learn to understand its sounds and motions. The animals want to communicate with men but *Wakan Tanka* - The Great Mystery of Life – does not intend they shall do so directly. Man must do the greater part in securing an understanding.

– MAKING MYSELF WORTHY OF MOCKINGBIRD –

Following the lead of wise men like Brave Buffalo and Chief Seattle, I began to wonder, "Ok! But how, Mockingbird might I make myself worthy of you and your people?"

One night, while lying on my cozy, four-seasons, outdoor wicker divan-bed, set beneath a tall Elm I called 'The Dream Helper', I began to chant aloud to the Great Spirit of Mockingbird.

"Heya yeh! Heya hey, ahey, hey, hey, hey!", I cried out, "Oh, wise flying one! Give me a dream. Tell me how to begin to use your people's lives as examples to live by."

In the dream that came that night, Mockingbird's spirit said:

Make your story a vehicle for the many voices of the new millennium's frontier of the spirit. Sometimes these voice will be mockingly-strident or full of satire. Sometimes they will be persuasive yet scolding or light-hearted and ecstatic with joy.

Without even consciously knowing it, these notations already had become heavily-influenced by these observations and telepathic dialogues with Mockingbird.

Learned while noting Mockingbird's curious mannerisms and some-times odd behavior was how he is unable to refrain from singing his dis-tinctive song all day long and sometimes even into the night. His life lived as if one continual motion, flitting from place to place, pouring out a ripple of song wherever he goes. Mockingbird rightfully enjoying his time-honored reputation for being a valiant warrior, who will doggedly fight to protect his homelands, often dying if need be in its defense.

"Did the dream", I wondered, while lying in my outdoor wicker bed one morning, watching the Sun break over the distant Petaluman hills to the East, "mean to follow the curious ways of Mockingbird, as the best way to purify my life? If Mockingbird is calling out to me, what different life forms are calling out to other New Frontier Breeds? Have these natural messengers also already become higher teaching lessons in their lives? Or am I all alone in trying to pick up these old ways?"

So, PILGRIM. Take this second opportunity to again close these covers and go off to some quiet natural place. Once there, ponder what non-human life form or forms have been attracted to you for some un-explainable reason. Have you made a study of them, as Brave Buffalo has suggested? What have you learned about their mannerisms? What have they taught you about yourself? How have they helped to purify your life?

Be Off With Ye! Go!

WELCOME BACK! The Old Wise Ones of Turtle Island say that in listening and watching for these natural messengers to come into our lives, we must remain ever-mindful of how to distinguish their real voices from those artificial ones we constantly manufacture within ourselves through our many self-delusions.

In recent decades, such cruel, illusory tricks of the mind have often caused the odyssey's of more than a few naive, gullible New Agers and White Shamans to end up in one mental or spiritual box canyon after another. The Old Wise Ones quick to point to these messengers as the best way to help them discover their own sacred names, rituals, symbols, ceremonies and stories to use among their people.

Previous to these telepathic contacts and observations of Mockingbird, the attempt had been made, numerous times, to artifically name that old chicken farmer's place. Yet each time the effort was made to 'rationally' come up with a 'meaningful' name, the fit seemed wrong until that day when Mockingbird's call instantly signaled the natural name for the house and its surrounds.

Mockingbird continued to encourage me to expand my listening and observational powers by tuning into the other 'Songs of Nature' that also inundated my senses, attempting to recount their own tales of life's trials and tribulations, marvels and joys.

– ANOTHER WALDEN POND IS BORN –

As time passed, the more I listened to the multitude of Nature's songs, all the more grew the realization that these halting attempts at journal-writing had become integral to the natural rituals, ceremonies and songs that were part of the ordinary, everyday lives of the wealth of human and non-humans who moved all 'round Mockingbird Lodge.

Before consciously being able to grasp the import of what all along was going on, Mockingbird Lodge turned into a modern 'Walden Pond', and I its would-be 'Thoreau'.

What began moving invisibly between each line and page of the journal's scribbles, were thousands of Walden-like experiences. Each experience a profoundly-moving one that simultaneously brought great pleasure as well as enormous agony since, as powerful as they all were, I knew not all of them could be written down.

Like rich stories woven into an old Navajo rug, that can never be known but only imagined, the life in-between these lines began to sing – to pulsate – with all those glorious, ever-shifting, subtle moods of Californian light at dawn and dusk, in the spring, summer, fall and winter.

Each line singing of the many gatherings of human and non-human relations who regularly assembled, in holy companionship, upon Mocking-bird Lodge's grounds. Each line pusating in honor of some of their relations dying and leaving behind bereaved families in sorrowful mourn-ing. Some singing and pulsating, in turn, on high, with the childlike bleating of young goats, crying sweet songs of innocence in harmony with the comical braying of a mule with loving eyes. Others singing, on low, with the gentle whinny of a young colt, greeting me each dawn with utter affection in her voice, as it mixed with the soft mews of a soulful Calico cat beside feet and hooves, who was convinced she was about to become human, any minute, and insisted we treat her accordingly.

Conveyed between these lines, as well, are the musical images of hummingbirds telegraph-dancing their hurried secret messages of love and life everywhere, as they rush all about the garden, assiduously-delivering life force to each and every flower. Hummingbird hovering inches before my face as I meditate every morning at dawn. While I, with eyes still closed, gleefully shout back at him or her in Spanish each time, "CHUPPAROSA! CHUPPAROSA! BUENOS DIAZ! GRACIAS AMOR!"

These lines filled to over-flowing with the images of timid ducks enjoying a daily water spraying. Pleasant little characters, their heads always cocked at right angles, eyeballing me to see if I can be trusted. Chicken brethren portrayed here, too, as they move within their complex, anxious, pecking-ordered world, who want to believe I don't care for them solely to eat them. Not to forget those frog brethren relations who, by splashing their croaking portraits upon each dawn and late evening's twilight canvas, encouraged me to keep my own written portraits simple. Furry black jumping spiders – their backs emblazoned with the deep scarlet-red of a mid-summer's day sunset – also hopping all across the journal's page onto my pen, their eyes reflecting a hundred mirrored-images of myself, each faceted image translating itself into a new telepathic thought of awe and wonderment. One declaring on a warm afternoon, "This is good, little brother, that you write of us. And just to let you know we approve and trust that what you say will be right and true, we now encircle you in a spidery network of silken communications lines, within which we enwrap you like a modern-day Gulliver."

Also moving between these lines, without beginning or end, are the invisible stories of ancient winds, traveling all the way from the Sun, following courses more ancient than even the Ganges, Danube or Nile. These ancient solor winds recounting cosmic tales that few would believe save for the leaves. Some of the invisible stories here speak of the Sun waking me each morn to the truth of the mystical heart of the galactic Christ-spirit. This cosmic spirit oft seen reflected in the rainbow shafts of new dawn light as it casts itself upon the dew-laden rose and camellia bushes that flourish at the foot of my wicker bed. Or those other invisible accounts of the many fleeting moments spent each night, staring up at the moon and stars who, in their own galactic way, forever encourage me to develop the necessary critical listening skills, in the hope that some night my ears might hear their tremulous celestial songs. The time taken to gape up at them, and marvel at their majesty, seemingly an eternity spent together while feeling Mother Earth's sensual movements underfoot, subtly shifting like a tiny cork in a vast, intergalactic sea.

This celestial feeling felt more like standing atop a giant surfboard than a planetary orb; 'hanging ten', on the edge of the universe's wild, creative powers that swirled all 'round Mockingbird Lodge.

So many other invisible, cosmic accounts, existant between these lines, revealed each day the transitoriness of life and how sad it is that in spite of how hard one tries, one constantly rushes past so much of it, with very little awareness of the majestic scope and breadth of it all.

– ONE SOFT GENTLE MOMENT SPENT IN TIME & SPACE –

Blossom was a four-legged relation who also daily spoke to me, telepathically. Each morning, as I entered a nearby paddock to give an Appaloosa mare her ration of hay, her foal *Blossom*, born one warm spring-time day in the tall grass, amidst a profusion of young blossoms of new life, took it upon herself to prance back and forth. Uh.......Huh, Huh, Huh, Huh, Huh, Huh, Huh, Huh!", she whinnied:

See! Look at me, little brother! I'm in this pasture night and day, day and night. I don't go anwhere. I don't have to go to work. I don't have to go to the supermarket. I don't have to go to the clothing store. I only stay here and eat this grass – your's and my ancestors – that lie below our feet. AND BEHOLD! As if by magic from the grass, I BECOME A HORSE! I am the grass you see. I am the sun and the moon, too, that we stand beneath. Is it no wondrous how I change before your very eyes each day? How my coat glistens and my eyes sparkle in the light, reflecting in them a mirrored-image of yourself. And all this, a gift – from the grass. Have you not wondered, little brother, why I become a horse from eating this grass, while my brothers and sisters over there, on the other side of the pasture, become sheep and goats? Or why, if you were to eat the grass, you would become something else again? There is big magic in these, our most ancient of related ancestors, that lie all around you. It's a sacred language you must learn to listen to more closely.

To watch Blossom playfully munching at the grass, was to recall all those hilarious times long ago spent with Grandma Ida Harrison on the Crow Creek Reservation in South Dakota; crawling amongst the tall grass, at her beckoning, like a new-born babe, searching for the blue blossom of the wild Indian *tipsila* turnip that Ida goaded me to dig up.

"Wherever you're at in the world beyond, Grandma Ida", I shouted aloud each time, "I love you and think of you often!"

Lingering before my mind's eye was that image of Ida and her yelping black Indian dogs by her side as she sat on a hillock, shaded beneath a tattered old black canvas umbrella, shouting at me in a playful, mocking voice, "No! No! Not that way, Jerry Vista! Over here! No! Dig here!"

As her memory returned to its place of honor within my brain's computer bank, I returned to watch Blossom quietly feed on the fresh young grasses as did her ancestors countless centuries before her.

"So, Blossom", I wondered, "For how many other lifetimes have you and I been together like this?" Flashing into conscious thought at that moment were all the times spent as a youth, galloping through Colma's labyrinth of sandy arroyos and surf of the Pacific Ocean. Or those later years, as an adult, tearing off on one wild-ass ride after another on a Lower Brulé Sioux chief's crazy cow pony, chasing down some errant cayuses, or just quitely plodding through yet another vast, noisy prairie dog village on the plains of South Dakota.

While searching for answers in some expressive motion of the wind in the trees, or strange cloud pattern as it passed overhead, The Voice would gently whisper, "Lad! There are still many more timeless lessons I have to teach you about all this, which you haven't even yet begun to discern."

– SIMPLE TEACHINGS OF MOCKINGBIRD LODGE –

This one-time chicken farmer's house was called 'a lodge' because it quickly became more of a base, lightly used, rather than a physical barrier that separated me from Nature, with the bulk of living, working and sleeping done out-of-doors.

Over the years, a primary teaching gleaned from Turtle Island medicine people, regarding one's daily holistic health and healing practices, is, "Fresh Air & Plenty of It!"

What can come from experiencing the simple joys of sleeping, eating and working amidst the elements all year 'round, regardless of the clime, was driven home during the sojourn at Mockingbird Lodge.

- Blossom and her Mother -
"A Soft Gentle Moment of Time Spent Among The Elements"

Yet the sounds and smells experienced around Mockingbird Lodge weren't always the natural ones of the sylvan glade.

Located near a major freeway, that served as a conduit to and from the Bay Area, with an industrial park, a stones-throw away, spreading fast like a cancerous growth, Mockingbird Lodge was often more a stressful challenge, than an adjunct, to the peace and tranquillity so eagerly sought after.

Given the way the wind was blowing, the deafening roar of commute-hour traffic, with its residue of toxic fumes and stench of industrial pollution, was nauseating.

During the early dawning hours of some mornings, the cacophony of mankind was so disconcerting as to wonder if there was an actual White Man's conspiracy afoot which sought to drown out every last natural sound left in the world.

The frustration felt at Mockingbird Lodge not unlike that earlier experienced in Hidden Valley, in the San Bruno Mountains, once the White Man cut that Guadalupe Highway straight through its heart and destroyed its own ancient legacy of silence.

To experience the stillness of the dawn at either place oftentimes required a deliberate act of volition rather than some passive, pleasurable sensate of all the natural sounds and smells. The ultimate challenge in both cases: to put into practice those Turtle Island 'centering' techniques that can help one tune out all the White Man's noise and confusion.

In Mockingbird Lodge's case, this meant tuning out the din of all the wrenching hulks of Detroit steel as they hurtled by, as well as block out the putrid smells of a nearby slaughter house or industrial park and instead listen for the uplifting cry of Red-Tailed Hawk and Mockingbird, the croak of Frog or sweet fragrances of dew-laden grasses.

The most important Turtle Island meditative technique of all: to acknowledge the power of our own free will and conscious desire *to simply allow* the ever-present healing powers of Earth, Sun, Water and Air to enter into our life and heal whatever dis-ease and imbalance caused by the haste and waste of the White Man's world.

– WHERE THE REAL PROBLEM LIES –

The simple healing powers of Nature are well-known to aboriginal peoples the world over, their homes more akin to temporary shelters than they are strongholds or castles, designed to keep out the natural world.

This was attested to by one Australian aboriginal man met up with
while at Chocuay, who had traveled to California as part of a cross-
cultural exchange program. He heard about my presence near Chocuay
and came to Mockingird Lodge.

During his brief visit, he recounted an anecdote that speaks to the
vast differences that still exist between indigenous and non-indigenous
peoples, especially regarding their forms of architecture and the
philosophies behind them that influence the type of living dwellings in
which they prefer to live.

"One day", said the Aboriginal, who was a Headman among his
people in New South Wales, "We Black's was given a brand spankin'
new government house t' live in. But th' government man who came to
see how we was gettin' on, got bloody crazy in the head th' day he seen
we'd took off all th' doors an' windows of th' house, an' made a small
hole in th' roof. When the White fella seen that he screamed, "Why in the
bloody hell did ya' do such a stupid thing to a perfectly good house?" I just
said, 'Why, t' let th' sky come in, fella!'"

This 'bizarre' response nearly sent the government official 'round
the bend, who demanded the Black's put everything back as it was. But
they couldn't because, as the Aboriginal man told it, "Cricky! I says t' th'
White fella, I'd do it, mate, if I could but I don't reckon that's possible
now 'cause we used 'em all up for our campin' fires instead of cookin'
on th' indoor kitchen stove."

Concluding his anecdote, the Aboriginal said, "What", screamed th'
White fella. "Ya' mean ya' burned 'em?" 'Yah I reckon', I says to him.
"Christ Almighty", he screamed. "You Blacks are gonna have t' wake up
some day an' realize ya' can't keep livin' in th' bloody Stone Age if ya'
want t' get ahead in this world, an' stop causing so many problems."

As the Aboriginal man spoke, I wondered who really has the
problem.

"Think about it, Twin Rainbow!", said the Headman, "Since th' day th'
White fella came t' our lands, not only have our problems been our
problems but th' White fella's problems have become our problems, too."

Willfred Pelletier, a spiritual man of the Odawa Nation in Eastern
Canada, once made a related observation as to why the Western mind
becomes so perplexed by the 'bizarre antics' of aboriginal peoples. He
noted:

> Because the Western intellect is so self-righteous, and thinks of its own
> interpretation of life as the only correct way to live, it judges our behavior as
> inferior and therefore primitive. When White people look at our unpainted, run-
> down houses on the reserves, they pass judgment on those of us who live in

them. When their own houses begin to crumble, thereby exposing them to the elements, they're usually so attached to them that they also begin to crumble and die because their houses have become part and parcel of their whole way of life. Not so with The Indian way of life. For our houses are only temporary shelters and nothing can happen to the dwelling that will destroy its owner because the owner is eternal.

'Eternal' peoples everywhere in the world are quick to note that the White Man's illness of body, mind and spirit are wedded to their choice of architecture and the way of life that it represents and demands of all those who adhere to it.

– A HOUSE IS FAR MORE THAN JUST A DWELLING –

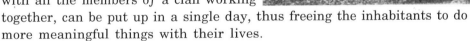

While at Mockingbird Lodge, Alta-Dena and I traveled to a State Park, near Olema, where a traditional village setting of the Coast Miwok and Pomo Indians was rebuilt in a Bear Valley place called 'Kulé Loklo'.

While lingering in one of Kulé Loklo's lodges, I grew saddened that this no longer is the simple way people build their dwellings. A dwelling that, with all the members of a clan working together, can be put up in a single day, thus freeing the inhabitants to do more meaningful things with their lives.

By comparison, the modern suburbanite in Petaluma and elsewhere in North America has virtually become an indentured slave to the money changers and financial houses. Today's citizenry forced into voluntary bondage, chained to however many jobs just to pay off a 30-year mortgage. Even to the point of foregoing their responsibilities of fatherhood and motherhood, or abandoning their sense of a sacred place. All for a dwelling that though, as the myth goes, a "man's home is his castle", is one but built on the shifting sands of an illusory legacy to future generations. A legacy predicated upon an ever more unaffordable, artifically-inflated price-tag, ever-rising prohibitive property taxes and the state's right, at any given moment, to exercise its privilege of eminent domain.

Pondering what distinguishes 'civilized' from 'barbaric' behavior, I recalled how this inherited legacy was cunningly shaped by the early kings. Especially during the time of the Great Clearances in England, when 'The Commons' were stolen from the people and they were forced into the cities to search for 'jobs' while in the grasp of greedy 'landlords'.

I grew ever more saddened the longer I dwelt upon how we've all somehow become hopeless captives of the White Man and a way of life based upon a particular style of architecture and world view that only values what is shiny, new, young, fleeting and superficial.

– A TRIP DOWN UNDER PUTS THINGS INTO PERSPECTIVE –

As the sojourn at Mockingbird Lodge drew to a close, a trip to Crystal Freesia's New South Wales homelands brought to a closure these 'Walden' ruminations.

Crystal Freesia and I decided to meet up in Sydney, visit her family in the Blue Mountains, and revisit the special natural places and homes where she spent her formative years.

Journeying to Australia was like entering into a time machine, traveling backwards to a North America of a distant yesteryear, when the natural landscapes and their indigenous life forms still flourished. The variety and vast numbers of Australia's wildlife, and especially its wild bird life, absolutely breathtaking.

Yet, at the same time. the so-called civilized 'White Australian' mentality, like its early North American counterpart, by then, also was in full-swing, hell-bent upon exterminating, pell-mell, as many levels of its own ancient, indigenous consciousness as was humanly possible.

The widespread extermination of its Kangaroo people, a 'down-under' version of the American Bison, was in high swing. As was the rapid elimination of those down-under versions of California's Grizzly Bear and Condor Nations – the Crocodile's and Emu's. The projected long-term fate of its First Peoples, like the Pitjantjatjarra and Gunwinggu, looking more and more like that of California's Coast Miwok and Ohlone, with each newly-expanded quota of Asian immigrants and U.S. corporate development throughout their tribal homelands.

AMWAY International's invasion of the Australian countryside, also a classic down-under version of the old Hudson Bay & Northwest Fur Trade Companies in North America. Those early 19th century North American railroad and land development syndicates, which mis-appropriated the sovereign territories of First Nation peoples, not to be outdone down-under, in the 21st century, by the Trilateral Commission's coal, uranium and other mineral-extraction conglomerates.

Over the years, as North America's resistance movement has stiffened against the incursions of such global conglomerates, these entities simply have followed the lines of least resistance and moved their operations elsewhere. Hence, places like Australia since have become but the newest casualties in the White Man's on-going death wish. A suicidal process as insidious and pervasive whether committed at a Hudson's Bay Trading Post in Canada, in the 1880's or an International AMWAY distributorship in Australia, in the 1980's.

Sitting in the window seat of a Jumbo 747, looking out at my last few glances of 'Australia Fair', I wondered, "Is it, ultimately, more painful, but healthier in the long run, for we humans to live in places like California in North America, where so many dimensions of consciousness already have been exterminated, but where the human awareness of the loss is more highly-evolved, and the consequent effort to preserve what little is left more intensely-focused? Or is it less painful, and so healthier for one's spiritual and psychic well-being, to be on a physical frontier, like that of Australia's Northern Territories or Canada's Far North, where the wholesale destruction of these dimensions is underway, but where the resistance within the human consciousness there isn't as well-organized or evolved? Yet where one can at least more easily tap into the manifold levels of consciousness that the still existant dimensions of the non-human world offers up to them?"

The conclusion finally reached was that the existential anguish is a trade-off either way. Faced with a choice between the two, the individual is left to decide what their own personal priorities and needs are that must be satisfied in the process.

Coming to terms with my own priorities and needs, the decision was finally made to take leave of Mockingbird Lodge and journey back across The Medicine Line to Canada, where the non-human consciousness is still more intact than in the South and the resistance movement among the humans more ethically-evolved.

– TO EVERY SEASON THERE IS A TIME –

Alta-Dena and I first went South, in search of a new 'Walden Pond', because Crystal Freesia and I previously decided that the time was fast approaching when we needed to permanently sink our roots down together somewhere. I said I would do a reconnoiter in the South for "our sacred spot", while she remained in the North and reconnoitered from her end.

From the time Alta-Dena and I first entered onto Mockingbird Lodge's dramatic stage, to the point where we finally exited from its magical surrounds, a cycle of two years and four months had come to pass.

I left with the same hopeful expectation as Thoreau's own entrance and exit from Walden when he wrote:

> I lived there two years and two months...At present, I am a sojourner in civilized life again...I left the woods for as good a reason as I went there. Perhaps it seemed to me that I had several more lives to live and could not spare any more time for that one...But why I changed? Why I left the woods? I do not think I can tell! I have often wished myself back. I do not know any better how I ever came to go there...I left as unaccountably as I went to it. To speak sincerely, I went there because I had got ready to go; I left for the same reason.

Preparing to leave this beloved Petaluman spirit place for good, painful last respects were paid to Blossom, feeding her one last handful of fresh, green grass for which she whinnied, gratefully. At the graveside of *Omogumph* – aka "OMO, Keeper-of-the-Sacred-Imperial Waters" – a black and white-pawed, true-blue Canadian-born, Short-Haired breed who was the mother of Little Meg – one last tobacco offering was made in her honor to the camellia bush, beside which OMO's remains were laid to rest. "FAREWELL, DEAR OMO! See you in the next great dreamtime life, for sure!"

My wild, gentle spirit soared one last time on the winds of Chocuay with Red-Tailed Hawk and Mockingbird, while more earth-bound spirit forces directed my feet upon a final walk along Chocuay's banks, bidding fond adieu to Frog, Turtle, Crayfish, Muskrat and Trout, cautioning each of them to, "BE WELL! Take care, little ones. I love you and will forever send my prayers skyward for you all."

Standing upon the sacred grounds of Mockingbird Lodge, I lit a braid of Sweetgrass and slowly encircled Alta-Dena in a clockwise manner, offering up blessings for another safe journey. Placing my medicine bundle of hawk feathers and herbs upon Alta-Dena's dash, I set off on a new path of discovery, perhaps, like Thoreau, to live yet several more lives elsewhere.

Before Alta-Dena and I could make the return trip to Canada, to report back to Crystal Freesia what all we learned in the South, we needed to make one more pilgrimage back to those San Bruno Mountains, on the southern edge of San Francisco, where this real-life fairy tale first began as a youth.

– A MEETING WITH THE MOUNTAIN'S RESIDENT HERMIT –

Word had reached me that that there was a man – referred to as, "the resident hermit *of* Owl Canyon", in the San Bruno Mountain's, who, years before, also withdrew from the 'civilized world' to create his own 'Walden'.

He built a lodge into the Mountain's side, that looked very much like a traditional Coast Miwok dwelling, gathered wild food stuffs and water from a natural spring on the Mountain for his sustenance, while establishing close relations with the resident wildlife.

I needed to seek him out and introduce myself, for the purpose of discussing the similarities and differences behind our motivations as outsiders to do what we did. I wanted to find out what wisdoms the Mountain and her resident wildlife had taught him.

So off Alta-Dena and I went on our short two hour jaunt South, passing quickly by the old Miwok village site *of* Olompali and the burial place *of* Chief Sem-Yet-To, that legendary 6'7" tall, chief of the Solano First Nation peoples. That sacred spot the same place where the Americans chose to fight their first battle *of* the Bear Flag Revolt, while torching part *of* Olompali and killing a Mexican officer. Back we went, as fast as Alta-Dena could go, to what the early Spanish explorers *of* the Mountain once called *Cañada de Guadalupe el Visitacion y Rodeo Viejo.*

CURCLE ISLAND

ROAD SIGN # 17

WHAT WISDOMS & HEALINGS
HAVE YOU RECEIVED
FROM RETURNING TO THE
VISIONARY PLACES
OF YOUR CHILDHOOD?

The Mountain writes poems on me whenever I'm quiet.
The Place in its own defining, informing energies
   – the buckling of an ancient seabed –
   – prehistoric summer fogs –
   leave records written minute
   in helical couplings of bearberry
   in great migrations of roots and seeds
   before advancing northern ice,
   Mianthemum Kamchtacum,
   a boreal huckleberry,
   a new-born hawk,
millions of tiny deaths and hatchings,
   creeks fed into the bay –
   And Man.

Man to fucus and names these energies,
   join them again with origins,
invest the Mountain with sacredness or use,
   heeding its articulations.
   And where heedless,
liable to scrape its slopes and canyons bare
   diminishing also himself.

(David Schooley)

– Yelamu Kuksuyu Dreamer Song –

(This natural breath-chant is repeated over and over as
the dancer gracefully dance-walks in place. With each
vocally-expelled breath-note, gently sway the dancer's
arms – held slack by ther side, with the hands open and
relaxed – back and forth across the body, one at a time,
like spiritual pendulums, gently extending symbolic
offerings to the invisible realm. With knee's slightly
bent, the dancers raise their feet off of Mothr Earth's
body and touch her again, as if they were drumsticks
gently beating-caressing her body, while in the presence
of all the dancer's ancestors who surround them. The
ancestors doing the same natural breath-chant-dance. The
dancer's bodies, minds and spirits harmoniously move as
if they were rhythmically breathing and swaying in a
trance or dream-like state)

NEW & OLD
HIDDEN VALLEY RELATIONSHIPS BECKON

"*PILGRIM*", challenges anew The Great Voice Of The Turtle, "*Return again to that place on my body where your childhood dreams and fantasies first began. Renew there your relationships with my wild children you once were attracted to. Renew your special connections with those sacred parts of me that you bonded with in the early days of your life. Be open for whatever new sacred parts of me or my wild children will reach out to your spirit and seek to become a new relation of yours. When you make these bonds, ask them and yourself how they speak to the realities of your adult life. Ask them what they would have you do with your life or where they would have you go from this point on.*"

As Alta-Dena approached the northern flank of San Bruno Mountain, Black Buffalo again entered my thoughts, seeking some acknowledgment for the important role all those wild denizens and sacred places I was attracted to as a youth, continue to play in my adult life.

The reasons and explanations behind why we each are attracted to so many different life forms and places in the natural world is truly one of life's greatest mysteries, but one which holds the key to why we are here.

To Crystal Freesia, the Bear and the Hawk, or places like San Bruno Mountain, hold little interest. Her spirit pulled more towards: eucalyptus trees that, in her childhood, were the residences of gumnut fairies and characters like Blinky Bill; three-hundred year-old Morten Bay Figs, whose massive roots systems were the secretive, cozy cottage dwellings of anthropomorphic Aussie bush figures, or; the bush, itself, alive with ferocious Banksia men, delicate Wattle babies and all manner of mysterious wild entities that emerged from the red Australian earth.

Thus, during the two years and four months just spent at Chocuay, and especially during those occasions when Crystal Freesia came for a visit, she never related to that old chicken farmer's ranch house as a lodge, dominated by the Mockingbird.

Instead, she saw it more as a 'cottage', whose spiritual signature was the nearby Pear Tree. So, to her, the essence of that place called itself 'Pear Tree Cottage' or, as I later dubbed it, to meld our two perceptions – *Mocking-bird-Atop-Pear Tree Cottage.*

We both easily could have made Mockingbird-Atop-Pear-Tree Cottage our spiritual base in the South, but, though we tried to make it happen, it seemed the spirit world had a different piece of sacred land and holy dwelling in mind for us to belong to.

Whether it was to be in the North or South we knew not. We only knew it to be somewhere so close by, in the spirit realm, that we could almost see it as we felt it pull us towards itself.

As Alta-Dena retraced the old Spanish *Cañada de Guadalupe el Visitacion y Rodeo Viejo* trail, drawing ever-closer to Buckeye & Owl Canyons, and the haunts of its mysterious 'resident hermit', The Voice declared, "Lad! You must learn to accept the fact that, like most of those immigrants who settled in Petaluma, few of the foreigners who settled along the Mountain's edges, consider the land there to be sacred in the same way that the old Yelamu Indian habitants once did. Fewer still would say they belong to the Mountain instead of the other way 'round. Find out how many of them have come to know the sacred name of the place on the Mountain where they live. Ask them how these spiritual names have influenced their lives."

As The Voice trailed off, I began to wonder aloud, "What about this hermit? Will I find a New Frontier Breed brother, who also is searching for some spiritual connection with the land and its wild residents? Or will he turn out to be just another confused, homeless, squatter in denial, trying to escape from the harsh realities of the modern-day world?"

When Crystal Freesia first learned of my plan to return to the San Bruno Mountains, where there exists large stands of eucalyptus, and the hermit's canyon homelands were close to the town of Brisbane, she squealed, "Brisbane! Eucalyptus! Gumnut fairies! Check it out, love. Maybe that's where the special house and land we seek awaits us."

– LIFE'S UGLY REALITY MANIFESTS UPON THE MOUNTAIN –

Before trying to find the hermit's haunts, the decision was made to first circumnavigate the Mountain's flanks to see how this largest urban open space in the United States, and 13th most important endangered species habitat in California, had fared over the years.

By then, the Mountain, as a test case of the Rare & Endangered Species Act (ESA) of 1973, had been pulverized by the developers. The

ESA's Habitat Conservation Plan (HCP) amendment of 1982, also craftily drafted for the Mountain as a test case, contained a host of legal loopholes, concoted by one Thomas Reid Associates and its cabal of environmental doublespeak, that turned into a truly laughable excuse for an ecologically-sensitive plan.

Large subdivisions and industrial developments, as well, were well on their way towards encroaching upon all the saddles and upper ridges of the Mountain. Her flanks everywhere under siege.

– AN IDEOLOGICAL BALKAN WAR ON THE MOUNTAIN –

- 1 -
San Bruno Mountain
grand looming symbol
will not be ignored
Who will listen?
Who will start to care?
Who will dare to
question smug plans of
short-sighted
bureaucrats?
Or cement schemes
of get-rich-quick
developers?

(Ellen Mark, poet)

- 2 -
The land cries out
for its rare and
ancient life
delicate, intricate
net of being.

- 4 -
Who will rise
to guard a park
from the bits of
bulldozers steel
blades, or a
predatory quarry's
devastating swipe?

- 3 -
Plants, insects, animals
abundant once,
now endangered,
 whose survival
depends upon a
 human whim.

- 5 -
On the steps of government
they gather
loyal lovers of the Earth.
 To save the mountain
 To save Life's green
 To save the green.
Life's truest color.

On the Mountain's northern San Franciscan flanks, the rare Levinson Marsh, botanically-rich Carter Street Ridge and Visitacion Valley's lush grasslands were in the process of being destroyed by housing developments that, like a slash-and-burn army, advanced ever-higher with each passing day. Her eastern, Brisbane flanks already also a grizzly scene of wide-spread destruction. 50 years of quarry mining in one of the Mountain's once most pristine, hidden canyons; huge subdivisions ever-expanding on her Northeast Ridge, destroying the invaluable habitat of a extremely rare buttterfly; the extermination of her Guadalupe Marshlands by a sprawling Crocker Industrial Park; were everywhere devastating the Mountain's wild integrity.

Not to be outdone, the humans on her South San Francisco flanks were also playing their part in the siege, causing a sweeping Southwest Diversified–W.W. Dean–Terra Bay Empire of sub-divisions and commercial development to obliterate her one-time 'Paradise Valley' surrounds.

If this wasn't enough, on her Western Colma flanks: the constant intrusive thrusts of a golf course and cemetary, as well as the illegal removal of 19 acres of conserved habitat for a garbage disposal site, were ruining her biologically unique ecozones, which was home to a rare 'albino' DNA strain among an endemic species of Red-Tailed Hawk and other rare species endemic to the Mountain.

The rest of her Western Daly City flanks already long-since carpet-bombed by the development community's: Cadillac Fairview West monstor condominiums atop Reservoir Hill and the Crocker Estates; the wholesale destruction of Colma Canyon's rare riparian ecosystem for still another uneeded intrusive highway and; the constant incursions onto the Mountain's highest points, to install yet the latest HD-TV Communication Towers that cut ever-deeper into the habitat of the rare and endangered San Bruno Elfin butterfly.

Each new development, as part of the White Man's conspiracy of consciousness, were playing its part in turning her body into another Scottish borderland–Balkanized war zone that some say is the scene of more drama and embattled politics than anywhere else in the Nation.

– A BEAUTIFUL NAME BECOMES AN UGLY CONCEPT –

It was while passing along San Bruno Mountain's southern flanks, near Paradise Valley, that Alta-Dena and I came face-to-face with one of the grimmest, battle-scarred scenes of wholesale destruction.

A Regimented Way of Life Amidst Nature

In a valley aptly named because of its paradisiacal qualities, an all-out, Man versus Nature war was undeniably underway. Yet the developer-combatants otherwise benignly dubbed the whole conflict as simply: *The Terra Bay Housing & Commercial Development Project.*

This understated White Man's battle plan, that hoped to realize yet one more conquest of the natural world, dreamt of an ever-expanding empire. Its open-ended objective: to legally or illegally remove as much of the Mountain's body as was possible, while slowly reducing her down to common landfill. Her body's remains to be disposed of in a nearby bay that once teemed with oysters, crustaceans and marine life, and so expand the plan's even more grandiose fantasies of dominion.

By then, the first stages of Terra Bay's mega-project had handily won the day when they received the 'democratically-approved' green light from the local, duly-elected city council.

"Everything was done according to Hoyle", proudly declared the developers and city planners. Translation: the usual strong-arm lobbying and 'holy-greasing-of-the-greedy palm' ritual had thus been completed; the usual tactics of cunning environmental doublespeak, to assure everyone the project would 'mitigate' the 'incidental taking' of all rare and endangered species, had been carried out to the letter of the law; while the obligatory nodding of heads around the conference tables and city council chambers, and the imprints of all their knee-jerk rubber-stamps had been duly affixed to the agreed upon 'Habitat Conservation Plan' A masterful plan everyone knew complied with every loophole purposely designed to declaw and defang the Endangered Species Act.

Alta-Dena and I could only stand by and helplessly watch while a phalanx of giant yellow earth-movers ripped away thousands of feet of the Mountain's thin skin at one fell swoop, exposing massive raw patches of her ancient red-sandstone flesh to the Sun's onslaught. Wondered again, as I did so many times before in other places where the same scene of destruction took place, was the question of who or why anyone would ever do such a thing.

With no less sense of horror or any more clarity as to the why's of it all, I rhetorically screamed aloud in Alta-Dena's cab, "What kind of ignorant, heartless, insensitive sonuvabitch would keep doing this? What kind of dialogue can I ever have with them that will convey how critical it is to keep the last of Turtle Island's sacred places sacrosanct? What is it that we possibly have left to talk about?"

Sensing the Mountain attempting to telepathically speak to me in that instant, I knew Alta-Dena and I had to retreat from that disturbing sight to some quiet place wthat offered a better chance at concentrating upon whatever subtle dialogue she had to give.

Alta-Dena gave a mighty rev and off we went, in search of some high vantage point along Oyster Road, to look back and visually feel the Mountain's whole mass all at once.

But no matter how hard we tried, we couldn't get far enough away from all the death and destruction. Huge, billowing clouds of red earth boiled and roiled from behind the ominous columns of 'blitzkrieging' earth-movers that moved in tandem as they continued to claw their way ever closer towards the site of the largest Indian shell mound ever found upon the Northern Franciscan peninsula.

Yet notwithstanding all the carnage committed against her, the Mountain still seemed strangely serene. In the face of her apparent doleful fate, her awe-inspiring dark-green aura still quietly pulsated like that of some huge slumbering Earth Goddess.

Humbled in the presence of such a stoic, magnanimous gentility, I just sat there in Alta-Dena, gaping out of her panoramic window at the harsh contrasts of what all I was being called upon to witness.

– IF ONLY THE MOUNTAIN COULD TALK –

Slowly, softly, into my mind's ear, whispered The Mountain:

Little One! I know you as one of my children. It is good that you have not forsaken me and take an interest in my well-being. I stand here as I must, accepting my fate decreed upon me by some among your species. For well over a century now, I have watched as these primitive, underdeveloped one's of your kind have continued to deface my ancient visage. So much so, that the day may soon come when I may not even be able to recognize myself.

I ask you, Little One, why can't your kind recognize how important it is to their lives to have someone as ancient as me, so close to them? Someone who they can look up to and marvel at each day, and say, 'You know something! Were so blessed and lucky because no matter what else changes in our insane, man-made hell of a world, it's always consoling to be able to look up at our sacred mountain and know she looks just the way she did to our ancestors'.

But instead they foolishly try to convince themselves that all life upon me was already headed towards extinction long before they began to violate me.

I ask you again, Little One, who will they turn to then? When they finally do wake up to what they have lost in me, it will be too late. And I am afraid for them, because when that day finally comes, and come-it-will, they might drop over dead-in-their tracks from sheer fright or a guilty conscience.

Go in peace, Little One! We are what we always have been together! CAH NAH! CAH NAH!, CAH NAH! CAH NAH! I AM WHAT I AM!

Those grandiose schemes of Southwest Diversified and W.W. Dean, that preceded Terra Bay, eventually became a nightmare of a scandal for the White Men involved, killed off by their greed and the collapse of the very S & L economic boondoggle upon which their greed was fueled.

Yet sadly, in the meantime, so, too, was killed off one whole side of the Mountain – with all her Lupine, S.F. Wallflowers, Johnny Jump-ups, S.F. Silverspot and Mission Blue Butterflies, Great Horned Owl, Red-Tailed Hawk and S.F. Garter Snake, not to mention the many micro-universes, above and below the ground, left to the further destructive forces of erosion and invasive, exotic plants.

Swinging around to the Western flanks of the Mountain, Alta-Dena entered into Colma Canyon. As we headed for the canyon's Indian Head Rock, where much quiet time was spent as a youth, I held gloomy thoughts about all the native plants and animals chances of survival. Not, that is, without a lot of militant, perhaps even violent, help from all the native human beings of the region. "Violence", I thought, "is sometimes the only way we natives can get through to all the violators and abusers."

– A MEETING WITH THE GENTLE MAN OF THE MOUNTAIN –

Upon rounding a bend on the canyon road, a husky, bearded man unexpectedly emerged from the dense eucalyptus forest through which that roadway passed.

It was his beaming face and intense stare, as much as anything else, that caused me to brake Alta-Dena to a halt and engage him in conversation.

This unusual-looking man conveyed a decidedly-bohemian look, what with him wearing: a heavy mackintosh covered in faded Indian designs; a thick, hand-made scarf draped loosely-round his neck, and; deeply-faded, threadbare blue jeans, below which stuck out dirty, sockless feet in old, worn leather thongs.

His ruddy, wind-blown red cheeks; ragged, sandy-blond beard and wild mop of hair to match; his piercing, green eyes that seemed to pass straight through my gaze; gave the stranger an even more bohemian look with a dash of mysticism thrown in.

"Hi! Welcome to the Mountain!", he gushed. "My name's Dave Schooley. I haven't seen you or your great-looking truck around these parts before."

"Twin Rainbow's my spirit name", I confided. "I actually was raised near here. These mountains are, what we kids once called, our 'Holy Black Hills', and this canyon is, what we referred to as, 'Hidden Valley'. I cut my spiritual teeth here. Alta-Dena and I've been traveling a lot between here and Canada for years. I just spent the past two years meditating at a place up north about what all this has meant , as time has gone on. I heard about a hermit guy, living somewhere on the mountain and came to see if I could find him."

Still somewhat taken aback by Alta-Dena's and my sudden presence, and what all was just revealed, Schooley just smiled for a time in a quiet, gleeful sort of way. "Oh, so you've heard about Dwight, have you!", he said. "Well, you're in luck, 'cause I know exactly where he lives and can show you how to get there."

"Wow, really? Shit, that's great!", I shouted. "'Cause I want to talk to him about why he's there and a whole lot of other stuff. Hey, by the way. Where are you going with all those strange-looking plants you've got in your hands?"

"These are some rare plants", he said, with an impish grin, "that I've never seen before in these Holy Black Hills, as you call them!" I'm takin' 'em down to my place in Brisbane to check out in my native botanical records. But what are you doin' here right this minute?"

"I'm about to climb up to ol' Indian Head Cave", I said, "where I spent a lot of time as a kid. It's just up aways."

Even more surprised by my latest revelation, Schooley gushed, with great gusto, "Oh, so you know about the cave, too, do you!"

The second he said that I queried, "Hey, Bro! Ya' wanna come with me up to Indian Head and sit for a spell?"

Without a moment's hesitation, Schooley bellowed, "Lead the way, my good Rainbow man!"

Once we'd clambored up to the mouth of Indian Head, I set out to do a smudging ceremony between us while Dave spontaneously chanted a mountan spirit song he said was in the tongue of the old Yelamu who once lived there.

"Kai istun xaluyaxe", went the chant, *"Kai mas ictunine, werena Kai, tceica Kai, eksena Kai"*, chanted Schooley over and over. Afterwards, he said the chant had something to do with a long-ago dreamer who dreamt of jackrabbits and quail.

Dave and I sat atop Indian Head for a long time in quiet solitude, looking down at that ugly Guadalupe Highway that totally destroyed Colma Canyon's once exquisitely beautiful Colma Creek and spring where the rare San Francisco Garter Snake and Red-Legged Frog once flourished.

"It's a cryin' shame what the White Man has done to this beautiful valley!", blurted Dave, as he broke the silence between us. "If James Roof were here now, he'd have a whole lot to say about what's happened to the Mountain?"

"Who's James Roof?", I queried. "Well, I'll tell you!", he said. "It's sort of because of Roof that I'm here doin' what I'm doin'."

– HE KNEW THE MOUNTAIN LIKE NO OTHER –

Listening to Schooley describe him, I thought, "James Roof would havee to be one of the Mountain's early 'New Frontier Breeds', or modern-day 'Yelamu Indians', if ever there was one, whose early voice in the wilderness inspired many to come to love the land as he."

After cutting his botanical teeth on San Bruno, Roof spent 35 years, fighting with every ounce of energy he had, to try to save the Mountain, and especially Colma Canyon, from annihilation.

As Schooley told it, "Roof always said that Franciscan Territory once was bounded by San Francisco's Mount Davidson, its Sunset Heights, Twin Peaks and Diamond Heights. But that now San Bruno Mountain, and its intact Colma Canyon, is that heart that we have to save at all cost, or we'll all one day lose our own hearts!"

When Colma Canyon, the last intact Franciscan Territory watershed system, and its natural spring-fed creek system were destroyed, Roof left in disgust, moved to the other side of the Bay and went to become a legend there, while creating the Native Botanical Garden at Tilden Park in Berkeley.

– A MODERN-DAY KEEPER-OF-THE-MOUNTAIN –

Soon after Schooley finished his tale of James Roof, we thanked Indian Head for all his lofty thoughts that came to us while atop him, and climbed back down the steep, poison oak-infested hillside to where Alta-Dena patiently awaited our return.

As Schooley slipped and slid his way down in front of me, I thought, "Wow, Jerome! For all you know, this new wayfarer-companion in front of you could just as easily be another Henry Thoreau or John Muir. Maybe you don't have to find the hermit! Maybe this is the strange dude that the Great Spirit wanted you to find all along."

Schooley, as I would come to learn, took it upon himself, eighteen years before, as his own inner voice's calling, to become a Keeper-of-the-Sacred Place, and so act as a spiritual town crier to wake the populace up to a deep ecological awareness of San Bruno Mountain and its many riches. As he, himself, humbly put it, "Someone had to begin doin' it. I guess I was the one who had to wake everyone up to the wonderful gifts they're squanderin' and the relations they'll never know if they don't do somethin' quick."

Schooley's efforts, as a deep ecologist, by that time already earned him the unofficial title – *Gentle Man of The Mountain*. He fit the description of a genuine New Frontier Breed in his role as a founding member, and early precursor, of the Mountain's new would-be band of natives, that she longed would once again reside upon her and cherish her as the Yelamu once did for thousands of years. David playing his part as he bathed in her winter gushets or frolicked amongst her spring-time flowers.

Before we parted company, Schooley exclaimed, "Twin Rainbow!. You're just the man I've been lookin' for. A bunch of us are having an Earth First strategy meeting about the Mountain's welfare tomorrow night in Brisbane. You've got to come. I'll tell you more about Dwight, or the hermit as you call him. He's gonna laugh when he hears about this. He was a public school teacher who also opted out of the system and decided that reinhabitin' the Mountain was the best thing to do."

Reaching into his mackintosh, he pulled out a crumpled, torn piece of paper and slapped it into my hand with a firm handshake. "Here", he said, "I wrote this a few years back. It'll give you somethin' more to think about 'til we meet tomorrow 'round about 9." The paper read:

– 1 –

Nothing need be proven
though something calls out
the murders of earth
and person;

– 2 –

Nothing need be said
though something asks
to be perfectly spoken into
a silence of seeing;

– 3 –

Were it only the
first doubled leaves
of the Blue Lupine
thru the crumpled
earth by the rock;

– 4 –

Or the opening, closing wings
of a Mission Blue butterfly
flashing thru the creekbed;

– 5 –

Or the hightened stillness
of the valley floor
beneath Blue Jay's gravely call –
from an oak-top.

Schooley's poem led to the recollection of all those happy times spent in dear ol' Blue, Alta-Dena's predecessor, and how I came to name her.

Long before I arrived, Schooley and his 'new Yelamu' associates cries of "SAVE SAN BRUNO MOUNTAIN!" served as a clarion call not only to those more conscious, highly-attuned local people in the Bay Area, but in other areas of North America, as well. Especially among those who were struggling with everything they had to save their own sacred sanctuaries in nature from the on-slaught of the same new forked-tongued breed of barbarians who only understood and spoke White Man's doublespeak.

As Alta-Dena wound her way out of Colma Canyon, I wondered what Schooley's meeting might hold in store. All at once, The Voice whispered in my ear, "Lad! Perhaps the personal healing and direction you seek in your life will naturally come about by assuming a responsibility to help heal the Mountain herself."

Little could I know but that this Earth First meeting of the Mountain's new natives was to become one of the odyssey's keynote benchmarks.

– THE SPIRIT WORLD SPEAKS IN STRANGE WAYS –

The next day found me lying in my bunk in Alta-Dena, suffering from the onslaught of one of the most sudden, severest cases of flu I'd ever known. Bedridden, I decided, even as much as I wanted to go, against attending Schooley's meeting.

Yet late that night, minutes before his meeting was scheduled to get underway, the image of a Gray Fox, from clear-out-of-the-blue, rushed into my thoughts and an overwhelming sense of urgency swept over me to nevertheless attend.

Quickly jumping out of my sickbed, and hastily throwing on some clothes, I revved up Alta-Dena and said, "Let's go, girl! Giddyup!" Away we eagerly went into the night, unaware of the fated meeting we were soon to have with one of the Mountain's spirit-soul mates who awaited us.

Driving back up Colma Canyon, past Indian Head Cave – through the dark, scary eucalypt forest which lay beyond – the images of a thousand childhood dramas once spent there darted and hovered before my mind's eye. The many Gray Foxes seen, as a youth, while tramping down the Mountain's animal paths, darted back and forth in front of Alta-Dena's panoramic windows.

Suddenly, a sixth sense told me to expect to once again see one of them, for real, at any moment. The feeling so intense that on every twist and turn in the road, I expected Alta-Dena's headlights to any second catch a pair of green eyes flashing back at them through the pitch-black darkness. Although few people today ever see the wild Gray Fox of Mount San Bruno, as some refer to it, they still exist in great numbers and, in the absence of the ancient Yelamu, are thought of, by deep ecologists, as the new 'Spirit Keepers' of The Mountain.

As my white Druid-Hippie-Spirit chariot reached the crest of the mountain and was about to start her way down the opposite side, **IT HAPPENED!** just as the spirit world said it would.

A pair of large green eyes suddenly flashed brightly from alongside the edge of the road. It was a road-kill which I took to be that of a jack rabbit and so didn't brake for it.

Yet as Alta-Dena lumbered down the mountainside, the haunting memory of a newborn fawn road-kill I was mystically drawn to just the year before, during my stay at Chocuay, came rushing into view.

Traveling along the northern edge of San Francisco Bay, on yet another mystical-twist-in-the-road, Alta-Dena and I had just passed by another road-kill, again thought to be a jack rabbit, but upon backing up to investigate if further, discovered it to be that of a tiny, day-old fawn.

The fawn had only just been killed, as attested to by his mother who I spotted standing rigidly still in a nearby field of tall corn, anxiously peering at us.

She watched my every move as I leapt from Alta-Dena to observe her baby more closely. I couldn't immediately get to her though, because she was lying in the middle of a major freeway and coming up fast were three huge eighteen-wheeler semi's and a half-dozen vehicles.

I took one glance at the frail little fawn lying there, who looked untouched, as if it were simply dozing. Looked back at the crunch of heavy tires that were about to pass over her in a few seconds and cringed at the thought of the mayhem they would do to her tiny body.

With that, I closed my eyes, shouted at the top of my lungs to the spirit world, "NO! SPIRITS! DON'T LET THIS HAPPEN! PROTECT THE DIGNITY OF THAT LITTLE ONE, EVEN IN DEATH!", and mentally threw around the fawn a protective bubble of psychic energy.

A heavy rush of wind jostled Alta-Dena and me as the traffic roared by, but my eyes kept themselves tightly closed, too apprehensive of what they might see once they opened. But when they tentatively peered through half-open slits to see what had happened, they couldn't believe what they saw. Because there was the little fawn, still lying there, completely untouched, without so much as a single hair on her head ruffled. Still in shock, I half-cried back at the spirit world, "**Aho**! Thank You Spirits! Thank You!"

With that, I walked into the middle of the freeway where the fawn lay, reverently picked up her limp body and motioned with its uplifted body held towards the doe who stood so woefully nearby in the field.

Spontaneously emitted was a short, wailing rendition of my New Dawn Chant made to the doe, the fawn and myself in that holy moment of time and space.

With the mother still staring, unblinkingly, our way like a statue, I continued to hold aloft her baby's frail, broken little body while chanting, "Heya, hey! Heya hey, ah hey, hey, hey, hey! Hear me, Spirits! I will honor well this, your tiny healing gift of love, gentleness, wildness and sensitivity that is embodied within this fawn."

Climbing into Alta-Dena's cab, I laid the fawn on my bunk and at once set out for Mockingbird-Atop-Pear Tree Cottage with the thought in mind to ceremonially skin and tan the fawn and use its cased body as a medicine bag, in which to keep the Medicine Pipe that Holy Dance and Joe Thunder Hawk helped me to consecrate so many years before.

It was then that this still vivid image of that spirit encounter with the fawn – and the final sacred scene of its skinned body lying in an open paddock, surrounded by a string of red-cloth tobacco ties and a sprinkled ring of bright orange bee pollen, with Blossom, curiously looking on, sniffing, snorting and whinning – rushed back into conscious thought. Alta-Dena at once wheeled around and we retraced the stretch of road just traveled.

BEFORE I KNEW IT, the two green eyes came flashing back at us through the dark. Slamming Alta-Dena's brake-pedal hard to the floorboard, we came to a sliding, lurching, screeching halt. I threw back her accordion door, leapt out and ran to the shoulder's edge in the direction of those still, shining green eyes that glared back at Alta Dena's headlights.

I stopped short once the realization dawned that there, lying alongside the roadway, was a young female Gray Fox, starkly gazing up at me.

Stunned by the accuracy of my earlier 'fox-sighting' premonition, and equally strange, sudden recollection of the fawn, I just stood there motionless for several moments, unable to move so much as a muscle.

Bending down to stroke its still warm, wonderfully-soft, furry body, I again sensed, as with the fawn, the unseen eyes of others watching my every move.

Gently picking it up, and cradling the tiny vixen's body in my arms, I let out a wailing, bemoaning chant to whomever might hear it. I knew this strange meeting with the she-fox wasn't by chance and, like the fawn, recognized her to be a messenger from the invisible realm, whose personal message was as yet to be discerned.

Still chanting when I arrived at Schooley's meeting place, I burst into the middle of their circle, cradling the she-fox as I had when I found her, while awkwardly trying to shift with the other hand and guide Alta-Dena the rest of the way.

"Hello!", I softly whispered to Schooley and his group. "Sorry to barge in on you folks this way, but I felt it important that I bring with me this Spirit-Keeper of the Mountain. I thought if anyone could appreciate the fox and what all just went on in the spirit world, it would be you folks."

The startling arrival of the fox in their midst galvanized the thoughts of those gathered upon the circle that night, causing them to ponder the individual and collective meaning she bore for us all.

The next day, my first impulse was to hop into Alta-Dena and return back to the paddock above Mockingbird-Atop-Pear Tree Cottage, where I could repeat the same ceremony that I did with the fawn. But something told me the ceremony had to instead take place somewhere on the Mountain herself.

That same day, a poem, written by Ellen Mark, one of the women in attendance at Schooley's meeting, magically ended up tucked under Alta-Dena's windshield-wiper with a sprig of Mountain Sage attached to it. It asked:

WHY COMES THE FOX?

– 1 –

A man stood before us,
a dead fox cradled
in his arms –
creature from San Bruno
our sacred mountain,
struck by a speeding vehicle
on a Guadalupe Canyon Road.

– 2 –

The man spoke,
head bowed in sorrow
"I sensed this had
happened before I
discovered her lying
on the damp highway.

– 3 –

We felt its body's
still warm, gradeful shape
bushy, gray winter coat,
and the blood on its jaw,
broken from the car's
fatal impact.
Another animal' victim
silent statistic
"We take these things for
granted", many would say.
"The price of progress".

– 4 –

A man stood before us
that dark night
of our December meeting
last of a vanishing year.

– 5 –

What does it mean,
For the man?
For all of us?
Why comes the fox?

– 6 –

San Bruno stands before us
Mountain wild and ancient
offering an answer.

While meditating upon Mark's poem, I heard The Voice gently declare, "Lad! Return to the Mountain to honor the foxes body the way I had you do with the fawn. This fox will serve as your *Voice of The Mountain* medicine bundle to put your sacred Buffalo Medicine Stone and other holy things in. The man you call Dwight, the hermit, will help you in this."

Traditional, aboriginal peoples the world over well understand that one's everyday life is an intimate part of the unseen, yet real realms of the many visible and invisible dimensions that surround them. They know, too, that animals are just spirits of a different sort who simply have animal names and embody qualities which we humans can know and recognize in ourselves and one another. They readily acknowldege that one can learn of such connections and relations through their inner voice, which constantly speaks to them through the natural world and their dreams. To reiterate what Brave Buffalo once said, "The animals want to communicate with men but *Wakan Tanka* – The Great Mystery of Life – does not intend they shall do so directly. Man must do the greater part in securing an understanding.

The night before returning the body of the she-fox back to the Mountain, a dream had come. A fragment of it depicted two Indians, one a young scout and the other an old, gray-haired elder, who sought to approach me from afar. They seemed to have just emerged from beneath a deep, still pool of black molasses-like water, and were ponderously making their way through it, in slow motion, in an effort to reach me. They wore on their heads, rounded buckskin hats, fashioned with the bright-orange feathers of the Red-Shafted Flicker. The Elder stopped directly in front of me, raised his open hand in the sign of peace and, while vibrating a split-stick clapper in  his right hand – which made a sharp, machine gun-like clacking sound – lowly chanted, over and over, "Ho-Ho, HOH! Ho-Ho, HOH! Ho-Ho, Ho-Ho, Ho-Ho, HOH!"

Finally he spoke, "Twin Rainbow! We desire to trade our Flicker feather headdresses with you in exchange for...." At that moment the dream faded and I awoke. Semi-conscious, I lay in Alta-Dena, pondering aloud the meaning of the dream's abrupt, unfinished ending. "Does it have something to do with the fox?", I wondered, "Or maybe it has to do with my work on behalf of the Mountain".

Bursting out in laughter, I thought, "Hey, maybe it's this Turtle Island journal idea that they want turned into a book someday. Could the dream's young scout and elder be different parts of me that they're showing, in exchange for putting them in the book?"

– A MEETING WITH THE MOUNTAIN HERMIT –

The next day, Alta-Dena, the She-fox and I drove through Brisbane's industrial park to a place, close to Buckeye Canyon's entrance, where Alta-Dena could pull off the road and stop for awhile.

With all the excitement of the foxes appearance, that took over Schooley's meeting, the chance never arose to ask him for any more details about Dwight or where exactly he lived, although I knew by now that he was somewhere up Buckeye Canyon. "Trust that you will be guided!", came the thought.

Saying goodbye to Alta-Dena, I gathered up the foxes body and walked towards Buckeye until I reached its base. Spotting a trail that meandered up the steep mountainside, I set out. After a time of passing amongst Live Oaks, Wild Islay Cherry and California Bay's, I came upon a fork in the trail, but didn't know where next to go.

"No worries!", came another thought, "Spirit will guide me! And when I find Dwight, he'll know exactly where the fox should be laid to rest."

At one point, as the trail climbed ever higher and deeper into Buckeye, I knew I was totally lost and didn't have a clue as to where next to go.

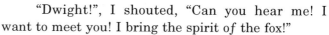

"Dwight!", I shouted, "Can you hear me! I want to meet you! I bring the spirit of the fox!"

All of a sudden, practically right beside where I stood, out jumped a wild-looking, barefooted man with long curly, dirty blond hair, his face covered by a bushy beard and moustache, who was dressed in tattered jeans and a khaki workshirt.

"Are you looking for me?", he said loudly, with a big grin.

'Dwight The Hermit's' sudden emergence, out-of-the-blue, from the thick scrub underbrush, and his unexpected loud greeting a few feet from my ear, that nearly caused me to jump out of my shoes, elicited among us much hearty laughter.

After a time, I raised up the body of the female fox in one hand, and a handful of Flicker feathers in the other, while exclaiming, "Hello! I'm Twin Rainbow! We haven't met before, but Dave Schooley told me a lot about you. I'm one of the natives of the Mountain, too. I've come to skin the fox and do ceremony with her body. I thought you'd be the one to show me a good place to do it."

"Good ol' Dave! You know him, do ya'! C'mon with me, Twin Rainbow. I know just the place!" Reverently placing the fox in his arms, I said, "Here, take her, Dwight. I know she is every bit your relation as she is mine. Lead the way!"

Without any further words or fanfare passing between us, I followed behind him as we strode, single-file, up the narrow trail past his secluded, open-air house that could barely be seen even if one were straining to spot it. "Is all this really happening?", I wondered as we went, "The fawn, now the fox, meeting David Schooley and now Dwight? What can I expect next?"

As we proceeded, I glanced back down the trail and could see Dwight's place. His totally organic home, cut into the earth, amongst the roots of a giant Live Oak, looked more like a cross between an Indian 'wickiup' and a hobo lean-to. The walls of its open air bedroom made of bound willow-reeds, a cozy cot in one corner and a mini-kitchen beside the cot. The kitchen a combination earth and rock-cairn wall, with cupboards and shelves notched into the hard-packed-clay earth, and a combo living-room–sun deck that was part automobile hood-ceiling, rock-terraced floor and a natural, open-pit fireplace, around which favored visitors were warmly enjoined to squat and chat for a spell.

His canyon home so secluded – sourrounded as it was by thick colonies of Islay Cherry, Buckeye's and Live Oaks – that one could virtually pass, as I just did, within a few feet of it without even having realized they'd passed straight through the hermit's extended living room-sun deck.

Briskly following Dwight by his house, we continued our, by now, joint pilgrimage further up Buckeye to where a natural rock-faced shrine existed, complete with an old Spanish–Mexican gold cross securely fastened to one of its sides. Beside the gilded cross was the sun-bleached skull of a fox, set within a small recess of the shrine. "Oh, yeah!", I thought upon spying the fox skull, "I'm in the right place, with the right guide!"

We stopped there for a time to offer up several prayers and chants, naturally created on the spot, in honor of the Mountain and Spirit of the fox, and then continued on.

Dwight stopped when we came to an opening in the scrub, high above the rock-shrine, and declared, "This is a good spot to do your ceremony with the fox."

The place he chose commanded a view of the entire Bay Area from where could be seen all of the Mountain's sister mountains: from Pechas Azul (Twin Peaks), Mt. Davidson and Mt. Tamalpais in the North; Mt. Diablo in the East; to the far-distant Pacific coastal ranges in the South and Farallone Islands in the West.

The two of us made silent tobacco offerings to the spot, at which point Dwight leaned over and whispered, "Hey, Twin! Spend some alone time here with the fox and I'll see yah back at the house." With that, he abruptly departed, disappearing into the thick scrub without so much as a backward glance.

The way he so easily could appear and disappear into the bush reminded me of some of those early accounts written by the first Spaniards who rode into places like San Bruno Mountains, or what the

Hermit's House on The Mountain

Hermit's Kitchen

White Man calls Mt. Diablo, and encountered those like the Yelamu and other Ohloné people. Wrote one explorer, "Jesus, Mary and Joseph! These black devils are like magicians who can appear and disappear right before your very eyes!" What that Spaniard didn't know was that instead of devils, hif he had likened them to clever angels or spirits he would have been closer to the truth.

– A COMMUNIQUE ARRIVES FROM THE SPIRIT WORLD –

Sitting beside the, by now, skinned-body of the fox – encircled by red-cloth tobacco ties and a sprinkling of orange bee pollen – I thought again about Ellen Mark's poem and the questions it raised.

As my eyes gazed out at the awesome expanse that surrounded us, staring once more at that tiny, skinless body that lay before me – I asked the fox a question, hoping her spirit would answer.

"So, why come you, little one?", I queried. "What clever, cunning, subtle, vulpine ways would you have me learn?"

Without any conscious desire to write anything, my fingers began hurriedly digging out the crumpled poem Schooley gave me, that was still in my pocket.

Turning it over, I feverishly scribbled down a stream of words which began to pour forth as if taking dictation from the fox herself. The Spirit of the Fox declared:

WHY COME I?

The Mountain now offers up an answer. I, its Spirit Keeper, wish to speak. I have sent you one of my children with this charge: without the help of you humans, I, and all like me, are doomed to disappear from sight forever. UNLESS you are prepeared to become as cunning and resourceful as I, and will work as hard in your world as I do in my world This you must do if you expect us to instruct your children and their children's children, as we now insruct you, in our ways and those of The Mountain. My body, that you now have turned into a spirit bag, will travel with you, wherever you go. Cherish it for it will help both you and us to live.

When the writing stopped I knew the ceremony with the fox was over. "Goodbye, Fox!", I said. "But it's not really goodbye because a part of you will remain with me always. So it's only, 'See you next time in the spirit world'!"

Returning back down the canyon to Dwight's house, I found him brewing a pot of tea on an open fire. "Sit down a spell, Twin!", he said,

"Tell me what all went on up there." Once I finished my tale, Dwight simply said, "This ol' Mountain sure is big medicine!"

– A NEVER-ENDING BATTLE WITH THE WHITE MAN –

Slowly sipping our tea, Dwight and I shared some of the key things that have happened to us in our lives and what made us do the many seemingly bizarre things we've done.

Dwight said that at one time he was a dedicated elementary school teacher who worked in Pacifica, before deciding that the sanest possible thing he could do in life was to reinhabit the Mountain as the native peoples before him had done for 10,000 or more years.

By the time we met, he already had spent eight years of daily silent bliss, enjoying a Spartan lifestyle and eating whatever native plants and berries he could gather, along with whatever other food stuffs friends from the surrounding human settlements were brought to him on occasion.

School children often made weekly trips up into his Buckeye Canyon home, not only to enjoy the natural beauty of the place but to bring the odd can of food, piece of fruit or loaf of bread as an offering with which to 'delight the hermit'.

If San Bruno Mountain, with all its valleys and canyons, served as a natural therapist for me as a youth, Dwight's similar efforts to heal himself led him to become, for a whole new generation of children, a modern-day human adjunct to the Mountain's healing powers.

Rather than seek out the unhealthy counterparts of the drug-addicted, hobo likes of 'Ol' Mr. Bear Tracks' of my day, many youngsters, over-wrought by their fast-paced, pressure-cooker way of life, in search of some solace, regularly beat a speedy retreat to the welcome haven of the hermit's enclave.

The day finally came, though, when local San Mateo County Park officials learned of his 'illegal presence' upon the Mountain and decided to take action. Yet when they attempted to remove Dwight, they suddenly found themselves besieged by hundreds of children and their families who rushed to his aid by initiating a huge grass-roots letter campaign and media blitz. Their strong support attested to his gentle nature and the invaluable educational resource he represented as the Mountain's *Resident Naturalist-Ranger*'.

It soon became abundantly clear to the authorities that this 'strange, homeless' man wasn't at all strange, nor was he homeless, but instead had come to symbolize – in the minds of at least those who enjoyed the

Mountain's wild beauty, and especially among those who enjoyed its ancient Yelamu human story – *"The Wild Freedom of A Lost Time"*. A lost time which this unusual man simply tried to reclaim for himself for however long a time and, in the process, came to symbolize, for some deep ecologists, not only the extinct Yelamu but the sixteen remaining rare and endangered species of plants and animals who also valiantly sought, as he, to remain free and wild upon the Mountain.

For still others of the Christian faith, Dwight came to symbolize the two 'hermit-saints', after which the Mountain originally received its Western name. The one a 12th century priest who sought out God in the wildernesses of France and Italy, while in the company of a community of monks, whose descendants founded the Carthusian Order which still resides on San Bruno Mountain in Italy. The other hermit-saint being Bordano Bruno, an Italian priest of the 1600's who, because of his animistic philosophy, was burned at the stake for his heresy.

In the end, with such a broad base of support against them, and in the face of an ever-mounting public outcry, the Park Service acquiesced and allowed Dwight to remain, indefinitely.

However, the White Man – always the two-faced, forked-tongued, double-dealing mongrels that they are – later did an about face, once it was politically expedient to do so. The Park officials subsequently dispatched a veritable army of park rangers, and their crony wrecking crews, or *Duchronaigh* (Doo-Kro-nee), as we Irish contemptuously once called such bastards in our own homelands, to evict Dwight and totally destroy whatever signs of his habitation existed.

When the truth finally came out as to why Dwight was removed, as is always the case with the White Man, it was because of a politically-motivated decision that was initiated by a disgruntled ex-mayor of Brisbane and his development-minded cohorts, supported by San Mateo County's senior environmental planners – who were all opposed to the deep ecological philosophy of Dwight and those who suppported him. Dwight simply became the most convenient object to do their axe-grinding on. As one park ranger tellingly put it, "We had to remove him because if we didn't the next thing you know there would be a whole tribe up there, pretending to be Indians. Those days are gone! No one, not even dreamers, can live like that anymore!"

– LIFE CAN PRESENT SOME FUNNY CONTRADICTIONS –

Several days after all the soul-talk with Dwight, I decided to return to the Mountain. This time it was to conduct an impromptu Turtle Island

'Earth Religion' Sunday service, of my own creation, at a another place Dwight showed after I'd gone back to his house and we'd drained another couple of big pots of tea while talking our heads off.

The proposed ceremony involved another visit to the rock shrine and the spot where the fox was laid to rest, followed by a contemplative hike to a sacred spot high atop one of the nearby ridges where the intent was to leave a prayer flag in a rock cairn.

The spot was a wild place of the spirit where other natural 'church goers', like at Hah-Kli-Luk in British Columbia, also previously traveled to many times, while leaving behind cairns of unusual rocks, brought there from the other sister mountains and sacred sites in the Bay Area. One could also find there many colorful *Wicca* prayer sticks – covered with feathers, tiny bells, bits of cloth and yarn of all patterns and colors – that pilgrims had everywhere stuck into the cleavages of the cairns and other natural rock formations.

As I headed up the canyon towards Dwight's place, who should be seen walking down the mountainside, but the people's *Resident Ranger* himself.

This time, though, Dwight looked completely different than I'd ever seen him. His tangled, fire-smoked, blond hair now clean and neatly brushed. He wearing his fresh *Sunday-go-to-Meeting* clothes, which, upon an earlier visit with him, I saw him wash in a nearby creek and let to dry in the sun, draping them helter-skelter all across the tops of the Islay Cherry trees which surrounded his place. Dwight proudly carrying in his hands – as the *piece de resistance* of this weekly Sunday pilgrimage of his – the brightly-polished black shoes he would put on once his feet hit the concrete edge of the modern world below.

We stopped and I gave him one of those customary big bear hugs often generously extended to all soul-mates met along the way. Once we finished exchanging some brief thoughts about the everyday travails of our native lives and that of the Mountain's, we gave each other one last bear hug before setting out again upon our separate journeys. Dwight had his own ceremony planned and I mine.

As I continued to climb up one of Buckeye's steep trails, which skirted the edge of a bright-green, moss-lined, creek bed, my mind pondered with bemusement, "Ah, this life is a strange one indeed, me bucko! Here you are, a wild, native city-dweller, who's on his way to church upon the mountain, while Dwight, the gentle, native mountain-dweller is on his way to church within the city. Two equally strange wayfarers, passing like the proverbial ships in the night, upon your own singularly unique odysseys."

SO, PILGRIM. Retreat to what you would call your own church in nature, wherever that is. As you sit against the spine of your spirit tree, or even the wooden pew in some man-made church that once was a tree in a great forest, ponder who or what have served as the 'Dwight' or 'Fox' in your life. What lessons of the White Man's world did they teach you? What ceremonies or rituals have they caused you to undertake? **Hurry Now! Be Off With Ye! Go!**

WELCOME BACK! Returning to the San Bruno Mountains in a sacred way; finding new meaning through the simple rituals, ceremonies and renewed spirit contact with the natural world there; while joining together with young and old alike who had the same spiritual connections; brought home to my rational, adult mind the real, living fairy tale that this natural sanctuary always has represented.

Recalling the many thrilling childhood challenges and arduous tests of courage this real-life saga posed, led me to wondering what still new spiritual tasks and personal–planetary healing work still lay ahead on behalf of the Mountain.

–THE SPIRIT MOVES IN STRANGE WAYS –

The answer to all these ruminations became clearer several years later, after having traveled once more to Mount Shasta, this time with Tai Situ Rinpoche, one of Tibet's most revered lamas, and his entourage of monks who were on the North American leg of their world-wide 'Pilgrimage For Active Peace'. Alta-Dena and I gathered together with the Tibetans in San Francisco for the honor to travel with them in their caravans to meet with the Great Mountain Chief and his wife.

The intent of our pilgrimage was to honor the mountain through a traditional Tibetan Lha Sang Ceremony, that was designed to promote harmony between environmental forces and human activity everywhere in North America. Runners had been extensively preparing themselves, as part of the ceremony, to take their Tibetan's prayer flags and offerings, as well as those others flags and offerings I carried from the San Bruno Mountains, to the summit of Mount Shasta.

However, once we arrived at the base of Mount Shasta, and the Tibetans became engrossed in their preparations, I immediately made contact, as is customary on Turtle Island when one travels into another's spiritual territory, with a local Wintu-Karuk woman to see if it was okay to do ceremony on Mt. Shasta.

What was soon discovered is that the local traditional spiritual people didn't know anything about the Tibetan's ceremony. No one had paid them the spiritual courtesy of clearing it beforehand. The Wintu-Karuk woman reminded me of their spiritual ways which consider the summit of Mount Shasta as the sacrosanct spiritual territory of the Creator and Creator's spirit forces, and so off-limits to we mortal humans.

Before things developed into a serious spiritual *faux pas*, I assured the native woman that it was all just an unfortuante oversight and that the Tibetans, no doubt, would abide by whatever Wintu-Karuk customs were appropriate. As the true, sensitive spiritual leaders that the Tibetan's are, they at once changed their plans, practically at the last minute, and gave their runners orders to only go to an agreed upon spot at an acceptable distance below the summit.

Before leaving with the Tibetans on their pilgrimage, I returned to Indian Head Cave to conduct a sage and cedar-smudging ceremony before carrying away a small stone and plant, found at the mouth of the cave, which I anticipated the Tibetan runners would also place some-where upon Mount Shasta's heights. The hope behind this ceremony was that by symbolically bringing Mt. Shasta and San Bruno's spirit forces together in this subtle way, they both would become bonded as one and so forever share in one another's well-being.

However, during Tai Situ Rinpoche's Lha Sang Ceremony nothing remotely earth-shattering, or even mildly startling occurred to either of the mountains during or after the ceremony's proceedings.

Yet, as I later would learn, some two months after the North American leg of the Tibetan's world pilgrimage had been completed, a small, yet significant positive event did occur upon San Bruno Mountain.

For in a subsequent meeting which transpired between Schooley's deep-ecological, Earth First commando forces and key private developers – who had been hopelessly bogged down for years, squabbling about whether or not to preserve any part or all of the Mountain – something almost inconceivable happened.

Schooley and the developers unexpectedly came to an agreement as to how best protect, in perpetuity, at least two of the Mountain's most treasured canyons – Buckeye and Owl – as State & County Park lands.

The second this news arrived, I wondered, "Hmm! Did the Tibetan's prayer flags, or the stone and plant from Indian Head Cave, have anything at all to do with this significant step in the healing of both the Mountain and ourselves? Are these juxtaposed events in time to be dismissed as mere coincidences, or are they rather reflections of that universal Law of Synchronicity hard at work again?"

Whatever the ultimate answer, a sixth sense suggested that these events were related. That forever more, the future welfare and fate of both mountains, henceforth, would remain bonded through prayer flag, stone and plant – spirit, mind and heart – as One.

– SOMETIMES SPIRIT GIVES MORE TANGIBLE FEEDBACK –

Still another time came when the odyssey drew me once more back to the San Bruno Mountains, to commemorate Earth Day while in the company of three more new-found soul-mates.

The one male and two female pilgrims happened to be met up with at the base of Buckeye Canyon. I carried in my hand another small stone and plant, which this time had been carried all the way from Mount Shasta to place upon that sacred *Place of The Fox*, as I called it, high atop one of Buckeye's ridges, where that long ago spontaneous Earth Religion ceremony had been conducted.

"This is my way", as I explained to those three new fellow pilgrims, "of completing the healing circle that's been started between the deva's of these two mountains and we humans."

Once again, the invisible realm of the spirit, at that moment, profoundly, yet simply made itself known to the four of us. The manifestation coming through the visitation of one of the Mountain's most humble, yet revered messengers – the San Francisco Silverspot Butterfly – a rare and endangered species found nowhere else on earth.

As we four 'earth medicine helpers' proceeded up one of Buckeye's animal trails, which led towards a 10,000 year-old Yelamu shell-midden, where we intended to conduct our Earth Day ceremony, we stopped to observe the wild scene.

Suddenly, directly in front of us, a lone Silverspot came to rest serenely in the grass, directly in front of our path. Unruffled by our presence near its cozy, basking place beneath the blazing hot sun, the

Silverspot allowed us to stoop down upon our hands and knees and peer closely at it from only a few inches away.

We four couldn't help but laugh as we tried to imagine how gargantuan and intimidating, or how ridiculously-funny we humans looked to that tiny butterfly, as we squatted there on all fours, our glaring faces and bulging eyes pressed flat to the ground in an attempt to make direct eye contact.

Finally I ever-so slowly placed my forefinger alongside its tranquil little body to see what would happen. When, much to our amazement, the Silverspot deliberately climbed off its grassy stalk and perched itself high atop my finger, placidly remaining there even as I raised my finger to eye level, practically at the tip of my nose. We all gasped with delight.

The Silverspot's deep-black eyes seemed to be peering deeply into my own as it conveyed a message to my spirit's ears. "Hello!", said the Silverspot, telepathically "I've come to you as an emissary from a world beyond your view. I will stay with you a while. Learn what you can."

Tumultuous winds, rushing down Buckeye's walls, began battering the Silverspot's fragile wings. Yet rather than fly away, it hunkered down all the more on my finger with a seemingly renewed resolve and sense of purpose. "This little guy", I chuckled with glee, "seems to want to come with us." So off we went, continuing our pilgrimage up to the Yelamu shell-midden site, still some hundred yards distant.

Though we twisted, turned and contorted ourselves through the tall, orange-blossomed Monkey Pods, the delicate, giant, white Queen Anne Lace, Wild Fennel and Poison Oak colonies that lined either side of the narrow trail – climbing up and down dry creek beds and over steep banks of Live Oaks and Islay Cherry trees – the tiny Silverspot remained hunkered on my finger tip. My forefinger all the while raised triumphantly at eye level, as Silverspot continued to happily sun itself as if it were leading the way.

At the shell mound, we humans formed ourselves into a medicine circle in the tall dry grass, with each of us taking positions at each of the four cardinal directions. Once settled, we again took to gazing upon our curious winged companion-traveler who steadfastly stayed with us the whole way.

Noemi, the elder woman-healer amongst us, who sat on the circle, to the North, noticed that one of the Silverspot's wings might have suffered some damage during our blustery journey together. "I'm going to give our little friend some contact healing", she declared.

With that she raised her crystal ring-bedecked hands to within a few inches above the tiny Silverspot, which still seemed not the least bit threatened by her actions, closed her eyes and quietly hummed a soothing tune.

Within seconds, the tiny emissary, who previously remained so stoic, all at once became highly-animated; its wings vibrating intensely, as if a current of electricity was rushing through them. Several minutes of this feverish healing ceremony passed before Noemi removed her hands, whereupon the frenetic vibrations of the Silverspot's wings just as quickly changed to a slow, relaxed, rhythmic fan. The butterfly continued to rhythmically wave its wings for a few seconds longer until, much to our surprise, it fluttered off my finger.

Airborne, it gracefully flittered and swirled in the wind's currents, weaving an ever-widening circle above our heads, before once more deliberately landing in the grass not more than two feet behind where I sat on the circle to the South. "Look!", I proclaimed, "our tiny spirit companion has decided to join us on the circle in the South – that symbolic place of perpetual growth and healing in the world."

The Silverspot's essence, itself, was a symbol that we readily acknowledged. The butterfly with her brilliantly-cloured, richly-patterned body a symbol of that which everywhere spreads beauty and life, with each new flower pollinated, in the most gentle, harmonious, natural way.

"The Silverspot", I said, "has come to us as a reminder that this is why we've come together on this special day and seek to do throughout the whole year." This tiny spirit messenger of that unique moment of time and space we five shared together, also reminded us of how always grateful we must always remain for life's beauty while, at the same time, acknowledging how forever fragile, fleeting and vulnerable it is.

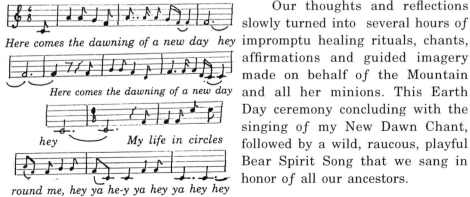

Here comes the dawning of a new day hey

Here comes the dawning of a new day

hey   My life in circles

round me, hey ya he-y ya hey ya hey hey

Our thoughts and reflections slowly turned into several hours of impromptu healing rituals, chants, affirmations and guided imagery made on behalf of the Mountain and all her minions. This Earth Day ceremony concluding with the singing of my New Dawn Chant, followed by a wild, raucous, playful Bear Spirit Song that we sang in honor of all our ancestors.

This Bear Spirit Song caused our tiny foursome to split into two sets of singers and drummers, with one man and woman assuming a place on the West side of the circle, while the other pair assumed a place on the East side. Our intent was to 'throw' the Bear Spirit song back and forth at one another.

One side of our medicine circle would suddenly thrust their bodies forward across the circle, with great animation, towards the other singers, as if to challenge them to reciprocate, while twice loudly chanting:

HAH!   Hah - Hah - Hah - Hah - Hah - Hah - Hah!

As soon as one side finished their chant they jerked their bodies back, as if to recoil in the face of the chanting reply they knew was about to explode in their faces. The other side just as animatedly chanting back:

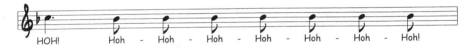

HOH!   Hoh - Hoh - Hoh - Hoh - Hoh - Hoh - Hoh!

Back and forth raged the Bear Spirit Song for what seemed like hours as our exchanges became evermore outrageously playful, our facial gestures and body talk growing all the more exaggerated and absurd as time went on.

At last exhausted, we began to clean up our ceremonial site, in preparation to leave the shell midden, when Naoemi shouted, "Oh, my God! Look! Our furry, winged friend all the while has been with us in the grass, as if to bear witness to our celebration of the Earth."

I walked over to the Silverspot, bent down and once more extended my finger alongside its outstretched body. To our utter amazement, it gingerly hopped back onto my finger. The four of us – half-laughing, half-gawking – gasped, in a mixed chorus of rising and falling voices, "Oh, My God! I don't believe this!".... "Wow! This is incredible!".... "Thank you, Mountain!"...."Thank you, Yelamu!"...."Thank you, Spirits!"

As we descended down the mountainside towards the White Man's cold, hard, concrete world that we knew awaited, we continued our noisy mixed chorus that was turning raucous again as we chanted, "Hooray To

The Magic Of Life! HAH! Hah-Hah-Hah-Hah-Hah-Hah-Hah!......HOH! Hoh-Hoh-Hoh-Hoh-Hoh-Hoh-Hoh!"

Tramping the trail with Silverspot once more leading the way, we humans, still gibbering muffled "HAH's and HOH's", laughed and cried as tears of joy and wonderment streamed down our faces.

San Bruno Mountain didn't experience that year the multitudes of Earth Day celebrants that other, more mass media-hyped venues in the Bay Area or elsewhere in North America enjoyed. Yet the power for good and planetary healing that we four humans and one non-human conjured up there was so mighty that the sense we had was that 100,000 celebrants couldn't have conjured up anything any better.

When we reached the point where we originally met up with our gentle, winged guide, we paused to place it back upon the stalk from whence it came. But it ignored all attempts to coax it back into the grass, resolutely refusing to budge from my fingertip. So down the mountainside we went, singing and laughing all the more 'til we reached the edge of the dreaded White Man's unreal world.

Yet the instant our feet touched its hard asphalt surface, the Silverspot, as if to make the point that this is where our two world's must always end, fluttered off, zigging and zagging 'round us before landing several yards back up along the Mountain's wild edge.

We walked back over to it, reverently bowed, as if in tribute to an almighty wise elder, knelt down and, with a quivering, awe-struck voice

paid our last respects. "Goodbye, dear Brother-Sister, whomever you are!", I whispered. "Thank's for the gift of your life's wild, gentle power. I'll never forget this moment. For you've taught me to always keep my eyes and heart open to enjoy the smallest, most precious moments. I vow to dedicate myself to help you and your people live and prosper. Goodbye again. See you in my dreams! The Yelamu are dead! Long live the Yelamu!"

With that, the Silverspot was airborne, disappearing back into the panoramic canvas of the Mountain's fog-swept, jewel of creation. The tiny butterfly once more caught up amongst a whirlwind of entwining eddy's of tiny Mission Blue's, Silverspot's and Elfin Butterflies who all seemed to at once join together in mid-air in one huge, tender, joyful, mating dance.

As I glanced back one last time at the whirlwind of fluttering wings, hoping to see them just once more before the Mountain's thick coastal scrub-brush world swallowed them up, I acknowledged that Gray

Fox and Silverspot now had been inducted into the pantheon of a real-life fairy tale to be shared with others. Like the Giant Pumpkin Spider, Red-Tailed Hawk, Grandfather Snake, Indian Head Cave, Mean Man & His Dogs and the Old Lady in the Haunted House of my youth, they had become mythic characters in an epic saga of my own creation.

– AT THE HEART OF THE ESA/HCP DEBATE –

Little could I know, as I left Buckeye Canyon and headed back to Alta-Dena, of the many return trips that would have to be made to help the Mountain survive as best she could. The objective of each return trip always the same: how to find yet another way to call the public's attention to what she symbolizes for the preservation of wild species and habitats throughout North America.

In 1995, during one trip, a furious debate arose within the U.S. 104th Congress over the reauthorization of its Endangered Species Act. Alta-Dena and I had just left Canada where an equally furious debate was raging over its *National Public Consultation on Endangered Species Conservation.* It was time to refocus the public's attention on the seminal role that San Bruno Mountain continues to play as a lightning rod in this on-going debate.

To sharpen the focus, six months was spent, as an investigative reporter, interviewing all the key players and extensively researching how the Mountain had fared under the ESA and its 1982 HCP amendment. The result was the publication and distribution of a monograph entitled, *A Voice in the Wilderness; San Bruno Mountain's Struggle For Survival.*

Out of the monograph emerged a whole slew of ESA/HCP issues. Was it the development or conservation community who originally selected the Mountain to become the national model for the ESA and its later HCP? Why San Bruno Mountain? Was it because certain Canadian-Amerian corporate syndicates – among some of the most powerful and ruthless in North America – had huge land holdings there? What drove the ESA/HCP legislation? Was it the billions of dollars in construction monies to be gained, or the protection of the last piece of wild Franciscan habitat left on the planet? Did the developer–moguls intend to use the Mountain as a Trojan horse to slowly, cunningly, gut, from within, the ESA/HCP concept and show how urban sprawl can continue, unabated, in spite of the Act's precepts? How has the Mountain's rare habitats, and their species of concern, in truth fared, over the past three decades, since the ESA/HCP's implementation?

The epic saga of the Mountain's two most endangered native species – the Mission Blue Butterfly & San Francisco Garter Snake – among the most ancient of archetypal symbols for personal transformation, quickly served as an ESA versus HCP call to action.

San Bruno Mountain soon called forth a widespread suspicion, especially held by the conservation community, that many of the biologists, herpetologists, zoologists and entomologists, supposedly involved in her care, were actually up to their eyeballs in the rapid, unexplainable crash of more and more of the Mountain's rare and endangered species. The collapse of these populations, curiously, occurred with greater frequency whenever that species, under the HCP's so-called 'protection', came in conflict with some powerful developer and their lucrative project.

These suspicions soon drew attention to the primary question as to whether or not the Mountain's HCP was a promising new vision for North America's spiritual and ethical reclamation or nothing more than the old Indian Reservation system, dusted off and rekindled for the last rare and endangered species in Canada and the United States? The cunning 'reservation system' that had been devised for the Mountain's species of concern seemed symbolic of the same historical conflict that has occurred in North America whenever some other native species – be it an Indian, Metis, buffalo, grizzly, wolf, spotted owl – has had the misfortune to come into harm's way of the corporate world's ever-expanding frontier?

In every case, the species in question, like the Indian of old, always the one who ends up either killed or shuffled off to some ever-dwindling, wasted parcel of land. The Mountain's seminal HCP a classic modern example of how to *reservationalize* and so neutralize all those new species who might dare to *get in the way of progress*. But instead of the Indian Agent, General Custer and War Department of yesteryear, the latest operative terms speak of 'HCP Plan Operators', 'Habitat Managers' or 'Interior Department' directives that pontificate on high of 'mitigation', 'incidental taking' and 'co-existence'.

The Mountain's HCP a case in point where no one law or precept, biblical or otherwise, can seemingly ever stem the tide or change the course of mankind's juggernaut collison with the Earth and its native denizens. The implication being that, "God's (i.e. The White Man's) providential law dictates that neither man nor beast ever has the right to interfere with mankind's (i.e. the eltitist classes) exercise of its dominion over the earth.

"   So many questions demanding answers constantly arose. Like what universal lessons can be learned from the way local, state and federal powers, historically, have dealt with the criticisms of the Mountain's HCP? How can the United States and Canada draw upon the lessons learned as a result of the bureaucratic pitfalls and philosophical shortcomings of the Mountain's HCP legislation? Will Canada's own ESA or HCP concept, unlike that of the United States, be wise enough to draw upon the spiritual wisdoms of its First Nation peoples and Christian faiths, as expressed through their *Sacred Assembly* that met in Hull, Quebec in 1995?

Since these questions first were asked, what has revealed itself over the years is the tip of an ugly Canadian–American political and philosophical iceberg. To pour over The Mountain's HCP and its environmental impact reports – as keenly as one would the Constitution's of Canada and the U.S., the Bible, Quran or some other holy book – is a most revealing exercise.

The tip of this iceberg suggestive of something so monolithic and sinister that it, by far, eclipses the corporate world's cynical manipulation of the ESA. This massive berg representative of the moral and ethical corruption of North American public life. Its visible tip a mere hint of the systemic ethos and pathos of North America and the still primitive experiment it represents as regards humankind's relationships with the natural world.

In the turbulent times of the late 20th and early 21st centuries – with public media and, ergo, public consciousness so tightly controlled and managed by a small elite cadre of people – who represent a very narrow, limited perspective on the political, religious and intellectual spectrum – it's next to impossible to go beyond the corporate success story spin that is given to the Mountain's Habitat Conservation Plan. The same applies for most every other HCP written in the United States.

The Mountain, in truth, representative of a political and scientific scandal, of mega proportions, over the way its ESA/HCP has been written and administered. Those politicians, scientists and academics responsible for overseeing the protection and preservation of the Mountain indeed guilty of what is, in the best or worst sense of the word, criminal negligence. But just try to ever legally prove that to judges and lawyers who are as much a part of the problem!

The thirty year 'War of The Roses' that since has raged upon San Bruno Mountain – that might better be dubbed 'The War of The Environmental Roses' or 'War of the Lupine' – provides more ominous twists than a Gothic novel or Tammany Hall exposé.

The goriest, messiest, battles in this war referred to as: the *South Slopes Washout*; *Pointe Pacific Lock-in*, and *Northeast Ridge Debacle*. Not to forget the *Terra Bay S & L Fiasco* and its curtain call *The Great Resolution Trust Corporation's Bailout*.

In the aftermath of all these battles, words like 'byzantine', 'conspiracy', 'kickback' and 'pay-offs' – or expressions like 'conflict of interests', 'rotten politics' and 'voodoo science' – litter The Mountain's natural landscapes. The unsung heroes and heroines in these battles cast as the *Crocker Wetland Warriors, The Protectoresses of the P G & E Marsh, Keepers-of-the-Wild Islay Cherry Forests of Buckeye Canyon, Guardians of Juncus Ravine* and *Protectors of the Shell Mounds*.

Yet the darkest windings of the Mountain's Gothic tale of tough, no-holds barred, trench warfare takes place behind the front lines, far away from the threatened habitats and endangered species daily struggles for survival. This even more deadly, covert war continues to occur unabated in hundreds of corporate board backrooms, closed council chambers and Congressional hallways.

In the meantime, local, state and federal politicans, and their lacky doublespeak 'environmental scientists', spin the story their way. "Our Plan", they say, "to protect San Bruno Mountain's species of concern and their habitats has proven itself a success. Thanks to the developers, and their HCP Trust Fund, the Mountain has been saved forever."

Over the past thirty years, slick puff-pieces of so-called 'wise use' and 'biology as ideology' journalism (i.e. propaganda) have been periodically planted in the local and national press to reinforce this premise. Each new puff-piece yet one more classic example of subtle hoodwinking by the corporate fascist mentality to ensure its spin remains as the perpetual public perception.

As a result, the Mountain's HCP has become the cancerous fountainhead of an endless supply of shrink-wrapped HCP's, sold to every developer and urban planner at $20.00 a pop. She the veritable motherlode of an ever-burgeoning cottage industry of *Environmental Consulting Firms* and Have-Gun-Will Travel HCP Plan Operators. The clever rhetoric of the Mountain's HCP part and parcel of the biggest swindle since the pilgrims bought Manhatten with a handful of beads.

Ever since, the Mountain, thanks to her HCP, has become hopelessly enmeshed in: the development community's endless bureaucratic sea of use permits; a constant gut-wrenching torque between four municipal-ities, two county governments, a state fish and game agency, another federal fish and wildlife service, as well as numerous environmental organizations, city or county planning commissions, not to mention the hosts of pseudo-scientific agencies who rubber-stamp the destruction of the rich diversity of the Mountain's habitats and wildlife. To make matters worse, these entities, as a rule, basically have remained antagonistic to one another as they've vied for hegemony.

Yet through it all, the Mountain remains steadfast as a stalking horse for whatever political, philosophical, economical, sociological, psychological, spiritual issue in the debate that one cares to explore.

Paul Reeberg, a one-time natural resources consultant for governmental agencies nationwide, and a former field biologist for San Mateo County, once said:

Everyone, Congress, the U.S. Fish & Wildlife Service, California Fish & Game, San Mateo County, Thomas Reid Associates, who administer the HCP on San Bruno Mountain, and the average concerned citizen, have something to learn by looking at San Bruno Mountain. It would be really worth it for the United States, as a country, and a society, if we're going to truly learn how to manage our rare and endangered habitats, to look at The Mountain as the first HCP, and drag over it with a fine tooth comb.

Reeberg poignantly ended with the question:

Is the HCP versus ESA debate we're seeing play itself out upon San Bruno Mountain a question of the lights being on in America's house but no one's home? The Fox in charge of the hen house? Or are we witnessing the difficult birth of a new way for we humans to try and live in harmony and balance with the rest of the planet's creatures?

If every berg, hamlet, village, town, city and metropolis in North America were to create, and then adopt, as part of their official trappings, their own version of the *Peoples Natural Nominees & Awards* that this writer once put forth to the citizenry for San Bruno Mountain, it would constitute a giant leap forward towards realizing the difficult birth that Reeberg suggests.

– THE PEOPLES NATURAL NOMINEES –

To the mayors, councils and citizenry of San Francisco, Brisbane, Daly City, Colma and South San Francisco, we, the Native Peoples of this sacred place, herewith nominate the following aboriginal representatives of the Mountain to become part of your city's official trappings:

The People's Bird — *Scrub Jay*

(Because it is still the flying 'knower and watcher' of our canyons from Colma Canyon to Noe Valley.)

The People's Insect — *Mission Blue, San Bruno Elfin, Callippe Silverspot & Bay Checkerspot Butterflies*

(Because they remain prime indicators of the ancient balance of the fragile wild Franciscan world still around us)

The People's Flower — *Coast Blue Blossom*

(Because it once flourished all along our region, from its bay slopes and hilltop heights to El Camino Real and Old Mission Road)

The People's Plant — *Dune Tansy*

(Because it once was found throughout our coastal dune country, from Sutro Baths and the Sunset to the sandy arroyos of Colma and Westlake, and still hangs on in a few isolated spots.)

The People's Tree — *Islais Cherry*

(Because it is an indigenous Franciscan forest tree which gave San Francisco the name of one of its largest creeks and still flourishes on the Mountain.)

The People's Reptile — *S.F. Garter Snake*

(Because its vibrant visage is rapidly vanishing from the last marshy areas of our peninsula.)

The People's Mammal — *Grey Fox* from

(Because for generations it has watched us its scrub and grassland haunts but seldom allowed itself to be seen.)

The People's Amphibian — *Rough-Skinned Newt*

(Because this orange-bellied pioneer of Franciscan pools, fogrocks and leafmold canyons still survives even in our inner-city canyon backyards.)

– THE PEOPLES NATURAL AWARDS –

The People also encourage your city to annually propose for nomination those within its jursidictions who would be most deserving of the following honors:

The *Flipped Bird of The Year* Award* —

(For those local developers who committed the greatest affront against the city's wildlands and endangered species.)

The *Proverbial Turkey of The Year* Award* — (For those legal consultants of city and county government most responsible for eroding away the laws and statutes that protect wild Franciscan habitat and its rare and endangered species.)

The *Messy Pigeon of The Year* Award* — (Awarded to the one corporate firm whose odious droppings, often mistakenly referred to as the positive by-products of progress, have rained down most heavily upon the heads of un-suspecting humans and non-humans of the Franciscan region while encrusting over the native countryside.)

The *Human Vegetable of The Year* Award* — (Awarded to the one mayor of the region who, because of his or her vegetable-like wisdom, gave new meaning to the term "environmental doublespeak" that allowed for even more death and destruction to the wild Franciscan world.)

The *Reptilian Human of The Year* Award* — (Awarded to those city council members who, because of dinosauric thinking above and beyond the reptilian norm, supported those development projects which destroyed even more wild Franciscan territory.)

The *Invasive Human Weed of The Year* Award* — (Awarded to those private citizens who have contributed the most personal and financial resources towards assisting the recipients of the above awards.)

*Awards are not meant to cast aspersions against Nature's genuine avian, reptilian and plant communities. They rather are intended to call to mind the derogatory ways in which humans themselves characterize the less desireable qualities of various non-humans and then apply these qualities to their own kind.

The indigenous peoples of the world have long understood the mutually symbiotic healing relationship that exists between we humans, the creatures and the land. Healthy human diversity and biodiversity one in the same! They know Mother Earth's *Ley System* to be part of a vast, inter-galactic network or grid of energy, like acupuncture points, which we humans can draw upon as radiant sources of higher spiritual energy and consciousness. IF, of course, that is, one has been properly trained and acquired the necessary disciplines through the kinds of experiences in Nature that sensitize one to its many subtle forms of communication.

A sixth sense said that Alta-Dena and I had yet one more healing journey still to make in the South before we could return North, back across The Medicine Line into Canada, and the renewal with Crystal Freesia of what we laughingly referred to as our *Movie Star On & Off Locations Relationship*. Yet one more acupuncture point within Mother Earth needed to be revisited and obtain a much sought-after healing.

This time the journey was about to take Alta-Dena and I to the East, back to that sacred *hanbleceya* earth altar atop Holy Hill in South Dakota where, eighteen years before, Joe Thunder Hawk put me to find out some big truth about this so-called reality we call life.

"Alta-Dena!", I shouted, "I know you're not gonna like to hear this! But this time we're gonna have to make it a fast trip, as in F–A–S–T! Not your usual plod! I'm anxious to be home again with Crystal Freesia, amongst the gentler people and softer vibrations *of* Grandmother's Lands. We've spent much too long a time in the South, away from her joyful, radiant spirit. C'mon, girl! Time to go! Giddyup!"

TURTLE ISLAND

ROAD SIGN # 18

WHAT WISDOMS & HEALINGS
HAVE YOU RECEIVED
FROM RETURNING TO THE
VISONARY PLACES
OF YOUR ADULTHOOD?

WE ARE SUCH STUFF AS DREAMS ARE MADE ON;
AND OUR LITTLE LIFE IS ROUNDED WITH A SLEEP

(Shakespeare, *The Tempest*, Act IV, Scene I)

– Song of The Turtle Come Full Circle –

Words & lyrics
by
Jerome Twin Rainbow Irwin

RECLIMBING HOLY HILL

"PILGRIM", warns The Great Voice Of The Turtle, *"To seek the dream of your authentic, intimate self, and so receive a healing through me, is to risk a dangerous journey. For though all my forests, mountains and rivers, or all my winged, finned, four-legged and rooted ones will listen to and respect who and what you are, your world is not so understanding. Far too many of the two-leggeds among you – whether they be Red. Black, White or Yellow – live in so much anger, fear and suspicion of one another, and towards that which is authentic within themselves, that to seek a dream-vision in some holy place upon me – and then follow that dream-vision to its end – is a lonely journey. But if you are strong and courageous enough to follow the beat of my heart, you will find the comfort and strength you need to continue your never-ending search for truth, beauty and wisdom."*

"**Pechas Azul! Pechas Azzzuuulll!**", I lovingly shouted one last time before those sacred spires of the South disappeared from view.

– RETRACING AN OLD TRACK IN THE NO MAN'S LANDS –

As Alta-Dena crossed the Bay Bridge, heading for the plains of South Dakota, I knew this wasn't going to be just a simple return visit, after an eighteen year absence. For what Holy Hill originally symbolized was the most intense stock-taking I'd ever spent, asking such basic questions as: who am I, where did I come from, why am I here now, where was I going. So this was one of those special times when the Holy Spirit was calling upon me to completely rethink what all had transpired over the years and what had been successfully learned or not learned.

It was no time at all before my thoughts were flooded with memories of Grand-da' William, and his epic survival tale through the 19th century's no man's lands of the New World. His life and death struggle as a firey Limerick Irishman – first as a coal and silver miner, cum crooner and clog dancer, champion pugilist and then Fire Chief of Leadville, Colorado – a truly legendary one.

The spectre of Great, Great Grandmother Brighitt Irwin's agonizing death by fire – on the infamous 19th century lanes of Limerick in Countae Claire, Ireland – also rushed to mind. It was Brighitt who, while suffering from extreme malnutrition due to the brutally oppressive policies of the English lords of her day, fell across the fire in her hearth and was horribly burnt before the odour of her burning flesh alerted those other poor wretchs who had the great misfortune to live on the lanes.

Drifting in and out of view as we went, were the haunting semblances of Joe Thunder Hawk, John Williams and Satiacum, who also had tasted the bitter salts of exilement as they struggled to harmonize the beat of their heart with that of the Great Turtle's.

Alta-Dena's tiny engine strained on Hwy 80, one of California's megalomaniacal 'Grand Prix' freeways, as she sought to keep up with the high-powered vehicles that recklessly cut in and around her – their drivers full of road rage, impatiently honking their horns, giving us the finger as they whizzed by. But Alta-Dena's turtle pace always afforded me the chance to slowly reflect upon my own ponderous journey as an exile and all the hostilities experienced along the way at the hands of both the White Man's and Indian's angry, violent cultures.

Especially disconcerting were those painful memories, that forced their way into conscious thought, around all the rejection and ridicule that first a spell-bound altar boy, then a questing teenage youth and later a defiant rebel adult had experienced whenever they ever tried in vain to assert something of their authentic spirit to those around them.

Before I knew it, Alta-Dena had started her ascent into the Sierra Nevada's, like Blue had done eighteen years before, and then, before I knew it, had begun to ply her way across the same blistering-hot Great American Desert that didn't look any different than the last time we'd passed this way.

Each familiar landmark revisited, every memorable benchmark reference point noted, dirged up still other memories of the entrance ways and exits of my life's past cycles. The sagely words of Shakespeare declaring as before, at each cycle's opening and closing, "All the world's a stage, and all men and women merely players. They each have exits and their entrances, and one man in his time plays many parts. His part being seven ages." It was Joe Thunder Hawk who, like Shakespeare, also often spoke of my being part of the return of the Seventh Generation and follower of the Seven Commandments of Turtle Island.

It wasn't long before Alta-Dena and I found ourselves in Wyoming, pulling up to Independence Rock, that lofty 'Ayers Rock' in the heart of Turtle Island, that native and non-native pilgrims alike, for centuries, have used as a sacred touchstone.

Scurrying back up to the top of Independence as before, I surveyed the long way Alta-Dena had just came. Once again, I was left dumbstruck by the immense, lonely, wind-swept expanse that those pilgrim-exiles, of another distant time, once knew.

Aside from Alta-Dena's lone presence far below, the landscape was devoid of the long columns of Indian ponies dragging their travois, or prairie schooners with tethered cows in tow, that once wound their way off into the distant haze, following the course of the Sweetwater towards the Rockies.

Before leaving, I clambered back amongst all the crevices to once more run my fingers over the names, dates and affirmations those unknown wanderers and exiles had painted or chiseled into the rock as a permanent record to say, to whomever would take the time to read it, "Look! We, Too, Once Lived and Passed This Way!"

Enquiring fingernails jabbed at each notched groove, in a desperate attempt to know something more about the authors of those brush strokes and chisel marks, while my mind's eye strained to see the same mysterious, vast, forbidding lands that their eyes once saw.

As my fingers traced their way back in time amongst all the notches, chips and dream-visions, I shouted aloud to those distant pilgrim-recorders, "Though my New Frontier covered wagon may seem slow to me, to you she no doubt would have been more like a rocketship on an asphalt slipstream. Especially compared to your travois poles and wagon wheels that once upon a time ponderously bumped and jolted, at a snail's pace, over every rock and hole of this vast landscape." Oh how I longed in that moment for the slowness and stillness of the world they once knew and were able to so intensely feel through all their senses.

When Alta-Dena crested that same Wyoming rise at dawn, and I caught another awesome, twilight glimpse of the sacred Black Hills of the Sioux, still far off in the distance, Joe Thunder Hawk's words rang out, when he once advised me not to dance in the Medicine Man's Sun Dance. "I know this is confusin' for yah, Twin Rainbow!", echoed Joe's voice, "But some day you'll come back here t' learn even more about what all I'm tryin' t' teach yah about all this."

As Joe's voice faded off, the strange way the odyssey led me to return to South Dakota, as he predicted, underscored life's great mysterious nature and how or why it is that we are led to do the sometimes outrageous or bizarre things we do.

Because prior to making the arduous journey back to South Dakota, a newly-completed journal passage about those early days spent with Joe and his family was rushed off to them in gratitude and thanksgiving for all the spiritual help they'd provided.

Once again, synchronicity came into play. For, as it turned out, my account reached the Thunder Hawk's virtually on the eve of them planning a Sun Dance and Ghost Dance in Joe's honor.

By then, some fifteen years had passed since that night when Joe mysteriously died in a bizarre head-on collision as he and another car recklessly drove with their lights off, in a deadly cat-and-mouse game, on the ridge near Holy Hill.

Joining together with their Red Bear Clan relations, they also intended to pay tribute to other venerated elders – like Ivan White Pipe, Hilda Red Bear, Angel Martinez and She-Takes-The Horse – who since had also passed into the invisible realm.

Sara Thunder Hawk's letter, informing me of the impending ceremonies and an invite to attend them, reached me as I was finishing up my ceremonial healing work on San Bruno Mountain. Without any hesitation, I knew at once that this was Spirit's way of communicating where next the odyssey should lead.

With only a hundred dollars in-hand, a tank full of gas, and over a thousand miles of hard desert, plains and mountain terrain to cover, I nevertheless made preparations to get underway.

Once Alta-Dena and I received the blessing of another braid of smoldering Sweet Grass, and the *Holy Rituals of The Road* checklist had been dutifully completed, I placed on Alta-Dena's dash the protective medicine bundle that Mrs. Koquitt's – a blind, 90 year-old Stoney Indian woman, who lived in an isolated house trailer way out in the middle of the Stoney Reserve in Alberta, Canada – had presented to me years before. Her bundle since had saved my life on more than one occasion.

Like the time I'd been driving non-stop, for 20 hours, after having celebrated with Metis peoples during their 'Back to Batoche' Centenary in Saskatchewan, and fell asleep at the wheel as we drove through the Rockies. It was Mrs. Koquitts medicine bundle that came to me in my reverie and woke me just in time before we drove off a cliff.

"Heya heh! heya heh! ahey! heh! heya hey!", I chanted, "Hear me, Spirits! I know you'll somehow provide me with a way to get their safely, but get there I will or bust!" As things turned out, that's exactly what they did. Without so much as a flat tire befalling the journey, Alta-Dena spirited me across the land.

– SPIRITS FROM THE BADLANDS COME FORTH –

As we entered into the Badlands, we were greeted by two spirit's who made their presence known in a curious way.

Alta-Dena was slowly pushing along a rough gravelled road, that wound and curved across one of the Badland's desolate plateau's, when suddenly, within minutes of one another, we were formally greeted by two of the Badland's Spirit-Keepers – *Rattlesnake* & *Buffalo*. Rattlesnake a symbol of The People's protection, and Buffalo a symbol of The People's survival and return.

It was when Alta-Dena crested a rise on the plateau, that revealed a stunning expanse of the Badland's stark, moon-like landscape, that Rattlesnake presented himself.

With its huge, thick body stretched out across our path, soaking up the Sun's rays and stored heat on the rocky road's hot-gravelled surface, Rattlesnake seemed not the least bit alarmed by our sudden intrusion.

Instead, as Alta-Dena slowly pulled up and stopped directly alongside his huge body, a mere few feet below Alta-Dena's open accordion door, Rattle-snake, still unperturbed, stared up at us and, as if by telepathy, seemed to say, "You may safely pass this way, Brother. Know you that your journey is watched over always by my people."

"Greetings, Grandfather Rattlesnake", I said back to it, telepath-ically, "I remember the dream of you that came to me on that ridge above Hah Kli-Luk in the Okanagan. Thank you for your protection."

With that, I took up the split-stick clapper, used by the native peoples of California as their drum, that was always kept in Alta-Dena's cab for just such special moments, and began to rattle it at Rattlesnake while singing to it a brief honoring song, spontaneously made up for the occasion. Rattlesnake lifted up when he heard my clapper and began to rattle back in a friendly way.

Alta-Dena continued onward until, not more than a few hundred yards distant, majestically standing atop a rise as he stoically stared out across his vast kingdom of eroded canyons far below, was Grandfather Buffalo Bull.

The moment he came into view him, I slammed Alta-Dena to a halt, jumped out of her cab and, without any thought of fear for my personal safety, reverently approached him while loudly chanting my New Dawn Song.

After paying tribute to 'His Regalness', I pulled up fifty yards short of where he stood, when he turned his massive. lordly head my way and mightily shook his whole body, that sent a huge dust cloud and swarm of insects airborne from out of his thick, matted hump.

We gazed intently into each other's eyes for a time until Grandfather Buffalo's wild stare telepathized the thought, "I stand here before you, Little Brother, as the living spirit of your ancestors who wish to tell you that they constantly watch over you. 'Our strength and power, even now', they say, 'is within you, waiting to be expressed. Watch for us in the coming days, for you will learn more of this.' I, your Grandfather, say go now, Little Brother, in a good way. "

Proceeding on through the Badland's, we wound our way up a narrow canyon track until we reached the top of Sheep Mountain Table, where my footsteps soon retraced the same narrow, precipitious ridge upon which Birgil Kills Straight, a Lakota spiritul man, once traveled with me years before. This time, though, a Hidden Valley Red-Tailed Hawk's cry was sent out in respect towards that one-time Ghost Dance stronghold of Kills Straight's ancestors.

The echoes of Red-Tailed Hawk served as affirmations of how right it was to return this long way round to Holy Hill.

– AS THINGS CHANGE, SO THEY REMAIN THE SAME –

When we finally pulled into the Thunder Hawk's compound in Porcupine, we were greeted by Joe's kids, who by now were grown with families of their own. So warm was their greeting that it felt like coming together with family, irrespective of the near two decades that since had passed between us. From the perspective of a natural sense of time – our time apart wasn't dictated by watches, clocks or calendars – for, in truth, it felt as if I'd never left.

No time passed again before I found myself once more pitching in with them, as if one big family, to complete the many awesome ceremonial tasks that needed doing. For the ensuing Sun and Ghost Dance demanded so many things of us: pine arbors and sweat lodges needed to be built; Grandfather Rocks for the Sweat Lodge yet had to be dug from out of their ancient embankment resting places; tipi lodge poles for the Sun Dance Medicine Lodge were waiting to be cut and scraped; a tall, straight Cottonwood first had to be touched by the Thunder Hawk and Red Bear Clan's maidens before the young men could cut it down and transport its body back to the Sun Dance grounds; a steer for the feast still had to be rounded-up and slaughtered; Sun & Ghost Dancers needed assistance in carrying out their final, complex spiritual preparations; whilst wild berries, medicine herbs and wild food stuffs for the celebration feast and the dancer's religious articles were still to be found and gathered in the hills.

Yet no time also seemed not to have passed since other less-positive aspects about reservation life and the Lakota people hadn't changed. The intense jealousies and rivalries between different clans at Pine Ridge, still as virulent as the day I left. Or as Homer Thunder Hawk, Joe's second eldest soon put it to me, "Its always been this way, Jerry, and always will be. There's nothing you or anyone else can do for us here, 'cause we're our own worst enemies." It was only days later that Homer's pithy comments were borne out.

For, as things started to reveal themselves, some of the clan's on Pine Ridge – for one reason or another, the depth and logic of which only an insider within their community can ever fully fathom – were going to great lengths to bad-mouth the ceremonies that the Thunder Hawk's and Red Bear's were about to conduct.

Vicious rumors started to fly about. Some traditionals suggested the Thunder Hawk's Sun Dance wasn't "properly prepared" in the "pre-scribed" traditional Lakota manner. While to some progressives, the Ghost Dance they planned to do, as the first of its kind to be openly-held on the rez in almost a hundred years, and the Shunka Feasting Ceremony that rumor had it would also be done, were ridiculed as "pagan rituals" that, if held, "will bring disgrace to our community."

Spiritual 'goon squads' and A.I.M. miltants menacingly drove by the Sun & Ghost Dance grounds, hurling threats at us to back up their verbal warnings with physical force if we didn't stop what we were doing.

The closed-hearted, closed-minded, glaring faces and rigid bodies of the passing goons – twisted and contorted by years of angry judgmentalness and paranoid suspicions towards whomever their latest fear happened to focus upon – brought so many distaseful memories back to mind.

Recalled were those stressful times, spent as a younger man, when I found myself caught in the middle of the same historically-complex, confusing, chaotic, spiritual–political scene of the Lakota. Like that time, prior to my first hanbleceya, when I sat in Wanagi Wacipi's beat-up silver and red trailer, awaiting his return, stewing over whether or not my undertaking such a vision-quest ceremony was a right thing for a white guy like me to do. "Holy Shit!", I thought, as all those images, like a high-speed tachistoscopic movie, rushed by my mind's eye, "It looks to me, Geronimo, like you're gonna have to again resolutely purify and steel yourself for this second go-around."

– A RIVER'S QUESTIONS ARE ANSWERED –

As my mind traveled ever more inward to prepare itself, the same telepathic questions posed before by Mni-sosé, as I sat upon one of her ancient banks near Crow Creek, again asked, "So why, over the years, have you undertaken to identify with First Nation aboriginal peoples? What has possessed you to travel the long distances required to seek them out to study and participate in their medicine ways instead of those of your own people? The native peoples you've sought to learn from, to be sure, have powerful medicine ways, through which their members keep in close contact with the invisible realm of Spirit. Yet, at the same time, many of them, for all their spirit contact, remain in woefully debilitating states of dis-ease and dissension, within themselves and between one another, for which even they cannot ever seem to find a cure. So again, why this persistence in the course you've taken?"

The answer to these questions already was partially known. The intervening years of trial and tribulation experienced in the no man's lands, had led to some simple realizations. One realization was that this personal desire to dance, sing and pray with different First Nation peoples, through their rituals and ceremonies, was because – even though I held no illusions about ever becoming one of them – the starving, authentic-self within me desperately needed to dance, sing and pray in the old way.

The White Man side of my authentic-self knew that, in this lifetime, this was one of the only ways it would ever be able to express itself in communion with others of like-mindedness, given that certain comparable cultural forms of spiritual expression in its world, at this sorry stage in its evolution or devolution, simply don't exist.

The Native side of my authentic-self also craved for the kind of reverential connections that flow between Nature and Natural Time, that the White Man's world is wholly ignorant of or insensitive to.

So I was forced to acknowledge, early on, that – no matter how incomplete, unsatisfying or alienating it might be, as I perpetually moved, back and forth, across the no man's lands – I had no other choice but to live the life of a renegade or maverick in both worlds.

Life otherwise lived like D.H. Lawrence's 'divided monstor' snake, writhing and twisting to try to shed the old skin while revealing tantalizing patches, here and there, of something of the authentic new skin which lies underneath.

Yet whenever finding myself on the White Man's side of the no man's lands, most attempts to share something of what all has been

Sun Dance and Ghost Dance Panorama
(Holy Hill in the Distance)

Sun Dance and Ghost Dance Await

IN MEMORY
OF
JOE THUNDER HAWK

EVELYNE THUNDER HAWK
ANGEL MARTINEZ
MRS TAKES THE HORSE
HILDA RED BEAR
EVAN WHITE PIPE

learned in this regard from such experiences with First Nation peoples, generally ends up ignored or rejected out-of-hand.

The White Man's world so lost within Homo sapiens lower stages of development – so alienated from Nature and Mother Earth – so bound up by the inelastic mental chains of its own ideological-driven reality – its divisive political, economic, cultural and spiritual institutions so devoid of moral compass – as to sometimes seem a hopeless hope-against-hope that anything other than self-destruction will ever come of Creation's grand experiment with our species.

Yet whenever finding myself on the Native side of the no man's lands, similar attempts often meet with similar results. Like, if ever I happen to use an Irish bodhran hand-drum, rather than an Indian drum, or identify myself as a 'Celtic tribesman' or 'New Frontier Breed', the response usually is the same, all-inclusive, "OH!" "Oh!", when translated, meaning, "Oh, then you can't possibly be a legitimate 'medicine person' or spokesperson for the spirit of this land. You must be just another one of those poor, damn, phony wannabe's!"

Rising out of all these contentous cross-cultural interactions – all the personal angst and self-doubts – has come a personal strength, resolve and confidence born from an authentic sense of who I'm supposed to be and what I'm supposed to do during this short time Creator has given me to share all this with others.

Out of the ensuing healing, forged from the fires of conflict, has also come an ever-deepening peace and inner-knowingness that who or what we New Frontier Breeds are, indeed needs no outside authentication or validation from anyone. If the gifts we have to offer either side of the no man's lands happen to be ignored or rejected, it's okay, because the *Natural Timing* simply isn't yet right for Spirit to share through us our healing gifts.

It was with this sense of acceptance and resignation that I once more prepared to reclimb Holy Hill and stand, for several days and nights – without food, water or protection from the elements – on the same spot where I stood as a younger man.

– SPIRITUAL HISTORY REPEATS ITSELF –

Once more, the Thunder Hawk's, Yellow Cloud and I found ouselves undergoing a Sacred Sweat Lodge Ceremony together, to prepare to receive whatever guidance and blessings The Great Mystery might grace us with in the private spaces of our minds and hearts.

Soon I was standing all alone as before, high atop Holy Hill, on that ridge that overlooked Thunder Hawk's Sun Dance grounds, where the pledge of an intimate name and its dream-vision first made itself known. Ready, at the same time, to keep myself open to whatever more clues might come to the mysterious path upon which the intervening years since had led me.

Fatigued from standing several days under a blistering-hot Dakota sun, and icy-cold, wind-swept Plains moon, I fell fast asleep within my circular prayer altar of red-cloth medicine herb ties.

During the sleeping reverie, I began to dance upon a circle of huge proportions – with many humans and non-humans gathered, side-by-side, on the circle's edge – for a ceremony of thanksgiving.

All manner of entities were present upon the circle: a black buffalo cloud; the same three spirit men from my first hanbleceya; my mother, father, brother, grandfathers, grandmothers and all those who came before them; Crystal Freesia and her own mother, father, sister, brother-in-law and spirit guides; Giant Pumpkin Spider, Gray Fox, Fawn, Silverspot, Red-Tailed Hawk, Mockingbird, Red-Shafter Flicker, Grizzly Bear, Stellar Jay, Bumble Bee, Dragonfly, Hummingbird; Dave Schooley and his mountain supporters; elders from different First Nations; all were massed upon the circle.

It was a celebration of great joy, with all of us aware that we were part of a great modern Iliad. The Turtle Island journal I carried indeed the documentation of this Iliad's tale.

In the dream, I'm asked to turn the journal into a book on behalf of all those, everywhere, from whatever mixed-breed heritage, who've ever become caught in the no man's lands, in-between the narrow cultures and spiritual traditions of their origins.

Suddenly, descending from out of the sky, from all points in the universe, came streams and streams of new-born infants from all races, colors, creeds as well as different times and periods of history.

These cosmic pilgrims *en masse* telepathically whispered:

Twin Rainbow! We come to your world already complete, ready to evolve you and ourselves into higher beings beyond your wildest dreams and imagination. Yet when we arrive, instead of you humans taking the time to acknowledge our completeness, the miracle we represent, or ask us why we have come and what gifts we bear, you instead socialize us into your still primitive ways with all your prejudices, biases and narrow misperceptions of what this beautiful orb, and the vast universe that lies beyond, really are all about. We have much to tell you of all this! But instead, in the end, you fragment us all and reduce us to the lowest common denominator among yourselves. All your parent-hosts, religious leaders, teachers, doctors, politicans and scientists brainwash us into believing that: we should be this or should be that; we should do this or shouldn't do that; we must believe this concept and doctrine but musn't believe that concept and doctrine; we must love these people, philosophies or beliefs, but hate those other people, philosophies and beliefs. You fill us so full of so many hateful, angry, limiting thoughts until we forget why we came in the first place and succumb to your cunning methods of indoctrination to the point that we are even willing to turn ourselves into weapons of mass destruction to do the bidding of whomever is in power and are even prepared to die or kill ourselves if we're called upon to do so. You really do not have even the remotest clues as to why we have come amongst you all.

When I awoke from the dream, I at once knew all the personal sacrifices that have been made to see the writing through to its end have been well worth it. I felt happy, grateful and honored to have been given the wherewithal to do it.

As I raised up from my tiny earth altar–dream pod, and began to sing again my New Dawn Chant to the Four Directions, a sea of joy swept over me; knowing that I've been so blessed to be able to stay the spiritual course that I came into this world to follow and abide by.

Mankind's lost, wretched, troubled, little world could do what it wanted with or to my body, because I knew the spirit that resides within this mortal coil, for the short time that it will function, is eternal.

It wasn't long before Joe Thunder Hawk Jr. came driving along the same roadless ridge that his dad traveled eighteen years before to escort me off of Holy Hill.

While I waited in his pickup, Joe Jr. cleaned up the ceremonial site and we then drove back down to where everyone was busy getting ready for the Sun Dance that was set to begin the next morning at sun-up.

In the hanbleceya's closing Sweat Lodge Ceremony, I spoke of my dream. No more words or interpretations needed to be spoken between us, though. For each of us knew to respectfully leave one another to ponder, in our own peculiar fashion, the mysterious ways the invisible realm communicates with we humans.

– THE ANCESTORS BLESS OUR DANCING –

During the Ghost Dance that proceeded our memorial Sun Dance to Thunder Hawk and the other deceased medicine people, yet another strange 'waking dream-encounter' with the invisible realm took place.

At one point in the Ghost Dance – after dancing for hours through the jet-black darkness, lit only by the glorious massive profusion of stars above – the singers took to chanting a powerful song.

My pounding feet, feverishly commiserating with the Earth in honor of all the ancestors, carried me 'round the circle's edge to a spot, close beside the singers, where I could dance in place and pay special tribute to their plaintive cries to the world beyond.

The rhythmic, hypnotic stamping of my feet soon moved the singers to beat the drum and cry out in ever-greater intensity, just as their wild chants caused my drumstick-feet to turn into ever more intense, piston-like pile drivers.

All at once the singers shrill pleas to the world of spirit caused my arms and hands, which at first were held tight against my body, to suddenly fling themselves heavenward, open palms reaching out to the vast starry Milky Way above, that stretched across the sky.

My outstretched arms as if antennae, eager to receive whatever subtle communiques from the eons of ancestral spirits and other distant intelligent life forms who still exist somewhere amongst the universe's billions of galaxies, their endless multitudes of stars and the even more countless numbers of planetary systems that orbit around them.

This exhilarating way of dancing, praying and communing with all our ancestors, however far off they've gone to the remotest of places, was similar to what I experienced on other occasions while dancing with the Wintu-Patwin people of California – in places like Grindstone, Colusa and Clear Lake during their Bighead–Kuksu Ceremonies.

The following morning, we singers and dancers partook in one of Sara Thunder Hawk's wonderful breakfast feasts – like the one she prepared in my honor so many years before after I'd finished my first hanbleceya. As we ate, we quietly spoke of the intense emotions and psychic impressions that, in different ways, we'd all felt during that key moment of transformation in the Dance.

The mood collectively expressed was one of knowing that, through all our movements and chants, we now were part of the living incarnation – the new vanguard – of something very old which sought to again re-enact itself through us.

Joe Thunder Hawk
Dancer/Rodeo Clown/Trickster

- Mrs. Red Bear & Sara Thunder Hawk -

Red Bear and Thunder Hawk Clan Birthday

Twin Rainbow, Irwin Pondering other Lifetimes

As our sharing drew to a close, The Voice took the opportunity to whisper in my ear, "And I say this to you, Lad! The Ghost Dancer's Dance isn't over yet!"

– HER SPIRIT IMAGE IS CAPTURED ON FILM –

On that same day, at the conclusion of the Ghost Dance, the Thunder Hawk and Red Bear Clan's gathered to celebrate Mrs. Red Bear's 88th birthday.

As part of the momentous sacredness of the moment, Mrs. Red Bear – who strongly believed, like the old-timers, that the White Man's looking-glass never should capture one's spirit, and so freeze it for all time for other strangers to gawk at – relented, and agreed to allow the first and only photographs of her ever to be taken.

It was so sweet to be a part of her shy, bashfulness, as she closed her eyes and winced in front of the camera, while we all laughed and jostled to become part of the historic moment.

Shortly after our group photo, I was called upon to assist one of the medicine men prepare the sacred Shunka Ceremony that was to be conducted in honor of the occasion.

– AN ANCIENT CEREMONY IS RENEWED –

In the old days, before the introduction of the horse into the Lakota way of life, the dog was king. The dog did almost everything that the horse did: acted as a pack animal; accompanied the hunt; warned the camp of intruders, and, most importantly; served as an emergency food source.

In fact, when the Lakota saw the first horse they named it in honor of their dogs. Their word for dog is *'Shunka',* and so the horse became know as *Shunka Wakan* ('Sacred Dog', or 'Mysterious Dog').

So valued was the dog in the old culture, that it was only in times of the most extreme famine, when no other food source was available, that they sacrificed their most prized possession and companion.

During those rare occasions that it did occur, the old-timers held a Shunka Ceremony, which to them was a most sacred ceremony, to honor the role that the dog played in the survival of the Lakota family.

The Shunka Ceremony involves the selection of some worthy family who the medicine man presents with a white puppy they are entrusted with to care and nurture for sometimes up to a year prior to the ceremony itself.

At the time of the ceremony, the family who cared for the puppy gathers with the medicine man. The white dog is then ceremonially killed in the most painless, respectful way possible as the honored family looks on. The holy dog's body is then ritualistically prepared in a soup which is shared by the whole community, starting with the elders and ending with the children.

In our Shunka Ceremony, the honored family was from the Red Bear Clan. It was such a solemn, precious sight to see that family standing there in a line, looking so innocent and humble, decked out in all their finery. The father wearing a suit from the 50's era. His wife in a similar period white dress with a matching headpiece, complete with white gloves, and a small white handbag. While their young son, standing beside them in what looked-like his catechism outfit, hair neatly-combed and greased, stood holding in his hands the dog's leash. Their young daughter in her favorite white party dress, with a bouquet of hand-picked wildflowers held in her tiny white-gloved hands.

I stood close by and watched in awe as the family looked on while the medicine man slowly bled the little white dog; so reverentially, that he never so much as whimpered or objected in the slightest as he slowly sank ever-deeper into a peaceful, eternal sleep.

The air so still around us at that moment, the presence of spirit so apparent, the mood so sacred, that it brought quiet tears to all our eyes as lumps rose in all our throats. "How could anyone", I thought, "ever call such a ceremony pagan, cruel or retarded?"

– ANOTHER COMMUNIQUE FROM THE SPIRIT WORLD –

It was while hauling a bucket of water from the Thunder Hawk's well, to where the medicine man was singeing the hair off of the white dog so it could be boiled in a soup, that I was stopped dead in my tracks.

As I walked through the Thunder Hawk living room with the bucket of water, on my way out back of their place, Sara Thunder Hawk called out.

"Jerry!", she said, "Stop what your doin' an' sit fer a minute, 'cause Mrs. Red Bear's got somethin' important she wants to tell ya' about your Ghost Dancin' last night. She don't speak English so I'll translate for her."

Setting the water bucket down between us, I sat and listened while Mrs. Red Bear, who sat quietly across the room, warmly staring at me, spoke in her native Lakota tongue. "When you, Jerry, was dancin'", said Mrs. Red Bear, through Sara's voice, "I seen someone dancin' right next t' yah an'thought at first it was one of your white friends. But when I seen your white friend, Dennis, dancin' on th' other side of the circle, I knew it was someone else. But when I looked back again that man dancin'next t' yah, Jerry, disappeared."

Aware that I was actually the only dancer, positioned next to the singers at that moment, I knew at once what Red Bear meant. Because in that same instant in the Dance, I, too, felt the presence of some strange force that encircled me. I had felt the presence of Joe Thunder Hawk near me at that moment, dressed out in all his traditional dance costume's splendor, eagle wand in his right hand fanning his prayers skyward as he danced. The intuitive feeling that rushed into my thoughts, at the time, was as if I were dancing in front of legions of other invisible people, of all colors and races, who all crowded tightly around we singers and dancers.

Mrs. Red Bear continued her tale, "It was then I fell into what yah might call a trance where I was sittin' under th' arbor on th' edge of th' Ghost Dance circle. While I was in th' trance, a voice said t' me, *'Wasté yelo, hetchétu yelo! Oh hey yuha tonya omani yo.* You folks here are just startin' out agin on th' old path like little babies just learin' t' crawl. Yer gonna make lots of mistakes along th' way, but it's okay. Just keep on adoin' what you're doin', an' in time you'll know even more about what all needs t' get done.'"

As Sara's translation trailed off, Mrs. Red Bear's deep black eyes continued to twinkle quietly, yet passionately at me from across the room. It was then that The Voice bellowed, "Lad! I say to you again that the Ghost Dancer's Dance isn't over yet. Your ancestors have a new strong step to teach you." With that, I picked up the water bucket in one hand and went over to Mrs. Red Bear and Sara, shook their hands, and thanked them. "Pilamaya", I said, "The spirit sure talks in strange ways."

– THE DOUBTING THOMASES RECEIVE VALIDATION –

Days later, the opportunity arose to talk with one old Lakota man, who was among those who had boycotted the Sun & Ghost Dance ceremonies. "Yeh!", he admitted, "A lot of us knew the Dance's was ahappenin' alright. We didn't show up but we was watchin' th' clouds all 'round th area, an' lookin fer other signs in Nature, day an' night, t' see what was goin' on. We could tell, alright, that somethin' mighty important was a happenin'."

The Thunder Hawk and Red Bear Clans took on an enormous risk and responsibility to conduct their contentious ceremonies. With Joe Sr. long since gone, Joe Jr., the ceremonies main organizer – as a young man still in-training – bit off perhaps way more than he was prepared to chew. The pressures were indeed enormous on everyone to come good.

As we sought to prepare ourselves, many highly-unorothodox, totally untraditional – absolutely gut-wrenchingly-hilarious, if they weren't so deadly-serious – incidents led up to the ceremonies themselves.

Like those that happened to Karma Tenzing Wangchuk – a haiku poet and practicing layman Tibetan Buddhist monk, who in another lifetime was 'Dennis Dutton', an editor for the Shaman's Drum magazine.

Karma Tenzing accompanied Alta-Dena and I out from the West Coast to attend the Sun & Ghost Dance ceremonies. He had participated in Ghost Dances elsewhere and was eager to know how the Lakota did it.

Karma helped Homer Thunder Hawk and several other clan members round-up the steer for slaughter and helped cut and transport the felled Cottonwood tree to the Sun Dance grounds. But, by his account, things were a lot different than one might expect such a traditional ceremony to be like. Said Tenzing:

It was the funniest damn sight you've ever seen in your life. Here we were trying to round-up this steer, that one of the Mean's brothers donated to us for the ceremony, and didn't have a clue as to how we were going to get it back to the Sun Dance grounds, many miles away. The plan at first was to tie it onto the back of the pickup and tow it. But we immediately dismissed that as a real dumb idea, given that it was the dead of summer, under a blazing Dakota sun. Then we tried to coax the steer into the bed of the truck.

Well, talk about a Keystone Cop scene! There we were, with the steer's front end in the bed and its ass end sticking out with all of us busting a gut, pushing from behind. And in the next minute there was the steer jumping off the side of the truck and, by this time, mad as hell, chasing us all 'round the pickup with us diving back into the bed for safety and the steer hot after us. Round an' 'round we went, with us jumping in and out of the bed and the steer following suit right behind us. Talk about hilarious!

Finally one of us managed to lasso the poor steer. But it became so freaked out that it got the rope all tangled up in the pick-up's rigging, and pulled it so taut around its neck, that it strangled itself and, with its huge, frothy tongue bulging out of its mouth, dropped dead right at our feet. I don't know if it was a heart attack or asphyxiation. So there we were, with a dead steer lying on the side of the road, trying next to figure out how to lift its dead weight onto the back of the truck.

Then there was the cutting down of the Cottonwood tree for the Sun Dance pole. Well. no one remembered to bring the ceremonial axe and so we had to use our native ingenuity to fall the tree, using the pulling power of the truck and what tools we had, which proved to be no small feat and definitely not the traditional way to do it. Then it turned out that no one properly notified the local tribal police of our activities and so, rather than risk an unwanted confrontation, we had to wait until nightfall to transport the tree, secretively, over back roads to the Sun Dance grounds. The whole thing was an unbelievable comedy of errors!

But, in the end, thanks to the eventual intercession of a highly respected local medicine man, the proper spiritual protocols were duly observed, the early hostilities expressed in opposition to the ceremonies soon subsided, and everything came good without a hitch.

So, PILGRIM. Our odyssey together is slowly drawing to a close. Yet there still is so much to share. Return to that quiet place of reflection within yourself. What do you call your authentic self? What has it caused you to do? Where has it taken you? What have you learned in the process? **Hurry Now! Be Off With Ye! Go!**

WELCOME BACK! With my return pilgrimage back to Porcupine, a new cycle in the odyssey's path began. I could feel this cycle pulling me hard back across The Medicine Line to Canada. This time it felt more permanent. I sensed my time in the South was at its end, at least for now. "Ha! Ha! Ha!", I laughed at this notion of thinking my time in the South had ended, "Can any of us humans ever know what the Spirit has in mind for us next?"

For months, Crystal Freesia and I had been synchronizing several positive affirmations and guided imagery exercises, that we agreed to do together each morning and evening, even though we were a thousand miles apart. Our intended purpose in doing so was to, hopefully, conjure into reality the sacred piece of land and spirit house that we long had dreamt about, for so many years. They both felt close to materialzing themselves at this point in time and so we set out to be active participants with all our helpers in the spirit realm.

As Alta-Dena and I prepared to leave Porcupine, we did so with a better sense of what Joe Thunder Hawk originally sought to share about the demanding path that all of us New Frontier Breeds have to travel. A path that demands we not become embroiled in all the long-standing jealousies, hatreds and age-old family–clan–tribal–national feuds that so many Europeans, Africans, Asians, Aboriginal peoples in North America, and in the world at large for that matter, still hold for one another.

Our primary task, as New Frontier trailblazers, being to learn the important spiritual lessons each race, culture and creed has to give us, while remaining aloof of all the debilitating, self-defeating aspects of their present ways of life. To then reflect back all these negative 'shadow' aspects of themselves and their cultures which they each need to somehow evolve beyond. To reflect, as well, those positive aspects of each which the others must assimilate in order for us all – First Nation natives, Old World Immigrants, New Frontier Breeds – to evolve towards a higher stage of human consciousness and development.

As Alta-Dena set out across the plains for the West Coast, I was anxious to wrap things up in the South so we could beat our way up to Grandmother's Lands and a much overdue reunion with Crystal Freesia.

There was so much to tell my medicine woman of this crazy Iliad and so much I needed still to learn from her about where next to go. I sensed the time was rapidly drawing nearer when Alta-Dena, my trusty New Frontier steed, like Ken Kesey's bus *Further*, had earned her right to be put out to pasture and return to Mother Earth in her own slow, inimitable way. A close friend, on a rural 'Salmagundi Farm' in Washington State, said she would be welcome to spend as long as she wanted there. We planned to stop on the way North and check his place out.

CURCLE ISLAND

ROAD SIGN # 19

WHAT PERSONAL VISION
DOES
THE HOUSE OF YOUR DREAMS
REPRESENT?

AS I WAS WANDERIN' O'ER THE GREEN
NOT KNOWING WHERE I WENT
BY CHANCE
I SPIED A PLEASANT SCENE
THE COTTAGE OF CONTENT

(old Irish poem)

– Fairy Dance –

As played by a Connaught Piper, who learned it from "The Little People."

RETURN TO GRANDMOTHERS LANDS:
AN ELF INN DREAM COMES TRUE

"*PILGRIM*", joyfully heralds The Great Voice Of The Turtle, "*There are many little spirit-keeper's of my meadows, fields, glens, streams, rivers, oceans, mountains, forests and deserts. To hear their music and song with your spirit ears is to realize the greatest of all gifts I have to offer. Once heard, their enchanting voices will never ever leave you. They will forever after act as a great force in your life, that will direct you to many more holy places upon me than you can ever dream. These special places, and the spirits who reside there, can help you realize your human dreams, too. They can teach you to become The Keepers of the place where you live. Have you ever heard their music and songs in that house you call home and upon the land where it sits? How have they so far shaped and directed your life?*"

N enchanting voice on the phone at 3 A.M., on the eve of a Winter's Solstice, shouts, "YIPPIE! We have The Elves Inn!"

The Elves Inn: a dream-like affirmation of two people's fairy ancestor's ideals made real. A visualization made manifest of a natural way of life put into motion; a holy meeting ground wherein a Twin Rainbow spiritual warrior and a Crystal Freesia healer meet up with an ordinary man and woman with feet made of common clay; where two soul-mates, looking for that ever-elusive pot-of-gold at the rainbow's end, discover it all the while lay at their very feet.

The years of wanderin' in Blue and Alta-Dena have cultivated an ever-deepening appreciation for the simpler things of life that are free for the taking. What also has come is a keen appreciation of the immense psychic impact that those special places one is drawn to can have upon one's spiritual growth and desire to creatively express what all that means.

In my life it happens to have been the different vital effluences, vibrations, chemical exhalations and polarities of places like: Mosquito Pass, high atop the Continental Divide of the Rockies, and its gift of solitude; Hidden Valley alongside San Francisco Bay, and its gift of silence; the ancient, eroded visage of the Missouri River, and its gift of

eternal change; the Pine Ridges of Porcupine and their gift of the living
spirit; tiny Chocuay in Kuksu Country, and its gift of simplicity. About to
be added to these places was The Elves Inn of Capilano River, that one
day would metamorphose into 'The Elf Inn', and its gift of rootedness.

There are those enlightened ones who know that just as there exists
no coincidental introductions to the significant people who touch our lives,
so, too, is it true with the significant blocks of land to which we are
drawn. Land, like people, a mirrored-image of a stage of consciousness
we each happen to be working through at any given cycle in our lives.

With each transformational shift made, we humans, in turn, are
drawn, as if by magic, to yet another special landscape or spot every bit
as much as the birds, in their migratory patterns, are pulled back and
forth, with the seasonal changes, to whatever distant nesting places
beckon. Each spot possessing its own special name and essence. One spot
perhaps called "the savoring place", another "the resting place", or still
another "the ebb before the flow place".

Mockingbird-atop-Pear Tree Cottage – with the softness of its surrounding Petaluman hills and peaceful nature of the ancient Miwok and
Pomo peoples who still permeate the story of the land there – earned the
right to be called all those names. As the odyssey's southern migratory
place "of introspective limbo", it served as the "calm before the storm".

With the advantage of years of hindsight as an aid, The Elves Inn
ala The Elf Inn, one day, would turn out to be the odyssey's northern
migratory "place of action".

A simple place that beckoned to us to one day put life into perspective
and finally realize that intangibles like love, beauty, joy, laughter, sharing, wonderment and innocence are the only real things that exist. All
the chaos and angst caused by the divisive forces of politics, religion and
the marketplace nothing more than a meaningless foreground that
constantly seeks to distract us from these fleeting yet eternal truths.

The Elf Inn about to become an affirmation of what author Leonard
Woolf meant, in *Down The Hill All The Way*, when he wrote:

> Facts about the houses in which one lives during the whole journey from the
> womb to the grave are not unimportant. The house – in which I include its
> material and spiritual environment – has an immense influence upon its
> inhabitants. The momentous or catastrophic events of one's life will mould,
> disrupt or distort the movement of one's life, but what has the deepest and most
> permanent effect upon oneself and one's way of living is the house in which one
> lives. The house determines the day-to-day, hour-to-hour, minute-to-minute
> quality, colour, atmosphere, pace of one's life; it is the framework of what one
> does, of what one can do, of one's relations with people.

I would only add to Woolf's description the phrase, "of one's relations, as well, with all the living non-human relations that live in and around the house's surrounds."

– LIFE IS OFTEN STRANGER THAN FICTION –

The story of how I came to realize all this begins some eight years before Crystal Freesia and I finally took possession of The Elves Inn, or it took possession of us.

At the time, when this magical Inn, that looked like it came straight out of some Old World storybook or mythic fairy tale, first made itself known, neither of us were ready for the kind of relationships and committments that this odd dwelling – completely hidden behind a wall of trees, with only a weathered-old driftwood sign visible that declared, 'The Elves Inn' – was prepared to offer up to us.

So, as things turned out, we let it pass us by as we wandered off in search of yet other 'sacred, holy places' and the answers they had to give of life's existential questions. But this is getting ahead of the story! It actually begins way back in '74, on 'The North Shore' of British Columbia's Lower Mainland. Local roadwork happened to be detouring a main North Vancouver 'Marine Drive' artery of traffic down a bumpy, pot-hole ridden, side road called, strangely enough, *Hope Road*. It was indeed strange for a number of reasons as this tale soon shall reveal.

For two years, prior to this 'minor' detour in the road of life, Crystal Freesia and I had traveled all about B.C. in Alta-Dena, searching for a place where we could make a fresh, new start.

Our "Northward, Ho!" dream to settle in the Queen Charlotte Islands and build Pelican sailboats with 'Pelican Pete' – a friend from the old Castro Street, Dave & Sago Benson-in-Blewett-days – never materialized.

Still, our dream to live free and clear in some setting as wild and pristine as the Queen Charlottes – away from all the political and ideological nonsense of the 'Melting Pot', 'Manifest Destiny' mob in the South – was the dream – the guiding light – which continued to fuel our northern search.

For two years, our travels led to and from the North Shore, to all points on the B.C. compass, yet we always found ourselves returning again, like homing pigeons, to the North Shore and a temporary respite in one of the cooking cabins of the old '303', a funky, forties-style, people-friendly motel that lay at the north end of the Lion's Gate Bridge. The '303' soon became a sort of home away from home.

However, we never realized, the whole time, that just a few short blocks away, patiently awaiting our discovery of it, was the real house of all our hopes and dreams.

So it was strange that Alta-Dena and I found ourselves one day being detoured onto a road, calling itself 'Hope', that, in the end, would turn out to be not a minor detour at all but one of those major, unexpected, unplanned crossroads which determine the entire course and fate of one's life.

It's even stranger, to the point of being eerie, because the driftwood sign that announced "The Elves Inn" – as it protruded through a thick clump of cedars, junipers and elms – happened to be at the corner of Hope Road and Phillips.

Both those names, eight years later, were to take on great import. Because at a crucial time when Crystal Freesia and I had all but run out of hope in trying to maintain our unorthodox, mostly apart yet always together, *Movie Stars On & Off Locations* relationship, we would find ourselves returning to that corner and, as fate would have it, discover a new sense of hope at precisely the place where Hope meets Phillips.

As if to make the whole tale even more mystical, 'Phillips' just happens to be Crystal Freesia's maiden surname and the numbers in the address of that corner also just happen to be the year of her birth.

But, on the day of that 'Twilight Zone' detour, eight years before this took on any import for us, Alta-Dena and I found ourselves innocently lumbering down Hope Road, weaving back and forth as we tried to dodge its many deep pot-holes, until we came to that corner and spotted its whimsical sign.

– ENTERING INTO THE LAND OF THE IMAGINATION –

Alta-Dena at once screeched to a halt and I eagerly bolted from her cab to see what lay beyond the sign's thick barrier of greenery.

At first glance, as I peeked through its ivy-covered front gate, The Elves Inn, and its over-grown block of land, looked like it just emerged from somewhere beneath the earth, or right off of one of Tolkien's pages in *The Lord of The Rings* or *The Hobbit*.

"Oh, my God!", I blurted, "I must meet whomever lives in that house!"

Smoke, lazily drifting from its stone chimney, gave notice that whomever the elf or elves were, they were presently within.

I didn't venture beyond the gate, however, because at that moment The Voice declared, "Lad! This is to be one of the most significant meetings you will ever make. Return to Crystal Freesia, tell her of your discovery, and dress in a manner befitting the occasion."

Hopping into my brilliantly-white New Frontier Conestoga Wagon, I sped back down Hope Road's obstacle course of pot-holes as fast as Alta-Dena's sprung-steel suspension system would allow, without sending me through the roof of her cab or shaking the eye-teeth right out of my head.

Back at the '303', I asked Crystal Freesia to help me quickly dress as The Voice directed. Once she braided my chest-length hair into two long-strands, she adorned them with a pair of red and white-beaded, thunder-and-lightning bolt-designed, buckskin wraps. I then quickly: slipped on a pair of thick elk-skin moccasins; tucked a red-plaid lumberman's wool shirt into a faded pair of rainbow-patched Levi's, that went all the way back to my early Crow Creek days; wrapped around my waist a hand-woven, orange and black, lightning-bolt patterned, mountain man's sash; snapped on a set of rainbow braces that sported the pins of three hallowed childhood heroes – Howdy Doody, Gumby and Alfred E. Neumann; tied a rainbow-abalone choker 'round my neck and topped off the outfit with a crocheted rainbow cap with a Red-Tailed Hawk feather pinned to its peak.

"Tah dah!", I said, while dramatically opening my arms wide as though a showtime curtain had been drawn, with me standing center stage. "Well? C'mon, Love! Whaddaya think?"

Crystal Freesia took one look at me, rolled her eyes, and giggled, "Crikey! All you need are moccasins with curled up, pointed toes. Now I know for sure you've gone right round-the-bloody-bend!"

"Don't worry, love!", I answered back, as I gave her one last fond peck on the cheek, "But if you hear of me getting thrown in jail or the looney bin, do be a good sort and come get me out!"

Feeling duly presentable and attired, I sped back to The Elves Inn as fast as Alta-Dena's two-ton, California flower-power, body would lumber.

Coasting to a halt, I gently pulled back Alta-Dena's accordion door so it wouldn't make its usual loud, squawking, metallic bang, stepped from her cab, slipped through the ivied-gate, and headed down a curved stone pathway that led to the Inn's dense purple wisteria-shrouded entrance.

– WE ARE SUCH STUFF AS DREAMS ARE MADE ON –

The Inn's entranceway looked more like an opening into a tree trunk, or dark, mysterious inner chamber of a cave, than it did the front door of a house.

Mounted to the upper-half of the rustic, hand-made wooden dutch door was a white plaster cast of a muse-like face in happy, tranquil repose, besides which was mounted a large Raven feather.

Feeling most Edgar Poeish, I made three slow, rhythmic knocks upon the wood-butcher door and then anxiously waited in anticipation of who or what would respond to its call.

A small peephole in the door soon slid open, a tentative, blood-shot eye peered out through the hole, and a feeble voice hesitantly-queried, "Yes? What do you want?"

Without so much as a word, I took two giant steps backward – and assumed a relaxed, crouching, Yoga-like, *Horse* stance – so whomever was behind the door could see what I was about to do with my hands.

As the, by now, puzzled eye stared intently, I slightly cocked my head to one side while beginning a slow, sweeping, Tai-Chi motion with my right hand that stopped in an upright position with the fingers signing the deaf expression for "I Love You!" My left hand simultaneously extending itself out, gracefully, in an open, friendly gesture – its palm facing upwards, fingers pointing upright – as it gave the old trad-itional Northwest Indian sign for, "I Come in Peace & Thanksgiving!"

There I silently stood, smiling – rainbow-peaked cap, choker necklace, hair wraps, Howdy Doody–Gumby-Alfred E. Neumann pins and all – peacefully-frozen in my 'Rainbow Breed–Buddha' position, awaiting the eye's response.

Unsure about the kind of reception that a complete stranger, from clear-out-of-the-blue, dressed as outrageous as I was, could expect to receive from such a bizarre, silent act; I prepared myself for everything from the barrel of a gun to be thrust through the peep hole, to the door all at once flying open and some crazed, mad dog rushing out to chase me clear off the property.

But no wait or anything untoward was forthcoming. For without a moment's notice, the old voice, with an English accent, this time sounding more sprightly, chuckled, "Hey! Heh! Heh! Wait just a minute, my good man!"

The noisy clacking of a wooden latch and lever being slid back and lifted announced that my 'cosmic hand signals' had achieved the necesary effect and earned me an audience with 'the elf' behind the voice, and at least a glimpse into the inner sanctums of his hobbit dwelling.

The top of the dutch-door creaked open and there appeared a white-haired, white-moustached, ruddy-faced, elderly man, wearing a heavy, monkish, brown robe, who looked every bit the part of the old innkeeper.

Curiously sizing up and down the colorful New Frontier Breed who stood before him, the old gent quizically posed, "Hello there, my good man! I'm Gordon Edwards, And so what, pray tell me, has brought a young chap like you to The Elves Inn?"

The second his question reached me ears, the spiritual telegraph began zinging messages up and down my spine as The Voice cried out, "You know, don't ye Lad, what has brought ye here. I believe you've just found a new 'Holy Hill' in life with a whole new set of challenges!".

I somehow knew this meeting between us to be something more than chance, that felt like one of those fated crossroads that one reaches at different stages in their life.

"Hi!", I said "My name's Jerome Twin Rainbow, Some people just call me 'Twin' or 'Rainbow'. The minute I saw your house and sign, I said to myself, 'Anyone who lives in such an organic house, with a name like that, has to be on my wave-length who I must meet.' So, Mr. Edwards! Here I am!"

His old eyes twinkled brightly and, with a boyish grin, he enjoined, "Twin Rainbow, you say. Is that an Indian name?" "No", I replied, "But then that's a long, long story which I could tell you something about if you're interested."

"Well.....", he hesitantly said, before gushing, "Yes, I do believe I would like to hear more about it. Come in! Come in!"

– TWO OLD SOULS ACHIEVE A TOUCHING –

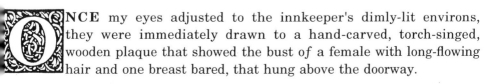

NCE my eyes adjusted to the innkeeper's dimly-lit environs, they were immediately drawn to a hand-carved, torch-singed, wooden plaque that showed the bust of a female with long-flowing hair and one breast bared, that hung above the doorway.

Pointing up to the plaque, he said, "Do you like my carving? She's *Ophelia* from Shakespeare's play, *The Tempest*. I don't know if you can make out the quote below her, that I also carved, but it says, 'We are such stuff as dreams are made on; and our little life is rounded with a sleep'."

All 'round the walls hung other carved wooden plaques which depicted different characters from Shakespeare's plays. The cardboard-lined walls and woodwork of the Inn were painted in a dark forest green, with blotches of gold paint scattered about the limbs and trunks.

"I did the forest scenes and gold with a brush and sponge.", he said, "It's the way I honor the royal colours of my people – the Leprechauns."

THE LEPRECHAUNS!", I gasped. "YOU MEAN, YOU MEAN! YOU, TOO!" the instant he said that, goose bumps rushed up and down my arms, while the hair on the back of my neck stood abruptly on end.

"Wow, Mr. Edwards!", I gasped again, "This amazing house doesn't seem like it's in Canada at all. It doesn't really seem like it belongs in any man-made country. It's like in this world but not of it, if you get what I mean. Like its more part of some fairy world or time-space warp. I feel like "I've just crossed over into the Twilight Zone. But any minute the whole thing might just as easily go, POOF, and disappear before my very eyes."

Responding to each of my gasped comments with a comical, deep-muffled belly laugh, this old wood-carver–artisan of the poets and fairies, warmly invited me to, "Drop the Mr. Edward's and just call me Gordon. Here, come with me and I'll show you around."

Gently holding onto one of my arms, Edwards directed me to walk with him to a tiny ante-room off his kitchen where he retrieved a couple of 8-proof, home-brewed beers from a rough-hewn, wood-butchered, green-and-gold splotched cold cupboard.

That cold-pantry was one of the many unique bits of carpentry that he everywhere built into his dwelling. The side of the pantry that faced the outdoors was covered by a wire screen that allowed cold air to circulate through its shelves. Thus, in the wintertime, his pantry became an effective refrigerator, whereas, in the summer, since it was located on a north face of the Inn, and so always in the shade, still kept everything cool.

His kitchen was unlike any thing I'd ever saw before, with its own unique symphony of natural sounds. Its brass section consisting of a relic of an old ice-box, with a large radiator coil on its top that happily whirled away in competition with the worn-out, rattling fan of the oil stove beside it.

The oil stove's long, bright-yellow pipe, which ran across the ceiling of the kitchen before it disappeared out a green and gold plastered chimney flume, made its own percussion sounds as it rhythmically rattled dislodged soot against the pipe all along its length.

Big, fat, cymbal-like drops of water, sizzling and popping as they dropped onto the hot surface of the oil stove below, added to the cacophany. The drops coming from driping-wet long-johns, socks, tea-towels and assorted garments that hung from a primitive, clothes-drying rack, suspended overhead by a rope pulley, upon which Edwards also hung bunches of roses and herbs that he sought to dry.

Edwards next gently guided me through a portal – framed by curtains with still more gold-splotched forest scenes hand-painted on them – that led from his tiny living room into what he said was his workshop.

One look at it caused me to instantly flash back to Grandpa John Saul's tiny bedroom-cum-workshop at Crow Creek, that always was similarly covered with bits and pieces of half-finished projects, jumbled all together in wild disarray.

The rough, wood-butchered walls of Edward's work space – its beamed-celing and hand-adzed work bench, that ran the length of the room, upon which were mounted a dozen, odd-shaped, primitive-looking, wood clamps – seemed even more so, than Grandpa John's place, like the storied workshop of 'Gepetto' in *Pinocchio*.

"This is where", he proudly declared, "I make all the plaques, cubby-hole nests, tiny doors and other things that I keep hoping will attract the squirrels, birds and little people to live here with me."

The old wood-carver guided me back into his living room and enjoined me to, "Sit here in my chair and let's talk for a spell."

The chair and other bits and pieces of furniture also reflected his amazing skills as a master carpenter and carver. Each one done without the use of nails, with all the pieces pegged and fitted together the way furniture was made in the old days. Each piece of furniture – chairs, end tables, dining tables, magazine racks – were made in the same fashion, with elaborate quotations and parables carved on every surface, along with the images of ships, clouds, plants and animals.

Adding to his Inn's organic symphony were the steel drum sounds
made by thick logs banging against metal as Edward stoked yet another
one of his home-made wonders: a glowing, red-hot, 50 gallon oil-drum
that he cleverly converted into a front-loading, engine-like, boiler of a
fireplace.

"How about getting us a couple more home-brews in my cold
cupboard!", Gordon insisted. "Jolly good show!", he said, as I returned
with the beers in-hand. "Now! Let's get comffy!", he added, as he swung
the oil drum's cast-iron door open, so we could watch the flames lick at
the thick rounds of red cedar that crackled and spat atop the dense
protective layer of sand that lined the drum's bottom.

As our animated conversation rose and fell in counterpoint to the
din of rattling pipes, a whirling fan, sizzling water and spitting
sapwood, I learned that this one-of-a-kind, Birkenhead–Liverpool-born,
English character before me once was everything from a Penny-farthing
bicycle-maker and a master shipswright, to a building contractor and
small-time inventor. His Jack-Of-All-Trades life, by then, already
having long since witnessed its octogenarian anniversary.

Drawing upon his skills as a shipswright, Edwards built The Elves
Inn along the lines of an upside-down boat, with a stout beam thrust, like
a keel, across the Inn's front room and two large, curved ribs, arching
out from it, which spanned either side of the girdled ceiling.

When I asked, "So tell me, Gordon, did you purposely intend the
Inn's interior to look somewhat ship-like?", he winked and paused to take
another long swig from his home-brew.

Quoting from Shakespeare's *Merchant of Venice*, that wily old
shipswright mused, "Ah, ships are but boards! But when one's ship comes
home! When one succeeds! When one's projects bear fruit.....Ah, now
there one will find peace!"

We continued to sit there for several hours, sipping on our potent
home-brews, stoking the glowing-red oil drum with more rounds of
cedar, as we recounted to each other the essence of our life's story. The
more Gordon revealed about who he was, and the many projects he'd
attempted around The Elves Inn, the more amazing grew his tale.

HE interior and exterior of his Inn was indeed built with the
discarded timbers and rough-cut mill ends once used as
supports in the building of hulls at the old Burrard Shipyard
on the North Shore where Edwards once plied his trade.

His small bedroom also had the look of a ship's cabin, what with
the deep storage drawers he set beneath his built-in, berth-like bunk, the

old milk-shaded ship's lantern that hung above it, and the hand-fashioned boatswain ladder attached to the wall beside his bunk that led to a large, upper storage compartment.

This unusual Englishman – who years later I would find myself often fondly referring to as 'Uncle Gordon', because of subsequent contacts with his surviving kin and the many warm, endearing tales they had to tell of him – was one of those characters one meets up with who deserves the accolade, "The Creator broke the mold when he was made!"

Like Buck Pomani of Crow Creek, Edwards life history would have made yet another fascinating book to tell in its entirety.

As an organic architect-builder, of the Frank Lloyd Wright school-of-thought, Edwards employed a wealth of novel, whimsical ideas in the creation of his otherworldly dream-vision of a house.

One idea was the alcoves, crannies and cubby-holes he set within the exterior of the Inn. "So", as he put it, "the birds, squirrels and other creatures will always have a handy place to nest if they need one."

Another idea was the tiny, 12-inch door he built to the side of the Inn's front entranceway, "Where the little people can come and go as they please!"

Then there were the plum trees, grape vines and wild berry shrubs he planted and reserved for the sole use of, as he said, "The little people of the forest!"

Edwards also attempted to follow the lead of the early Romans – who ingeniously had designed the world's first central heating system beneath their tiled-floors – by endeavoring to adapt their two-thousand year-old design in the heating of The Elves Inn, itself.

Though some of his architectural brainstorms, like the Roman idea, proved less successful than others, so unique was his manifested dream-vision of the way he chose to live, that the Canadian Broadcasting Commission (CBC) once had became so enraptured by it that they made a documentary for television on him that they appropriately entitled, *The Wood Butcher Man & His House.*

While polishing off yet a couple more home-brews, I came to learn that his favorite pastime – when he wasn't doing dramatic readings of Shakespeare for the raccoons, squirrels, birds and young children, womanizing about the neighborhood, or playing an intense game of chess – was watching, day and night, around The Elves Inn for the Leprechauns and UFO's he so avidly believed one day would show themselves to him.

So intense was his belief in extra-terrestrial life, that he once had taken to hand-grind a superb, high-resolution 12-inch telescopic lens. Then he designed the roof of The Elves Inn so a portion of it could easily be removed, thereby, in effect, turning his living room into a mini astronomical observatory from which to scan the heavens in search of intelligent life.

By the time we met, however, Edward's was in his 90's and feeling down-hearted – what you might even call 'betrayed' – that neither the little people of the forest nor any space traveler from another dimension ever saw fit to show themselves to him.

"Twin Rainbow", he confided, "so strong are my beliefs in them that I truly thought if ever they chose to show themselves to any human it would have been me. I feel so...." "Well, Gordon", I interjected before he could continue, "You WERE right on both counts! 'Cause, guess what! HERE I AM! As living proof!" With that, Uncle Gordon let out a huge gruffaw! But my attempt to both console him, as well as remind him of the subtle ways in which these entities often communicate with we humans, soon caused us both to laugh, heartily.

Later, we began to delve deeper into one another's sixth sense of these things and the different ways we already expreienced many encounters with such entities. We also shared between us how, since we first could remember, somehow always knowing that we originally came from some otherworld, extra-terrestrial place.

"Yah know, Gordon", I confided, "It's real odd that we two almost complete strangers, should be talking like this, right off the bat, 'cause whenever I'm asked my nationality, I honest-to-God feel like I'm part Leprechaun, with the other part coming from *Epsilon Bootes*, a twin, red giant star system some 200 light years away. Of course, whenever I talk like this, the young souls, as I call them, always think I'm kidding and laugh their heads off. I don't go on with it and instead just laugh right along with them. But the old souls always know exactly what I mean!"

This line of inquiry lifted Edwards spirits, who giggled gleefully before going on to share some personal thoughts about his own similar 'other-worldly' origins. Stopping at one point, he mysteriously pointed up to the plaque that hung over the doorway and paused, as if to gather within himself a huge sea of latent emotion, and, with great dramatic elocution, spoke each of the plaque's words, slowly and deliberately, as if it were the most sublime thing that anyone could ever say about such matters.

"My dear Jerome", he bellowed, "No Matter What! Always....Always Remember!....We Are....Such Stuff...As Dreams...Are Made On;...And... Our Little Lives...Are Rounded...With A Sleep!"

By the end of our first meeting, we both felt high-as-kites, Gordon's home-brews certainly having done nothing to detract from the natural high we achieved through our old soul-talk together.

Edwards summed up the mood when he declared, "Jerome, you're definitely a young counterpart of myself who's after my own heart. So you must promise to come again for another chat and, perhaps, a game of chess and some more Shakespeare over a home-brew or two. What say you to that?"

"Well, Gordon", I replied, "You, too, unquestionably are an elder counterpart of my own heart. You've given me a most clear vision for the way I want to live in the future, and the kind of legacy that I also wish to leave as you shall do through this wondrous house and its surrounds. But as far as my ever coming 'round again, I can only answer you with these three conundrums: Does the Bear shit in the woods? Does the Hawk soar through the air? Does the Salmon, indeed, swim in the sea?" We both chuckled heartly once last time and I departed.

– THE SPIRIT WORLD GUIDES US IN STRANGE WAYS –

VER the next several months which followed, the two of us made contact a few more times: drinking home-brews; playing chess; swapping parodies of Shakespeare; and generally sharing our mutual love of women and the search for truth.

Edwards personal search led his life's odyssey on any number of fascinating wanderings. Like the time he found himself standing on a lonely beach in Nova Scotia, with nothing but his old kit bag on his back, after having just returned to Canada from France on a cattleship at the end of 'The Great War To End All Wars'.

After serving several years with distinction, under murderous machine-gun fire, as a Red Cross corpsman with the 6th Brigade, 29th Battalion, Edwards decided that he needed to see and experience, first-hand, the country he, and so many of his dead mates, sought to defend. So he set out on foot and took almost two years to walk from Nova Scotia to British Columbia.

During one of our soul-visits, I took it upon myself to orally deliver to Edwards a letter Crystal Freesia and I composed. The letter – a calligrapher's masterpiece, drafted upon romantically-ethereal Victorian stationery, covered with cherubs floating through the bluest of skies on white clouds – was a long soliloquy about how much we admired him for his all-important statement to the world through The Elves Inn.

"Dearest Gordon, your magical home", began the letter, "is a simple, yet crucial affirmation about those eternally real things in life. It represents to us the very best of ways to counter the pathological dystopias which everywhere seem to be emerging, with ever–greater savagery, upon the North American scene, and indeed the world."

Our sililoquy began as it ended, "Dearest Gordon, we would be most honored if you would allow us the great privilege to carry on, through The Elves Inn, your life's statement of something incredibly pure, clean and healthy which needs to be passed on to those who, in turn, will come after us.

The offer we made to the old Englishman was that he need never again have to worry about being forced to vacate his sacred Inn due to lack of funds, because we were prepared to help him out with a most unusual proposition.

All we asked of him was that he enter into an agreement of understanding with us that we would pay him a regular monthly payment, as if we actually were living in The Elves Inn, for however many years as he so chose to remain there. In return for which, we would assume occupancy on the day he decided, for whatever reason, to give it up.

Edwards, like the stalwart elf he was, declined the offer. "NO!", he sternly cried, as he agitatedly-waved his hands and head all about. "I mean you no offense, but NO! NOT UNDER ANY TERMS OR CIRCUMSTANCES! You see, I'm an old socialist from the word go, who doesn't believe in the modern, capitalistic way of grossly inflating land and property values for whatever the market will bear. I want no part of that greedy, scheming philosophy. I built The Elves Inn, in the first place, precisely to hold out the insane, mental-ward-of-a-prison world that's out there, and instead create around me a reality of my own choosing."

Noticing how dejected I was, Gordon softened his tone. "Look! It's this way, dear boy. I don't see that The Elves Inn really is worth anymore than the same $500 dollars it originally cost me to build it – lock, stock and barrel, with the bath tub and sink thrown in for good measure. But if I took up your truly kind, generous offer, and eventually sold it to you two for what my conscience dictated it was worth, where do you suppose I could go and live in this absurd world on so little money. No, Jerome. Tell your dear, sweet wife that I plan to live here 'til the day they finally carry me out feet first."

– THE SPIRIT DIRECTS ME BACK TO THE ELVES INN –

Several months passed since the day I shared our letter of intent with that old staunch socialist, which, as things turned out, was the last time I would ever see him again.

One late afternoon, as Alta-Dena and I were returning to the '303' from one of our spiritual jaunt's into the Okanagan Valley, an over-powering urge arose, like a bolt-from-the-blue, to first stop by The Elves Inn to see how it and Edwards were faring.

As Alta-Dena pulled up to the heavily-treed edge of the Inn's grounds, an eerie feeling crept over me. Electric impulses, transmitted by the spiritual telegraph, rippled all across my arms and up and down the back of my neck.

This time, instead of jerking open Alta-Dena's accordion door as I usually did, I slowly pushed it open. There was an altogether different, awkward, heavy feeling surrounding the Inn than I ever knew there before.

Even the wild Plum, Peach and Cherry trees – the Concord grape vines, Huckleberry and Salmonberry bushes – that surrounded the Inn, all manifested a melancholic energy as if something that was once integral to them, now was missing.

Rather than gingerly leap from Alta-Dena's cab, as was my bent, I quietly stepped out of her, so as not to disturb whatever unseen force it was that I sensed, and pensively passed through The Elves Inn gate towards its tree trunk–cave opening of a front door.

As I proceeded up the curved stone pathway, I suddenly noticed the thick, richly hand-painted, forest-scene curtains were missing from the Inn's diamond-shaped, leaded-glass windows.

My heart sagged, for I knew 'Uncle Gordon's' animated face and twinkling eyes – his always comical, deep-muffled belly laughter – wouldn't be there to receive my customary 'cosmic' Hippie-Druid-Buddha hand signals and 'Horse' pose, which had become my own inimitable way to comically greet him each time I stopped by.

For the longest time I stood transfixed, in the middle of the curved stone pathway, as if caught in a time-space warp, sandwiched in-between two dimensions, in a sort of suspended state of weightlessness that dictated my every move.

I didn't really walk so much as I felt 'transported' to a leaded-glass side window, through which a view of the Inn's living room presented a forsaken, empty scene, stripped bare of all its furnishings, save for the, by now, cold, lifeless fifty-gallon oil drum – with its thick, soot-blackened cast-iron door swung idly open – which stood out starkly amidst the lonely surounds of the once cozy room.

After making some general inquiries with the neighbors, I soon met up with one of Edwards surviving kin – a niece – who lived close by in another of the many houses that Edwards built in his lifetime.

However, the reaction I received upon introducing myself to her was a startling one. For no sooner had I uttered, "Oh, hello. I hate to bother you, but my name is Jerome Twin Rainbow and....", when her mouth practically dropped to the floor and she struggled as if to catch her breath while grasping hold of my arm.

As I stopped mid-sentence, wondering if she was about to have some kind of nervous fit, she yelped, "My God!" Seizing hold of my other arm she gasped, "So your Jerome Twin Rainbow! I'm Barbara, Gordon's niece. But just call me Babs! Come in! Come in!"

So emphatic was her outburst, given the solemnity of the occasion, that I was momentarily taken aback. Before I could even ask Babs how she came to know my name, she firmly clutched hold of both my hands, led me into the house and practically plunked me into a chair.

"Hallelujah! God Almighty!", she cried, "Am I glad to see you! My dear, just as Uncle Gordon always said to us, he was going to live in that house 'til the day they carried him out feet first. And that's exactly what happened. But he went real peaceful. I actually found him dead in the bath tub. He apparently died several days before of natural causes. But he lived a long, good, full life doing exactly what he always wanted to do."

By this time, it was my mouth's turn to drop to the floor. "But I still don't get it, Babs!", I said, "How do you know who I am?"

Gulping down another quick breath, she continued in her staccato manner. "After Uncle Gordon died, I was going through his things when I came across a tin under his bed that had lots of letters from his old flames in it. That's when I came across that lovely one you and your wife wrote to him. You know the one! On that beautiful stationery with all the clouds in the blue sky, with cherub's, roses and hearts around them!

Well, anyway, Uncle Gordon saw fit to keep it in that special tin of his. But the envelope was missing. And since there wasn't a return address on the letter, I had no way to track you two down to let you know what happened." I sat there, numb. Everything was happening too fast. I just wanted to immediately rush back to the '303' and inform Crystal Freesia of the sad news.

Babs continued with her tale, "I looked up Twin Rainbow and Crystal Freesia in every kind of directory I could think of, asked around the neighborhood, put a small advertisement in the North Shore News, in the local laundromat and several other bulletin boards to try to find you two."

Meanwhile, as I came to learn, her phone almost rang off the hook from the number of people who were on to her, night and day, trying to buy The Elves Inn. Apparently there were countless other people – developers, real estate brokers, artists, artisans, poets, writers – who all had long since coveted The Elves Inn for many different reasons. Some because its corner lot, that could accomodate several large condominiums or townhouses, was prime for redevelopment. Others because it spoke to their soul's they way it did to our's.

"I was so taken by your letter", continued Babs, "that I've been putting them all off in the hope of somehow reaching you. And now, here you are! This all, I guess, is somehow meant to be. I know Uncle Gordon would like to see you have his wonderful old place, and I'll certainly do everything in my power to help you get it."

Never able to get more than a few words in edgewise, with my head by now reeling from the unexpectedly sad yet, at the same time, incredibly wonderful turn of events, I soon bade Babs good-bye and hurried back to tell Crystal Freesia of the sweet and sour news.

– IT WASN'T MEANT TO BE AT THAT MOMENT IN TIME –

Crystal Freesia and I knew we, unquestionably, were drawn back to The Elves Inn, by some mysterious force, that sought to help us fulfill a big part of both our heart's desire in life. Returning to its grounds, we held hands and thanked the fairies and whatever other unseen spirits there caused us to return to it in the nick of time.

Gordan's niece didn't say we could have The Elves Inn for what Edwards once said it was worth, but she did offer it to us at the lowest market price, with the most generous terms imaginable.

But as strange and contradictory as it seems, when it came down to the actual moment to commit ourselves, after several weeks of soul-searching and hand-wringing anguish, we let the chance to take possession of The Elves Inn pass us by.

The reasons for our unexpected decision were manifold and complex ones, some of which we couldn't even completely verbalize to ourselves or one another. In spite of what seemed fated to be, we decided before we could fully commit ourselves to any one place, our two separate, yet joint, odyssey's still had other distant places and lessons we yet had to learn.

Gordon's niece was as shocked and disappointed as we were by our decision. "I'm desperately sorry to hear that", she moaned. "The Elves Inn seemed so right for you two kids. But I guess if your mind's are made up, there must be some reason why you're not supposed to have it."

As we bade her good-bye, and were about to close the door behind us, she suddenly shouted, "HOLD IT YOU TWO!", before mysteriously disappearing down a dark hallway before turning into a back room of her home. She finally returned several minutes later carrying one of Edwards carved wooden plaques.

Our eyes suddenly flashed wide, the size of full moons, once we realized it was the bust of *Ophelia* that hung over The Elves Inn doorway and announced, "We are such stuff as dreams are made on....!"

"I don't know why, but something just came over me to want to give this to you kids. I know deep down in your hearts you really would like to have The Elves Inn if you could. But since it doesn't seem destined to be, I think Uncle Gordon would at least like you to have a small piece of its spirit to take away with you. I hope one day, when the time is right it will, in some way, help you find the house of your dreams. Once you do find it, I just somehow feel again that Uncle Gordon would like you to place this plaque on one of its walls as a reminder of him and The Elves Inn."

We thanked her for the unexpected gift and departed, little knowing that this simple carving was an amulet. A magic charm that one day not only would help us find the house of our dreams but **THEE** very house from which it came and upon whose walls it was destined to return.

– ANOTHER MAGICAL CYCLE TAKES ITS COURSE –

Eight years passed, while the two of us, like wandering wild geese in search of a sacred nest, continued our migratory passages in Alta-Dena, traveling back and forth, with the seasons of our lives, between the North and South, never certain where our ultimate resting place would be.

At one point, Crystal Freesia returned to British Columbia while I remained in California. She was the ship's anchor or spiritual homing device, to which I knew to continually return. My role that of the 'hunter ship', in constant search of a new spiritual port of call.

There finally came a point when we both grew weary of our long, physical separation from one another, and were equally fed up with the odious intrusions of landlords in our intensely-private lives.

We deliberately set out to coordinate our joint northern and southern search by devising a daily meditative ritual. One that, though our meditative outposts were a thousand miles apart, we faithfully agreed to conduct, at precisely the same time each morning and evening.

The synchronized, introspective ritual we devised was meant to affirm one of life's truisms which is that if one concentrates long and diligently enough upon any one image to be realized, the universe will, in due course, as if by magic, physically manifest either that image or something entirely different, yet even better.

Our ritual to 'image-into-being' our dream place employed a regimen of guided-imagery exercises. An image of The Elves Inn served as the primary affirmation that went, "Creator, may we find a place, as exquisitely beautiful as this, to put our whole heart and soul into as a statement to the world of the way life should be."

Another key image used was that of the carved wooden plaque of Ophelia that so long ago was placed in our keeping. During each ritual we envisaged ourselves placing the plaque upon the wall of a house that looked just like The Elves Inn.

Yet never once, during our visual-izations, did we ever, consciously, entertain the thought that our 'conjuring' would actually produce The Elves Inn itself.

For the next several months, we 'religiously' conducted our meditative ceremony, periodically contacting one another by phone or letter to further boost the power and strength of our joint imagery.

From my end, every time this meditative ritual was undertaken, I couldn't help but note the strange similarity between the way Babs mysteriously disappeared down a dark hallway of her home, before returning with her gift of Gordon's carving of Ophelia, and the way Lucy Swift Hawk-Sargent at Crow Creek also once disappeared into a back bedroom of her home, before returning with Drifting Goose's medicine bundle that contained his Sun Dance stick and pouch of red ceremonial earth. "Are these two mysterious old men", I wondered, "somehow mystically connected to me in a Dreamtime that knows no boundaries of time and space?"

One early Sunday morning, in the dead of a cold December Winter's Solstice night, I was startled awake by the phone jangling next to my ear. It was Crystal Freesia, incoherently blurting out something about,"OH, MY GOD! IT WORKED! IT REALLY DID! THE INN! A SIGN!"

Still half-asleep, trying to gather my wits about me, I cut her off. "Hold it! Hold it! Love!", I cried, "Not so fast. Slow down. Take a deep breath! Now, run that by me one more time from the top."

"OH, MY GOD, LOVE! I CAN'T REALLY BELIEVE IT!", she squealed with another burst of uncontrollable excitement. "Well, you'll never guess in a million years what I saw tonight. You know how much I hate parties of any kind because of their impersonal nature. Well, anyway, tonight a teacher friend on the North Shore invited me to her house-warming party. And for some unexplainable reason, I accepted. Well, Love! At about two this morning I was just about to cross Lion's Gate Bridge, on my way back home to Tudor Manor, when I suddenly had an overwhelming, compelling urge, like the one you had to return to The Elves Inn years ago, to instead drive by it just to see how it looked after all these years. As I pulled up to its front gate, you'll never guess what I saw in the dark."

Pausing in her tale, as if to prolong my anxiety, she teased, "Guess!" "Listen, Love!", I sighed, "At two in the morning, still dozy, I'm in no mood to play guessing games. Don't stop now. I can't stand it. Just tell me for God's sake!" "WOULD YOU BELIEVE – A GIANT FOR SALE SIGN?", she screamed at the top of her lungs.

In the next few moments, if someone had accidentally crossed our lines and overheard what followed, or had a cell phone and could have watched all our antics, they no doubt would have thought they'd just tuned into some bizarre scene of two Neanderthals primitively communicating with one another. Because all they would have heard or seen, at either end of the line, for several long minutes, was an exchange of guttural 'Aggghhh's' and 'Yaaahhh's', interspersed by a number of weeping sobs and high-pitched 'Lee-Lee-Lee-Lee' tremolos, with both of us doing our own version of a St. Vitus Day Dance.

Still incoherent with excitement, Crystal Freesia struggled to describe how, upon seeing the *For Sale* sign, she at once jumped out of her white VW 'bug' and did an ad-libbed, impromptu dance of sheer ecstatsy on The Elves Inn grounds, while ritually encircling it several times and everywhere doing a 'laying on-of-hands' ceremony, before rushing home to inform me of the incredible news.

By now wide-awake, yet still half-incredulous, I questioned, "Huh? What? Get serious! You're putting me on! Aren't you, Love?" Yet after a number of frustrated, "No, I'm not! Honest! I'm dead serious! Really, Love!", from Crystal Freesia, we both resorted again for a time to our Neanderthal grunts, bellows and temolos. "OH, MY GOD!", I screamed, "If only I could jump through this phone right now and rush back with you so we could do a St.Vitus Day Dance together upon its hallowed grounds."

"Don't worry, Love", she squealed, "I know exactly how you feel. The minute I hang up, I'm going to have a good, strong, hot cup of Billy Tea, and then rush back to the Inn, do our meditative ritual on its grounds and then stay camped out on its door-step 'til the real estate people arrive in the morning." We synchronized our watches and agreed to do our meditative ritual at precisely the time when the sign said the Inn would be open for inspection.

What ensued over the next several weeks was a series of strange 'coincidences' which proved, beyond any shadow of a doubt, that someone or something, far beyond the two of us, was powerfully directing us back to The Elves Inn and Canada as our place of destiny. A tiny piece of Grandmother's Land was opening up its arms to us, welcoming us to her bosom.

– ONWARD CANADA –

Words & Music
By T.L. Richardson

– THE WHOLE THING IS IN THE HANDS OF THE SPIRIT –

The first 'coincidence' involved the developer, who'd recently acquired The Elves Inn. He was known as *The King of Knockdowns* because of his reputation for bulldozing architecturally-beautiful, constructionally-sound heritage homes to make way for ugly, cheaply-built, high-priced 'Monstor' dwellings and glitzy townhouses.

But no sooner had he made plans to callously do the same to Uncle Gordon's exquisite creation when, curiously, his whole heady dream of economic empire instead suddenly turned into a nightmare of ruin when bankruptcy proceedings were brought against him and he was forced to not only liquidate The Elves Inn but virtually all his holdings.

The second 'coincidence' was that the real estate agency only just put up the for sale sign on the night of the party Crystal Freesia so mysteriously, out-of-character, attended. Thus, no one had yet been shown The Elves Inn.

Next, one legal or financial snag after another made it seem as if The Elves Inn once again was going to slip through our fingers. The final blow almost came when no insurance company would underwrite The Elves Inn because of its non-conforming, wood-butchered-nature, which every company referred to as "a shack!" or "fire-trap!"

That was the third 'coincidence'. Because on the very day our deal was set to fall through, one company agreed to underwrite it in the most bizarre way. It happened as Crystal Freesia dejectedly stood on The Elves Inn's grounds, fresh out of hope, when a middle-aged man approached her. "Hello", he said. "I saw the for sale sign and thought I'd stop to take a look at the old house. I've loved this place since I was a kid, when I used to walk by it on the way to school. But why do you look so sad?"

The instant he learned our deal was about to collapse because we couldn't find an insurance company, he said, "Well this must be your lucky day, because I'm in the insurance business and I'll underwrite it, without a doubt. I want to see this place preserved forever."

As one seasoned bank manager put it at the time, "In all my years of experience in this field, I've never seen anything quite like this before. Someone, somewhere, obviously very badly wants you two to have this house." Or as another bank official succinctly commented, "You both must have a guardian angel up there who is watching over you."

Still a fourth 'coincidence' occurred once the deal closed – and we took possession of The Elves Inn, or it took possesion of us – when we were approached by the owner who originally bought it when we turned it down, years before. Her divorce had led her to sell it to the developer.

Curious to see who we were, and unaware of our past history with Gordon Edwards, she nervously began to relate how, over the past eight years that she lived there, she was "strangely prevented" from, as she put it, "ever making any drastic changes to this house."

Furtively glancing all about, as if concerned that some invisible force might be listening, she continued her tale in a low whisper. "I don't want to unduly scare you two, but I should tell you that this house is haunted. It's haunted by an old man. Friends and workers who've come here have actually seen him and I think I even caught a glimpse of him once, too. But the whole time I lived here, I felt his scary presence. And every time I, or a worker, ever tried to make some big changes to the place we felt a strange forebodingness. It was as if he was hovering over us all, trying to take the saw or hammer right out of our hands." We didn't say anything to her about once having ever known Edwards, but politely continued to listen and validate her fears.

It wasn't long after we moved in, before we, too, felt 'the ghost's' presence, of which she spoke. It wasn't at all scary, though, but rather gentle and benign, as if it were simply overseeing things there for a time 'til we settled in.

One day, after nearly six months of digging our way out of boxes and crates, the ghost noticeably vanished. To us it was as if Gordon's spirit, by drawing us back to The Elves Inn, had accomplished what it set out to do and now was ready to continue onward towards wherever its own 'cosmic odyssey' next was headed.

– THE ELVES INN METAMORPHOSES INTO THE ELF INN –

At that moment, it was as if a solemn transfer of spiritual ownership had occurred and a holy torch placed in our hands.

With his spirit's departure, Crystal Freesia declared, "You know, Love. When Gordon was here by himself, the name he chose fit because there was only one elf – Him! But now there's two, with more elves and fairies coming. So I think we should hold a ceremony and rename this place *The Elf Inn*."

With that, we lit a mixed-braid of Sweetgrass and Sage and passed through every room in the house, blessing each space as we went with affirmations about our intent to preserve the spirit of The Elf Inn and carry on Gordon Edwards work. The same ceremony was repeated outside, as we made a pilgrimage to every plant, flower and shrub around the Inn.

"How do you do! I'm Twin Rainbow and this is my lady, Crystal Freesia!", we said, as we took turns introducing one another to all the rooted, winged, crawly life forms in the garden.

Our impromptu ceremony concluded with a kiss, a toast to 'Uncle Gordon' and then a procession to a place in the living room, close to the front door, that we designated as The Elf Inn's 'Spirit Post'.

There we prominently displayed a photo of Edwards – as a handsome, dashing young W.W. I corpsman – beside his carved wooden plaque of Ophelia. "Thank you, Spirits", we said in tandem, "for this talisman carving that guided us back to assume our sacred role as the new caretakers of The Elf Inn and the Keepers of its legacy."

– CONTINUING ANEW THE LEGACY –

With the rechristened Elf Inn came the enormous legacy we discovered it represents to the community of Lower Capilano at large.

Passerby's on foot or in a car often approach its tree-lined edge, sit on an old weathered log or park for a time in quiet contemplation. Some lean over its latched wood-butcher gate as far as they can to peer into the Inn's secluded grounds. Others, if they see us in the garden, engage us in conversation. Each has an overwhelming need to share some personal story or feeling concerning their past or present connections with it.

Beaming like an awe-struck 'Alice in Wonderland', while using descriptive phrases like 'The Magic Kingdom' or 'Fairyland' to describe the Inn and its grounds, each struggles to put into words how the spot acts for them as a signpost to the fantasies of another time. It engenders within each of them a professed desire to somehow escape from the alienating modernity of the new world order in which they live, and return to the atmosphere of a simpler age that the spirit of the Inn harbors.

Observing our daily activities, they often speak of similar longed-for things, like: being busy in their own gardens; happily pruning, weeding, feeding and conversing with all the plants, birds and other critters, as if they were their own beloved flesh and blood; chopping and stacking a winter's supply of firewood as a natural form of mental, physical and spiritual therapy; reverently partaking in all the wonderment and magic of each passing season's changing dispensations; joining in sonorous communion with others on some project to beautify, embelish or renew their place and its surrounds; or just regularly gather with family and friends, especially during holiday events and anniversaries, to celebrate – through song, dance and colloquy – the ordinary passing of life.

Some seek to briefly recount what it was like, as a child, to ever come near The Elves Inn's grounds and meet, as one put it, "The nice old man who always gave us kids candy, flowers or shared some dramatic passage from Shakespeare." A few dirge up how thrilling and scary it once was to ever dare to sneak into the Inn's yard in the dark, especially, as one recounted, "On a moonless night to peer into one of the old house's leaded-glass windows and try to catch a glimpse of the elf inside." The intensity of emotions these experiences once elicited, still vitally alive in the verve with which each of their accounts is related.

More than a few pilgrims are always eager to recount the sense of mystery and fear of what it once was like to approach The Elves Inn every Halloween night because of, as one said, "All the bizarre, creepy pieces of driftwood the old man scattered around his place, sticking them in the bushes, hedges or hanging from the trees. These scraps of wood, especially in the dark, were made all the scarier by the blood-shot eyes, sharp teeth, strands of matted hair or gruesome scars and fake blood that he put on them."

One 'victim' of Uncle Gordon's elfish pranks declared, "Getting up enough courage every 31st of October to approach the old haunted house was one of the scariest rituals of my youth that I still can remember as if it was only yesterday. Each year, as The Eve of Old Hallows rolls around again, I still get goose bumps whenever I think about it."

It wasn't long before I found myself taking up where Edwards left off to carry on the legacy of his elfish 'Feast of Samhain' tradition, for succeeding generations of young and old alike. I, too, avidly looking forward each year for the chance to: dress up as a haggard-old banshee or hobgoblin; turn out all the lights around the Inn, with only glowering pumpkins and ghoulish jack-o-lanterns suspended from tree branches and grape vines to light the way; lying in wait near the Inn's dark tree trunk-cave of an entrance; praying for some unsuspecting Trick-or-Treater to be foolish enough to venture within its grounds so I can jump out from my dark haunt and scare the living be-Jesus out of them.

Some years the decision is made to simply wait for the unsuspecting Trick-or-Treater to knock upon the Inn's wood-butcher door, whereupon the peephole slids open, a blood-shot eye peers out at them and a high-pitched, whining-shriek of a voice from within calls out, "Yes Dearie!

Who is it?" And as the door creaks open, the voice continues to whine, "Come in, little boy! Come in, little girl!" At which point, most Trick-or-Treaters, wisely more concerned with their own self-preservation than with satiating a sweet tooth, are sent fleeing into the pitch-black night as they scream to other Trick-or-Treaters behind them, "Don't go in there! It's hella creepy! Aggghhh! It's haunted!"

In the meantime, while standing within the shadows of The Elf Inn's inner sanctums, listening to all their shrill forewarnings, fondly patting Edwards wood-carving of Ophelia on the Inn's Spirit Post, I smilingly mutter, "Ahhh, Uncle Gordon! Wherever you or your spirit may be! I, as you once did, have instilled within yet another generation, still more fresh, gripping terrifying tales that they can recount to all those who come after them, of a wild Eve of Old Hallows once spent at The Elf Inn."

Then there are all those other passerby's, eager to tell their tales of the 'elementals' they've seen around The Elf Inn, or the psychic effect the Inn's 'earth consciousness' has upon them whenever the occasion arises to enter or leave its grounds. As one visitor put it, "I have to catch my breath each time I come here because it's like I just passed through a time barrier into an earlier century or some bygone era. It's like being in some kind of real-life archival film or storybook."

With each new tale, we two lucky inheritors of all this intangible wealth have come to realize how such simple tales represent the real meaning of the concept and practice of *deep ecology* and *spiritual bio-regionalism* where one lives. Slowly, the realization dawned that Gordon Edwards, in his own inimitable way, had provided for his Lower Capilano community the same mythic function as my own San Bruno Mountain encounters with The Mean Man & his Dogs, The Old Lady in the Haunted House, and even Ol'Bear Tracks and Indian Head Cave.

The Elf Inn's old-soul passerby commonly has the same need to seek us out, as potential fellow soul-mates, and inform us about all those once-upon-a-time mythic characters and sacred places of their own Canadian youth on the North Shores of Vancouver. The Elf Inn seemingly serving as a tabula rasa place upon which local 'once-upon-a-time' tales filled with unusual characters needed to be told.

There were the accounts of characters like 'Johnny One Ear', the mad barber who, so it's said, always cut everyone's hair in the same bizarre way and could be seen walking the streets clutching fast to his scissors, clicking away, waiting to clip some unsuspecting youth who happened by.

Napoleon *"The Mystic Gardener"*

— The Great Mystery, Capilano, B.C. —

Napoleon's Magic Topiary Gardens

The Great Mystery, Capilano Garden, B.C.
"Quebecois Heroine Tale & Squamish Indian WHIHCH-in-TAWL Tale Side-by-Side"

Napoleon's Magic Topiary Gardens

LIVING MONUMENT TO THE HERO

Then there was 'Thump Drag', who, on special occasions, could be seen proudly wearing his faded-old World War One greens and beret, covered in metals. His legendary nickname created by children, too frigthened to approach him, as they listened to the eerie sounds he made as he walked the woods, at all hours of the night, dragging behind him his paralyzed right leg. The legendary 'Thump! Drag! Thump Drag!' sound he made becoming the source of outrageous tales and wonderings about how he came by all his medals or what horrific war-time battle scene led to his injury or queer behavior.

Then there was 'Squeaky', the hobo with the high-pitched voice that always sounded like he'd just swallowed a mouthful of helium, who lived as a recluse somewhere in the wild bush. Squeaky scaring half-to-death the unsuspecting passerby as he unexpectedly burst from the bush and squealed like some cartoon-character, "Nice day, hey! Got any spare change?" Squeaky, like ol' Mr. Bear Tracks in my youth, the buyer of beer and cigarettes for the troubled youth of his time and place.

Never to forget the tale of the one-and-only, eccentric 'Lady In Red', an equally strange character who is said to have nary spoken a word to anyone in the community yet who, throughout her mysterious life, could be seen walking everywhere bedecked in one mad, outlandish red outfit after another.

Last, but by no means least, was Napoleon St. Pierre with his 'House of Mystery' & 'Mysterious Garden', that once existed a short stone's throw from The Elves Inn. Napoleon, a Quebec native, became Lower Capilano's first white settler in 1909 on the eve of old Joe Capilano's death. Capilano one of the Squamish Nation's most illustrious chiefs of yesteryear who, just the year before, led a contingent of chiefs to petition King Edward VII to honor the aboriginal title of their homelands.

Napoleon, for decades – prior to when Gordon Edwards set out, in his own way, to continue onward some of the local traditions of Lower Capilano that he began – labored tirelessly to create a house and garden of natural and man-made antique oddities. His topiary garden a wonderment of unusual figures, among which was a: four-sided monument dedicated to the Universal Hero, Canadian Maple Tree, Beaver and Moose; a mourning heroine, draped upon a cross, in tribute to a mythic tale from his French Canadien Roman Catholic origins; a huge snake in honor of the Squamish Nation's creation mythology, as well as; a myriad collection of driftwood that resembled bizarre human and non-human forms.

So captivating to the imagination were his creations, that Napoleon was well-known to every settler and traveler, young or old, rich or poor, famous or infamous, who ever ventured onto the North Shore. People are said to have traveled from far and wide just to have their fortunes told by this strange transplanted Quebecois psychic–gardener–outspoken mystic orator–oral historian.

Touched by the sacred power of the nearby Capilano River and all its canyons and mountainous surrounds, I soon realized that – like Joe Capilano, Napolean St. Pierre, Gordon Edwards and the cavalcade of rare souls who came before them– I, too, was one of the relay runners in some ancient human race in the Dreamtime. Another storyteller-runner carrying in his hand a baton mysteriously passed on, as it has by so many other's hands before, for a short while until it comes my time to pass it on to still others.

The North Shore has had many such relay runners who have had their own mythic tales to tell of all its magical spots in Nature. Places like 'Indian Head Rock' and 'The Mysterious Pool of Bubbles'.

Indian Head Rock, to the imaginations of many young Canadian pilgrims, who found themselves standing within its awesome presence in a secluded mountain canyon, was said to have been the petrified remains of an old Indian Chief or Medicine Man. Indian Head Rock of the North Shore the source of as many legendary tales as once was my Indian Head Rock in the South.

The Mysterious-Pool-of-Bubbles, a hidden place in nature far more demanding to reach than my own Indian Head Cave, was where young Canadian youth often heard, as they tell it, "voices speaking and singing in strange tongues." That mysterious, dark-green pool only accessible to those brave-hearted souls willing to make the necessary difficult swim upstream through treacherous, fast-moving currents and glacier-fed waters. A feat said to have been, "a veritable rite of passage within itself." Its deep waters only reachable during those times of the year when the water level was low enough, and the pilgrim a strong-enough swimmer, to undergo this rigorous, watery challenge. Such were the many timeless stories of the land around and beyond The Elf Inn that became part and parcel of its legacy.

However, when most people take possession of a house they seldom realize the legacy they're buying into is much more than the limits of their immediate walls or the edge of their property. They seldom concern themselves with the 'polarities' or 'vibrations' of the house, its land and the story of the human community around it. Did anyone ever enjoy the

Capilano River

Twin-Rainbow Irwin engrossed in some Water Spirit Talk

benefits or suffer from the consequences of whatever unique physical, emotional or spiritual powers or debilitations they didn't have before living in that house? Did anything good or bad ever happen to the former owners for which the house should be blessed or cleansed? Where the former occupants happy or unhappy living there? Did that have to do with them or the place itself? Is the house resting on the site of some historical incident which might act as a positive or negative influence upon anyone who ever has or ever will live there? What is the name that the house and its lands would give to themselves? These and still other questions often never addressed, save for writer-artists of the spirit like Leonard Woolf.

Like Leonard Woolf, my sense is that that lad who once lived: in a shack on the Crow Creek Reservation in South Dakota; in a log cabin among the Lil'Wat of British Columbia; in a Mockingbird Lodge in Kuksu Country; or in the Elf Inn of Lower Capilano are four related yet different people. The most powerful molders of their lives neither the universities they attended, the jobs they held, the acclaim they received from the work they did nor the political movements and civic activism they had a hand in, but the houses and lands upon which they each lived. The evolutionary phases of their lives determined by each house and its surrounding landscape.

Commenting upon her own relationships with the houses in which she lived, Crystal Freesia once noted, "As a child, I was raised on May Gibb's stories of Gum-Nut Fairies and tales of Beatrix Potter. I've always envisoned one day living in a Brambly Hedge-type tree trunk–cave of a house. So the Elf Inn, at some stage in my life, simply had to be. It was a fantasy I had to realize, But I often wonder, at the same time, why all those other children around me, who were raised on the same stories, didn't grow up with the same longings. Why, I wonder, did I end up in The Elf Inn while many of them ended up satisfied to live in plastic, ticky-tacky, match-box houses? Why did such Elf Inn images imprint upon me and not them? How Come? How Come?"

Such questions could be said to be among the great imponderable mysteries of life. Their answers, perhaps, have something more to do with we humans who, metaphysically, are sometimes referred to as 'young souls' or 'old souls'. It's as if we 'young' or 'old' souls, unconsciously responding to some mysterious 'homing beam', attempt – through the houses in which we choose to live, or through the urban or rural lands upon which we settle – to relive, reintegrate or resolve some karmic aspect of our ancestral or 'cosmic' origins.

Some of us becoming, in the process, 'Water People', who settle on or near some body of water. 'River and Lake People', though, as distinctive from one another as are 'Ocean and Seashore People'. Those urban 'Hill People' who choose to live in: dense inner-city, man-made box canyons; sprawling suburban homes on the side of steep arroyos; or postage-sized, bee-hive, high-rise apartments; as distinctive again from one another as those living high atop a ridge or meadowed foothill. Alta-Dena, as a mobile house unique unto herself, also as distinctive from those who would choose a giant Winnebago as they from us.

Each time Alta-Dena and I found ourselves passing through yet another community, The Voice would whisper in my left ear, "Hmmm, Lad! Now look at, will yah, the strange way all those people live over here. And would you look, too, at the odd way their living over there. Yah know, don't yah, that yah couldn't possibly ever live in such places. But isn't it curious that these strange people, whomever they might be, and wherever they originally came from, love their places as much as you and Crystal Freesia do The Elf Inn. They, no doubt, would be just as puzzled and mystified as to who would ever choose to live in such a house as yours. Think long about what mysterious genealogical, biological or metaphysical longings drive you all to live in such disparate places? "

– GRANDFATHER ELK SPIRIT LODGE MATERIALIZES –

The Elf Inn satisfied Crystal Freesia's longings but not all of mine. I needed a 'Lodge' where I could be surrounded, in private, by the many objects, images and personal effects, gathered at each of the odyssey's twists and turns, that hold intense, spiritual meaning for no one else but me.

Once surrounded by the sympathetic vibrations of kindred spirits of other times and places – the mounted heads of deer, bear–wolf–coyote–wolverine skins, elk antlers, a buffalo bull skull, medicine bundle, eagle and hawk feathers, Rocky Mountain Man's sash; peyote stick, ancestral photographs, spirit paintings, sacred statues, medicine hats and medicine stones, a turtle's shell and sculpture – my mind, body and soul then able to receive the inspiration and spiritual sutenance they need to survive and flourish.

As synchronicity would have it, almost on the day when I began to wonder where to even start looking for such a lodge, it all but found me. About the time Edwards spirit presence vanished, Crystal Freesia and I decided to go for a drive, along the Sea-To-Sky Highway that connects the interior of British Columbia with the Lower Mainland. As we passed through Brittania Beach, once the stie of one of the world's largest copper mines, about an hour's drive north of The Elf Inn, there, alongside the road, was an old historic log cabin that just that day had been moved down to the coast, on a Low Boy truck and trailer, from the place in the Interior where it stood for over a century and a quarter. Tacked onto its side was a big sign that read – *For Sale*.

Within days a deal was cut, the cabin was loaded back onto the Low Boy and just the right place for it was found on The Elf Inn's grounds.

GRANDFATHER ELK SPIRIT LODGE

Built in 1858 with one foot thick, hand-adzed, squared and dove-tailed cedar logs, the cabin soon announced itself to be *Grandfather Elk Spirit Lodge*; so-named in honor of the spirit's of Grandpoppa Louie and the Bull Elk who once passed from this world onto the next together.

Historically, it served as the *10 Mile House*, where gold-miners once received overnight room and board as they made their long trek, ten miles each day, from one road house to another, until they finally reached the rich gold fields of Barkerville fame. The cabin's weathered granite and quartz rock foundation, itself, quarried from high atop a place in B.C.'s interior called Gold Mountain.

Legend has it that this 10 Mile House was where the infamous Judge Begbie – known as 'The Hanging Judge', for his quick death sentences for the smallest of infractions in British Columbia's early wild history – often stayed as he traveled his circuit. In a later evolution, it became home to many generations of Indian families who shared its one large, 12 foot by 20 foot room and two lofts.

So, from that point on, Crystal Freesia had her tree trunk fantasy of a house and I my lodge – two quiet eddies amidst the world's maelstrom, where time could stop and eternity begin – sitting side-by-side one another, atop the ancient diluvium flood plains of the Capilano River.

Grandfather Elk Spirit Lodge one of the places where, in the early hours of morning and night – while lying in one of its lofts beds – yet another fresh *'Life on Turtle Island'* entry can be duly noted.

The Elf Inn's sleeping loft another place of retreat eagerly sought out to jot down still more entries. Ah, such simple bliss, to be able to: scramble up an old ship's ladder; fling open the loft's tiny window to feel the rush of ice-cold Northern night air; stare out at the stars and await some new, inspired thought to come from out of the heaven's vast, dark, stillness and descend upon yet another fresh, blank page.

Meanwhile.....inside the Inn, the pendulum of an old Grandfather Clock slowly ticking back and forth, chimes with each passing hour as it has faithfully done for over 200 years. While outside, the powerful diesel hum of tugboats, pushing and pulling their loads through heavy seas, mix with the drone and groan of seaplanes that struggle to become airborne. The loud wailing horns and whistles of distant trains, struggling to find their way through heavy rains or snowfalls, plying towards untold imagined frontier places in British Columbia's interior, serve as yet another counterpoint to this whole timeless scene.

With each horn's wail and whistle's blast – each diesel's surge and propeller's rev – that echo off the heights behind the Inn and Lodge, there

Grandfather Elk Spirit Lodge Interior

Grandfather Elk Spirit Lodge Interior

sounds yet another "SWEET JESUS!" thought in my head. "SWEET JESUS!", goes one thought's wail, "Is it chance or cosmic force that has led us to this strange inn and lodge, and tiny patch of sacred Grandmother's Land?" "SWEET JESUS!", comes another thought's great blast, "Will some other mystical inn and lodge, elsewhere upon the Great Turtle's back, one day draw you away to them, with as much passionate force as The Elf Inn, to teach even loftier lessons?" These noisy ruminations always spiking one last puzzled, "SWEET JESUS! Could it be that this strange Inn and Lodge is where the odyssey must end?" It wasn't long before Inn and Lodge cried out for us to take on the role of leaders in their defense.

– THE INN BECOMES A PLACE OF ACTION –

Suddenly our community turned into a battle-zone, with The Elf Inn and Grandfather Elk Spirit Lodge two of its main command posts.

First, there were a series of extensive development plans along a nearby commercial 'Marine Drive' corridor, by insatiable predator-developers, who sought to turn the whole area into a 'Hong Kong' strip of high rises and shopping malls. Then a huge influx of Asian and Persian immigrants into Lower Capilano – and the tensions that soon arose between them, the earlier European immigrants and Squamish Indians over developmental, environmental and societal issues – threatened to pit neighbor against neighbor. Then came the construction of a huge 'Save On' shopping complex, one block away, on the grounds of a vacated 'Schlage Lock' plant, that cunningly was traded between developers for the sum total of $1.00. A city planner's hair-brain scheme soon proposed to use Hope Road as a major thoroughfare, to and from this commerical corridor and its huge shopping complex. Excessive noise, pollution and physical danger was being caused by more and more transient motorists who used our community as a short-cut speedway. The proposed draft of an 'Official Community Plan' for the Lower Capilao community, that sought to radically alter the integrity and character of our small-scale, low-key, single-family neighborhood, turned into a multiple unit, illegal in-law suite controvery. This encouraged an array of insensitive building codes, expedient council by-laws and arrogant architectural biases that encouraged the demolition of perfectly-sound, single-family heritage homes in favor of ugly townhouses, condominiums and 'Monstor' houses. The abuse to and potential loss of what was left of an old historic Squamish Indian trail and its greenbelt which skirted Lower Capilano, as well as the woeful lack of park and recreational facilities for our youth all cried out for our help. Suddenly, it was Action Time!

Like the Williams clan among the Lil'Wat, our tiny community of 500 strong also found ourselves dubbed *The Mouse That Roared*. But for all our good intentions, we earned, like the Williams, not the praise but the ire of local district planners, building inspectors, by-law enforcement officers, as well as local and foreign development investment interests and their bevy of high-priced lawyers and lobbyists. Cast as "the enemy", we had to take a crash '101' course on *How To Quickly Tell Your Friends From Foes & Your Allies From Adversaries*.

In the meantime, one heritage home after another fell like so many trees in a clear-cut forest.

– Typical Knockdown & Its Replacement in Lower Capilano –

– BEFORE –   **– AFTER –**

What rose to the fore, was the harsh reality of the White Man's avaricious, capitalism-gone-mad way of life that constantly takes rather than gives. The rights of community-controlled neighborhoods seldom ever given precedence over those government bureaucrats, loose cannon entrepreneurs and corporate syndicates who seek to dominate them.

Underlying this age-old struggle for the soul of a people, a nation and, indeed, an entire civilization – so commonly repeated in every tiny hamlet, berg, village, town or city in North America – are several major, as yet unresolved issues between the moral and ethical value systems of Turtle Island and North America. Namely, whether *smaller is beautiful* or *bigger is better* and whether *less growth* ultimately is preferable to *more growth*. These fundamental conflicts the veritable tip of the iceberg of a dramatic morality play that has been acted out between these two antagonistic world views since the first days of contact.

The major lesson offered up by The Elf Inn was that in the White Man's mindless, progress-giddy society, the simple act of buying a block of land or house – not for the purpose of outright speculation or other

Chief Joe Capilano

Joe Capilano & Other B.C. Chiefs Gather To Petition King Edward VII in England

ulterior profit motive, but with the intent of assuming one's sacred stewardship responsibilities towards its preservation as a legacy to those still to come – is the most revolutionary act one can ever undertake.

Yet though Lower Capilano's borders parallel the *Sk wx wú7mesh* people's Capilano Reserve, and only a narrow drive divides them, the gulf between them may as well be many miles, if not centuries, for how little day to day contact or relationships they have with one another.

Overnight, much to Crystal Freesia's chagrin, like the true elfin she is, who desires to forever keep the crazed world out of The Elf Inn's magical confines, I became the founding president of a militant community resident's association to foster this consciousness. As its point man, came the realization that our Association – like that of any clan, tribe, nation or union – is only as strong as its weakest link, especially when that link puts its own vested self-interests ahead of that of the collective's.

As 'The Mouse That Roared', the starting point of our community's consciousness-raising–solidarity-building process began with a renewed historical awareness of ourselves as one of the North Shore's oldest non-Indian communities. This naturally led to the symbolic act of first reclaiming our much-beloved, indigenous name of *Lower Capilano*.

– A STRONG SPIRIT NAME LIVES ON –

Still, though our two communities lead separate yet parallel lives, to some of us in the Association, our name became fused with the spirit of old Chief Joe 'Saapluk' Capilano and the great river of his people, and its even more ancient spirit name *Xwmlch'sen* (hoh-MUL-chee-son). "Xwmlch'sen", say the Squamish, "is where the spirit of Salmon, Bear and Killer Whale still are strong. It's where we live in the peaceful shadows of Che-che-yoh-ee – The Power Above All Others – and our Twin Sister's – Lolum & Waimatha – who represent peace, harmony and respect for all."

In a slower, less-complicated time, the name *Lower Capilano*, once was used by its early inhabitants, on all their letters, to identify the place where they belonged and the natural heritage that it represented. For years many even refused to conform to the White Man's attempt to instead call it 'Lower Pemberton', after a British lord and naval explorer.

Protection, *Preservation* and *Stewardship* at once became the watchwords that symbolized The Elf Inn and Grandfather Elk Spirit Lodge's main teaching to the community.

The two years of blissful 'Walden Pond' calm once spent at Mockingbird-Atop-Pear-Tree Cottage was quickly engulfed by 'The Tempest' of this strange Inn and Lodge. The original fantasy of The Elf

Inn – as that old proverbial Irish poem's 'Cottage of Content' – instead thrust us into the role of a modern-day 'Ophelia' and 'Hamlet', wondering whether our fates would turn out to be not unlike what befell those two Shakespearean characters.

– THE ODYSSEY TAKES ON A NEW FORM –

Alta-Dena and The Elf Inn proved to be perfect foils of one another. Alta-Dena, as the talisman who spirited me away to many places atop the Great Turtle, encouraged me, as we lumbered slowly along, just *TO THINK*! To Think about who I am, where I came from and where I'm going and so, in the process, to constantly remember that wherever one travel's to in life is a sacred place. Whereas, The Elf Inn, as an earth amulet, eagerly sought to teach what realities are involved in becoming 'The Keepers' of just one sacred place. To become a native, indigenous person, of one clan with one tiny homeland piece of Mother Earth.

The years spent in Alta–Dena's company now were at an end. 'Salmagundi Farm' – on the outskirts of Coupeville, in Washington State – was to be the place where Spirit chose Alta-Dena's gleaming white body to return back to Mother Earth's womb in a dignified manner.

With one last go-around of our *Ritual of The Road* checklist, a final smudge of smoldering Sweetgrass and chant of thanksgiving duly completed, I revved her up one last time and coasted her into a field behind Salmagundi Farm's outbuildings. Everything left inside her like a time capsule: the woodcut image of the prophet Ezekiel mounted above her dash; Allen Ginsburg's 'Science Fiction–Magic' declaration; the Grateful Dead 'American Beauty' Rose painted on her steering wheel and horn; the Peter Max artwork and framed Batik hanging on her

ceiling; all the Indian-collaged cabinets, rugs, bedding; left just as they were.

Peering into her inner chambers one last time caused so many memories to flash into view. Especially the one of the woman who, on her honeymoon, did the framed Batik that depicted a rainbow springing from a snow-capped mountain of the Olympic Peninsula, with the other end spill-ing onto a pebbled beach of the Juan De Fuca's as a rainbow king, with an orb in his hand, steps from the rainbow's end. "See you in the next life, for sure, Alta-Dena!", I cried out, as my hand made one final passing caress of her suicide knob that had safely guided me to so many wondrous places.

– ALTA-DENA IS DEAD! LONG LIVE ALTA-DENA! –

Those who knew Alta-Dena often said of her that if ever the Smithsonian Museum had dedicated a special wing entitled, *Hippie America; A Different Dream,* to capture this unique period in American History, then Alta-Dena would have been the perfect candidate to be inducted as a representative artifact of those times. But then again, her ending was fitting and appropriate. For the Earth she returned to is the greatest museum of them all. As a Lakota elder once so aptly put it – when a group of well-intended white people wanted to construct a lofty monument at Wounded Knee to commemorate the massacre there – he declined to support it because, as he said, "The wild Buffalo Grass itself is the greatest tribute of all to them, and says it all!"

Within a few days of leaving Alta-Dena to herself, a friend approached me with a strange offer. "Say, Jerome!", he said, "I hear you've finally put dear old Alta-Dena, bless her heart, out to pasture! She was one great truck! But everything has its day, right! Anyway, I don't know if you're interested, but a friend, out in Port Coquitlam, has a '79 VW Rabbit he bought new, but is willing to let go to someone he knows will respect it. It's a great car, with a great heart, that he calls his *Timex Watch*, because, as he says, 'It can take a lickin' but keeps on tickin'!' It's not as big and roomy as Alta-Dena, nor quite as unique, but you might like it. It's a real beautiful sky blue!"

"What color did you say it was?", I queried. In that instant, the spiritual telegraph sent goose bumps rippling up and down my arms, as the hair on the back of my neck stood on end. "This is another one of those fated crossroad moments!", whispered The Voice in my left ear, "Pay close attention to everything that is about to happen!"

"Holy Moly!", I thought. "You don't suppose this is Spirit's way of presenting me with yet another 'Blue' to take up where my old Crow Creek sidekick left me years back? Could this mean a whole new, maybe even wilder, more magical odyssey may already be a done deal somewhere in the spirit realm?" "Thanks!", I said to my friend, "I think I will check out his trusty Timex Watch first thing in the morning. Who knows, this might be Ezekiel's new spirit chariot, beckoning me forth!"

With my goodbye ceremony to Alta-Dena concluded, the time had come to go off into nature to do a mini-Holy HIll ceremony where I could be alone to think. Once there, I cried out to the spirit world. "Grandfather! Grandmother!, your grandson speaks. Time flies and yet stands still! A short yet long time we all live! There is still so much to tell you – to ask you – about this journey and its endless epiphanies to be found amongst the darkness and light. Wait for me!"

In the next breath I shouted, "Buck, Lucy, Bessie, Napoleon, Drifting Goose, Thunder Hawk, Wanagi Wacipi, Joe Capilano, Gordon Edwards and all you other new-old soul mate-pilgrims along the open road up ahead! Just let me throw a few things in my wicker steamer and I'll be with you in no time a'tall!"

In that instant, everything became manifestly clear. Like the plight of other New Frontier Breeds, I saw myself as a tribal man without a tribe in time. Another 'Ishi', who Fate decreed should wander alone, forever trying to recall and recount the long memories of his people. I knew, too, that as such a tribal man, my 'people' and 'clans', who I searched so long and hard for, on so many wild goose chases, weren't of any one culture, nation, religion, race or region but were scattered throughout endless time and space.

I knew then that perhaps the best way we New Frontier Breeds could begin to identify the citizenry of our 'new nations' would be to simply focus upon those loved ones around us towards whom we pledge our allegiance. The true, undying love for just one person equal to all the expressed clan wisdom that ever was or ever will be.

The Voice singing in that moment of clarity, "There was a boy....A ver-y strange, en-chanted boy....They say he wan-dered ver-y far, ver-y far....O-ver land and sea....A lit-tle shy....and sad of eye....But ver-y wise....was he....And then one day....A ma-gic day he passed my way....And while we spoke of man-y things....Fools and Kings....This he said to me....The great-est thing....you'll ever know....Is just to Love....And be Loved....in re-turn."

So, Pilgrim! Our odyssey together finally is at its end. Before your journey takes whatever turn it will, return to your quiet listening place in nature and ask yourself these last questions. What have the houses you've lived in taught you about the basics of life? What mysteries have they revealed? What legacies have they bequeathed? So, now! **Be off with ye, I say, in the most loving way possible! GO!**

WELCOME BACK! As The Voice trailed off, I knew we New Frontier Breeds need look no further for holy hills to climb, vision-questing places to seek or shamanic scenes to sensate than commit to places like The Elf Inn. Each of our 'Elf Inn's' the embodiment of tiny mystical webs of life found everywhere on Mother Earth. The quest to protect, preserve and proclaim them all – one in the same. Sharing a quiet walk, a nurturing caress or soft utterance with a loved one while maintaining an on-going dialogue with one's wild yet gentle spirit voice, is, in truth, all there really is. This, the Great Turtle's dream for itself and all its denizens.

Keeping forever foremost in mind, in everything one does, the old Navajo *Pollen Path Chant To Life*. A chant that goes, "Beauty in front of me! Beauty behind me! Beauty to the left of me! Beauty to the right of me! Beauty above me! Beauty below me! Beauty within me!"

When first I set out to walk this Pollen Path, I knew that, at some point, it would have to lead me back to the ancestral lands of my people. Back to Countae's Mhaigh Eo and Claire, the Burrens and Cnoc-Aine of Western Ireland. Back to the Dolomiten Alps and Oetzi's homelands of South Tyrol. To explore the lands my ancestors once walked, lived, laughed, cried and died upon. To find out if the land and all its human and non-human relations there had something good to give to the odyssey's quest. To find still another great tree to sit beneath and learn of its subtle, oracular wisdoms. Some great tree to align my spine to, that could act as an ancestral bridge, linking all things that possess duality: man and woman, day and night, life and death, sky and earth, heaven and hell. I knew at once where the odyssey's next leg should lead.

"And The Great Migration Atop the Turtle's back", whispers The Voice, **"Isn't Over YET!"**

AHO! ALL MY RELATIONS!

– POSTSCRIPT –

Long, long ago, the first wave of pilgrims assembled on distant shores and looked towards an Isle of the Turtle far across the sea for fresh hope and vision – for a new tree of life. The next great wave gathered on the edges of the Turtle's vasts forests and looked towards a mythic land of 'Milk & Honey' somewhere far beyond its distant mountains and the ancient cultures of its still wild, free peoples.

Now, facing the unknowns of another vast millennium of time and space, still more pilgrims go forth. Looking back beyond those ancestral seas traversed – those native cultures, mountains and forests breached – they anxiously ask, "Which of our great migration's is the most perilous? What forecasts of the future would the scholars make of our quest for yet new havens of liberty and happiness?"

Dare we new pilgrims claim for ourselves the promise in Genesis – given by The Creator to that ancient Old World pilgrim, Abraham – *'Get thee out from thy country and thy kindred unto a goodly land that I will show thee, and I will bless thee, and thy children after thee, and in thee and thy children shall all the families of the earth be blessed'*?

Or will the next great wave of pilgrims go forth across the Turtle's back with an equally ancient yet harsher vision of life that expects all who would follow it to take up an oath that goes, *"I pledge allegiance to the flag of aggression, and to the new world order for which it stands! One Nation, divided by fraud, with hypocrisy and deception for all!"*

So, PILGRIM! Prepare now to return to your quiet place in Nature. Before you leave, reread this work's dedication page. How has your odyssey confirmed any of those hopeful affirmations? What curious blend of ancestral myth and legend, new world history, personal story and quest has come to light? How much more stranger than fiction or fable does the truth of your life seem? What part of the ancient oak tree and youthful acorn within yourself has been revealed?

And where'er the road may lead in search of yet a new revelation of this tree of life, recall what that other stalwart pilgrim of another space and time, Appleseed Johnny, knew so well in his day; succinctly put by the poet William Blake, in *Human Abstract*, when he posed:

> The Gods of the earth and sea
> Sought through nature to find this Tree;
> But their search was all in vain:
> There grows one in the Human brain.

Hope to see you somewhere up ahead at the next roadsign. 'Til then....